TWO-STORY HOMES

Design 2662

460 Designs
For 1½ and 2 Stories
1,059 to 7,275 square feet

HOME PLANNERS, LLC
Wholly owned by Hanley-Wood, Inc.

Published by Home Planners, LLC
Wholly owned by Hanley-Wood, Inc.
Editorial and Corporate Offices:
3275 West Ina Road, Suite 110
Tucson, Arizona 85741

Distribution Center:
29333 Lorie Lane
Wixom, Michigan 48393

Rickard D. Bailey, CEO and Publisher
Cindy Coatsworth Lewis, Director of Publishing
Paulette Mulvin, Senior Editor
Amanda Kaufmann, Project Editor
Paul D. Fitzgerald, Book Designer

Photo Credits

Front Cover: Andrew D. Lautman

Back Cover: Bruce Arant
          courtesy of Design Basics, Inc.
          Builder: Paradise Homes, Inc.
                  Omaha, NE

10 9 8 7 6 5 4 3 2

Printed in the United States of America.
Library of Congress Catalog Card Number: 96-075928
ISBN: 1-881955-31-1

On the front cover: Bold and beautiful, this plan will answer all the needs and desires of your family. See page 153 for floor plans.

On the back cover: The heritage and romance of an authentic Colonial is captured in this graceful plan. See page 117 for floor plans and more information.

Table of Contents

Editor's Note

For generations Americans have "gone upstairs to bed." This comfortable living pattern has been around since the early Colonial period and continues today in the form of economical and thoroughly livable designs. With the "stacked livability" features of the two-story house producing lower costs in construction and operation, and up to twice the amount of livable square footage, two-story homes present not only the best return per construction dollar spent but also a budget-smart residence option in the long-run.

In this new collection of *Two-Story Homes*, 460 designs span the style spectrum, ranging from Colonial to contemporary and Sun-Country to down-home country—all designed to make your dreams come true!

Whatever style you desire or size specifications you require, *Two-Story Homes* covers all the bases and will provide plenty of options from which to choose for building an outstanding home. With the addition of the many home designs offered by the Blue Ribbon Network of Designers, realizing your dream has never been easier. To help you plan the cost of your dream home, our Quote One® estimation service is available for many of our designs—see page 374 for more information. Complete ordering instructions, along with many helpful additional products, are also available at the back of the book.

About the Designers

The Blue Ribbon Designer Series™ is a collection of books featuring home plans of a diverse group of outstanding home designers and architects known as the Blue Ribbon Network of Designers. This group of companies is dedicated to creating and marketing the finest possible plans for home construction on a regional and national basis. Each of the companies exhibits superior work and integrity in all phases of the stock-plan business including modern, trendsetting floor planning, a professionally executed blueprint package and a strong sense of service and commitment to the consumer.

Design Basics, Inc.

For nearly a decade, Design Basics, a nationally recognized home design service located in Omaha, has been developing plans for custom home builders. Since 1987, the firm has consistently appeared in *Builder* magazine, the official magazine of the National Association of Home Builders, as the top-selling designer. The company's plans also regularly appear in numerous other shelter magazines such as *Better Homes and Gardens, House Beautiful* and *Home Planner*.

Design Traditions

Design Traditions was established by Stephen S. Fuller with the tenets of innovation, quality, originality and uncompromising architectural techniques in traditional and European homes. Especially popular throughout the Southeast, Design Traditions' plans are known for their extensive detail and thoughtful design. They are widely published in such shelter magazines as *Southern Living* magazine and *Better Homes and Gardens*.

Alan Mascord Design Associates, Inc.

Founded in 1983 as a local supplier to the building community, Mascord Design Associates of Portland, Oregon began to successfully publish plans nationally in 1985. With plans now drawn exclusively on computer, Mascord Design Associates quickly received a reputation for homes that are easy to build yet meet the rigorous demands of the buyers' market, winning local and national awards. The company's trademark is creating floor plans that work well and exhibit excellent traffic patterns. Their motto is: "Drawn to build, designed to sell."

Larry E. Belk Designs

Through the years, Larry E. Belk has worked with individuals and builders alike to provide a quality product. After listening to over 4,000 dreams and watching them become reality all across America, Larry's design philosophy today combines traditional exteriors with upscale interiors designed for contemporary lifestyles. Flowing, open spaces and interesting angles define his interiors. Great emphasis is placed on providing views that showcase the natural environment. Dynamic exteriors reflect Larry's extensive home construction experience, painstaking research and talent as a fine artist.

Larry W. Garnett & Associates, Inc.

Starting as a designer of homes for Houston-area residents, Garnett & Associates has been marketing designs nationally for the past ten years. A well-respected design firm, the company's plans are regularly featured in *House Beautiful, Country Living, Home* and *Professional Builder*. Numerous accolades, including several from the Texas Institute of Building Design and the American Institute of Building Design, have been awarded to the company for excellence in architecture.

Home Planners

Headquartered in Tucson, Arizona, with additional offices in Detroit, Home Planners is one of the longest-running and most successful home design firms in the United States. With over 2,500 designs in its portfolio, the company provides a wide range of styles, sizes and types of homes for the residential builder. All of Home Planners' designs are created with the care and professional expertise that fifty years of experience in the home-planning business affords. Their homes are designed to be built, lived in and enjoyed for years to come.

Donald A. Gardner, Architects, Inc.

The South Carolina firm of Donald A. Gardner was established in response to a growing demand for residential designs that reflect constantly changing lifestyles. The company's specialty is providing homes with refined, custom-style details and unique features such as passive-solar designs and open floor plans. Computer-aided design and drafting technology resulting in trouble-free construction documents places the firm at the leading edge of the home plan industry.

The Sater Design Collection

The Sater Design Collection has a long established tradition of providing South Florida's most diverse and extraordinary custom designed homes. Their goal is to fulfill each client's particular need for an exciting approach to design by merging creative vision with elements that satisfy a desire for a distinctive lifestyle. This philosophy is proven, as exemplified by over 50 national design awards, numerous magazine features and, most important, satisfied clients. The result is an elegant statement of lasting beauty and value.

Home Design Services, Inc.

For the past fifteen years, Home Design Services of Longwood, Florida, has been formulating plans for the sun-country lifestyle. At the forefront of design innovation and imagination, the company has developed award winning designs that are consistently praised for their highly detailed, free-flowing floor plans, imaginative and exciting interior architecture and elevations which have gained international appeal.

American Atmosphere:
Traditional family designs

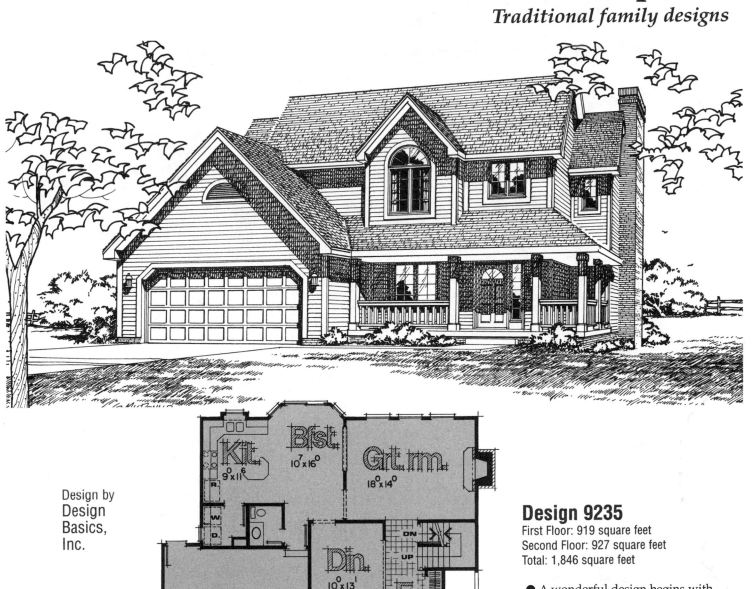

Design by
Design Basics, Inc.

Width 44'
Depth 40'

WRAPAROUND PORCH

Kit. 9⁰x11⁶
Bfst. 10⁷x16⁰
Grt. rm. 18⁰x14⁰
Gar. 20⁰x19⁸
Dn. 10⁰x13¹

Mbr. 12⁰x16⁰ 9'-4" CEILING
Br. 10⁰x11⁶
Br. 10⁰x11⁶
Br. 10⁰x11⁸ 10'-0" CEILING
WHIRLPOOL
LIN.
OPEN TO BELOW
PLANT SHELF
DN

Design 9235
First Floor: 919 square feet
Second Floor: 927 square feet
Total: 1,846 square feet

● A wonderful design begins with the wraparound porch of this plan. Explore further and find a two-story entry with a coat closet and plant shelf above and a strategically placed staircase alongside. The island kitchen with a boxed window over the sink is adjacent to a large bay-windowed dinette. The great room includes many windows and a fireplace. A powder bath and laundry room are both conveniently placed on the first floor. Upstairs, the large master suite contains His and Hers walk-in closets, corner windows and a bath area featuring a double vanity and whirlpool tub. Two pleasant secondary bedrooms have interesting angles and a third bedroom in the front features a volume ceiling and arched window.

Quote One®
Cost to build? See page 374
to order complete cost estimate
to build this house in your area!

5

Design 7296

First Floor: 1,300 square feet
Second Floor: 1,070 square feet
Total: 2,370 square feet

● There is plenty of charm to be found in this two-story home. From the covered front porch and transom windows to the attractive through-fireplace between the living room and the family room, this design offers many amenities. The large, efficient kitchen is convenient to both the formal dining room and the sunny breakfast room and offers plenty of storage space via a pantry and many cabinets. The nearby laundry room presents access to both the rear yard and the two-car garage. Upstairs, four bedrooms include a deluxe master suite complete with a large walk in closet and a pampering bath with a whirl-pool and twin vanities. The three secondary bedrooms share a full hall bath with a dual-bowled vanity.

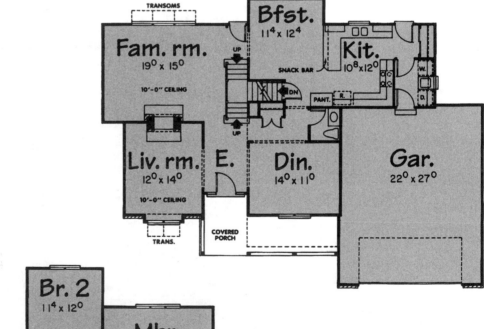

Width 59'-4"
Depth 46'-8"

Design by
Design Basics, Inc.

Design 9591

First Floor: 1,176 square feet
Second Floor: 994 square feet
Total: 2,170 square feet

Design by
Alan Mascord
Design Associates, Inc.

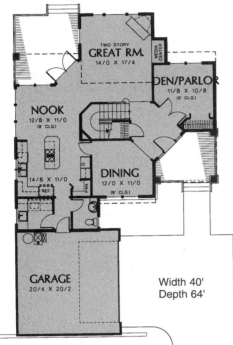

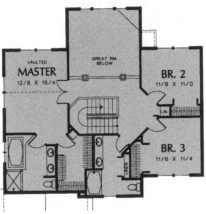

Width 40'
Depth 64'

● This home's covered, angled entry is elegantly echoed by an angled door to a rear covered porch, thus setting the style for this amenity-filled design. Flanking the foyer to the left is the formal dining room and to the right, through double French doors, is a cozy den. The great room opens out into the comfortable breakfast nook, giving this plan a spacious feeling. Gourmets will enjoy the large island kitchen. Upstairs, the master suite is located away from two secondary bedrooms for privacy and offers a luxurious bath and a walk-in closet.

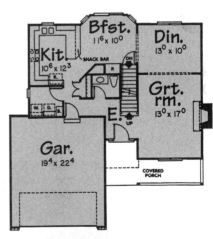

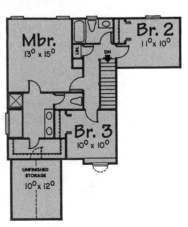

Design 7291

First Floor: 862 square feet
Second Floor: 780 square feet
Total: 1,642 square feet

● A wide gabled porch welcomes you to this comfortable home. Inside, the great room and dining room flow together to create wonderful entertaining space. The kitchen has direct access to the bay-windowed breakfast nook by the use of a snack bar. A convenient laundry room is near by. Upstairs, two family bedrooms share a hall bath while the master suite offers a pampering compartmented bath, a large walk-in closet and access to lots of unfinished storage space.

Design by
Design
Basics,
Inc.

Width 40'
Depth 44'

7

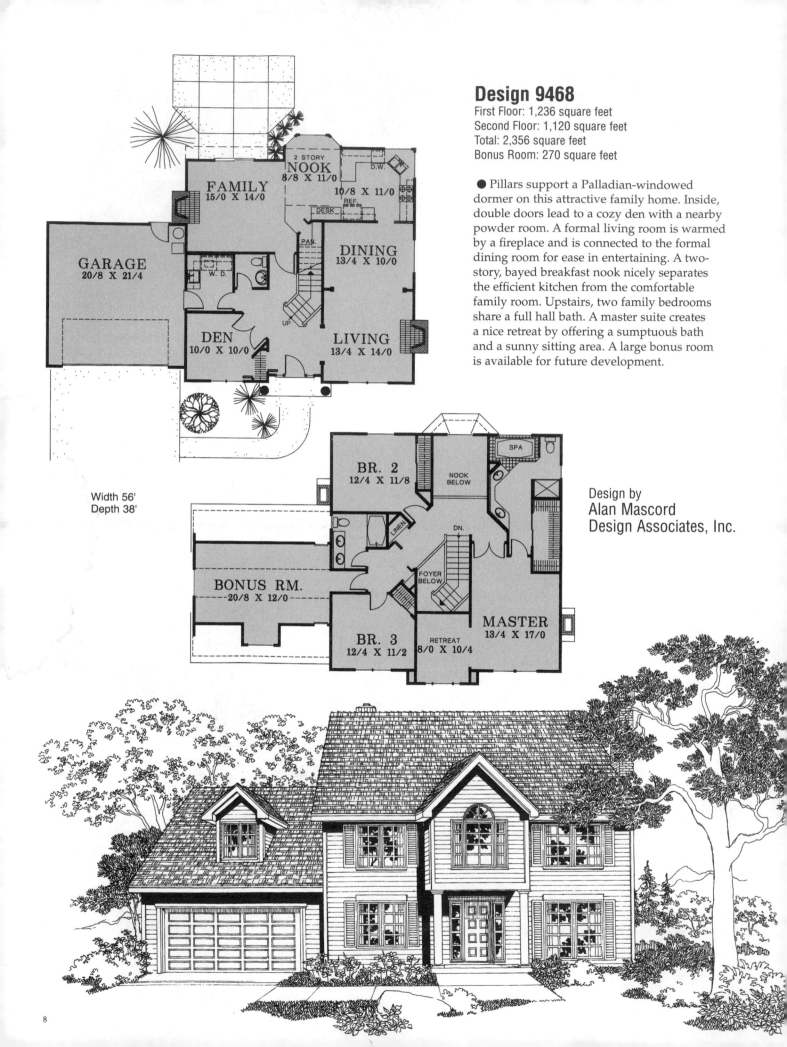

Design 9468

First Floor: 1,236 square feet
Second Floor: 1,120 square feet
Total: 2,356 square feet
Bonus Room: 270 square feet

● Pillars support a Palladian-windowed dormer on this attractive family home. Inside, double doors lead to a cozy den with a nearby powder room. A formal living room is warmed by a fireplace and is connected to the formal dining room for ease in entertaining. A two-story, bayed breakfast nook nicely separates the efficient kitchen from the comfortable family room. Upstairs, two family bedrooms share a full hall bath. A master suite creates a nice retreat by offering a sumptuous bath and a sunny sitting area. A large bonus room is available for future development.

FAMILY 15/0 X 14/0

2 STORY NOOK 8/8 X 11/0

10/8 X 11/0

D.W.

REF.

DESK

PAN.

DINING 13/4 X 10/0

GARAGE 20/8 X 21/4

W.D.

DEN 10/0 X 10/0

UP

LIVING 13/4 X 14/0

Width 56'
Depth 38'

SPA

BR. 2 12/4 X 11/8

NOOK BELOW

LINEN

Design by
**Alan Mascord
Design Associates, Inc.**

BONUS RM. 20/8 X 12/0

DN.

FOYER BELOW

MASTER 13/4 X 17/0

BR. 3 12/4 X 11/2

RETREAT 8/0 X 10/4

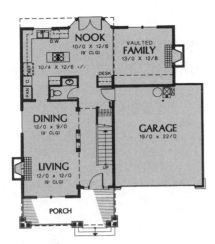

Design 9593

First Floor: 968 square feet
Second Floor: 837 square feet
Total: 1,805 square feet

Design by
Alan Mascord
Design Associates, Inc.

Width 40'
Depth 46'

● A charming covered porch welcomes you into this three-bedroom home. The living room and dining room are accessed through a columned hallway just off the two-story foyer. The large kitchen is convenient to both the dining room and a bay-windowed breakfast nook, with the cozy family room nearby. On the second level two secondary bedrooms share a full hall bath and access to the laundry facilities. The luxurious master suite is entered through double doors and offers a walk-in closet and a pampering bath.

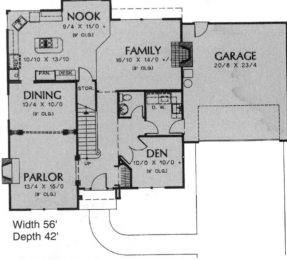

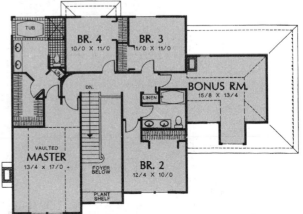

Design 9477

First Floor: 1,308 square feet
Second Floor: 1,141 square feet
Total: 2,449 square feet
Bonus Room: 266 square feet

Design by
Alan Mascord
Design Associates, Inc.

Width 56'
Depth 42'

● Quietly stated elegance is the key to this home's attraction. Its floor plan allows plenty of space for formal and informal occasions. The rear of the first floor is devoted to an open area serving as family room, breakfast nook and island kitchen. This area is complemented by a formal parlor/dining room combination. A private den could function as a guest room with the handy powder room nearby. There are four bedrooms on the second floor. Bonus room over the garage could become an additional bedroom or study.

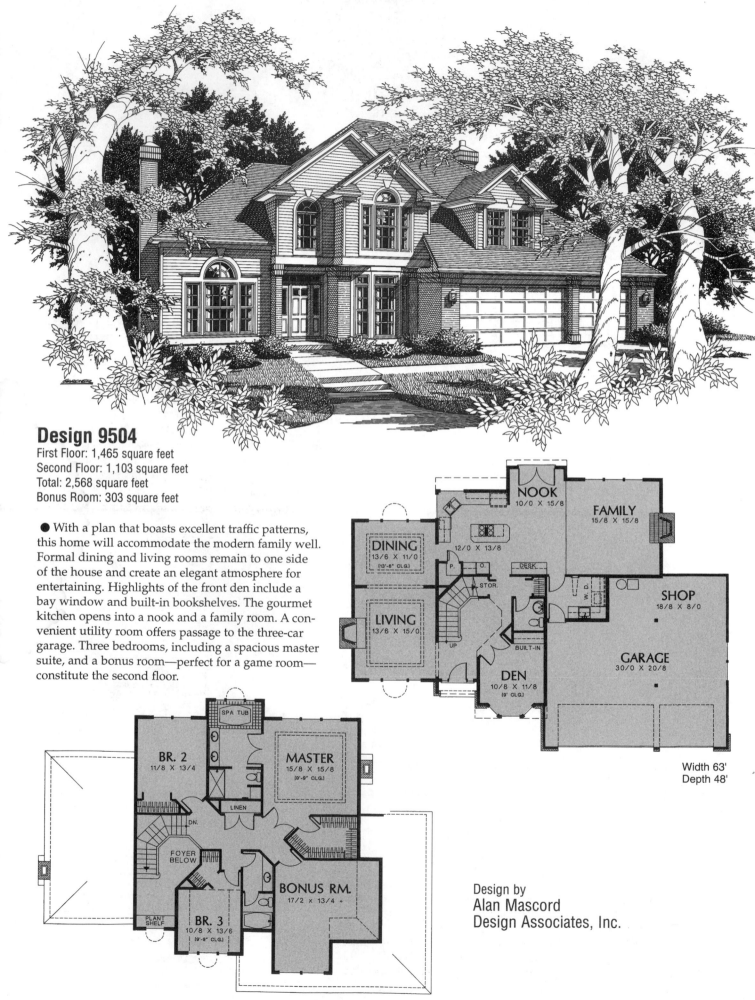

Design 9504

First Floor: 1,465 square feet
Second Floor: 1,103 square feet
Total: 2,568 square feet
Bonus Room: 303 square feet

● With a plan that boasts excellent traffic patterns, this home will accommodate the modern family well. Formal dining and living rooms remain to one side of the house and create an elegant atmosphere for entertaining. Highlights of the front den include a bay window and built-in bookshelves. The gourmet kitchen opens into a nook and a family room. A convenient utility room offers passage to the three-car garage. Three bedrooms, including a spacious master suite, and a bonus room—perfect for a game room—constitute the second floor.

NOOK
10/0 X 15/8

FAMILY
15/8 X 15/8

DINING
13/6 X 11/0
[13'-8" CLG.]

12/0 X 13/8

DESK

SHOP
18/8 X 8/0

LIVING
13/6 X 15/0

STOR.

UP

BUILT-IN

DEN
10/8 X 11/8
[9' CLG.]

GARAGE
30/0 X 20/8

Width 63'
Depth 48'

SPA TUB

BR. 2
11/8 X 13/4

MASTER
15/8 X 15/8
[9'-9" CLG.]

LINEN

DN.

FOYER
BELOW

BONUS RM.
17/2 X 13/4 +

PLANT
SHELF

BR. 3
10/8 X 13/6
[9'-9" CLG.]

Design by
**Alan Mascord
Design Associates, Inc.**

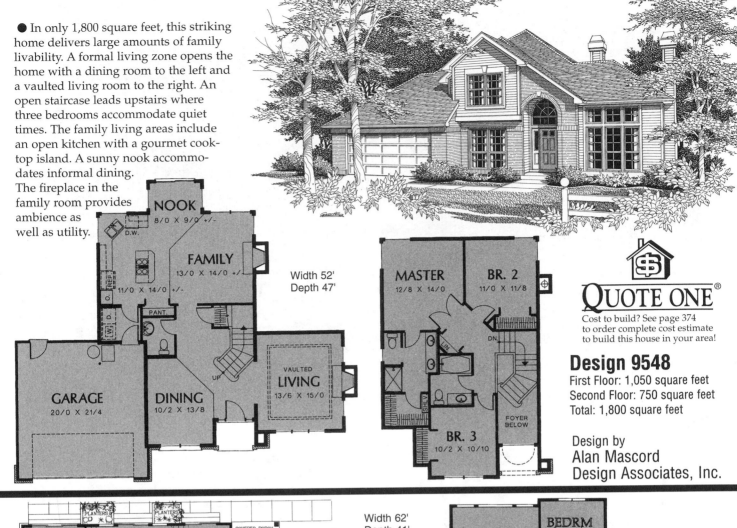

● In only 1,800 square feet, this striking home delivers large amounts of family livability. A formal living zone opens the home with a dining room to the left and a vaulted living room to the right. An open staircase leads upstairs where three bedrooms accommodate quiet times. The family living areas include an open kitchen with a gourmet cooktop island. A sunny nook accommodates informal dining. The fireplace in the family room provides ambience as well as utility.

Width 52'
Depth 47'

NOOK 8/0 X 9/0 +/-
FAMILY 13/0 X 14/0 +/-
11/0 X 14/0 +/-
GARAGE 20/0 X 21/4
DINING 10/2 X 13/8
VAULTED LIVING 13/6 X 15/0
MASTER 12/8 X 14/0
BR. 2 11/0 X 11/8
BR. 3 10/2 X 10/10
FOYER BELOW

Quote One®
Cost to build? See page 374 to order complete cost estimate to build this house in your area!

Design 9548
First Floor: 1,050 square feet
Second Floor: 750 square feet
Total: 1,800 square feet

Design by
Alan Mascord Design Associates, Inc.

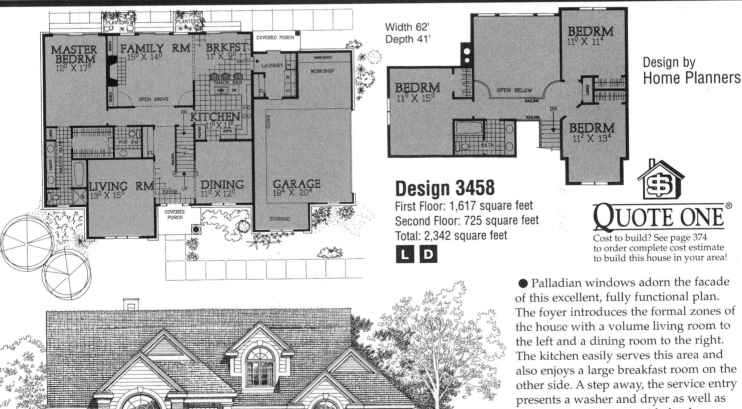

Width 62'
Depth 41'

MASTER BEDRM 12° X 17⁸
FAMILY RM 15° X 14°
BRKFST 11° X 9°
COVERED PORCH
LAUNDRY
WORKSHOP
WORK BENCH
SNACK BAR
KITCHEN 11° X 11⁸
OPEN ABOVE
MASTER BATH
LIVING RM 13° X 15°
FOYER
DINING 11° X 12°
GARAGE 19⁴ X 20⁴
STORAGE
COVERED PORCH

BEDRM 11° X 11⁴
BEDRM 11° X 15°
OPEN BELOW
BEDRM 11² X 13⁴
BATH
RAILING

Design by
Home Planners

Design 3458
First Floor: 1,617 square feet
Second Floor: 725 square feet
Total: 2,342 square feet
L D

Quote One®
Cost to build? See page 374 to order complete cost estimate to build this house in your area!

● Palladian windows adorn the facade of this excellent, fully functional plan. The foyer introduces the formal zones of the house with a volume living room to the left and a dining room to the right. The kitchen easily serves this area and also enjoys a large breakfast room on the other side. A step away, the service entry presents a washer and dryer as well as passage to the two-car, side-load garage. Four bedrooms include a master suite with terrace access. Upstairs, a balcony overlooking the two-story family room leads to the secondary bedrooms.

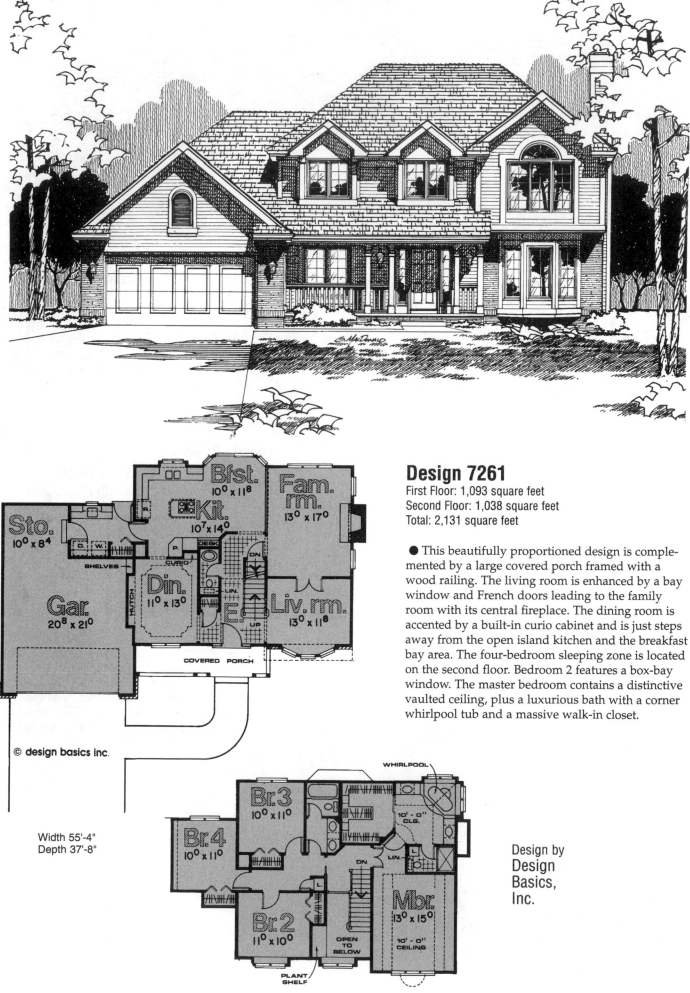

Design 7261

First Floor: 1,093 square feet
Second Floor: 1,038 square feet
Total: 2,131 square feet

● This beautifully proportioned design is complemented by a large covered porch framed with a wood railing. The living room is enhanced by a bay window and French doors leading to the family room with its central fireplace. The dining room is accented by a built-in curio cabinet and is just steps away from the open island kitchen and the breakfast bay area. The four-bedroom sleeping zone is located on the second floor. Bedroom 2 features a box-bay window. The master bedroom contains a distinctive vaulted ceiling, plus a luxurious bath with a corner whirlpool tub and a massive walk-in closet.

Design by
Design
Basics,
Inc.

Width 55'-4"
Depth 37'-8"

© design basics inc.

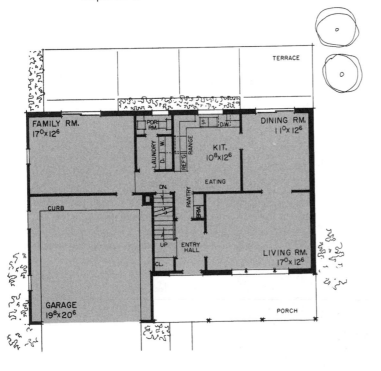

Width 46'-5"
Depth 34'-3"

FAMILY RM.
17⁰x12⁶

DINING RM.
11⁰x12⁶

LAUNDRY

KIT.
10⁸x12⁶

EATING

PANTRY

GARAGE
19⁸x20⁶

CURB

ENTRY HALL

LIVING RM.
17⁰x12⁶

PORCH

TERRACE

MASTER BED RM.
15⁰x11⁶

BATH

BATH

BED RM.
11⁰x10⁰

BED RM.
11⁰x13⁰

Design 1361

First Floor: 965 square feet
Second Floor: 740 square feet
Total: 1,705 square feet

L D

● An abundance of livability is offered
by this charming, traditional adaptation. It
will be most economical to build. The
entry hall gives way to a central, L-shaped
kitchen. The formal dining room opens to
the right. The spacious living room affords
many different furniture arrangements. In
the family room, casual living takes off
with direct access to the rear terrace. Note
the first-floor laundry conveniently located between the kitchen and the family room.
Upstairs, three bedrooms include a master
bedroom with a private bath. Double closets guarantee ample space for wardrobes.
One of the secondary bedrooms features a
walk-in closet. Don't forget the handy
broom closet and the pantry located just off
the kitchen.

Design by
Home Planners

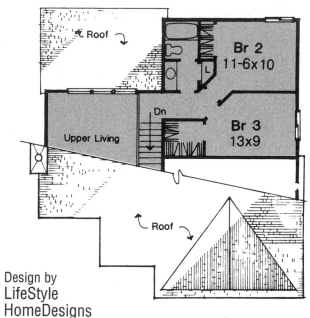

Design 8894

First Floor: 846 square feet
Second Floor: 400 square feet
Total: 1,246 square feet

Roof

Br 2
11-6x10

Upper Living

Dn

Br 3
13x9

Roof

Design by
LifeStyle
HomeDesigns

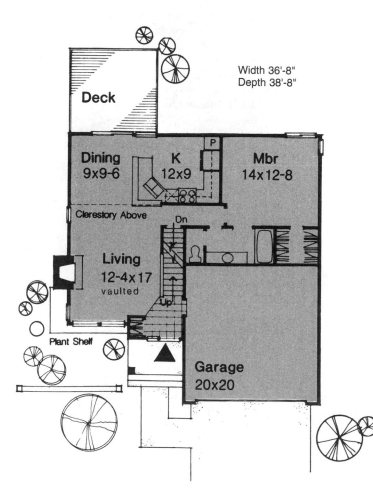

Deck

Width 36'-8"
Depth 38'-8"

Dining
9x9-6

K
12x9

P

Mbr
14x12-8

Clerestory Above

Dn

Living
12-4x17
vaulted

Up

Plant Shelf

Garage
20x20

● A sloping roofline and wood siding lend a
fresh look to this stunning starter home. Inside,
a tiled entryway reveals a vaulted living room
with a fireplace and clerestory windows. An
efficient kitchen serves a dining room that accesses a rear deck for outside enjoyment. The
first-floor master-suite enhancements include
corner windows, a walk-in closet and private
passage to a full bath. Two bedrooms on the
second floor include one with a walk-in closet.
They share a full hall bath.

ALTERNATE ELEVATION
9437A

Design 9437

First Floor: 1,009 square feet
Second Floor: 1,049 square feet
Total: 2,058 square feet

Design by
**Alan Mascord
Design Associates, Inc.**

● This efficient two-story home incorporates all of the features demanded by today's discriminating home buyer. Check out the gracious two-story foyer featuring a comfortable L-shaped stair and dormered window filling the area with an abundance of natural light. The spacious kitchen includes an island, a large pantry, a desk and a bayed-out nook area. Opening directly off the nook is a large family room with fireplace and glass doors leading to the outdoor living space. The upper floor of this home includes four generous bedrooms. An alternate plan, 9437A, provides the same wonderful floor plan with a different exterior look.

Width 50'
Depth 40'

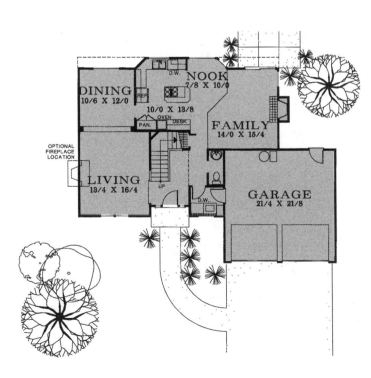

DINING
10/6 X 12/0

NOOK
7/8 X 10/0

10/0 X 13/8

OPTIONAL FIREPLACE LOCATION

OVEN
PAN.
DESK

FAMILY
14/0 X 15/4

LIVING
13/4 X 16/4

UP

GARAGE
21/4 X 21/8

D.W.

REF.

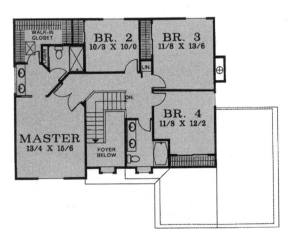

WALK-IN CLOSET

BR. 2
10/3 X 10/0

BR. 3
11/8 X 13/6

LIN.

DN.

MASTER
13/4 X 15/6

BR. 4
11/8 X 12/2

FOYER BELOW

SPA

WALK-IN CLOSET

ALTERNATE
MASTER W/
SPA TUB

13/4 X 17/2

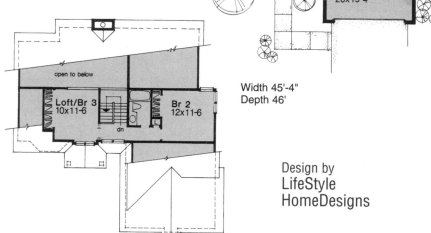

Design 8892

First Floor: 1,105 square feet

Second Floor: 460 square feet

Total: 1,565 square feet

● Enter this home to find the kitchen with a charming bayed breakfast area. A window-lit sink and ample counter space are highlights. In the dining room, sliding glass doors lead to a rear deck for added livability. The great room, with a warming fireplace, acts as the heart of the home. The luxurious first-floor master suite features a large walk-in closet, a platform tub and a separate stall shower. Upstairs, two bedrooms—or one bedroom and a handy loft—accommodate family or guests. A full hall bath is nearby. The two-car garage accesses the first floor near a convenient powder room.

Width 45'-4"
Depth 46'

Design by
LifeStyle
HomeDesigns

Design 8897

First Floor: 834 square feet

Second Floor: 722 square feet

Total: 1,556 square feet

● In this contemporary interpretation of the traditional cottage, wood and stone accents create a homey feel. The foyer leads to a vaulted living room with a three-sided fireplace, which can be viewed from the dining room. The country kitchen provides a great family focus on outdoor living with a nearby deck. On the second floor, three bedrooms comfortably accommodate the family. The master bedroom enjoys a relaxing, private bath.

Width 40'-4"
Depth 41'-8"

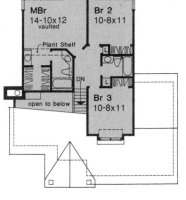

Design by
LifeStyle
HomeDesigns

Design 8896

First Floor: 668 square feet
Second Floor: 691 square feet
Total: 1,359 square feet

● A raised foyer gives the inside of this home added dimension. A bright, vaulted living room includes a fireplace and easy access to the rear dining room—perfect for entertaining. The kitchen and breakfast room offer efficiency in meal preparation and serving. A coat closet and a powder room are situated near the two-car garage. The master bedroom suite is removed from two family bedrooms—or one bedroom and a loft.

Design by
LifeStyle
HomeDesigns

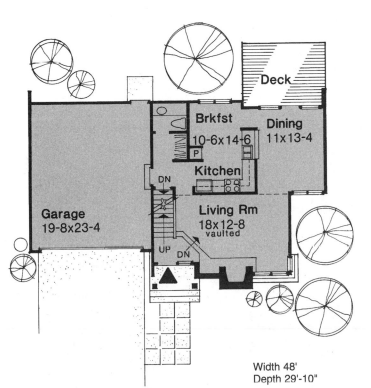

Deck

Brkfst
10-6x14-6

Dining
11x13-4

Kitchen

Living Rm
18x12-8
vaulted

Garage
19-8x23-4

DN

UP DN

Width 48'
Depth 29'-10"

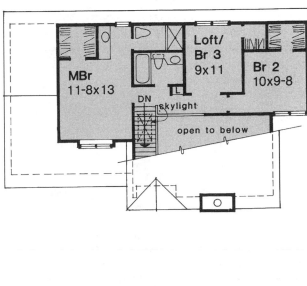

MBr
11-8x13

Loft/
Br 3
9x11

Br 2
10x9-8

DN

skylight

open to below

Design 9230

First Floor: 1,303 square feet
Second Floor: 1,084 square feet
Total: 2,387 square feet

Design by
**Design
Basics,
Inc.**

● It's hard to get beyond the covered front porch of this home, but doing so reveals a bright two-story entry open to the central hall. Just to the left, an enticing bay window enlivens a living room featuring French doors which connect to the family room. The efficient kitchen with snack bar and pantry is open to the bay-windowed breakfast area with planning desk. The salad sink and counter space double as a service for the formal dining room. The master bedroom features a raised ceiling and arched window. Its adjoining bath contains a walk-through closet/transition area and a corner whirlpool. Three family bedrooms and a hall bath complete this level.

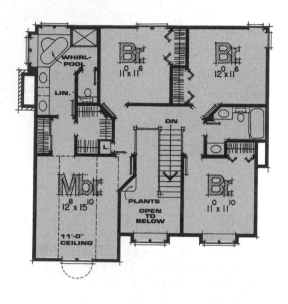

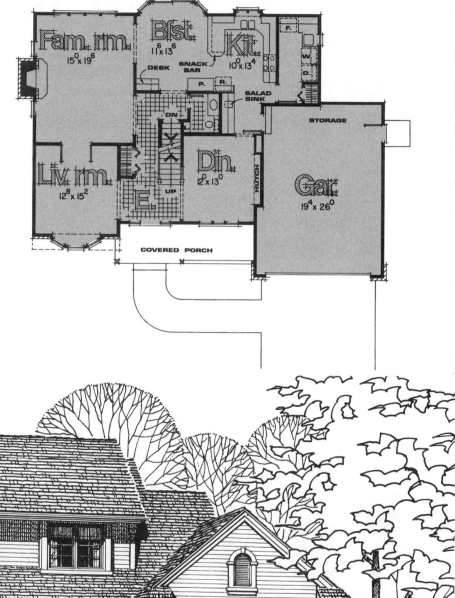

Width 54'
Depth 42'

Photos by Jon Riley

DECK

seat

spa

arched window above door

GREAT RM.
15-4 × 18-0
(cathedral ceiling)

fireplace

KIT./BRKFST.
16-8 × 16-0

master
bath

walk-in
closet

walk-in
closet

pd.
rm.

up

sto.

cl

MASTER
BED RM.
13-0 × 13-6

FOYER
7-8 × 9-0

DINING
12-4 × 12-4

UTILITY
10-0 × 6-4

w

d

up

storage

PORCH

GARAGE
20-0 × 20-0

Quote One®

Cost to build? See page 374
to order complete cost estimate
to build this house in your area!

Width 58'-3"
Depth 68'-9"

BED RM.
10-4 × 11-9

walk-in
closet

down

bath

cl

BED RM.
12-4 × 13-6

down

BONUS
RM.
11-0 × 20-0

Design by
Donald A.
Gardner,
Architects, Inc.

Design 9661

First Floor: 1,416 square feet
Second Floor: 445 square feet
Total: 1,861 square feet
Bonus Room: 284 square feet

● An arched entrance and windows provide a touch of class to the
exterior of this plan. The foyer leads to all areas of the house minimizing corridor space. The dining room displays round columns at
the entrance while the great room boasts a cathedral ceiling, fireplace and arched window over exterior doors to the deck. The large
kitchen is open to the breakfast nook and sliding glass doors present
a second access to the deck. In the master suite is a walk-in closet
and lavish bath. On the second level are two bedrooms and a full
bath. Bonus space over the garage can be developed later.

Design 9385

First Floor: 1,195 square feet
Second Floor: 1,034 square feet
Total: 2,229 square feet

● This majestic-looking home offers a delightful floor plan. The foyer reveals a winding staircase and double doors to the den. In this versatile room, a spider-beamed ceiling and built-in bookshelves lend style and appeal. The great room rises into a sixteen-foot ceiling and also supports a fireplace flanked by a built-in media center. The kitchen features a snack bar to the breakfast area where a door opens to the covered stoop outside. Double doors connect this whole area to the dining room. Upstairs, the master bedroom showcases a built-in dresser and entertainment center. The master bath offers a unique angle on luxury with its fabulous whirlpool and walk-in closet. Two family bedrooms share a hall bath and a delightful loft over-looks the great room below; you may decide to build a bedroom in its place.

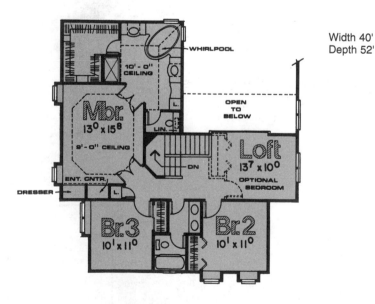

Width 40'
Depth 52'

Design by
**Design
Basics,
Inc.**

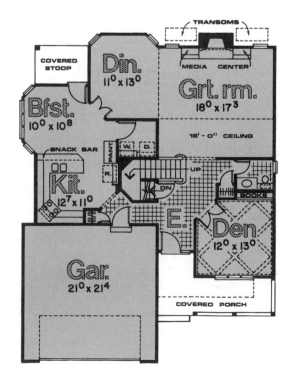

Design 9592

First Floor: 1,168 square feet
Second Floor: 1,157 square feet
Total: 2,325 square feet

● A covered front porch and multi-paned windows combine to present a pleasing facade for this three-bedroom home. The two-story foyer leads directly to the columned living and dining rooms, with a fireplace gracing the living room. Farther in, double doors lead to a cozy den. A large family room with a second fireplace opens to the breakfast nook and the L-shaped kitchen. Upstairs, two family bedrooms share a full hall bath. A large bonus room can be developed at a later date. The master suite is entered through double doors and offers a walk-in closet and a pampering bath.

Design by
Alan Mascord
Design Associates, Inc.

Width 40'
Depth 49'

Design 9327

First Floor: 1,032 square feet
Second Floor: 743 square feet
Total: 1,775 square feet

● Sleek roof lines, classic window details, and a covered front porch tastefully combine on the exterior of this three-bedroom home. A bright living room with an adjoining dining room is viewed from the volume entry. Meals will be enjoyed in the bayed breakfast area, which is served by a comfortable kitchen. A raised-hearth fireplace adds warmth to the family room. The second-level hall design provides separation between two secondary bedrooms and the luxurious master suite with a boxed ceiling. Two closets, a whirlpool bath with plant sill, and double lavs are featured in the master bath/dressing area.

Design by
Design
Basics,
Inc.

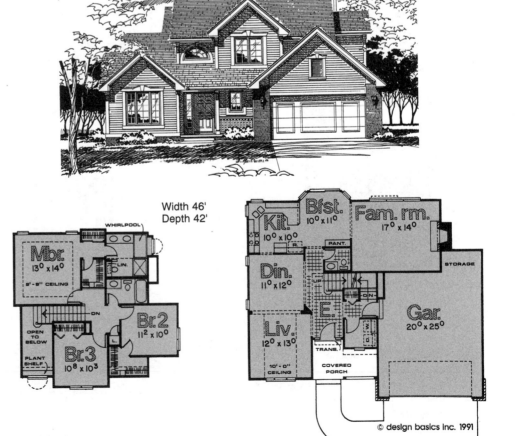

Width 46'
Depth 42'

© design basics inc. 1991

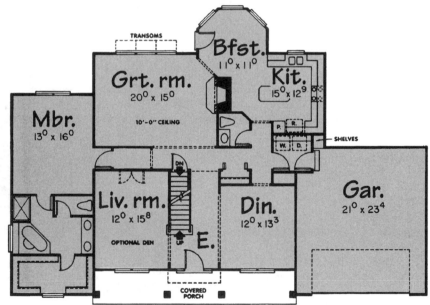

Design 7298

First Floor: 1,767 square feet
Second Floor: 795 square feet
Total: 2,562 square feet

● The abundance of amenities generates a lot of appeal in this four bedroom home. Flanking the two-story foyer is the formal living room on the left and the formal dining room on the right. A large great room with transom windows and a fireplace has direct access to an octagonal breakfast room. The U-shaped kitchen has a work island and a nearby powder room. A handy washer and dryer are found in the passageway to the two-car garage. Separated from family bedrooms for privacy, the first floor master suite offers a luxurious bath and a spacious walk-in closet. Upstairs, two secondary bedrooms share a full hall bath and access to a walk-in linen closet. A third bedroom has its own private bath and a walk-in closet. It could serve as the guest suite.

Design by
Design Basics, Inc.

Width 68'
Depth 46'-8"

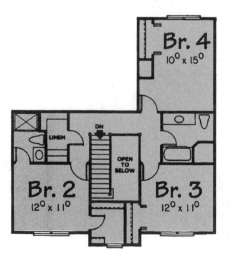

Design 2905

First Floor: 1,342 square feet
Second Floor: 619 square feet
Total: 1,961 square feet

L **D**

● All of the livability in this plan is in the back! With this sort of configuration, this home makes a perfect lakefront or beachfront home. Each first-floor room, except the kitchen, maintains access to the rear terrace via sliding glass doors. However, the kitchen is open to the breakfast room and thus takes advantage of the view. The master bedroom delights with its private bath and walk-in closet. Two secondary bedrooms comprise the second floor. One utilizes a walk-in closet while both make use of a full hall bath. A lounge overlooks the foyer as well as the gathering room below.

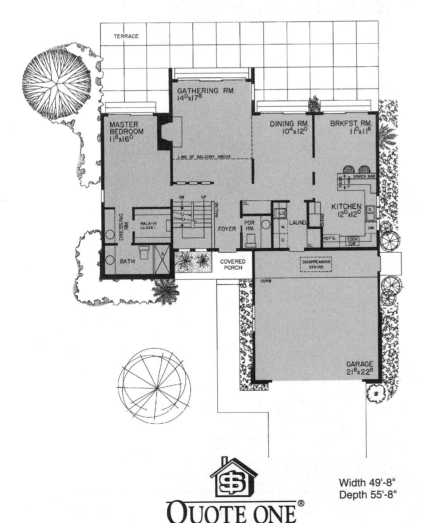

Width 49'-8"
Depth 55'-8"

Design by
Home Planners

Design 7297

First Floor: 925 square feet
Second Floor: 960 square feet
Total: 1,885 square feet

● A covered porch leads to a corner entry in this appealing four-bedroom home. A formal dining room opens directly off the foyer and a family room with a fireplace is toward the rear. A bayed breakfast nook accents the efficient island kitchen that offers a nearby laundry room. Upstairs, three family bedrooms share a full hall bath while the master suite has its own pampering bath and two large walk-in closets.

Width 44'
Depth 42'

Design by
Design Basics, Inc.

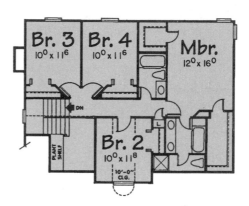

Design 8898

First Floor: 1,075 square feet
Second Floor: 816 square feet
Total: 1,891 square feet

● The vaulted entry of this home will impress visitors. The great room features a vaulted ceiling shared with the dining room. The U-shaped kitchen serves the family room with a pass-through. A bay window and deck access make the family room extra special, as does the warming hearth. Upstairs, three bedrooms include a master suite with a private bath and two closets. The secondary bedrooms share a full hall bath.

Width 43'-4"
Depth 46'

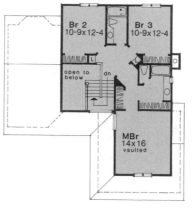

Design by
LifeStyle HomeDesigns

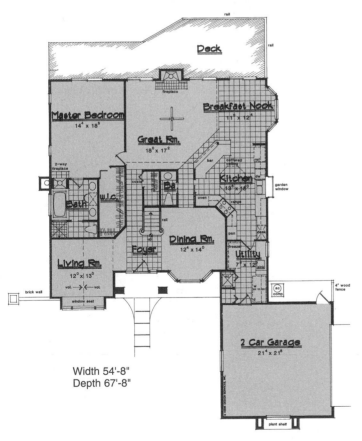

Width 54'-8"
Depth 67'-8"

Design by
**Home Design
Services, Inc.**

Design 8689

First Floor: 1,810 square feet
Second Floor: 922 square feet
Total: 2,732 square feet

● A Palladian window crowns this impressive entry and brings you into the foyer which separates the formal living and dining rooms. Efficient planning keeps the casual living area to the rear where the breakfast nook, the great room and the huge kitchen share views of the deck and backyard beyond. A fireplace flanked by sliding glass doors is the focal point of the great room, as is the bay window in the breakfast nook. The master suite features a large bedroom and a deluxe bath containing a spacious walk-in closet and a soaking tub with a through-fireplace. Upstairs, Bedroom 2 has a private bath and a walk-in closet, while two other bedrooms share a full bath.

Design 9590

First Floor: 1,205 square feet
Second Floor: 1,123 square feet
Total: 2,328 square feet

Design by
Alan Mascord
Design Associates, Inc.

● A covered porch, multi-paned windows and shingle-and-stone siding combine to give this home plenty of curb appeal. Inside, the foyer is flanked by the formal living room and an angled staircase. The formal dining room shares space with the living room and the kitchen is accessible through double doors. A large family room is graced by a fireplace and opens off a cozy eating nook. The second level presents many attractive angles. The master suite has a spacious walk-in closet and a sumptuous bath complete with a garden tub and separate shower. Three bedrooms share a full hall bath.

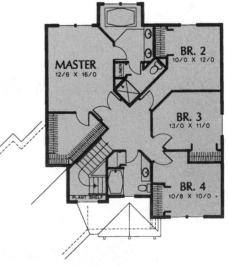

Width 57'-2"
Depth 58'-7"

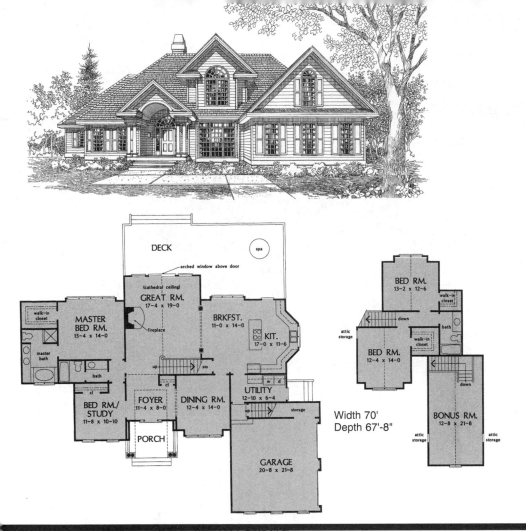

Design 9736

First Floor: 1,839 square feet
Second Floor: 527 square feet
Total: 2,366 square feet
Bonus Room: 344 square feet

● An arched entrance and windows combine with round columns to develop a touch of class on the exterior of this four-bedroom plan. The foyer leads to all areas of the house, minimizing corridor space. The large, open kitchen with an island cooktop is convenient to the breakfast and dining rooms. The master bedroom suite has plenty of walk-in closet space and a well-planned master bath. A nearby bedroom would make an excellent guest room or study, with an adjacent full bath. An expansive rear deck boasts a location for a spa tub and generous space for outdoor living. The second level offers two bedrooms, with sloped ceilings and walk-in closets, and a full bath. A bonus room is available over the garage.

Design by
Donald A. Gardner, Architects, Inc.

Width 70'
Depth 67'-8"

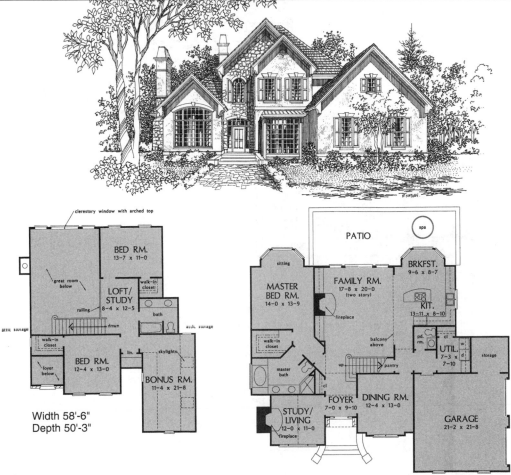

Design 9757

First Floor: 1,715 square feet
Second Floor: 620 square feet
Total: 2,335 square feet

● With its curved, multi-paned windows and shutters, this two-story home features family living at its best. The foyer opens to a study or living room on the left and includes a warming fireplace. The dining room on the right offers large proportions and full windows. The family room, offering yet another fireplace, remains open to the kitchen and breakfast room. In the master suite, a bayed sitting area, a walk-in closet and a pampering bath are sure to please. Upstairs, two bedrooms have their own walk-in closets and flank a loft or study area.

Design by
Donald A.
Gardner,
Architects, Inc.

Width 58'-6"
Depth 50'-3"

Design 9272

First Floor: 1,520 square feet
Second Floor: 1,334 square feet
Total: 2,854 square feet

Design by
**Design
Basics,
Inc.**

● Dramatic details and nine-foot main level walls make this home worthy of building consideration. An enormous great room with spider-beamed ceiling, built-in bookcases and a fireplace connects directly to the sun room with attached wet bar. This skylit area leads to the breakfast room and island kitchen. Complementing these informal gathering areas are the formal living room and dining room. A luxurious master suite features His and Hers walk-in closets and a volume dressing area with an angled, oval whirlpool. Generous bath arrangements are made for the three secondary bedrooms.

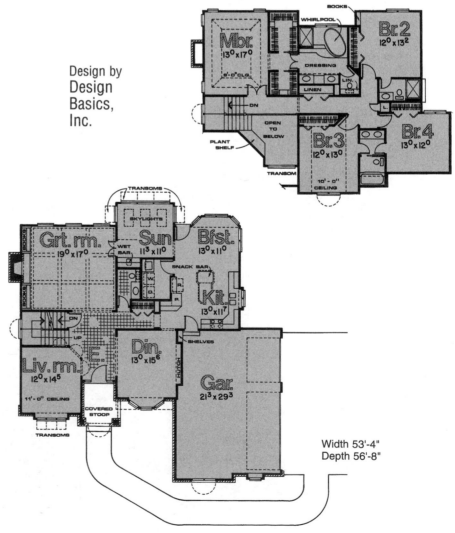

Width 53'-4"
Depth 56'-8"

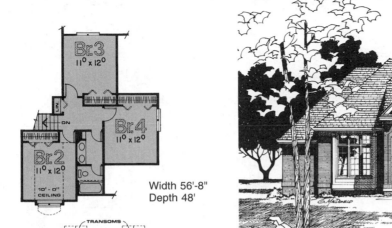

Width 56'-8"
Depth 48'

Design 7239

First Floor: 1,701 square feet
Second Floor: 639 square feet
Total: 2,340 square feet

Design by
Design Basics, Inc.

● The impressive entry into this graceful 1½-story home boasts a high ceiling and a built-in curio cabinet. To the left, the den offers built-in cabinets. Between the dining room and the kitchen is a wet bar. The great room features a raised-hearth fireplace flanked by floor-to-ceiling windows. The first-floor master suite is highlighted with vaulted ceilings, a walk-in closet and a bath with a tunneled skylight above an oval whirlpool tub. Three family bedrooms and a full bath are located on the second floor

Design 9243

First Floor: 1,320 square feet
Second Floor: 1,270 square feet
Total: 2,590 square feet

● Four bedrooms, garage space for three cars and separate formal and informal living areas are all found in this wonderfully compact design. The central corridor leads back to the large family room with fireplace and wet bar. Note how conveniently the kitchen is placed, with easy access to the formal dining room and bay-windowed breakfast room. Four bedrooms upstairs include a master bedroom with tray ceiling and skylit master bath with a whirlpool tub. Three family bedrooms share a full bath.

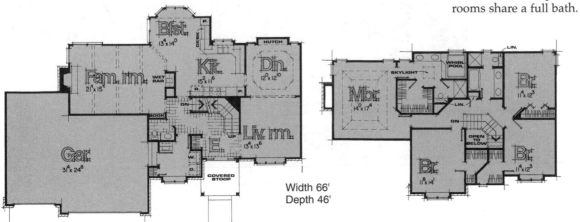

Width 66'
Depth 46'

Design by
Design Basics, Inc.

Design 9287

First Floor: 944 square feet
Second Floor: 987 square feet
Total: 1,931 square feet

● An inviting front porch complements this elevation's combination of brick and siding. Family and friends alike are welcomed into the volume entry with an interesting staircase. A formal dining room with bayed window is to the right. On the left, a noteworthy great room features a ten-foot ceiling, a wall of windows and a handsome fireplace. Serving the great room and bayed dinette is an island kitchen with pantry, snack bar and planning desk. On the upper level, three secondary bedrooms share a hall bath. The segregated master bedroom features a dressing area, a compartmented stool and shower plus a whirlpool under a boxed window.

Design by
Design
Basics,
Inc.

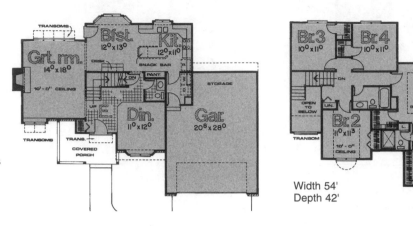

Width 54'
Depth 42'

Design 9221

First Floor: 1,204 square feet
Second Floor: 1,075 square feet
Total: 2,279 square feet

● This elegant four-bedroom is a sophisticated addition to any neighborhood. Formal living areas are at the front of the plan—a living room with arched window and through-fireplace to the family room and a dining room with a beautiful bay window. The well-planned kitchen includes a work island and a breakfast area. The highlight of the four bedroom upstairs is the master suite with high ceiling, sumptuous bath and a giant walk-in closet.

Design by
Design
Basics,
Inc.

Width 54'
Depth 46'

Design 9705

First Floor: 1,675 square feet
Second Floor: 448 square feet
Total: 2,123 square feet

Width 53'-8"
Depth 69'-8"

● This attractive three-bedroom house projects a refined image with its hip roof, brick veneer and arched windows while offering a touch of country with its covered front porch. The entrance foyer, flanked by a dining room and a bedroom/study, leads to a spacious great room with sloped ceiling and clerestory above to add impressive vertical volume. The dining room and breakfast room have cathedral ceilings with arched windows flooding the house with natural light. The master bedroom boasts a cathedral ceiling and a bath with a whirlpool tub, a shower and a double-bowl vanity. The second floor allows for two additional bedrooms along with a bonus room. The plan is available with a crawl-space foundation.

Design by
Donald A.
Gardner,
Architects, Inc.

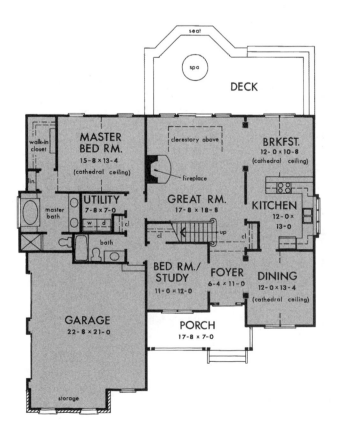

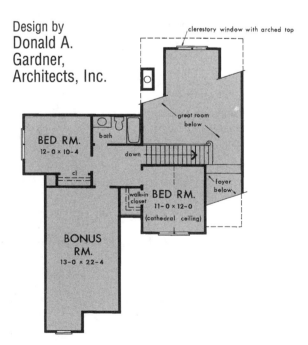

Design 9286

First Floor: 1,583 square feet
Second Floor: 1,331 square feet
Total: 2,914 square feet

● A dramatic elevation with bright windows hints at the luxurious floor plan of this four-bedroom, two-story home. Upon entry, a beautiful staircase and formal living spaces are in sight. To the right, transom windows and a volume ceiling grace the living room. The dining room was designed to accommodate a hutch. The large family room includes elegant bowed windows and a showy three-sided fireplace. A bright dinette and snack bar are served by the open, island kitchen. Step up a half-flight of stairs to a private den with double doors and a special ceiling treatment. All secondary bedrooms have access to either a Hollywood bath or a private bath. A tiered ceiling, a sumptuous bath and two closets highlight the master suite.

Width 58'
Depth 59'-4"

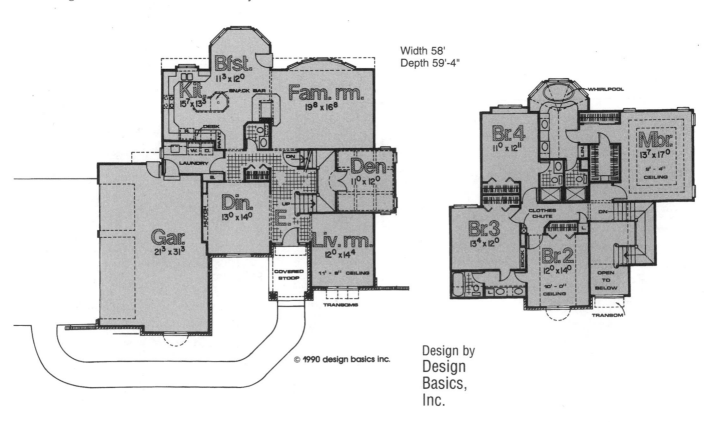

© 1990 design basics inc.

Design by
Design
Basics,
Inc.

Design 8037 First Floor: 1,930 square feet
Second Floor: 791 square feet;Total: 2,721 square feet

● A delightful elevation with swoop roof captures the eye and provides just the right touch for this inviting home. Inside, an angled foyer with a volume ceiling directs attention to the enormous great room. The dining room is detailed with massive round columns connected by arches and shares a through-fireplace with the great room. The master suite includes an upscale master bath and access to a private covered porch. Bedroom 2 is located nearby and is perfect for a nursery or home office/study. The kitchen features a large cooktop island and walk-in pantry. The second floor is dominated by an oversize game room. Two family bedrooms, each with a walk-in closet, a bath and a linen closet complete the upstairs.

QUOTE ONE®
Cost to build? See page 374
to order complete cost estimate
to build this house in your area!

Design by
**Larry E. Belk
Designs**

Width 64'-4"
Depth 62'

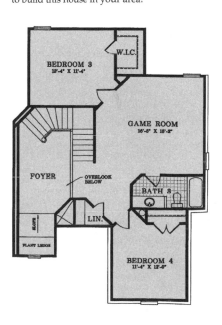

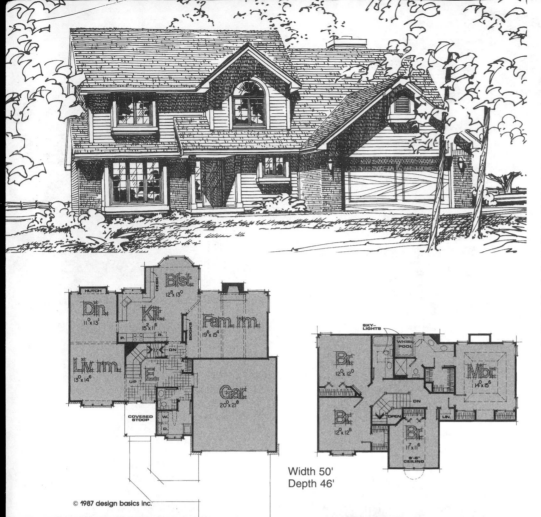

Design 9213

First Floor: 1,247 square feet
Second Floor: 1,183 square feet
Total: 2,430 square feet

● A dramatic entry with a soaring angled staircase greets visitors to this two-story home. To the left are the formal living areas—a living room with a boxed window and a dining room with hutch space. Just steps away is the kitchen with a wraparound counter, desk and bay-windowed breakfast room. Highlighting the family room is a beautiful fireplace, built-in bookcases and beamed ceiling. Upstairs are three family bedrooms and a master suite with tray ceiling and bath with a whirlpool, twin vanities and a walk-in closet.

Design by
Design Basics, Inc.

Width 50'
Depth 46'

© 1987 design basics inc.

Design 9186

First Floor: 1,340 square feet
Second Floor: 514 square feet
Total: 1,854 square feet

Design by
Larry W. Garnett & Associates, Inc.

● This quaint brick home excels in livability. The front porch gives way to a multi-faceted living area emphasized by a fireplace. The kitchen serves this area through a pass-through, making entertaining a breeze. Defined by columns, the dining room presents a simply elegant atmosphere for meals. The rear of the house is made up of the master bedroom suite. A full private bath with dual lavatories, a compartmented toilet and a separate tub and shower enhance this retreat. Upstairs, two bedrooms each sport walk-in closets and share a full bath. A detached two-car garage rests to the rear of the plan.

Width 30'-8"
Depth 61'-8"

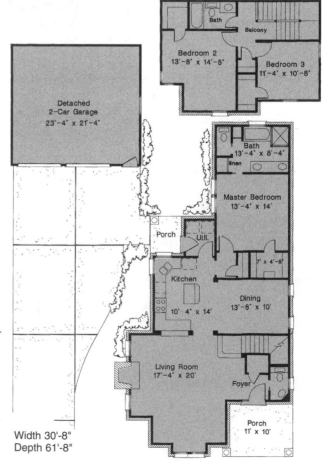

Design 9245

First Floor: 1,132 square feet
Second Floor: 1,087 square feet
Total: 2,219 square feet

● A front porch graces the entry to this charming traditional design. It hints of the great floor plan inside. Note the central core staircase, around which revolve the formal dining room with tiered ceiling, huge great room with fireplace and an island kitchen with breakfast room. A convenient powder room is found in the hallway to serve guests. Upstairs are four bedrooms, including a master suite, with a double vanity and a whirlpool, which is buffered from the family bedrooms. Secondary bedrooms share a full bath with double vanity.

Design by
Design Basics, Inc.

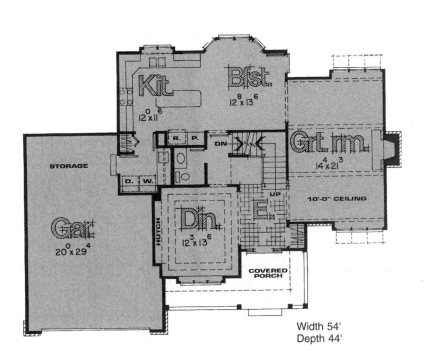

Width 54'
Depth 44'

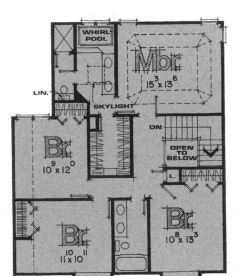

Design 8227

First Floor: 2,361 square feet
Second Floor: 974 square feet
Total: 3,335 square feet

● Stately columns and a covered porch invite visitors and family alike to partake of this home. Attractive angles in the large kitchen help to tie this room into the nearby family and breakfast rooms. The master suite is secluded on the left side of the first floor and offers His and Hers walk-in closets, a double-bowl vanity, a garden tub and a separate shower. The formal living and dining rooms are convenient to one another for ease in entertaining. A secondary bedroom is also located on this level and could be used as a guest suite. Upstairs, two large family bedrooms each have spacious walk-in closets, share a hall bath and have access to a game room. Please specify crawlspace or slab foundation when ordering.

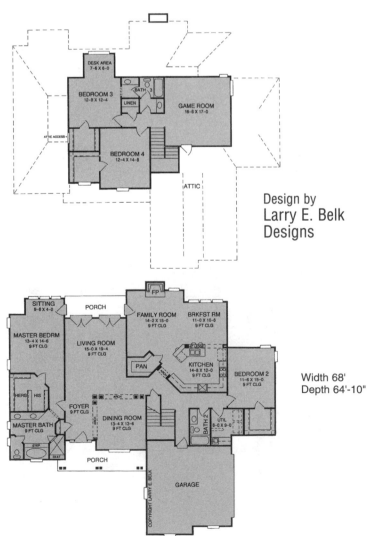

Design by
Larry E. Belk
Designs

Width 68'
Depth 64'-10"

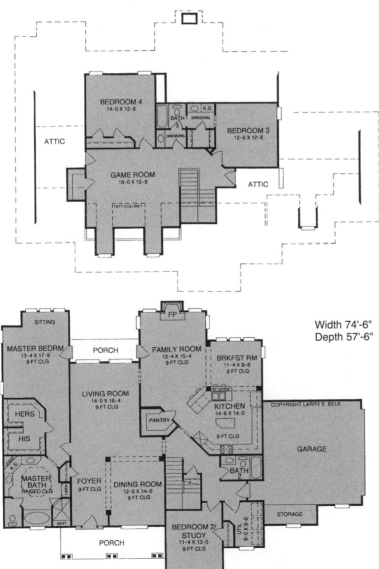

Design 8228

First Floor: 2,346 square feet
Second Floor: 972 square feet
Total: 3,318 square feet

● Varied rooflines, multi-pane windows and elegant columns combine to create a pleasing facade for this wonderful home. Great livability is evident from the minute you set foot in the elegant foyer. A dining room is defined by continuing the column theme inside, while the nearby formal living room offers plenty of blank wall space for easy furniture placement. For those informal times, a family room, sunny breakfast room and efficient kitchen have plenty to offer. Three bedrooms include the sumptuous first floor master suite and two large family bedrooms located on the second floor. An enormous game room is available for the children's enjoyment. Please specify crawlspace or slab foundation when ordering.

Width 74'-6"
Depth 57'-6"

Design by
Larry E. Belk
Designs

37

COPYRIGHT LARRY E. BELK

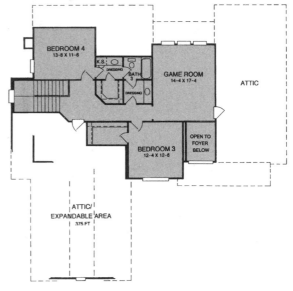

Design 8223

First Floor: 2,121 square feet
Second Floor: 920 square feet
Total: 3,041 square feet

● A two-story foyer is just the first sign of the elegance of this fine home. The formal dining room is to the left, through graceful arches. The formal living room looks out onto the rear covered porch and is well situated for entertaining. A family room with a fireplace and a bright breakfast room open off the large gourmet kitchen, creating ease in serving the family. The luxurious master suite and another bedroom complete with a nearby full bath finish out the main level. Upstairs, two comfortable family bedrooms, both with walk-in closets, share a full bath and a huge game room. Access to the attic and future expandable space is also located on this level. Please specify crawlspace or slab foundation when ordering.

Design by
Larry E. Belk
Designs

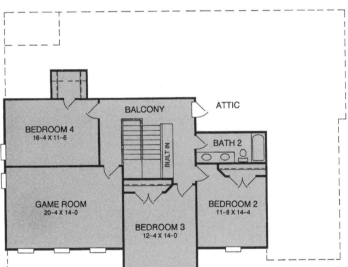

BEDROOM 4
16-4 X 11-6

BALCONY

ATTIC

BATH 2

BUILT IN

GAME ROOM
20-4 X 14-0

BEDROOM 3
12-4 X 14-0

BEDROOM 2
11-8 X 14-4

Width 60'-6"
Depth 45'-10"

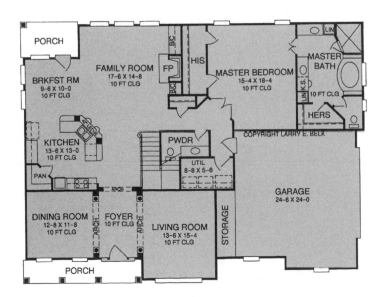

PORCH

FAMILY ROOM
17-6 X 14-8
10 FT CLG

FP

HIS

BRKFST RM
9-6 X 10-0
10 FT CLG

B/C

MASTER BEDROOM
15-4 X 18-4
10 FT CLG

MASTER BATH

LIN

KITCHEN
13-6 X 13-0
10 FT CLG

PWDR

L.IN.S.O.

10 FT CLG

HERS

PAN

UTIL
8-8 X 5-6

COPYRIGHT LARRY E. BELK

DINING ROOM
12-8 X 11-8
10 FT CLG

FOYER
10 FT CLG

LIVING ROOM
13-6 X 15-4
10 FT CLG

ARCH

STORAGE

GARAGE
24-6 X 24-0

PORCH

Design 8226

First Floor: 1,935 square feet
Second Floor: 1,170 square feet
Total: 3,105 square feet

● The formal areas are right up in front in this handsome brick home. Elegant arches lead to all areas from the inviting foyer, with the formal dining room to the left and the formal living room—with no cross-room traffic worries—to the right. Toward the rear of the plan, the welcoming kitchen with its snack bar looks out onto the cozy family room where a fireplace and built-in bookcases dominate. A sunny breakfast room has access to a small covered porch. Located on the first floor for privacy and entered through double doors, the huge master suite has many amenities to tempt you. Upstairs, three family bedrooms share a full hall bath and have direct access to the large game room. Please specify crawlspace or slab foundation when ordering.

Design by
Larry E. Belk
Designs

Design 8675

First Floor: 1,747 square feet
Second Floor: 879 square feet
Total: 2,626 square feet

● An outstanding floor plan graces this traditional home. From the covered front porch, the foyer gives way to formal living areas that include a dining room with an elegant, tiered ceiling. Nearby, the informal family room features a fireplace, a skylight and double doors to the covered patio out back. The tiled kitchen and breakfast nook are both bright and efficient. In the master bedroom, ample proportions, along with a super master bath, provide a fine retreat. Upstairs, three family bedrooms offer privacy. Overlooking the family room below, the balcony adds a touch of drama. A two-car garage and a laundry room make this plan even more functional.

Design by
**Home Design
Services, Inc.**

Width 64'
Depth 59'-4"

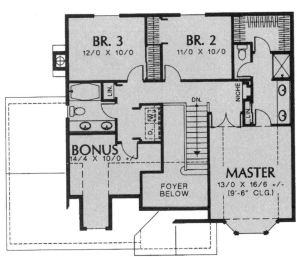

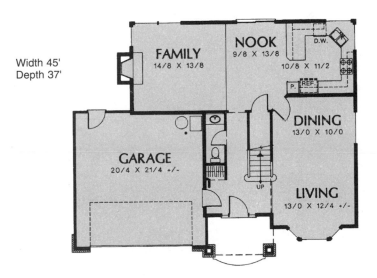

Width 45'
Depth 37'

Design 9582

First Floor: 972 square feet
Second Floor: 843 square feet
Total: 1,815 square feet
Bonus Room: 180 square feet

● A brick arch and a two-story bay window adorn the facade of this comfortable family home. Inside, the formal bayed living room and dining room combine to make entertaining a breeze. At the rear of the home, family life is easy with the open floor plan of the family room, nook and efficient kitchen. A fireplace graces the family room and sliding glass doors access the outdoors from the nook. A powder room is conveniently located in the entry hall to make it easily accessible. Upstairs, three bedrooms include the master suite with pampering bath. A full hall bath with twin vanities is shared by the family bedrooms. A bonus room is available for future development as a study, library or fourth bedroom.

Design by
**Alan Mascord
Design Associates, Inc.**

Design 9584

First Floor: 1,308 square feet
Second Floor: 1,141 square feet
Total: 2,449 square feet
Bonus Room: 508 square feet

● Set at an angle, this home starts off
with distinction. Just off the foyer and
down a step, the formal parlor presents a welcoming atmosphere with
its large window and warming fireplace. The island kitchen has convenient access to both the formal dining
room and the sunny nook and looks
out onto the large family room graced
with yet a second fireplace. A den
with double French doors completes
this level. Upstairs, three secondary
bedrooms share a hall bath with a
double-bowl vanity while the vaulted
master suite is replete with luxuries.

Design by
**Alan Mascord
Design Associates, Inc.**

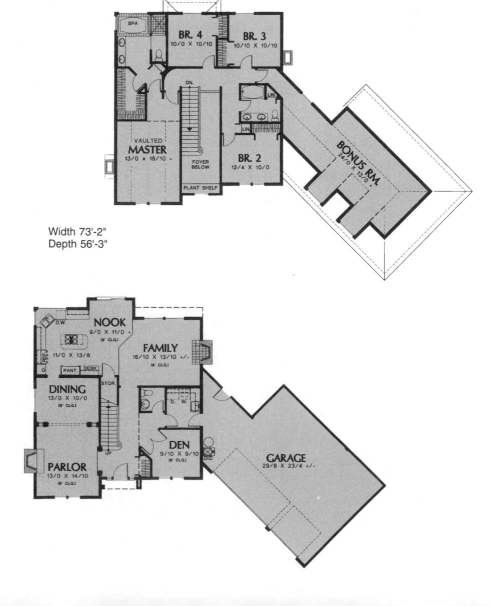

Width 73'-2"
Depth 56'-3"

Design 7295

First Floor: 1,319 square feet
Second Floor: 1,173 square feet
Total: 2,492 square feet

● Elegant columns define a covered front porch which leads to a two-story foyer. The formal dining room is to the left and the formal living room is to the right, with the large family room opening off the rear of this room. A through-fireplace shares its warmth with a bayed hearth room and the family room, while the island kitchen offers plenty of counter and cabinet space. Upstairs, four bedrooms include a deluxe master suite filled with pampering amenities.

Width 56'
Depth 40'

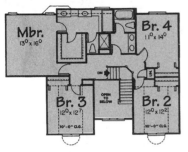

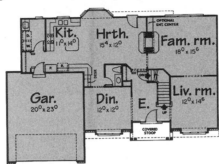

Design by
Design
Basics,
Inc.

Design 9790

First Floor: 1,799 square feet
Second Floor: 730 square feet
Total: 2,529 square feet
Bonus Room: 328 square feet

● A multi-pane dormer, shutters and a covered front porch invite you to call this house a home. Inside, to the left of the foyer is a room which could function as either a formal living room or an elegant study. To the right through a pair of columns, a formal dining room has direct access to the U-shaped kitchen. For informal meals, a breakfast room is just off the kitchen via a snack bar. With a cathedral ceiling and a warming fireplace, the family room is sure to please. The first-floor master suite is full of pleasing details, including a large walk-in closet, a garden tub and a separate shower. Upstairs, three family bedrooms share a full hall bath with dual vanities.

Width 55'-4"
Depth 61'-4"

Design by
Donald A.
Gardner,
Architects, Inc.

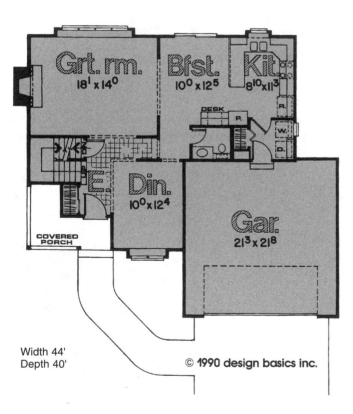

Grt. rm.
18¹ x 14⁰

Bfst.
10⁰ x 12⁵

Kit.
8¹⁰ x 11³

DESK

Din.
10⁰ x 12⁴

Gar.
21³ x 21⁸

COVERED PORCH

Width 44'
Depth 40'

© 1990 design basics inc.

Design by
Design Basics, Inc.

Design 9260

First Floor: 891 square feet
Second Floor: 759 square feet
Total: 1,650 square feet

● This modest-size home provides a quaint covered front porch that opens to a two-story foyer. The formal dining room features a boxed window that can be seen from the entry. A fireplace in the great room adds warmth and coziness to the attached breakfast room and the well-planned kitchen. Sliding glass doors lead from the breakfast room to the rear yard. In a nearby utility room, a washer and dryer reside and a closet provides ample storage. A powder room is provided nearby for guests. Three bedrooms are on the second floor; one of these includes an arched window under a vaulted ceiling. The deluxe master suite provides a large walk-in closet and a dressing area with a double vanity and a whirlpool. A two-car garage will protect the family vehicles.

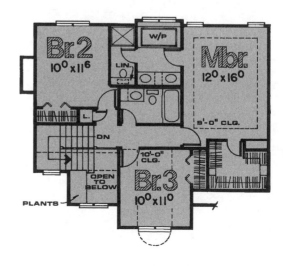

Br. 2
10⁰ x 11⁶

W/P

LIN.

Mbr.
12⁰ x 16⁰

9'-0" CLG.

L.

DN

10'-0" CLG.

OPEN TO BELOW

Br. 3
10⁰ x 11⁰

PLANTS

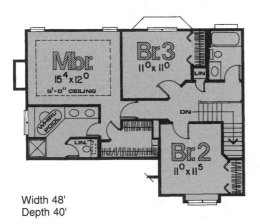

Width 48'
Depth 40'

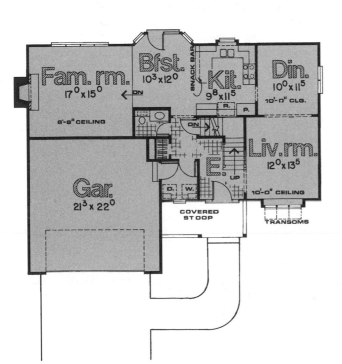

Design 9282

First Floor: 1,042 square feet
Second Floor: 803 square feet
Total: 1,845 square feet

● At 1,845 square feet, this classic two-story home is perfect for a variety of lifestyles. Upon entry from the covered front porch, the thoughtful floor plan is immediately evident. To the right of the entry is a formal volume living room with ten-foot ceiling. Nearby is the formal dining room with a bright window. Serving the dining room and bright bayed dinette, the kitchen features a pantry, Lazy Susan and window sink. Off the breakfast area, step down into the family room with a handsome fireplace and wall of windows. Upstairs, two secondary bedrooms share a hall bath. The private master bedroom has a boxed ceiling, walk-in closet and a pampering dressing area with double vanity and whirlpool.

Design by
**Design
Basics,
Inc.**

45

Photo by Laszlo Regos

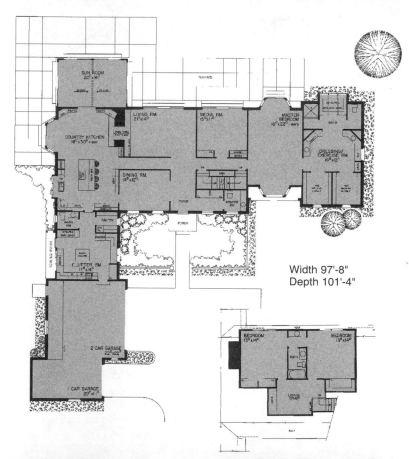

Width 97'-8"
Depth 101'-4"

Quote One®

Cost to build? See page 374
to order complete cost estimate
to build this house in your area!

Design 2921

First Floor: 3,215 square feet
Second Floor: 711 square feet
Total: 3,926 square feet
Sun Room: 296 square feet

L **D**

● Organized zoning makes this traditional design a
comfortable home for living. A central foyer facilitates
flexible traffic patterns. Quiet areas of the house include
a media room and luxurious master bedroom suite with
fitness area, spacious closet space and bath, as well as a
lounge or writing area. Informal living areas of the
house include a sun room, large country kitchen and an
efficient food preparation area with an island. Formal
living areas include a living area and formal dining
room. The second floor holds two bedrooms and a
lounge. Service areas include a room just off the garage
for laundry, sewing or hobbies.

Design by
Home Planners

A Fondness For Farmhouses:
Country-style homes

Photo by Carl Socolow

Design by
Home Planners

Width 59'-6"
Depth 46'

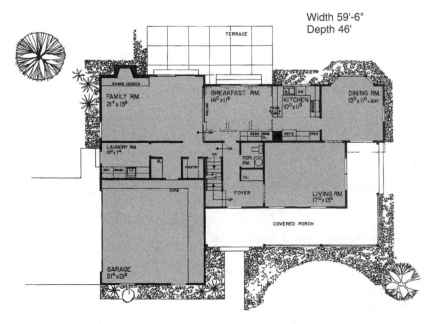

Design 2774
First Floor: 1,366 square feet
Second Floor: 969 square feet
Total: 2,335 square feet

L **D**

● Here's a great farmhouse adaptation with all the most up-to-date features. There is the quiet corner living room which has an opening to the sizable dining room. This room will enjoy plenty of natural light from the delightful bay window overlooking the rear yard and is conveniently located near the efficient U-shaped kitchen. The kitchen features many built-ins and a pass-through to the beam-ceilinged nook. Sliding glass doors to the terrace are found in both the family room and nook. The service entrance to the garage is flanked by a clothes closet and a large, walk-in pantry. Recreational activities and hobbies can be pursued in the basement area. Four bedrooms and two baths are located on the second floor. The master bedroom has a dressing room and double vanity.

QUOTE ONE®
Cost to build? See page 374
to order complete cost estimate
to build this house in your area!

Design 9557

First Floor: 1,371 square feet
Second Floor: 916 square feet
Total: 2,287 square feet

Design by
**Alan Mascord
Design Associates, Inc.**

● The decorative pillars and the wraparound porch are just the beginning of this comfortable home. Inside, an angled, U-shaped stairway leads to the second-floor sleeping zone. On the first floor, French doors lead to a bay-windowed den that shares a see-through fireplace with the two-story family room. The large island kitchen includes a writing desk, a corner sink, a breakfast nook and access to the laundry room, the powder room and the two-car garage. The master suite provides ultimate relaxation with its French-door access, vaulted ceiling and luxurious bath. Two other bedrooms and a full bath complete the second floor.

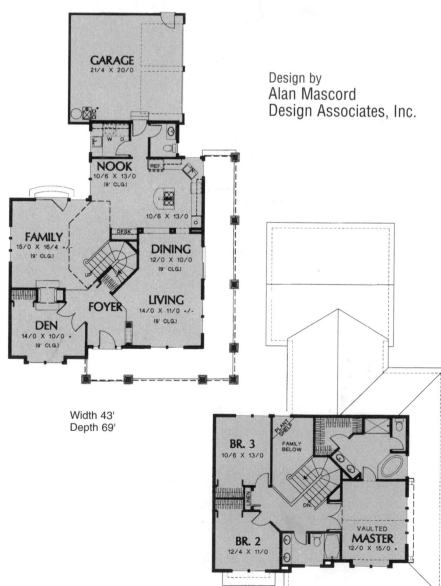

Width 43'
Depth 69'

QUOTE ONE®

Cost to build? See page 374
to order complete cost estimate
to build this house in your area!

Design 2946

Width 74'
Depth 46'

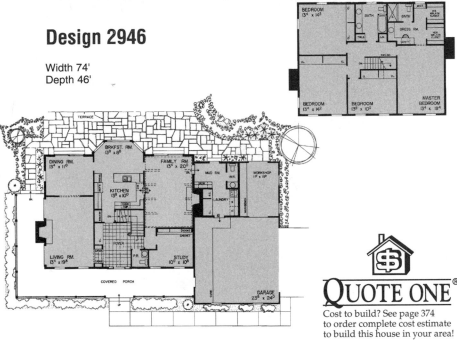

Quote One®

Cost to build? See page 374
to order complete cost estimate
to build this house in your area!

Design 2946/3324

First Floor: 1,581 square feet/1,762 square feet
Second Floor: 1,344 square feet/1,311 square feet
Total: 2,925 square feet/3,073 square feet

L D

● This delightful family farmhouse is even better with the availability of two unique floor plans. In the four bedroom adaptation you'll find a comfortable living room, dining room, breakfast room and an oversize family room. Utilitarian areas include a mud room and a workshop. In the three-bedroom adaptation, the floor plan is reversed and an office replaces the workshop. A grand, two-story entry with an open staircase welcomes visitors. Both designs offer a large master retreat with His and Hers walk-in closets and a dressing room. The secondary bedrooms remain spacious. Whichever you choose, you're sure to feel right at home!

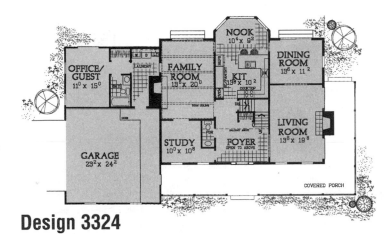

Design 3324

Width 66'
Depth 47'-6"

Design by
Home Planners

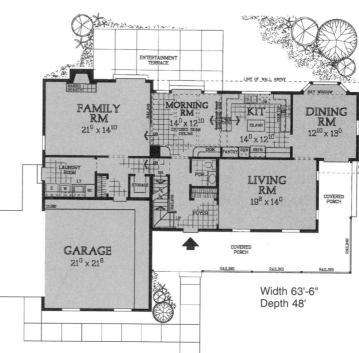

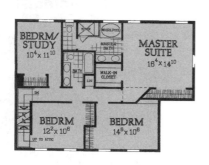

BEDRM/STUDY
10⁴ x 11¹⁰

MASTER SUITE
18⁴ x 14¹⁰

WHIRLPOOL

MASTER BATH

BATH

WALK-IN CLOSET

LIN

BEDRM
12² x 10⁶

DN

BEDRM
14⁸ x 10⁶

UP TO ATTIC

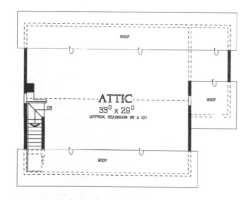

ATTIC
39⁰ x 29⁰
(APPROX. HEADROOM 39' x 12')

DN

ROOF

ROOF

ROOF

ENTERTAINMENT TERRACE

LINE OF WALL ABOVE

FAMILY RM
21⁰ x 14¹⁰

RAISED HEARTH

MORNING RM
14⁰ x 12¹⁰
EXPOSED BEAM CEILING

KIT
14⁰ x 12¹⁰
ISLAND

DINING RM
12¹⁰ x 18⁰

BAY WINDOW

RAILING

DESK

PANTRY

OVN

REFG

LAUNDRY ROOM

D W

LT

INC

STORAGE

DN

DN

PDR.

LIVING RM
19⁸ x 14⁰

COVERED PORCH

CURB

RAILING

UP

FOYER

GARAGE
21⁰ x 21⁶

COVERED PORCH

RAILING   RAILING   RAILING

RAILING

Width 63'-6"
Depth 48'

Design 3325

First Floor: 1,595 square feet
Second Floor: 1,112 square feet
Total: 2,707 square feet

L **D**

Design by
Home Planners

QUOTE ONE®

Cost to build? See page 374
to order complete cost estimate
to build this house in your area!

● Horizontal clapboard siding, varying roof planes and finely detailed window treatments set the tone for this delightful family farmhouse. The living and dining rooms are free of unnecessary cross-room traffic and function very well together. For informal occasions, a spacious family room and breakfast room extend a wealth of livability. In the family room, a raised-hearth fireplace acts as the focal point. Large glass doors provide an extra measure of natural illumination and direct access to the rear terrace. The U-shaped kitchen, with a tile floor,

utilizes a work island supplemented by plenty of cabinet, cupboard and counter space. The sleeping accommodations of this plan include a master bedroom suite with a walk-in closet in addition to a long wardrobe closet. The master bath has a tub plus a stall shower and twin lavatories. The rear bedroom will make a fine study, guest room or fourth bedroom.

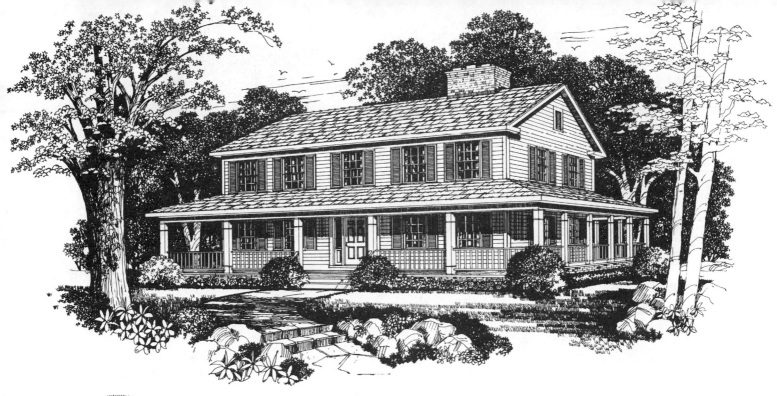

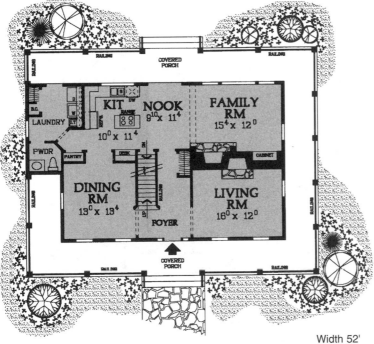

Width 52'
Depth 40'

Design by
Home Planners

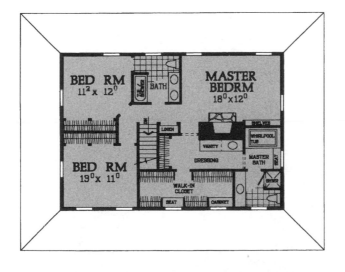

Design 3514

First Floor: 1,216 square feet
Second Floor: 1,120 square feet
Total: 2,336 square feet

● Simple, expansive roof planes, symmetrically placed windows, effectively
stationed columns and a massive brick
chimney help set the appeal of this
farmhouse. Horizontal siding, wood
railings and a paneled front
door with side-lites add to the charm.
Its rectangular shape means economical construction, too. The central foyer
is flanked by the formal living and
dining rooms. The living room with its
central fireplace is completely
free of cross-room traffic. The dining
room is but a step or two from the
kitchen. The corner family room has
the second fireplace and a built-in cabinet for games storage. The L-shaped
kitchen with its island cooking range
functions well. The second floor features two secondary bedrooms and a
master suite. The master bath is compartmented and has a whirlpool, a
stall shower and a built-in seat.

Cost to build? See page 374
to order complete cost estimate
to build this house in your area!

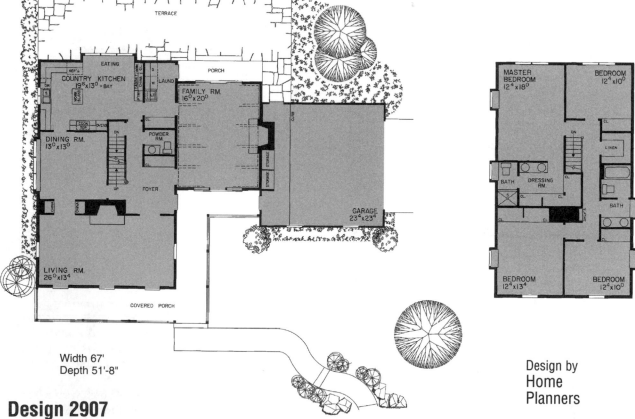

Width 67'
Depth 51'-8"

Design 2907
First Floor: 1,546 square feet
Second Floor: 1,144 square feet
Total: 2,690 square feet

L

Design by
Home Planners

● This traditional, L-shaped farmhouse is charming, indeed, with its gambrel roof, dormer windows and covered porch supported by slender columns and side rails. A spacious country kitchen with a bay provides a cozy gathering place for family and friends, as well as a convenient place for food preparation with its central work island and size. There's a formal dining room also adjacent to the kitchen. A rear family room features its own fireplace, as does a large living room in the front. All four bedrooms are isolated upstairs, away from other household activity and noise. Included is a large master bedroom suite with its own bath, dressing room and abundant closet space. This is a comfortable home for the modern family who can appreciate the tradition and charm of the past.

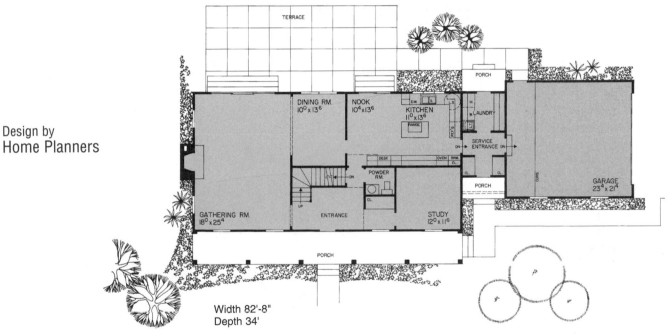

Design by
Home Planners

TERRACE

DINING RM.
10⁰ x 13⁶

NOOK
10⁴ x 13⁶

KITCHEN
11⁰ x 13⁶

RANGE

PORCH

LAUNDRY

SERVICE
ENTRANCE

GARAGE
23⁴ x 21⁴

DESK

OVEN

BRM.

POWDER
RM.

CL.

GATHERING RM.
18⁰ x 25⁴

UP

ENTRANCE

STUDY
12⁰ x 11⁶

PORCH

Width 82'-8"
Depth 34'

WALK-IN
CLOSET

DRESSING
RM.

BATH

BED RM.
11⁴ x 10⁰

BATH

MASTER
BED RM.
18⁰ x 14¹⁰

DN

BED RM.
17⁰ x 12⁶

LINEN

SHELVES

ROOF

Design 2650

First Floor: 1,451 square feet
Second Floor: 1,091 square feet
Total: 2,542 square feet

L **D**

● The dormers and the covered porch with pillars introduce this house to friends and family. Inside, the appeal is also outstanding. Note the size (18 x 25 foot) of the gathering room which is open to the dining room. The kitchen-nook area is very spacious and features a cooking island, built-in desk and more. Great convenience is having the laundry and the service area close to the kitchen. Imagine, a fireplace in both the gathering room and the master bedroom! Make special note of the service entrance doors leading to both the front and back of the home.

Design 7288

First Floor: 1,400 square feet
Second Floor: 584 square feet
Total: 1,984 square feet

● The wrapping covered front porch of this home leads to an oak foyer showcasing an elegant U-shaped staircase. The formal dining room to the right is enhanced by intricate ceiling detail. Double French doors lead into an island kitchen with an attached bay-windowed breakfast nook. With a cathedral ceiling, transom windows and a warming fireplace, the family room is sure to please. Located on the first floor for privacy, the deluxe master suite offers a large walk-in closet and a sumptuous bath complete with a whirlpool tub, separate shower and twin vanities. Upstairs, three family bedrooms share a full hall bath.

Design by
Design
Basics,
Inc.

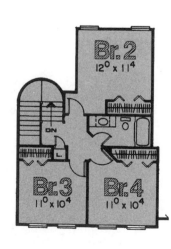

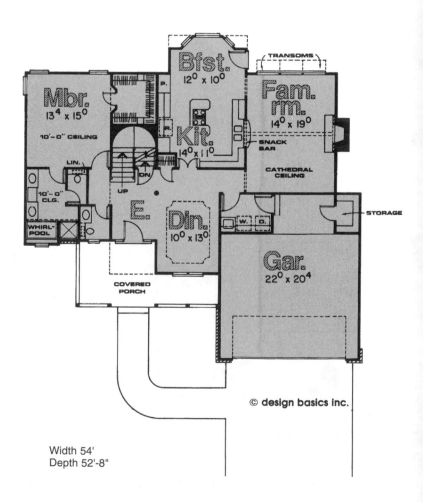

Width 54'
Depth 52'-8"

54

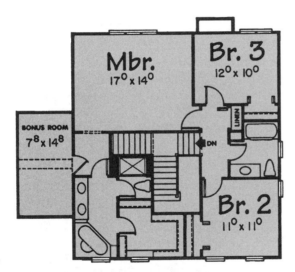

Width 52'
Depth 38'

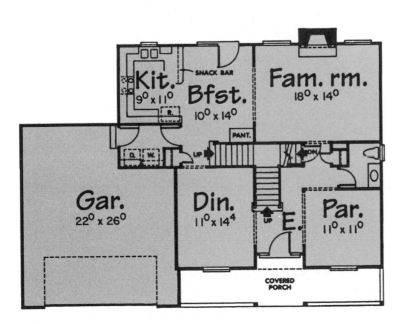

Design 7290

First Floor: 1,111 square feet
Second Floor: 886 square feet
Total: 1,997 square feet

● An elegant parlor, open to the foyer, invites guests to relax and feel at home. Open planning at the rear of this plan gives the kitchen, breakfast room and family room a spacious yet connected feeling. Upstairs, the luxurious master suite offers a huge walk-in closet, a corner tub, a separate shower and twin vanities. Also accessible from the suite is a small bonus room that can be used as an exercise room, office or deluxe storage. Two family bedrooms share a full hall bath and a large linen closet.

Design by
Design
Basics,
Inc.

Design 2945

First Floor: 1,644 square feet
Second Floor: 971 square feet
Total: 2,615 square feet

ATTIC 29⁴ x 26⁴
(HEADROOM 29⁴ x 10⁴)

Width 59'-8"
Depth 56'

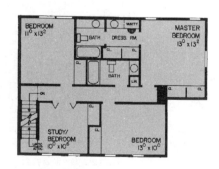

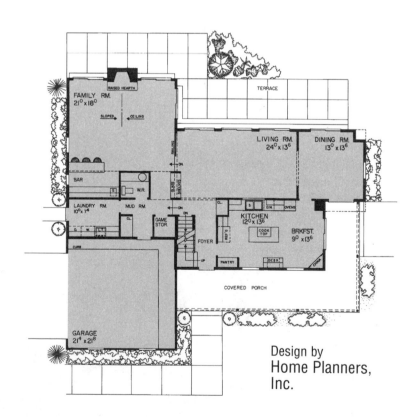

Design by
Home Planners,
Inc.

● This masterfully affordable farmhouse manages to include all the basics—then adds a little more. Note the wraparound covered porch, large family room with raised-hearth fireplace and wet bar, spacious kitchen with island cooktop, formal dining room and rear terrace. Upstairs, the plan is as flexible as they come: three or four bedrooms (the fourth could easily be a study or playroom) and plenty of unfinished attic just waiting to be transformed into living space. This area would make a fine sewing room, home office or children's playroom. Special amenities make this home a stand-out from others in its class. Note the many built-ins, the sliding glass doors to the terrace, and the wealth of closets and storage space.

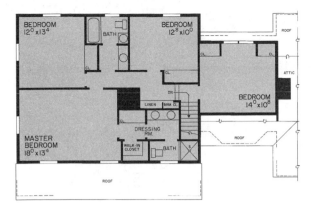

BEDROOM
12⁰x13⁴

BATH

BEDROOM
12⁸x10⁰

CL

ROOF

ATTIC

DN

BRM CL

LINEN

MASTER
BEDROOM
18⁰x13⁴

DRESSING
RM.

WALK-IN
CLOSET

BATH

BEDROOM
14⁰x10⁸

ROOF

ROOF

Width 70'
Depth 34'

Cost to build? See page 374
to order complete cost estimate
to build this house in your area!

Design 2908

First Floor: 1,427 square feet
Second Floor: 1,153 square feet
Total: 2,580 square feet

L **D**

● This Early American farmhouse offers plenty of modern comfort with its covered front porch with pillars and rails, double chimneys, building attachment and four upstairs bedrooms. The first-floor attachment includes a family room with bay window. The upstairs is accessible from stairs just off the front foyer. Included is a master suite. Downstairs is a modern kitchen with breakfast room, a dining room and front living room. Special features of this home include fireplaces in the family room and living room, a laundry/sewing room with freezer and washer/dryer space, a large rear terrace and an entry-hall powder room.

Design by
Home Planners

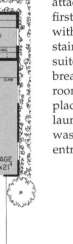

TERRACE

DINING RM.
12⁰x13⁴

KITCHEN
11⁰x13⁴

BRKFST. RM.
9⁸x11⁰

D.W.

S.

REF.

LAUNDRY / SEWING
14⁸x8⁰

LT.

W.

D.

CL

FREEZER

SEWING

DN

BRM
CL.

OVEN

COOK
TOP

STOR.

PDR.
RM.

PANTRY

DN

DN

DISAPPEARING
STAIRS

CURB

BOOKS

CL.

RAILING

FAMILY RM.
14⁰x17⁰+ BAY

LIVING RM.
18⁰x13⁴

FOYER

GARAGE
21⁴x21⁴

COVERED PORCH

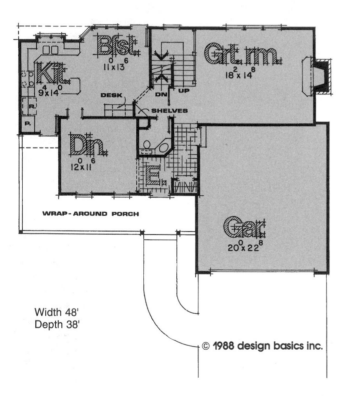

WRAP-AROUND PORCH

Width 48'
Depth 38'

© 1988 design basics inc.

Design by
Design
Basics,
Inc.

Design 9289

First Floor: 927 square feet
Second Floor: 1,163 square feet
Total: 2,090 square feet

● If you've ever dreamed of living in a country home, you'll love the wrapping porch on this four-bedroom, two-story home. Comfortable living begins in the great room with windows and nearby staircase. Just off the entry, a formal dining room was designed to make entertaining a pleasure. The large kitchen includes a pantry, island counter, a roll-top desk and a lazy Susan. Don't miss the bright dinette. Upstairs, secondary bedrooms share a centrally located bath with double vanity. The deluxe master bedroom is accessed by double doors. In the master bath, you'll enjoy the whirlpool, transom window and sloped ceiling.

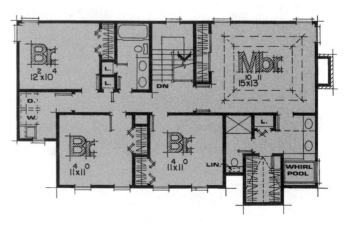

Width 58'
Depth 40'

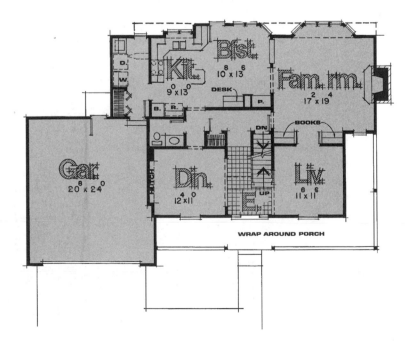

WRAP AROUND PORCH

Design 9214

First Floor: 1,188 square feet
Second Floor: 1,172 square feet
Total: 2,360 square feet

● Beginning with the interest of a wraparound porch, there's a feeling of country charm in this two-story plan. Formal dining and living rooms, visible from the entry, offer ample space for gracious entertaining. The large family room is truly a place of warmth and welcome with its gorgeous bay window, fireplace and French doors to the living room. The kitchen, with island counter, pantry and desk, makes cooking a delight. Upstairs, the secondary bedrooms share an efficient compartmented bath. The expansive master suite has its own luxury bath with double vanity, whirlpool, walk-in closet and dressing area.

Design by
Design
Basics,
Inc.

Design 9212

First Floor: 1,096 square feet
Second Floor: 975 square feet
Total: 2,071 square feet

● "Country charm" is the keynote for this delightful three-bedroom home. Create a very large great room or place a strategically located wall to provide a living room toward the front. The dining room features extra hutch space. The roomy kitchen is complete with large island counter/snack bar, pantry and desk. The gazebo-shaped breakfast room shares a through-fireplace with the great room. The three-bedroom upstairs includes a master suite which boasts an eye-catching arched transom window and bath with whirlpool.

Width 54'
Depth 40'-8"

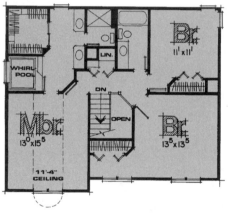

Design by
**Design
Basics,
Inc.**

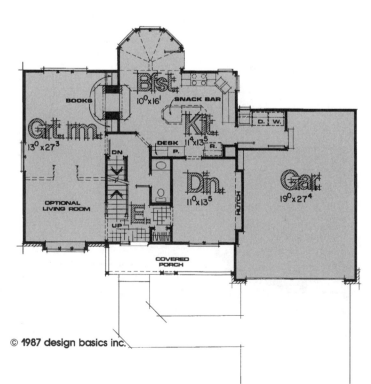

© 1987 design basics inc.

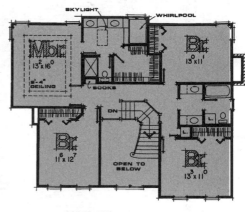

Width 58'
Depth 41'-4"

Design 9215 First Floor: 1,386 square feet
Second Floor: 1,171 square feet; Total: 2,557 square feet

Design by
Design Basics, Inc.

● Amenities for casual family living and entertaining abound in this attractive farmhouse. A charming, covered front porch makes for an inviting exterior. Inside, the two-story entry with a flared staircase opens into the formal dining and living rooms. French doors connect the living room with the more informal family room for expanded entertaining space. A spacious kitchen handily serves both the family and dining rooms. Also note the bay-windowed breakfast area. Upstairs are four bedrooms, one a master suite with a skylit bath including a whirlpool and a large walk-in closet.

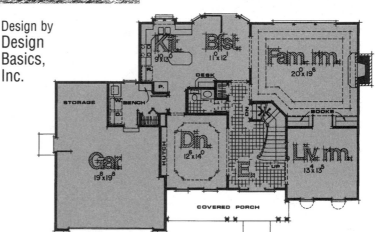

QUOTE ONE®

Cost to build? See page 374
to order complete cost estimate
to build this house in your area!

Width 44'
Depth 38'

Design 3733 First Floor: 1,300 square feet
Second Floor: 1,251 square feet; Total: 2,551 square feet

Design by
Home Planners

L **D**

● The covered front porch with columns and railings provides a sheltered front entrance. Straight ahead from the foyer is the hub of the family's informal living activities. The morning/breakfast room has a bay window, which looks out onto the rear terrace. The U-shaped corner kitchen will be a delight in which to function. It has a wide counter snack bar, built-in cooking units, a pantry and a view of the terrace. For the development of additional recreational space and bulk storage facilities, there is the full basement. There are four sizeable bedrooms and two full baths, each with a double lavatory.

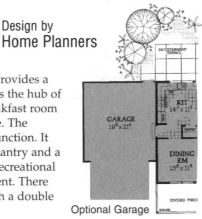

Optional Garage

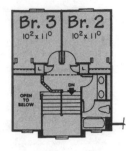

Design 7292

First Floor: 1,210 square feet
Second Floor: 405 square feet
Total: 1,615 square feet

Design by
**Design
Basics,
Inc.**

● An expansive great room, enhanced by a warming
fireplace, will be the focus of this attractive three-bedroom home.
The kitchen will please even the fussiest of gourmets with its
large pantry, abundance of counter space and the snack bar which
opens to the sunny breakfast room. Located on this floor for privacy, the master suite is definitely a place to pamper yourself. On
the second floor, two comfortable family bedrooms share a full
hall bath with twin lavatories.

Width 50'
Depth 48'

Design 9312

First Floor: 1,150 square feet
Second Floor: 1,120 square feet
Total: 2,270 square feet

● A covered porch enhances the elevation of this popular farmhouse. An
entertainment center, through-fireplace and bayed windows add appeal
to the great room. Families will love
the spacious kitchen, breakfast and
hearth room. Enhancements include a
gazebo dinette, wrapping counters, an
island kitchen and planning desk. Upstairs, comfortable secondary bedrooms and a sumptuous master suite
feature privacy by design. Bedroom 3
is highlighted by a half round window, volume ceiling and double closets while Bedroom 4 features a built-
in desk. The master suite has a
vaulted ceiling, large walk-in closet,
compartmented toilet/shower area
and an oval whirlpool tub.

Design by
**Design
Basics,
Inc.**

Width 46'
Depth 48'

Design 7286

First Floor: 1,366 square feet
Second Floor: 1,278 square feet
Total: 2,644 square feet

● A covered porch and a front door with sidelites create an inviting facade to this four-bedroom house. Inside, the formal dining room and formal living room flank a two-story foyer. The rear of the home holds the informal areas. A large kitchen with a cooktop island opens to a bay windowed breakfast area which shares a through-fireplace with the bay windowed family room complete with built-ins. Upstairs is the sleeping zone. Three family bedrooms share a full hall bath with twin vanities. A sumptuous master suite offers an abundance of closet space with twin walk-ins and presents an elegant bath designed to pamper.

FIRST FLOOR PLAN

BOOKS
ENT. CENTER

Kit.
10⁰ x 14⁰

Bfst.
18⁰ x 13⁰

Fam. rm.
17⁰ x 18⁰

Gar.
20⁸ x 25⁰

Din.
13⁰ x 13⁰

Liv. rm.
12⁰ x 13⁰

DN

UP

COVERED PORCH

© design basics inc.

Width 54'-8"
Depth 42'

Design by
Design Basics, Inc.

SECOND FLOOR PLAN

WHIRLPOOL SKYLIGHT

Mbr.
14⁰ x 16⁰

10'-0" CLG.

9'-0" CEILING

LINEN

Br. 2
12⁰ x 13⁰

DN

Br. 4
12⁰ x 12⁸

Br. 3
12⁰ x 13⁰

OPEN TO BELOW

PLANT SHELF

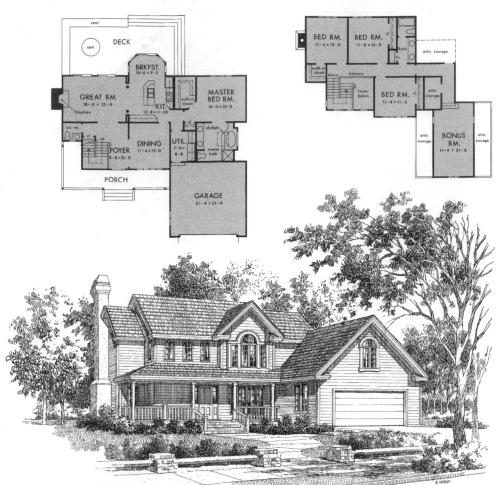

Design 9717

First Floor: 1,377 square feet
Second Floor: 714 square feet
Total: 2,091 square feet

● An inviting covered porch and roundtop windows offer an irresistible appeal to this four-bedroom plan. The two-story foyer allows a more spacious feeling uncommon to plans of similar size. The generous great room, with a fireplace, and the breakfast bay both provide access to a rear deck. The master bedroom, located on the first level, has a large walk-in closet and a bath consisting of a double-bowl vanity, a shower and a garden tub with a skylight overhead. The second level has three bedrooms and a full bath with a double-bowl vanity. As an added feature, the bonus room over the garage does not take away from any of the attic storage space.

Width 55'-8"
Depth 62'-4"

Design by
Donald A.
Gardner,
Architects, Inc.

Design by
Donald A.
Gardner,
Architects, Inc.

Design 9644 First Floor: 943 square feet
Second Floor: 840 square feet; Total: 1,783 square feet
Bonus Room: 323 square feet

● Roundtop windows and an inviting covered porch offer an irresistible appeal for this three-bedroom plan. A two-story foyer provides a spacious feeling to this well-organized open layout. Round columns between the great room and kitchen add to the impressive quality of the plan. An expansive deck promotes casual outdoor living to its fullest. The master suite with walk-in closet and complete master bath is on the second floor along with two additional bedrooms and a full bath. The bonus room over the garage offers room for expansion.

Width 53'-4"
Depth 64'-4"

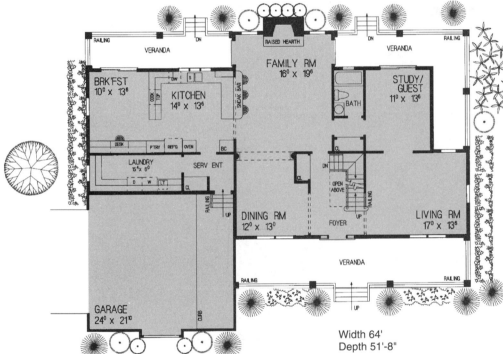

RAILING   VERANDA   DN   VERANDA   RAILING

RAISED HEARTH

FAMILY RM
16⁰ x 19⁶

BRK'FST
10⁰ x 13⁶

KITCHEN
14⁰ x 13⁶

STUDY/
GUEST
11⁰ x 13⁶

BATH

DESK PTRY REF'G OVEN

LAUNDRY
15⁴ x 6⁰

SERV ENT

BC

CL

DN

OPEN
ABOVE

RAILING

DINING RM
12⁰ x 13⁰

FOYER

UP

LIVING RM
17⁰ x 13⁶

VERANDA

RAILING   RAILING

UP

GARAGE
24⁰ x 21¹⁰

Width 64'
Depth 51'-8"

WHIRLPOOL

MASTER
BEDROOM
16⁸ x 13⁴

MASTER BATH

SKYLIGHT VANITY

WALK-IN CLOSET

DN

OPEN
BELOW

RAILING

CL

LINEN

BEDROOM
12⁰ x 11⁰

BEDROOM
12¹⁰ x 13⁶

BATH

Design 3307
First Floor: 1,765 square feet
Second Floor: 1,105 square feet
Total: 2,870 square feet

L **D**

● Classically styled, this charming design brings together the best in historical styling and modern floor planning. Special exterior features include three verandas, multi-paned windows and arch-topped windows. Inside, the first-floor plan boasts formal living and dining areas on either side of the entry foyer, a study that could double as a guest room with nearby full bath, a large family room with raised-hearth fireplace and snack bar pass-through, and a U-shaped kitchen with attached breakfast room. Two family bedrooms on the second floor share a full bath; the master bedroom has a thoughtfully appointed bath and large walk-in closet.

Design by
Home Planners

QUOTE ONE®
Cost to build? See page 374
to order complete cost estimate
to build this house in your area!

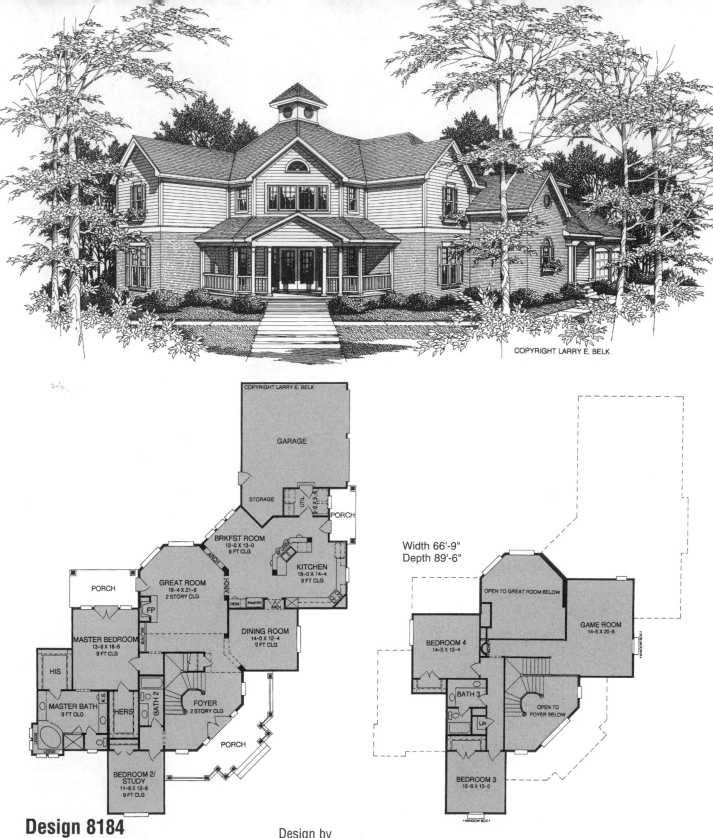

COPYRIGHT LARRY E. BELK

GARAGE

STORAGE

UTIL

PORCH

BRKFST ROOM
12-0 X 13-0
9 FT CLG

KITCHEN
15-0 X 14-4
9 FT CLG

PORCH

GREAT ROOM
18-4 X 21-8
2 STORY CLG

FP

DESK   PANTRY

DINING ROOM
14-0 X 12-4
9 FT CLG

MASTER BEDROOM
13-8 X 16-8
9 FT CLG

HIS

MASTER BATH
9 FT CLG

HERS

BATH 2

FOYER
2 STORY CLG

PORCH

BEDROOM 2/
STUDY
11-6 X 12-6
9 FT CLG

Width 66'-9"
Depth 89'-6"

OPEN TO GREAT ROOM BELOW

GAME ROOM
14-6 X 20-6

BEDROOM 4
14-0 X 13-4

BATH 3

LIN

OPEN TO
FOYER BELOW

BEDROOM 3
12-6 X 13-0

WINDOW BOX

Design 8184

First Floor: 2,276 square feet
Second Floor: 1,049 square feet
Total: 3,325 square feet

Design by
Larry E. Belk
Designs

● Elegant angles and an abundance of space make this a most appealing design. A grand two-story foyer greets you and displays a graceful staircase. Columns define the parameters of the formal dining room and are echoed to separate the well-proportioned great room from the kitchen/breakfast room. The sumptuous master suite is replete with luxuries ranging from His and Hers walk-in closets to a pampering bath and is secluded for privacy on the first floor. Upstairs, two family bedrooms—each with walk-in closets—share a full hall bath and access to a large game room. Plenty of storage can be found in the two-car garage. Please specify crawlspace or slab foundation when ordering.

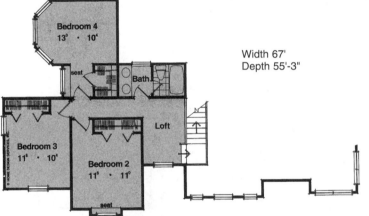

Bedroom 4
13⁰ · 10⁴

Bath.

seat

Loft

Bedroom 3
11⁴ · 10⁴

Bedroom 2
11⁸ · 11⁰

seat

Width 67'
Depth 55'-3"

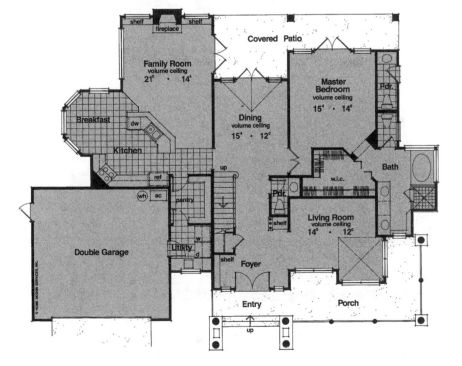

shelf   fireplace   shelf

Covered Patio

Family Room
volume ceiling
21⁰ · 14⁴

Breakfast

dw

Kitchen

Dining
volume ceiling
15⁴ · 12⁰

Master Bedroom
volume ceiling
15⁴ · 14⁰

Pdr.

ref

wh   ac

pantry

up

Pdr.   w.i.c.

Bath

Double Garage

Utility   w   d

shelf

up

Pdr.   shelf

Living Room
volume ceiling
14⁰ · 12⁰

shelf   Foyer

Entry

Porch

up

Design 8622

First Floor: 1,820 square feet
Second Floor: 700 square feet
Total: 2,520 square feet

● Expansive interior space, a porch and a patio are found in this country-style plan. Front-to-back views begin at the double doors that open to the foyer and extend through the dining room to the covered patio. To the right, the foyer spreads into the living room, which opens to a tower. The pass-through kitchen is linked to the sunny bayed breakfast area and has a large walk-through pantry nearby. The family room includes a fireplace flanked by windows and built-in shelves. French doors provide access to the covered patio from the family room, the dining room, and the master bedroom. A lower-level master bedroom includes a private full bath a walk-in closet, double vanity and spa tub. Three additional bedrooms and a loft are located upstairs

Design by
Home Design
Services, Inc.

Design 9588

First Floor: 1,032 square feet
Second Floor: 870 square feet
Total: 1,902 square feet
Bonus Room: 306 square feet

● A wraparound covered porch and symmetrical dormers produce an inviting appearance for this farmhouse. Inside, the two-story foyer leads directly to the large great room graced by a fireplace and an abundance of windows. The U-shaped island kitchen is convenient to the sunny dining room and has a powder room nearby. The utility room offers access to the two-car garage. Upstairs, two family bedrooms share a full hall bath and have convenient access to a large bonus room. The master suite is full of amenities including a walk-in closet and a pampering bath.

Design by
Alan Mascord
Design Associates, Inc.

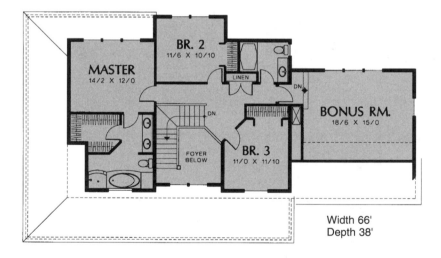

Width 66'
Depth 38'

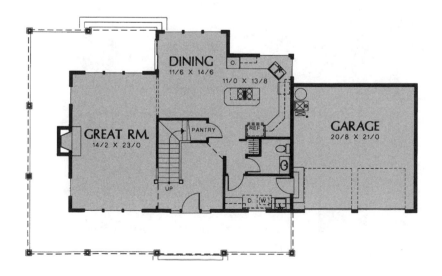

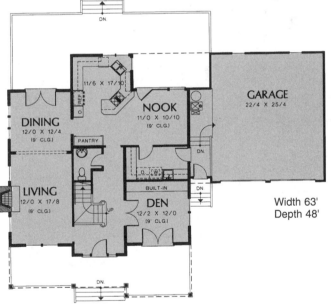

DINING
12/0 X 12/4
(9' CLG.)

NOOK
11/0 X 10/10
(9' CLG.)

11/6 X 17/10

GARAGE
22/4 X 25/4

PANTRY

LIVING
12/0 X 17/8
(9' CLG.)

DEN
12/2 X 12/0
(9' CLG.)

BUILT-IN

Width 63'
Depth 48'

BR. 3
11/4 X 12/0
(8' CLG.)

BR. 2
12/0 X 13/0
(8' CLG.)

LINEN

MASTER
14/8 X 17/2
(8' CLG.)

COVERED
DECK

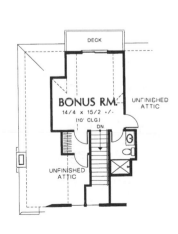

DECK

BONUS RM.
14/4 X 15/2 +/-
(10' CLG.)

UNFINISHED
ATTIC

UNFINISHED
ATTIC

Design 9589

First Floor: 1,225 square feet
Second Floor: 1,116 square feet
Total: 2,341 square feet
Bonus Room: 300 square feet

● The amenities of this home begin on the outside, with its covered porch and balcony, and continue inside with its wonderful layout. To the right of the foyer is a cozy den with access through double French doors to the front porch. To the left of the foyer is the living room which is graced by a warming fireplace and many windows. An efficient kitchen has direct access to both the informal eating nook and the formal dining room. Upstairs, two secondary bedrooms share a full hall bath. The master suite overflows with amenities, including a walk-in closet, a garden tub, a separate shower and a private covered porch. A bonus room with a balcony is located over the garage and can be developed into a mother-in-law or guest suite at a later date.

Design by
Alan Mascord
Design Associates, Inc.

Design 7294

First Floor: 1,365 square feet
Second Floor: 1,185 square feet
Total: 2,550 square feet

● With its brick and siding facade, this farmhouse presents a strong and solid image while its covered front porch offers a cool place to relax. Inside, flanking the foyer, the formal living room and the formal dining room express elegance in a subtle manner. The family room at the rear of the home is graced by a warming fireplace and has direct access to the bay-windowed breakfast room and island kitchen. The sleeping zone is upstairs and is made up of three secondary bedrooms that share a full hall bath with twin vanities and a master bedroom with a pampering bath and a large walk-in closet. A bonus room is accessible from the master bedroom and can be used for an office, an exercise room or storage.

Design by
**Design
Basics,
Inc.**

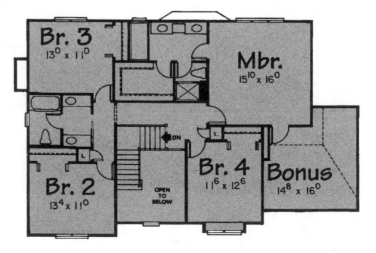

Width 59'-4"
Depth 45'-4"

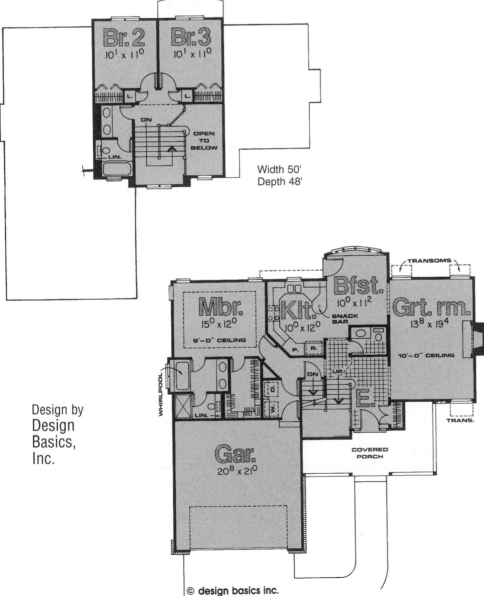

Width 50'
Depth 48'

Design by
Design
Basics,
Inc.

Design 7215

First Floor: 1,191 square feet
Second Floor: 405 square feet
Total: 1,596 square feet

● This charming country-style elevation features a wrapping porch and oval window accents. The spacious great room, directly accessible from the two-story entry and the bowed breakfast area, has a warming fireplace and transom windows. An angled wall adds drama to the peninsula kitchen and creates a private entry to the master suite. In the master suite, a boxed, nine-foot ceiling, a compartmented whirlpool bath and a spacious walk-in closet assure modern livability. The second-level balcony overlooks the U-stairs and entry. Twin linen closets just outside the upstairs bedrooms serve a compartmented bath with natural light.

© design basics inc.

RAILING

VERANDA

GREAT RM
18⁰ X 15⁴

KITCHEN
9⁰ X 11⁸

MASTER
BEDROOM
11⁰ X 15⁰

WHIRLPOOL

BATH

SNACK BAR

DW. REF.

REFRG.

DN

UP

LAUNDRY
W. D.

PANTRY

CL.

DINING
ROOM
11⁰ X 11⁰

FOYER

LIVING
ROOM
12⁰ X 13⁴

GARAGE
23⁰ X 24⁸

VERANDA

RAILING

Width 53'-8"
Depth 57'

QUOTE ONE®

Cost to build? See page 374
to order complete cost estimate
to build this house in your area!

Design by
Home Planners

Design 3462

First Floor: 1,395 square feet
Second Floor: 813 square feet
Total: 2,208 square feet

L

● Horizontal siding with corner
boards, muntin windows and a raised
veranda enhance the appeal of this
country home. Twin carriage lamps
flank the sheltered entrance. Inside,
the central foyer delights with its two
sets of columns at the openings to the
formal living and dining rooms. In the
L-shaped kitchen, an adjacent snack
bar offers everyday ease. Open to the
kitchen, the great room boasts a centered fireplace, a high ceiling and access to the veranda. Sleeping accommodations start off with the master
bedroom; a connecting bath will be a
favorite spot. Upstairs, the bedrooms
share a full bath with twin lavatories.

BEDROOM
11⁰ X 13⁰

OPEN BELOW

STORAGE

BATH

DN

LINEN

BEDROOM
12⁸ X 12⁰

DESK

BEDROOM
12⁰ X 14⁴

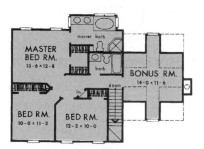

MASTER BED RM. 13-6 × 12-8

master bath

bath

BONUS RM. 14-0 × 11-6

down

BED RM. 10-0 × 11-2

BED RM. 12-2 × 10-0

in.

Width 45'
Depth 69'-2"

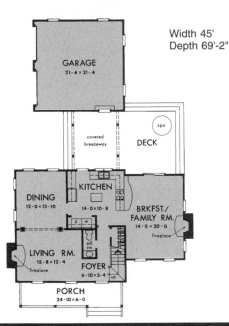

GARAGE 21-4 × 21-4

spa

covered breezeway

DECK

DINING 12-0 × 13-10

KITCHEN 14-0 × 10-8

BRKFST./ FAMILY RM. 14-0 × 20-0

fireplace

LIVING RM. 15-8 × 12-4

pd. rm.

FOYER 6-10 × 5-4

up

fireplace

PORCH 24-10 × 6-0

Design 9687

First Floor: 1,044 square feet
Second Floor: 719 square feet
Total: 1,763 square feet

Design by
Donald A.
Gardner,
Architects, Inc.

● This two-level, three-bedroom country home is ideal for narrow lots. The spacious living room and the family room, both with fireplaces, add flexibility to entertaining. The U-shaped kitchen with island counter offers maximum efficiency for food preparation. A covered breezeway connects the garage to the main house and provides a partially sheltered deck area. The second level boasts a master bedroom with master bath having a double-bowl vanity, whirlpool tub and shower. In addition, two family bedrooms with a full bath and a bonus room are located on the second floor.

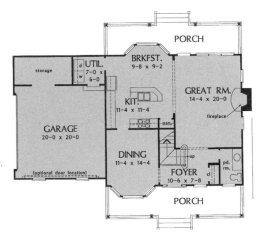

PORCH

UTIL. 7-0 × 6-0

storage

BRKFST. 9-8 × 9-2

KIT. 11-4 × 11-4

GREAT RM. 14-4 × 20-0

fireplace

GARAGE 20-0 × 20-0

DINING 11-4 × 14-4

pan.

up

FOYER 10-6 × 7-8

pd. rm.

(optional door location)

PORCH

Width 52'-6"
Depth 42'-8"

Design 7600

First Floor: 959 square feet
Second Floor: 833 square feet
Total: 1,792 square feet

Design by
Donald A. Gardner,
Architects, Inc.

attic storage

BED RM. 10-4 × 10-0

bath

MASTER BED RM. 13-6 × 15-8

BONUS RM. 20-0 × 14-2

cl

down

walk-in closet

master bath

attic storage

BED RM. 11-4 × 11-10

walk-in closet

● From its covered front porch to its covered rear porch, this farmhouse is a real charmer. The formal dining room is filled with light from a bay window and has direct access to the efficient kitchen. A matching bay is found in the cozy breakfast room. The large great room is graced with a warming fireplace and even more windows. An L-shaped staircase leads up to the sleeping zone containing two family bedrooms sharing a full bath and a master suite full of luxuries. A bonus room extending over the garage can be developed into a game room, a fourth bedroom or a study at a later date.

Design 8993

First Floor: 1,731 square feet
Second Floor: 758 square feet
Total: 2,489 square feet

● The charm of this farmhouse is clearly evident at first glance. Its huge wraparound porch welcomes everyone to come and sit a spell. Inside, a formal dining room is defined by elegant columns and is convenient to the island kitchen. A sunny breakfast room is open to a large living room, thus making casual entertainment easy. Secluded on the first floor for privacy, the master suite is a sight to behold with its enormous walk-in closet and skylit bath. Upstairs, Bedroom 2, with its own full bath and walk-in closet, could be used as a second master suite or a guest suite. Bedrooms 3 and 4 share a full hall bath with a double-bowl vanity.

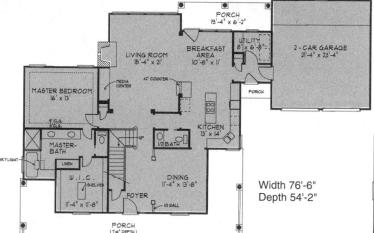

Width 76'-6"
Depth 54'-2"

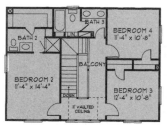

Design by
Larry W. Garnett & Associates, Inc.

Design 3654

First Floor: 1,378 square feet
Second Floor: 912 square feet
Total: 2,290 square feet

L

● The combination of shutters, multi-pane windows and a luxurious wrap-around porch makes this farmhouse a real winner. The formal living room is accented by columns and offers access to the covered porch. At the rear of the plan, the formal dining room shares a through-fireplace with a large family room and both have convenient access to the efficient kitchen. The private first-floor master suite has plenty to offer; a walk-in closet, an ultra tub, a separate shower and access to the covered porch. Upstairs, three family bedrooms share a full hall bath with a compartmented toilet. A large utility room is conveniently located just off a multi-media loft.

Width 74'
Depth 46'

Design by
Home Planners

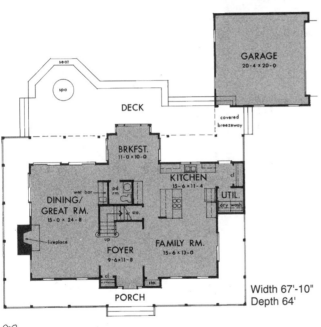

GARAGE
20-4 x 20-0

DECK

covered breezeway

BRKFST.
11-0 x 10-0

KITCHEN
15-6 x 11-4

UTIL.
dry wash

DINING/
GREAT RM.
15-0 x 24-8

wet bar

pd rm

sto.

FOYER
9-6 x 11-8

FAMILY RM.
15-6 x 13-0

fireplace

up

cl

sto.

PORCH

Width 67'-10"
Depth 64'

Design 9668

First Floor: 1,254 square feet
Second Floor: 1,060 square feet
Total: 2,314 square feet

Design by
Donald A. Gardner, Architects, Inc.

● This stylish country farmhouse shows off its good looks both front and rear. A wraparound porch allows sheltered access to all first-level areas along with a covered breezeway to the garage. On the first floor, the spacious, open layout has all the latest features. A fireplace graces the large great room/dining room area and a breakfast room revels in the sun near the kitchen. The master bedroom on the second level has a fireplace, large walk-in closet and a master bath with shower, whirlpool tub and double-bowl vanity. Three additional bedrooms share a full bath with double-bowl vanity.

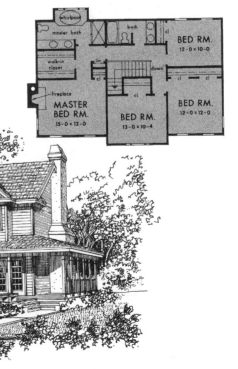

whirlpool

master bath

bath

cl

BED RM.
12-0 x 10-0

walk-in closet

lin.

down

fireplace

MASTER
BED RM.
15-0 x 12-0

BED RM.
13-0 x 10-4

BED RM.
12-0 x 12-0

Design 3461

First Floor: 1,391 square feet
Second Floor: 611 square feet
Total: 2,002 square feet

 L

● Muntin windows, shutters and flower boxes add exterior appeal to this well-designed family farmhouse. The high ceiling, open staircase and wide, columned opening to the living room all lend themselves to an impressive entry foyer. In the living room, a long expanse of windows and two, long blank walls for effective furniture placement set the pace. Informal living takes off in the open kitchen and family room. An island cooktop will be a favorite feature, as will be the fireplace. On the way to the garage, with its workshop area, is the laundry room and its handy closet. Sleeping accommodations are defined by the master bedroom where a bay window provides a perfect sitting nook. The master bath has a large, walk-in closet, a vanity, twin lavatories, a stall shower and a whirlpool tub. Three bedrooms reside upstairs.

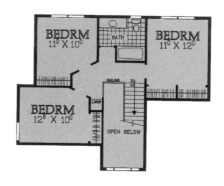

Design by
Home Planners

Width 64'
Depth 44'

QUOTE ONE®

Cost to build? See page 374
to order complete cost estimate
to build this house in your area!

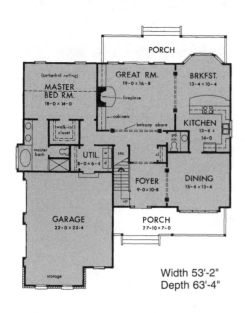

Width 53'-2"
Depth 63'-4"

Design 9701

First Floor: 1,720 square feet
Second Floor: 652 square feet
Total: 2,372 square feet
Bonus Room: 553 square feet

● This elegant country home, with both front and rear porches, offers a pleasing appearance with its variety of materials and refined detailing. The open floor plan is reinforced by the vaulted great room and entrance foyer with clerestory windows in dormers above. Both spaces are open to a balcony/loft area above. The master suite, with a cathedral ceiling and a large walk-in closet, is located on the first floor for privacy and accessibility. Nine-foot ceilings grace much of the first floor. The second floor, with its eight-foot ceilings, has two large bedrooms, a full bath and a bonus room over the garage with space available for another bath.

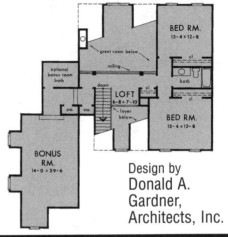

Design by
Donald A.
Gardner,
Architects, Inc.

Design 9747

First Floor: 1,335 square feet
Second Floor: 488 square feet
Total: 1,823 square feet

● This farmhouse exudes welcoming charm. Inside, the large great room with cathedral ceiling, fireplace and rear deck access is convenient to the efficient kitchen. The breakfast room has sliding glass doors to a screened-in porch for carefree outdoor dining. The location of the master bedroom downstairs and two other bedrooms upstairs maintains privacy.

Design by
Donald A.
Gardner,
Architects, Inc.

Width 61'-6"
Depth 54'

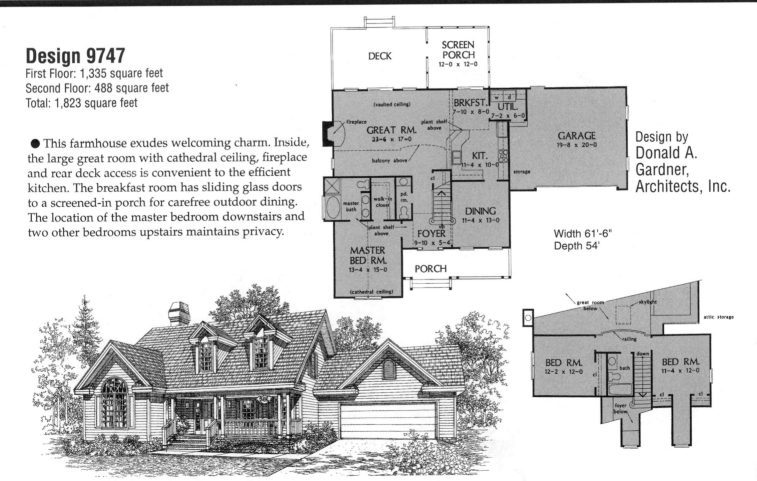

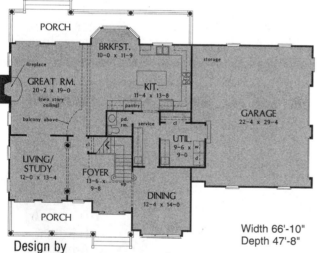

PORCH

BRKFST.
10-0 x 11-9

storage

fireplace

GREAT RM.
20-2 x 19-0
(two story ceiling)

KIT.
11-4 x 13-8

pantry

GARAGE
22-4 x 29-4

balcony above

pd. rm.

service

LIVING/
STUDY
12-0 x 13-4

cl

FOYER
13-6 x
9-8
up

UTIL.
9-6 x
9-0
w
d

PORCH

DINING
12-4 x 14-0

Design by
Donald A.
Gardner,
Architects, Inc.

Width 66'-10"
Depth 47'-8"

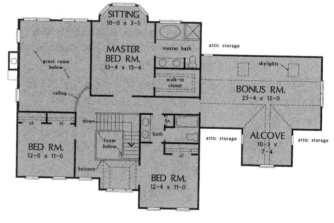

SITTING
10-0 x 3-5

MASTER
BED RM.
13-4 x 15-4

master bath

attic storage

great room
below

skylights

walk-in
closet

BONUS RM.
25-4 x 15-0

railing

cl

down

lin.

cl

BED RM.
12-0 x 11-0

foyer
below

bath

attic storage

ALCOVE
10-3 x
7-4

attic storage

cl

balcony

BED RM.
12-4 x 11-0

Design 9791

First Floor: 1,484 square feet
Second Floor: 1,061 square feet
Total: 2,545 square feet

● With two covered porches to encourage outdoor living and an open layout, this farmhouse has plenty to offer. Columns define the living room which could also be a study. The great room is graced by a fireplace and has access to the rear porch. A sunny, bayed breakfast room is convenient to the U-shaped island kitchen. A formal dining room is located to the front of the design and is enhanced by a boxed-bay window. Three bedrooms upstairs include a deluxe master suite complete with a bay-windowed sitting area, a lavish bath and a walk-in closet. Two secondary bedrooms share a full hall bath. A large bonus room can be developed into a guest suite or game room at a later date.

REAR

Design 9672

First Floor: 1,410 square feet
Second Floor: 613 square feet
Total: 2,023 square feet

● This four-bedroom, 1½-story farmhouse offers special features in an up-to-date plan. Windows at the second level of the two-story foyer allow penetration of natural light. The generous great room with fireplace is accessible from a covered porch and a carefully designed deck with seating and spa location. A kitchen with an island counter serves the breakfast and dining rooms while a wet bar provides an added dimension. Located on the first level for convenience, the master bedroom offers a large walk-in closet and a spacious master bath with double-bowl vanity, whirlpool tub and shower. The second level includes three bedrooms sharing a full bath and ample storage space.

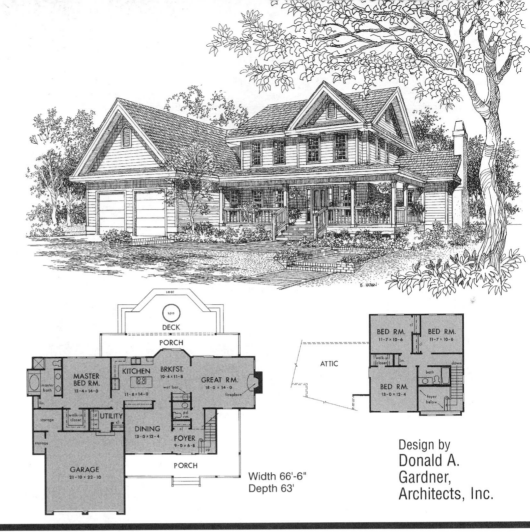

Width 66'-6"
Depth 63'

Design by
Donald A. Gardner, Architects, Inc.

Design 3605

First Floor: 1,622 square feet
Second Floor: 900 square feet
Total: 2,522 square feet

L **D**

● An abundance of country charm creates a welcoming facade to this comfortable two-story home. Living centers around a two-story family room which offers a warming fireplace, a built-in desk and access to the rear covered porch. The U-shaped kitchen efficiently serves a bay windowed dining room and a sunny nook with yet a second bay window. The first-floor master bedroom has many amenities, including two closets and a deluxe bath. On the second floor, two family bedrooms share a hall bath while a third bedroom has its own full bath and could be used as a guest suite.

Design by
Home Planners

Width 70'-6"
Depth 41'-5"

Quote One®

Cost to build? See page 374 to order complete cost estimate to build this house in your area!

79

Design by
**Donald A.
Gardner,
Architects, Inc.**

Design 9798

First Floor: 1,483 square feet
Second Floor: 1,349 square feet
Total: 2,832 square feet

● With two covered porches to encourage outdoor living, multipane windows and an open layout, this farmhouse has plenty to offer. Columns define the living room/study area. The great room is graced by a fireplace and has access to the rear porch. An adjacent sunny, bayed breakfast room is convenient to the U-shaped island kitchen. A formal dining room is nearby for ease in serving elegant meals. Four bedrooms upstairs include a deluxe master suite with a detailed ceiling, a luxurious bath with a tub surrounded by a bay window, and a walk-in closet. Three secondary bedrooms share a full hall bath and offer plenty of storage space. A large bonus room with skylights can be developed at a later date.

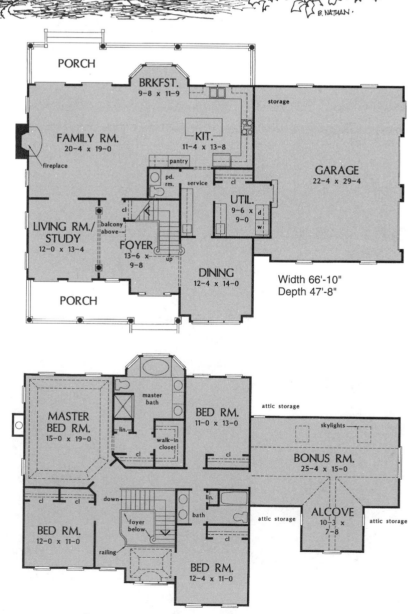

PORCH

BRKFST.
9-8 x 11-9

storage

FAMILY RM.
20-4 x 19-0

KIT.
11-4 x 13-8

GARAGE
22-4 x 29-4

fireplace

pantry

pd. rm.

service

cl

UTIL.
9-6 x 9-0

d
w

LIVING RM./
STUDY
12-0 x 13-4

cl

balcony
above

FOYER
13-6 x
9-8

up

DINING
12-4 x 14-0

PORCH

Width 66'-10"
Depth 47'-8"

MASTER
BED RM.
15-0 x 19-0

master
bath

BED RM.
11-0 x 13-0

attic storage

skylights

lin.

walk-in
closet

cl

cl

BONUS RM.
25-4 x 15-0

cl

cl

down

lin.

bath

attic storage

ALCOVE
10-3 x
7-8

attic storage

BED RM.
12-0 x 11-0

foyer
below

railing

cl

BED RM.
12-4 x 11-0

Design 9667

First Floor: 1,357 square feet
Second Floor: 1,204 square feet
Total: 2,561 square feet

● This grand four-bedroom farm-house with wraparound porch has eye-catching features: a double-gabled roof, Palladian window at the upper level, arched window on the lower level and an intricately detailed brick chimney. The exceptionally large family room allows for more casual living. Look for a fireplace, wet bar and direct access to a porch and deck here. The lavish kitchen boasts a cooking island and serves the dining room, breakfast and deck areas. The master suite on the second level has a large walk-in closet and a master bath with a whirlpool tub, shower and double-bowl vanity. Three additional bedrooms share a full bath.

Design by
Donald A.
Gardner,
Architects, Inc.

Width 80'
Depth 57'

Quote One®

Cost to build? See page 374
to order complete cost estimate
to build this house in your area!

Width 55'
Depth 59'-10"

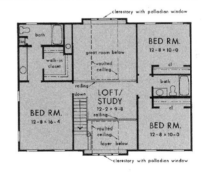

Design 9616

First floor: 1,734 square feet
Second floor: 958 square feet
Total: 2,692 square feet

Design by
Donald A.
Gardner,
Architects, Inc.

● A wraparound covered porch at the front and sides of this home and the open deck with a spa and seating provide plenty of outside living area. A central great room features a vaulted ceiling, fireplace and clerestory windows above. The loft/study on the second floor overlooks this gathering area. Besides a formal dining room, kitchen, breakfast room and sun room on the first floor, there is also a generous master suite with a garden tub. Three second-floor bedrooms complete sleeping accommodations.

Design 3653

First Floor: 1,216 square feet
Second Floor: 1,191 square feet
Total: 2,407 square feet

L **D**

● This home's simple rectangular plan means relatively economical construction costs. Formal areas are located to the front of the plan. Each of the major living areas has direct access to the wraparound porch. The living room is free of annoying cross-room traffic. It even has good blank wall space for effective furniture placement. Upstairs are three bedrooms and a bath with twin lavatories for the kids and a deluxe master suite with a lavish bath. A basement is available for the development of additional recreational and storage space.

Design by
Home Planners

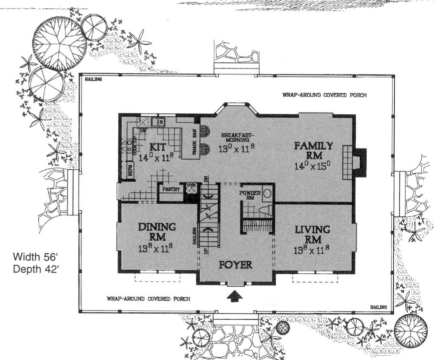

Width 56'
Depth 42'

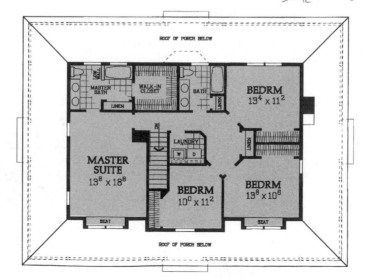

QUOTE ONE®

Cost to build? See page 374 to order complete cost estimate to build this house in your area!

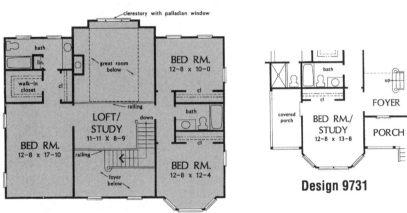

bath
lin.
walk-in closet
cl
BED RM.
12-8 x 17-10
railing
clerestory with palladian window
great room below
LOFT/ STUDY
11-11 X 8-9
down
railing
foyer below
cl
BED RM.
12-8 x 10-0
cl
bath
cl
BED RM.
12-8 x 12-4

bath
cl
covered porch
BED RM./ STUDY
12-8 x 13-8
up
FOYER
PORCH

Design 9731

Width 58'-8"
Depth 66'-4"

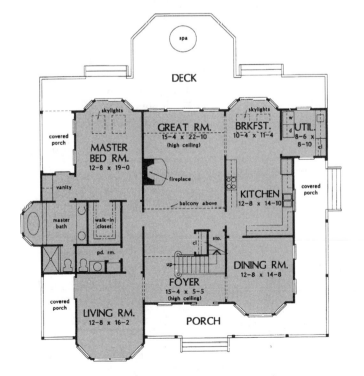

spa
DECK
skylights
covered porch
MASTER BED RM.
12-8 x 19-0
vanity
master bath
walk-in closet
pd. rm.
fireplace
GREAT RM.
15-4 x 22-10
(high ceiling)
balcony above
cl
sto.
up
FOYER
15-4 x 5-5
(high ceiling)
skylights
BRKFST.
10-4 x 11-4
UTIL.
8-6 x 8-10
w d
KITCHEN
12-8 x 14-10
covered porch
DINING RM.
12-8 x 14-8
covered porch
LIVING RM.
12-8 x 16-2
PORCH

Design 9730/9731

First Floor: 1,976 square feet
Second Floor: 970 square feet
Total: 2,946 square feet

● This stylish country farmhouse offers flexibility in the total number of bedrooms while maximizing use of space. Choose between a living room with a half bath (Design 9730) or a bedroom/study with a full bath (Design 9731) depending on your family needs. A loft/study on the second floor overlooks the elegant foyer and great room below. The master bedroom and breakfast area admit natural light through bay windows and skylights. Private covered porches are accessible from the master bedroom and the living room/study. Three bedrooms and two full baths occupy the second floor.

Design by
Donald A.
Gardner,
Architects, Inc.

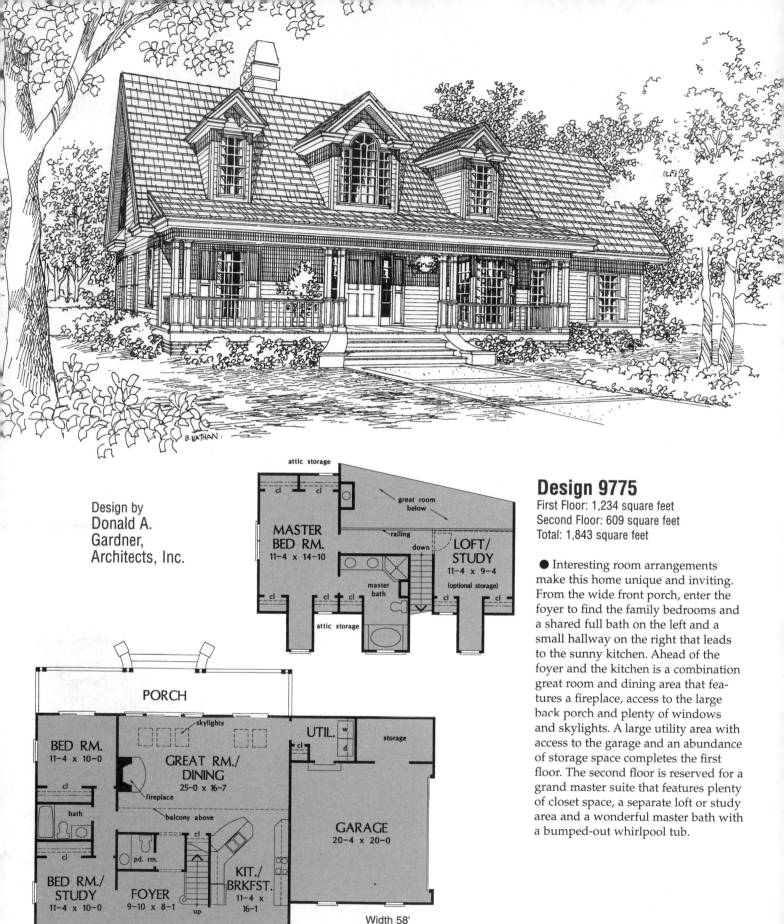

Design by
Donald A.
Gardner,
Architects, Inc.

attic storage

cl | cl

great room
below

MASTER
BED RM.
11-4 x 14-10

railing

down

LOFT/
STUDY
11-4 x 9-4

(optional storage)

master
bath

cl | cl | cl

cl | cl

attic storage

PORCH

skylights

BED RM.
11-4 x 10-0

cl

bath

cl

BED RM./
STUDY
11-4 x 10-0

GREAT RM./
DINING
25-0 x 16-7

fireplace

balcony above

pd. rm.

FOYER
9-10 x 8-1

up

KIT./
BRKFST.
11-4 x
16-1

UTIL.

w

storage

d

cl

GARAGE
20-4 x 20-0

Width 58'
Depth 44'

PORCH

Design 9775

First Floor: 1,234 square feet
Second Floor: 609 square feet
Total: 1,843 square feet

● Interesting room arrangements
make this home unique and inviting.
From the wide front porch, enter the
foyer to find the family bedrooms and
a shared full bath on the left and a
small hallway on the right that leads
to the sunny kitchen. Ahead of the
foyer and the kitchen is a combination
great room and dining area that features a fireplace, access to the large
back porch and plenty of windows
and skylights. A large utility area with
access to the garage and an abundance
of storage space completes the first
floor. The second floor is reserved for a
grand master suite that features plenty
of closet space, a separate loft or study
area and a wonderful master bath with
a bumped-out whirlpool tub.

clerestory with arched window

(cathedral ceiling)
great room below

skylight   skylight

railing

BED RM.   LOFT   BED RM.
12-8 x 11-6   11-10 x 7-8   12-8 x 11-6

down

foyer below

clerestory with palladian window

Design by Donald A. Gardner, Architects, Inc.

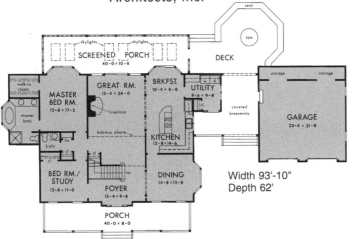

seat
spa

DECK

skylights   skylights

SCREENED   PORCH
40-0 x 9-6

storage   storage

GREAT RM.   BRKFST.   UTILITY
15-4 x 24-0   10-4 x 6-8   9-6 x 9-6

walk-in closet

covered breezeway

MASTER BED RM.
12-8 x 17-2

fireplace

balcony above

GARAGE
23-4 x 21-8

master bath

bath

KITCHEN
12-8 x 14-6

BED RM./ STUDY
12-8 x 11-0

up

FOYER
15-4 x 9-6

DINING
14-8 x 12-8

PORCH
40-0 x 8-0

Width 93'-10"
Depth 62'

Design 9712
First Floor: 1,766 square feet
Second Floor: 670 square feet
Total: 2,436 square feet

Quote One®
Cost to build? See page 374
to order complete cost estimate
to build this house in your area!

● This four-bedroom farmhouse celebrates sunlight with a Palladian window dormer, a skylit screened porch and a rear arched window. The clerestory window in the two-story foyer throws natural light across the loft to a great room with a fireplace and a cathedral ceiling. The central island kitchen and the breakfast area open to the great room through an elegant colonnade. The first-floor master suite is a calm retreat and opens to the screened porch through a bay area. A garden tub, dual lavatories and a separate shower are touches of luxury in the master bath. The second floor provides two bedrooms with private baths and a loft area.

Width 55'
Depth 53'-10"

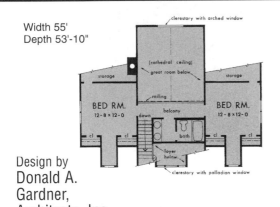

clerestory with arched window

(cathedral ceiling)
great room below

storage   storage

BED RM.   railing   BED RM.
12-8 x 12-0   balcony   12-8 x 12-0

down

bath

Design by Donald A. Gardner, Architects, Inc.

foyer below

clerestory with palladian window

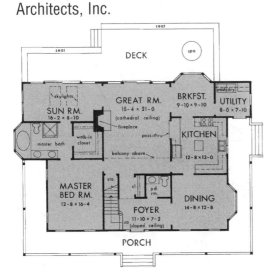

seat

DECK
spa

seat

skylights

SUN RM.
16-2 x 8-10

GREAT RM.
15-4 x 21-0
(cathedral ceiling)

BRKFST.
9-10 x 9-10

UTILITY
8-6 x 7-10

wash/dry

fireplace

master bath

walk-in closet

pass-thru

KITCHEN
12-8 x 13-0

balcony above

MASTER BED RM.
12-8 x 16-4

sto.

pd. rm.

DINING
14-8 x 12-8

FOYER
11-10 x 7-2
(sloped ceiling)

up

PORCH

Design 9623
First Floor: 1,651 square feet
Second Floor: 567 square feet
Total: 2,218 square feet

Quote One®
Cost to build? See page 374
to order complete cost estimate
to build this house in your area!

● A wonderful wraparound covered porch at the front and sides of this house and the open deck with a spa at the back provide plenty of outside living area. Inside, the spacious great room is appointed with a fireplace, cathedral ceiling and clerestory with arched window. The kitchen is centrally located for maximum flexibility in layout and features a food preparation island for convenience. Besides the master bedroom with access to the sun room, there are two second-level bedrooms that share a full bath. Please specify a basement or crawlspace foundation when ordering.

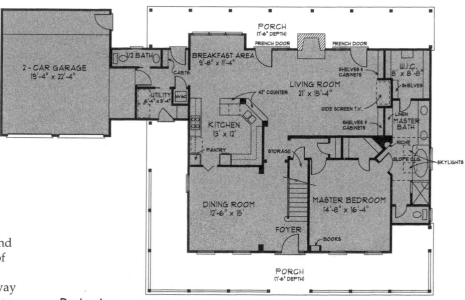

Design 8996

First Floor: 1,748 square feet
Second Floor: 880 square feet
Total: 2,628 square feet

● Three dormers and a wraparound porch give this farmhouse plenty of down-home charm. Inside, a large formal dining room is just steps away from the efficient kitchen. At the rear of the plan, the living room is graced by a fireplace and a French door to the covered porch. A nearby breakfast area is easily served by the snack bar off the kitchen. Secluded on the first floor for privacy, the master bedroom offers many amenities including two walk-in closets, a built-in bookcase and a skylit bath. Upstairs, two bedrooms share a full hall bath while a third bedroom has its own bath. A cozy study area with built-ins completes this level.

Design by
Larry W.
Garnett &
Associates, Inc.

Width 78'-6"
Depth 51'-8"

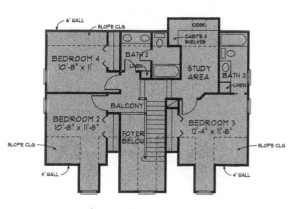

Design 2776

First Floor: 1,134 square feet
Second Floor: 874 square feet
Total: 2,008 square feet

● This board-and-batten farmhouse design has all of the country charm of New England. The large covered front porch will be appreciated for outdoor enjoyment. Immediately off the front entrance is the delightful corner living room. The dining room with bay window will be easily served by the U-shaped kitchen. The informal family room features a raised-hearth fireplace, sliding glass doors to the rear terrace and easy access to the powder room, laundry and service entrance. The second floor contains a master bedroom with private bath and walk-in closet, as well as two other bedrooms sharing a full bath.

Design by
Home Planners

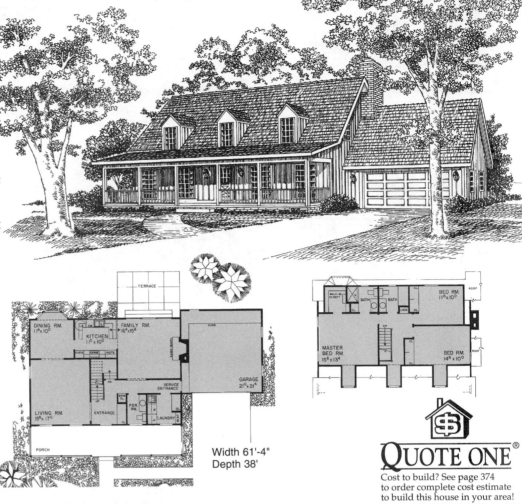

Width 61'-4"
Depth 38'

Q̲UOTE ONE®

Cost to build? See page 374
to order complete cost estimate
to build this house in your area!

Design 8114

First Floor: 1,785 square feet
Second Floor: 830 square feet
Total: 2,615 square feet
Bonus Room: 280 square feet

Design by
Larry E. Belk
Designs

Width 68'-10"
Depth 65'-3"

● Looking to the past for style, the character of this winning plan is vintage Americana. A huge great room opens through classic arches to the island kitchen and the breakfast room. A corner sink in the kitchen gives the cook a view to the outside and brings in sunlight. Nearby, a small side porch provides a charming entry. The master suite is found on the first floor for privacy and features a luxury bath with separate vanities, His and Hers walk-in closets and a corner tub. The three bedrooms upstairs feature dormer windows and share a full bath. Please specify crawlspace or slab foundation when ordering.

Design 9669

First Floor: 1,759 square feet
Second Floor: 888 square feet
Total: 2,647 square feet

● This complete four-bedroom country farmhouse encourages both indoor and outdoor living with the well-organized open layout and the continuous flowing porch and deck encircling the house. Front and rear Palladian window dormers allow natural light to penetrate the foyer and family room below as well as adding exciting visual elements to the exterior. The dramatic family room with sloped ceiling envelopes a curved balcony. The master suite includes a large walk-in closet, a special sitting area and a master bath with whirlpool tub, shower and double-bowl vanity. Two secondary bedrooms share a full hall bath while a third has its own private bath. A bonus room over the garage adds to the completeness of this house.

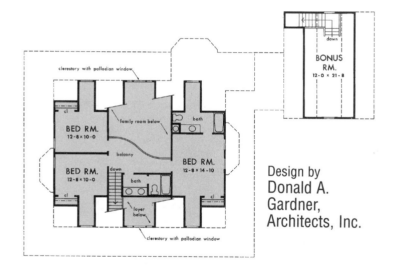

Design by
Donald A. Gardner, Architects, Inc.

Width 85'
Depth 67'-4"

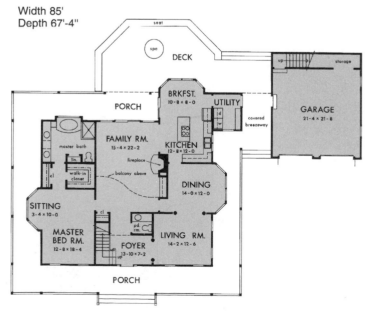

Design 9621

First Floor: 1,325 square feet
Second Floor: 453 square feet
Total: 1,778 square feet

● For the economy-minded family desiring a house with lots of distinction, this compact design has all the amenities available in larger plans. A wraparound covered porch, a front Palladian window and dormer and rear arched windows all provide exciting visual elements to the exterior. The spacious great room has a fireplace, a cathedral ceiling and arched clerestory windows. The kitchen is centrally located for maximum flexibility in layout and features a pass-through to the great room. Besides the generous master suite with a full bath, there are two family bedrooms located on the second level sharing a full bath with a double vanity. Please specify basement or crawlspace foundation when ordering.

QUOTE ONE®

Cost to build? See page 374
to order complete cost estimate
to build this house in your area!

Design by
**Donald A.
Gardner,
Architects, Inc.**

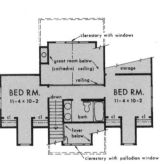

Width 48'-4"
Depth 51'-10"

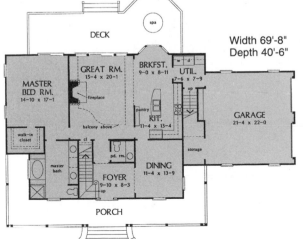

Width 69'-8"
Depth 40'-6"

Design 9773

First Floor: 1,499 square feet
Second Floor: 665 square feet
Total: 2,164 square feet

● This home offers as much on the outside as the inside. A wraparound front porch and a rear deck with a spa provide plenty of space to enjoy the surrounding scenery. Inside, a two-story foyer and a great room create a feeling of spaciousness. The great room leads to a breakfast area and an efficient kitchen with an island work area and a large pantry. The master bedroom is situated on the left side of the house. It features deck access, a large walk-in closet and a bath that includes dual vanities, a whirlpool tub and a separate shower. Three bedrooms, a full bath and bonus space are located upstairs.

Design by
**Donald A.
Gardner,
Architects, Inc.**

Design 9708

First Floor: 2,238 square feet
Second Floor: 768 square feet
Total: 3,006 square feet

● This grand country farmhouse with
wraparound porch offers comfortable
living at its finest. The open floor plan
is reinforced by a vaulted great room
and an entrance foyer with Palladian
clerestory windows in dormers above.
A large country kitchen has a cooktop
island and is convenient to the nearby
bay-windowed breakfast area. The master suite has beautiful bay windows and
a well-designed master bath with cathedral ceiling, His and Hers vanities,
shower, whirlpool tub and spacious
walk-in closet. The second level has two
large bedrooms, a full bath and plenty
of attic storage. An elegant balcony
overlooks the lavish great room.
The three-car garage will easily take
care of the family fleet.

Design by
**Donald A.
Gardner,
Architects, Inc.**

Width 94'-1"
Depth 59'-10"

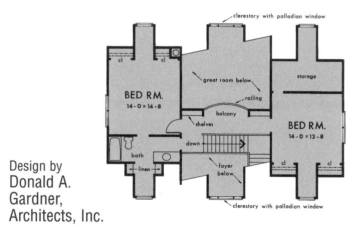

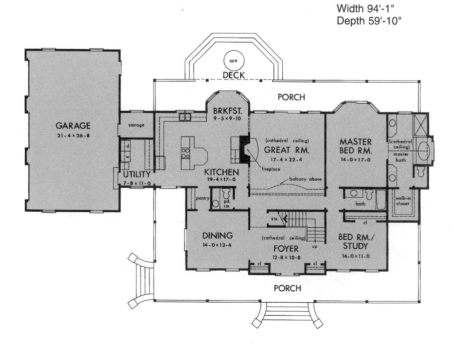

Design 9745

First Floor: 1,576 square feet
Second Floor: 947 square feet
Total: 2,523 square feet
Bonus Room: 405 square feet

● Enjoy balmy breezes as you relax on the wraparound porch of this delightful county farmhouse. The foyer introduces a dining room to the right and a bedroom or study to the left. The expansive great room—with its cozy fireplace—has direct access to the rear porch. Columns define the kitchen, with its large island cooktop, and a sunny breakfast area. A built-in pantry and a desk are additional popular features here. A powder room and a utility room are located nearby. The master bedroom features a tray ceiling and a luxurious bath. Two additional bedrooms share a skylit bath.

Design by
Donald A. Gardner, Architects, Inc.

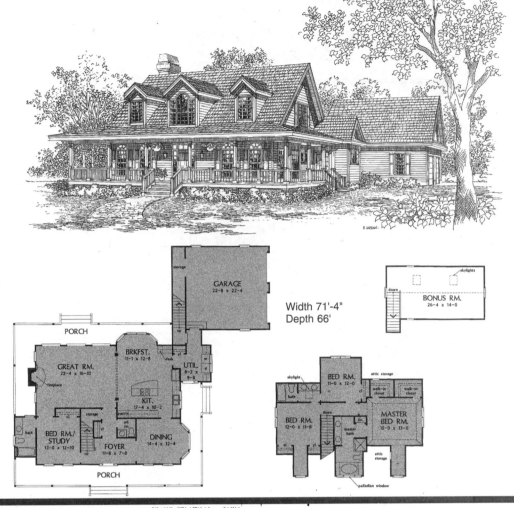

Width 71'-4"
Depth 66'

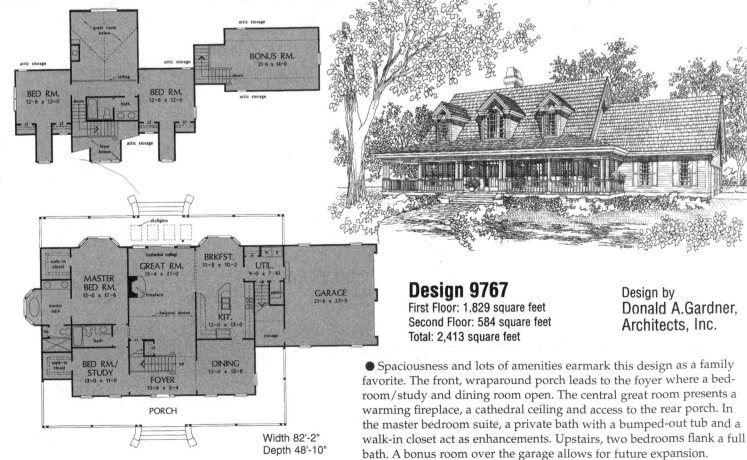

Design 9767

First Floor: 1,829 square feet
Second Floor: 584 square feet
Total: 2,413 square feet

Design by
Donald A. Gardner, Architects, Inc.

● Spaciousness and lots of amenities earmark this design as a family favorite. The front, wraparound porch leads to the foyer where a bedroom/study and dining room open. The central great room presents a warming fireplace, a cathedral ceiling and access to the rear porch. In the master bedroom suite, a private bath with a bumped-out tub and a walk-in closet act as enhancements. Upstairs, two bedrooms flank a full bath. A bonus room over the garage allows for future expansion.

Width 82'-2"
Depth 48'-10"

91

Design 7602

First Floor: 2,097 square feet
Second Floor: 907 square feet
Total: 3,004 square feet
Bonus Room: 373 square feet

● This wonderful farmhouse offers a casually elegant facade with arched windows, multi-pane dormers and a welcoming front porch. A formal living room and dining room flank the foyer, with pillars defining the dining room. The large great room is graced by a fireplace and access to the rear screened porch. A luxurious master suite boasts a walk-in closet and a master bath with twin vanities, a separate shower and a sumptuous garden tub nestled in a bay window. A second-floor balcony and loft overlook the spacious great room. Three family bedrooms share a full bath.

Design by
Donald A.
Gardner,
Architects, Inc.

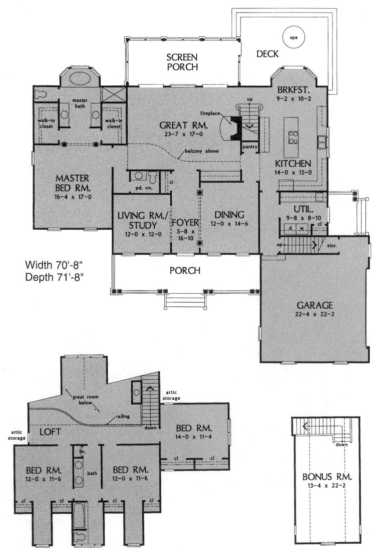

SCREEN PORCH

DECK

spa

BRKFST.
9-2 x 10-2

master bath

walk-in closet

walk-in closet

GREAT RM.
23-7 x 17-0

fireplace

up

balcony above

pantry

KITCHEN
14-0 x 15-0

MASTER BED RM.
16-4 x 17-0

pd. rm.

cl

LIVING RM./ STUDY
12-0 x 12-0

FOYER
5-8 x 16-10

DINING
12-0 x 14-6

UTIL.
9-8 x 8-10

d w

up

stor.

Width 70'-8"
Depth 71'-8"

PORCH

GARAGE
22-4 x 22-2

great room below

attic storage

railing

down

attic storage

LOFT

BED RM.
14-0 x 11-4

cl

cl

lin.

bath

down

BED RM.
12-0 x 11-6

BED RM.
12-0 x 11-6

cl

cl

cl

cl

BONUS RM.
13-4 x 22-2

Design 9706

First Floor: 1,585 square feet
Second Floor: 731 square feet
Total: 2,316 square feet

● This complete farmhouse projects an exciting and comfortable feeling with its wraparound porch, arched windows and dormers. A Palladian window in the clerestory above the entrance foyer allows an abundance of natural light. The large kitchen with cooking island easily services the breakfast area and dining room. The generous great room with fireplace offers access to the spacious screened porch for carefree outdoor living. The master bedroom suite, located on the first level for privacy and convenience, has a luxurious master bath. The second level allows for three bedrooms and a full bath. Don't miss the garage with bonus room—both meet the main house via a covered breezeway.

Width 80'-4"
Depth 58'

Design by
Donald A.
Gardner,
Architects, Inc.

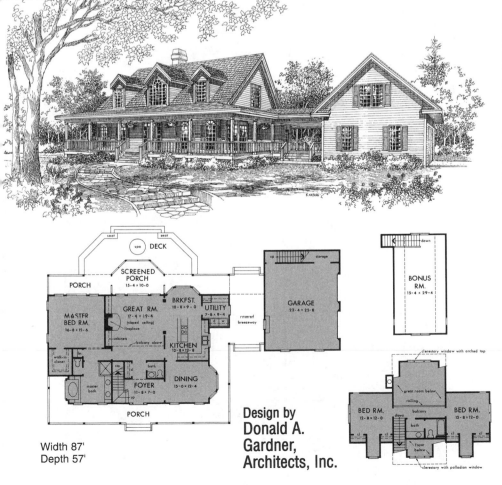

Width 87'
Depth 57'

Design by
Donald A.
Gardner,
Architects, Inc.

Design 9702

First Floor: 1,618 square feet
Second Floor: 570 square feet
Total: 2,188 square feet
Bonus Room: 495 square feet

● A wraparound covered porch, open deck with a spa and seating, arched windows and dormers enhance the already impressive character of this three-bedroom farmhouse. The entrance foyer and great room have Palladian window clerestories to allow natural light to enter. The spacious great room boasts a fireplace, built-in cabinets and bookshelves. The kitchen, with a cooking island, is conveniently located between a dining room and a breakfast room with an open view of the great room. A generous master bedroom has plenty of closet space as well as an expansive master bath. Bonus room over the garage allows for room to grow.

Cost to build? See page 374
to order complete cost estimate
to build this house in your area!

Design 9707

First Floor: 1,632 square feet
Second Floor: 669 square feet
Total: 2,301 square feet
Bonus Room: 528 square feet

● This open country plan boasts front and rear covered porches and a bonus room for future expansion. The entrance foyer with a sloped ceiling has a Palladian window clerestory to allow natural light in. The spacious great room has a fireplace, cathedral ceiling and a clerestory with arched windows. The second-floor balcony overlooks the great room. A U-shaped kitchen provides the ideal layout for food preparation. For flexibility, access is provided to the bonus room from both the first and second floors. This plan is available with a crawlspace foundation.

Design by
Donald A.
Gardner,
Architects, Inc.

QUOTE ONE®

Cost to build? See page 374
to order complete cost estimate
to build this house in your area!

First Floor Plan

PORCH

GREAT RM.
15-4 × 19-2

BRKFST.
9-10×11-10

KIT.
10-10 ×
16-4

up

storage

MASTER
BED RM.
13-2 × 19-2

fireplace
(cathedral ceiling)

balcony above

wet bar

sto.

pantry

cl

walk-in
closet

cl

pd.
rm

DINING
12-4×12-8

d   w

GARAGE
21-8 × 21-0

master
bath

FOYER
10-0 × 7-4

up

PORCH

Width 72'-6"
Depth 46'-10"

Second Floor Plan

clerestory with arched window

great room below

railing

storage

down

BED RM.
13-2 × 15-4

balcony

BED RM.
12-4 × 15-4

cl

cl

down

bath

cl

cl

BONUS
RM.
13-0 × 33-2

foyer
below

clerestory with palladian window

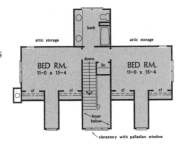

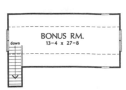

Width 65'-8"
Depth 70'

Design 9694

First Floor: 1,537 square feet
Second Floor: 641 square feet
Total: 2,178 square feet
Bonus Room: 418 square feet

● The welcoming charm of this country farmhouse is expressed by its many windows and its covered wraparound porch. The two-story entrance foyer has a Palladian window in a clerestory dormer above for natural light. The master suite, with its large walk-in closet, is on the first level for privacy and accessibility. The master bath includes a whirlpool tub, a shower and a double-bowl vanity. The second level has two bedrooms, a full bath and plenty of storage. Please specify crawlspace or basement foundation when ordering.

Design by
Donald A. Gardner, Architects, Inc.

Design 9645

First Floor: 1,356 square feet
Second Floor: 542 square feet
Total: 1,898 square feet

● The welcoming charm of this country farmhouse is expressed by its many windows and its covered, wraparound porch. A two-story entrance foyer is enhanced by a Palladian window in a clerestory dormer above to allow natural lighting. A first-floor master suite allows privacy and accessibility. The master bath includes a whirlpool tub, a shower and a double-bowl vanity along with a walk-in closet. The second floor provides two additional bedrooms, a full bath, and plenty of storage space. Please specify basement or crawlspace foundation when ordering.

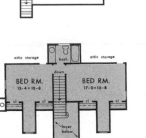

Width 59'
Depth 64'

Design by
Donald A. Gardner, Architects, Inc.

QUOTE ONE®
Cost to build? See page 374 to order complete cost estimate to build this house in your area!

Design 9792

First Floor: 1,480 square feet
Second Floor: 511 square feet
Total: 1,991 square feet

● This farmhouse has plenty to offer, from its covered front porch to its rear deck with a spa. Inside, the amenities continue, including a bayed formal dining room, a great room with fireplace and a bayed breakfast nook. A deluxe master bedroom pampers you with a luxurious bath made up of a whirlpool tub, a separate shower, twin vanities and a walk-in closet. Upstairs, away from the master bedroom for privacy, two family bedrooms share a full hall bath and a balcony overlooking the great room.

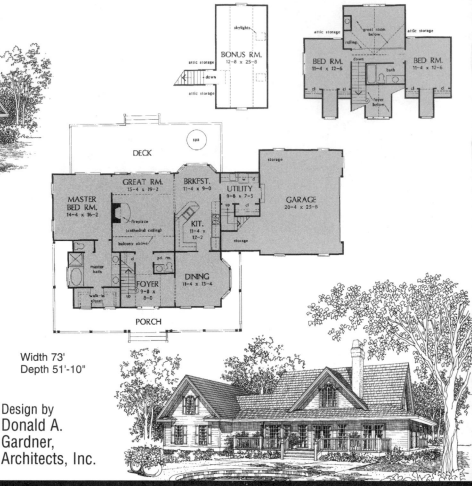

Width 73'
Depth 51'-10"

Design by
Donald A.
Gardner,
Architects, Inc.

Design 9796

First Floor: 1,395 square feet
Second Floor: 489 square feet
Total: 1,884 square feet

● Indoor and outdoor living are a pleasure in this attractive farmhouse. The cathedral ceiling in the great room accents the view to the rear porch, while a fireplace warms those cool evenings. Formal or informal dining will be very enjoyable with the convenience of the gourmet kitchen to the dining room and the sunny bayed breakfast room. Two family bedrooms share a full hall bath. Upstairs, the master bedroom reigns supreme and offers many ways to pamper the homeowner. Also on this level is a large bonus room with skylights.

Width 54'-2"
Depth 53'-5"

Design by
Donald A.
Gardner,
Architects, Inc.

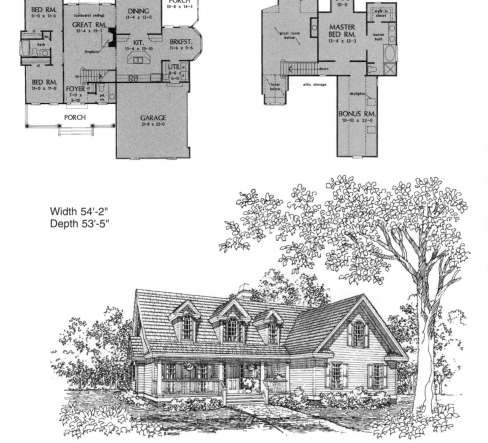

Design 9632

First Floor: 1,756 square feet
Second Floor: 565 square feet
Total: 2,321 square feet

QUOTE ONE®

Cost to build? See page 374
to order complete cost estimate
to build this house in your area!

● A wraparound covered porch at the front and sides of this house and an open deck at the back provide plenty of outside living area. The spacious great room features a fireplace, cathedral ceiling and clerestory with an arched window. The island kitchen has an attached, skylit breakfast room complete with a bay window. The first-floor master bedroom contains a generous closet and a master bath with garden tub, double-bowl vanity and shower. The second floor sports two bedrooms and a full bath with double-bowl vanity. An elegant balcony overlooks the great room. Please specify basement or crawlspace foundation when ordering.

Width 56'-8"
Depth 54'-4"

Design by
Donald A. Gardner, Architects, Inc.

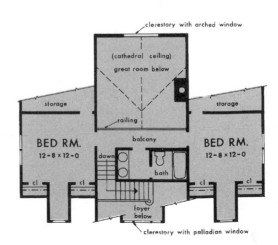

Design 3608

First Floor: 2,347 square feet
Second Floor: 1,087 square feet
Total: 3,434 square feet

L

● Dutch gable roof lines and a gabled wraparound porch with starburst trim provide an extra measure of farmhouse style. The clerestory window sheds light on the stairway leading from the foyer to the upstairs bedrooms and loft. On the main level, the foyer leads to the study or guest bedroom on the left that connects to the master suite, to the formal dining room on the right and to the massive great room in the center of the home where a warming fireplace creates a cozy centerpiece. The kitchen conveniently combines with the great room, the breakfast nook and the dining room. The master suite includes access to the covered patio, a spacious walk-in closet and a master bath with a whirlpool tub.

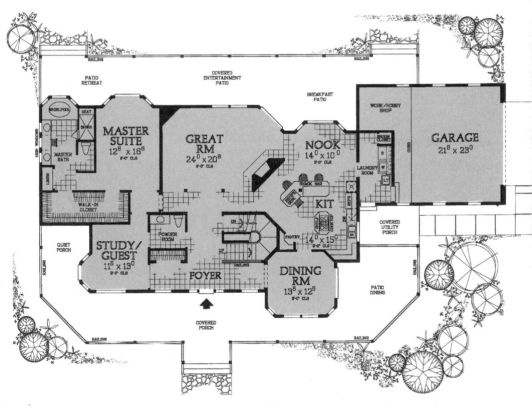

Cost to build? See page 374 to order complete cost estimate to build this house in your area!

Design by
Home Planners

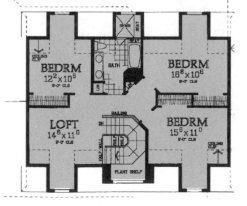

Width 93'-6"
Depth 61'

Design 9723

First Floor: 2,064 square feet
Second Floor: 594 square feet
Total: 2,658 square feet
Bonus Room: 464 square feet

● A front Palladian window dormer and rear clerestory windows at the great room add exciting visual elements to the exterior while providing natural light to the interior. The large great room boasts a fireplace, bookshelves and a raised cathedral ceiling, allowing a curved balcony overlook above. The great room, master bedroom and breakfast room are accessible to the rear porch for greater circulation and flexibility. Special features such as the large cooktop island in the kitchen, the wet bar, the bedroom/study, the generous bonus room over the garage and ample storage set this plan apart.

Design by
Donald A.
Gardner,
Architects, Inc.

Width 92'
Depth 57'-8"

Cost to build? See page 374
to order complete cost estimate
to build this house in your area!

Design 9690

First Floor: 1,145 square feet
Second Floor: 518 square feet
Total: 1,663 square feet

● Look this plan over and you'll be amazed at how much livability can be found in less than 2,000 square feet. A wraparound porch welcomes visitors to the home. Inside lies an enormous great room with a fireplace. To the rear of the home, the breakfast and dining rooms have sliding glass doors to a large deck with room for a spa. The master bedroom contains a walk-in closet and an airy bath with a whirlpool tub. Two bedrooms are found on the second floor, as well as a bonus room over the garage.

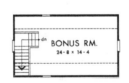

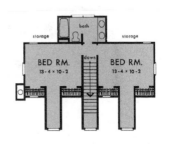

Width 59'-4"
Depth 56'-6"

Cost to build? See page 374
to order complete cost estimate
to build this house in your area!

Design by
Donald A.
Gardner,
Architects, Inc.

99

Design 9662

First Floor: 1,025 square feet
Second Floor: 911 square feet
Total: 1,936 square feet

● The exterior of this three-bedroom home is enhanced by its many gables, arched windows and wraparound porch. A large great room with impressive fireplace leads to both the dining room and screened porch with access to the deck. An open kitchen offers a country-kitchen atmosphere. The second-level master suite has two walk-in closets and an impressive bath. Two family bedrooms share a full bath and plenty of storage. There is also bonus space over the garage.

Design by
Donald A.
Gardner,
Architects, Inc.

Width 53'-8"
Depth 67'-8"

QUOTE ONE®
Cost to build? See page 374
to order complete cost estimate
to build this house in your area!

Design 3609

First Floor: 1,624 square feet
Second Floor: 596 square feet
Total: 2,220 square feet

L **D**

● This home's front-projecting garage allows utilization of a narrow, less expensive building site. The wraparound porch provides outdoor living access from the family kitchen. Open planning and an abundance of windows highlight the formal dining room/great room area. Notice the second bay window in the dining room. The great room has a centered fireplace as its focal point. The master bedroom has a big walk-in closet and the master bath has twin lavatories, a garden tub and a stall shower. Upstairs are two bedrooms, a bath with twin lavatories, plus an outstanding computer/study area.

Design by
Home Planners

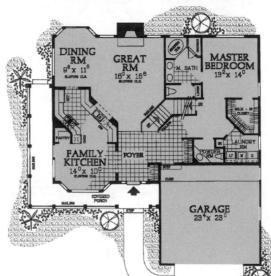

Width 54'-4"
Depth 56'-4"

QUOTE ONE®
Cost to build? See page 374
to order complete cost estimate
to build this house in your area!

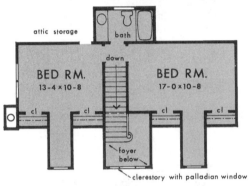

attic storage

bath

BED RM.
13-4 × 10-8

down

BED RM.
17-0 × 10-8

cl cl cl cl

foyer
below

clerestory with palladian window

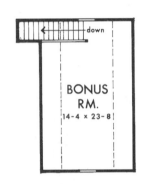

down

BONUS
RM.
14-4 × 23-8

Design by
**Donald A.
Gardner,
Architects, Inc.**

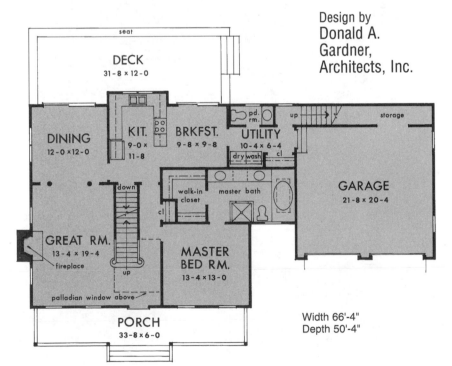

seat

DECK
31-8 × 12-0

DINING
12-0 × 12-0

KIT.
9-0 ×
11-8

BRKFST.
9-8 × 9-8

pd.
rm.

up

storage

UTILITY
10-4 × 6-4

dry wash

cl

GARAGE
21-8 × 20-4

down

walk-in
closet

master bath

cl

GREAT RM.
13-4 × 19-4

fireplace

up

MASTER
BED RM.
13-4 × 13-0

palladian window above

PORCH
33-8 × 6-0

Width 66'-4"
Depth 50'-4"

Design 9606

First Floor: 1,289 square feet
Second Floor: 542 square feet
Total: 1,831 square feet
Bonus Room: 393 square feet

● This cozy country cottage is perfect for the growing family—offering both an unfinished basement option and a bonus room. Enter through the two-story foyer with a Palladian window in a clerestory dormer above. The master suite is on the first floor for privacy and accessibility. Its accompanying bath boasts a whirlpool tub with a skylight above and a double-bowl vanity. The second floor contains two bedrooms, a full bath and plenty of storage. Note that all first-floor rooms except the kitchen and utility room boast nine-foot ceilings. Please specify basement or crawlspace foundation when ordering.

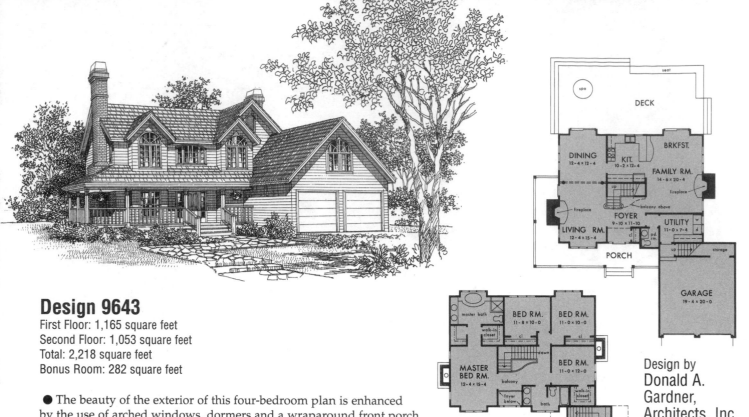

Design 9643

First Floor: 1,165 square feet
Second Floor: 1,053 square feet
Total: 2,218 square feet
Bonus Room: 282 square feet

● The beauty of the exterior of this four-bedroom plan is enhanced
by the use of arched windows, dormers and a wraparound front porch.
Both the living and family rooms have fireplaces. The U-shaped kitchen
is centrally located between the breakfast area and dining room for
maximum efficiency. A large rear deck enhances outdoor living. A master
suite with a generous master bath shares the second floor with three
other bedrooms and a bonus room.

Design by
**Donald A.
Gardner,
Architects, Inc.**

Width 53'
Depth 70'-8"

Design 3620

First Floor: 1,295 square feet
Second Floor: 600 square feet
Total: 1,895 square feet

● This Southern country farmhouse seems to
reach right out and greet you. The octagonal
entry hall is balanced by two bay windows.
Inside, Colonial columns and pilasters provide
a charming entrance to a family/great room
enhanced by a fireplace and French doors. The
L-shaped country kitchen is highlighted by a
bay-windowed eating area with a window
seat. The spacious first-floor master suite is
complemented by French doors opening onto
the porch and a wealth of closet space. A bay
window in the master bath effectively surrounds an old fashioned claw foot tub. The
second floor holds two secondary bedrooms
and a full bath. Plans for an optional indoor
swimming pool/spa and detached garage are
included.

Width 50'
Depth 55'-3"

Design by
Home Planners

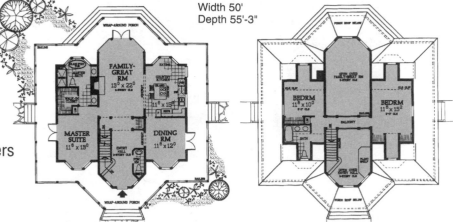

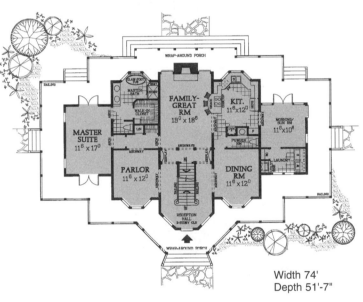

Width 74'
Depth 51'-7"

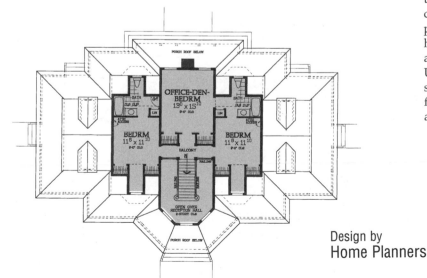

Design by
Home Planners

Design 3621

First Floor: 1,752 square feet
Second Floor: 906 square feet
Total: 2,658 square feet

L **D**

● Delightfully proportioned and perfectly symmetrical, this Victorian farmhouse has lots of curb appeal. The wraparound porch offers appealing columns and railings and broad steps present easy access to the front, rear and side yards. The panelled front door opens to a dramatic two-story reception hall. Archways, display niches and columns catch the eye on the way to the large family/great room with a fire-place. Flanking the reception hall are the formal parlor and the dining room. Each has a bay win-dow and good blank wall space for flexible and effective furniture placement. The left wing of the plan is devoted to the master suite. French doors provide direct access to the front and rear porches. The master bath is compartmented and has a bay with a claw-foot tub, twin lavatories, a walk-in closet and a stall shower with a seat. Upstairs, a perfectly symmetrical layout pre-sents a big office/den (or make it a bedroom) flanked by two bedrooms, each with a full bath and nine-foot ceilings.

Design 9852 First Floor: 1,840 square feet
Second Floor: 950 square feet; Total: 2,790 square feet

Design by
Design Traditions

● The appearance of this Early American home brings the past to mind with its wraparound porch, wood siding and flower-box detailing. The uniquely shaped foyer leads to the dining room accented by columns, a vaulted ceiling and a bay window. Columns frame the great room as well, while a ribbon of windows creates a wall of glass at the back of the house from the great room to the breakfast area. The asymmetrical theme continues through the kitchen as it leads back to the hallway, accessing the laundry and two-car garage. Left of the foyer lies the living room with a warming fireplace. The master suite begins with double doors that open to a large living space with an octagonal tray ceiling and a bay window. The spacious master bath and walk-in closet complete the suite. Stairs to the second level lead from the breakfast area to an open landing overlooking the great room. Three additional bedrooms with large walk-in closets and a variety of bath arrangements complete this level. This home is designed with a basement foundation.

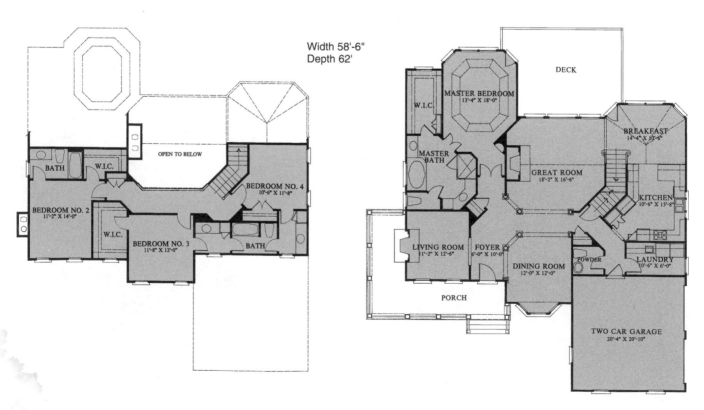

Width 58'-6"
Depth 62'

Design 9822

First Floor: 1,944 square feet
Second Floor: 954 square feet
Total: 2,898 square feet

● This story-and-a-half home combines warm informal materials with a modern livable floor plan to create a true Southern classic. The dining room, study and great room work together to create one large, exciting space. Just beyond the open rail, the breakfast room is lined with windows. Plenty of counter space and storage make the kitchen truly usable. The master suite, with its tray ceiling and decorative wall niche, is a gracious and private owners' retreat. Upstairs, two additional bedrooms each have their own vanity within a shared bath while the third bedroom or guest room has its own bath and walk-in closet. This home is designed with a basement foundation.

Width 51'-6"
Depth 73'

Design by
Design Traditions

Rear Elevation

Design 9242

First Floor: 1,322 square feet
Second Floor: 1,272 square feet
Total: 2,594 square feet

● Here's the luxury you've been looking for—from the wraparound covered front porch to the bright sun room at the rear off the breakfast room. A sunken family room with fireplace serves everyday casual gatherings, while the more formal living and dining rooms are reserved for special entertaining situations. The kitchen has a central island with snack bar and is located most conveniently for serving and cleaning up. Upstairs are four bedrooms, one a lovely master suite with French doors into the master bath and a whirlpool tub in a dramatic bay window. A double vanity in the shared bath easily serves the three family bedrooms.

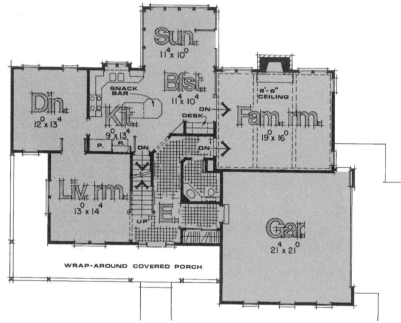

Width 56'
Depth 48'

Design by
Design
Basics,
Inc.

QUOTE ONE®

Cost to build? See page 374 to order complete cost estimate to build this house in your area!

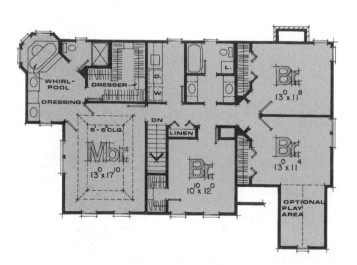

Clearly Colonial:
Early Americana designs

Design 2659 First Floor: 1,023 square feet; Second Floor: 1,008 square feet; Third Floor: 476 square feet; Total: 2,507 square feet

L D

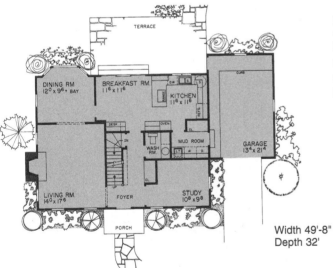

Width 49'-8"
Depth 32'

● The facade of this three-story, pitch-roofed house has a symmetrical placement of windows and a restrained but elegant central entrance. The central hall, or foyer, expands midway through the house to a family kitchen. Off the foyer are two rooms—a living room with a fireplace and a study. The windowed third floor attic can be used as a study and a studio. Three bedrooms are housed on the second floor, including a deluxe master suite with a pampering bath.

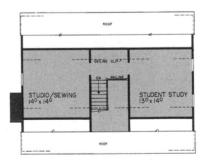

Design by
Home Planners

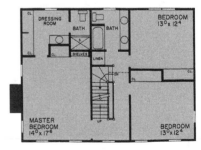

Design 9719

First Floor: 1,168 square feet
Second Floor: 917 square feet
Total: 2,085 square feet

● This elegant, three-bedroom Colonial has an inventive, well-zoned, solar floor plan. Perfect for entertaining, the sun room with ventilating skylights shares its wet bar with the adjoining great room. A contemporary center island kitchen services the dining and breakfast areas. Notice how both the breakfast area and the sun room open to a large rear deck. Upstairs, the master bedroom acts as a calm retreat with a luxurious bath featuring a whirlpool tub, a separate shower and a double-bowl vanity. The two family bedrooms enjoy privacy by design—one even features a walk-in closet. A two-car garage extends a storage space as well as entrance to the house through a utility area.

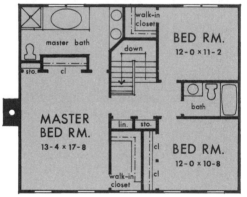

master bath

walk-in closet

down

BED RM.
12-0 × 11-2

sto. cl

bath

MASTER BED RM.
13-4 × 17-8

lin. sto.

cl

BED RM.
12-0 × 10-8

walk-in closet

cl

Design by
Donald A. Gardner, Architects, Inc.

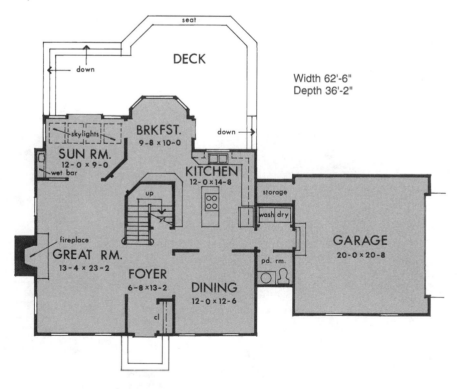

seat

DECK

down

down

skylights

BRKFST.
9-8 × 10-0

SUN RM.
12-0 × 9-0

wet bar

KITCHEN
12-0 × 14-8

up

storage

wash dry

fireplace

GREAT RM.
13-4 × 23-2

FOYER
6-8 × 13-2

pd. rm.

GARAGE
20-0 × 20-8

DINING
12-0 × 12-6

cl

Width 62'-6"
Depth 36'-2"

Design 9691

First Floor: 1,044 square feet
Second Floor: 719 square feet
Total: 1,763 square feet
Bonus Room: 206 square feet

● Colonial through and through, yet
with an added attraction—an addition
containing a family room complete
with a fireplace and access to a rear
deck and spa. The formal living room
has a second fireplace and opens
through pillars to a formal dining
room for ease in entertaining. Upstairs, three bedrooms include a
sumptuous master bedroom with a
pampering bath and walk-in closet. A
bonus room is also located on this
floor for future expansion.

Design by
Donald A.
Gardner,
Architects, Inc.

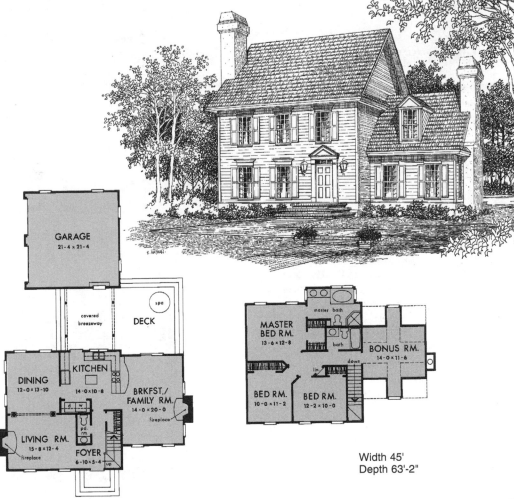

Width 45'
Depth 63'-2"

Design 2622

First Floor: 624 square feet
Second Floor: 624 square feet
Total: 1,248 square feet
Bonus Room: 247 square feet

L **D**

● This Colonial adaptation provides a functional design
that allows for expansion in the future. A cozy fireplace in
the living room adds warmth to this space as well as to
the adjacent dining area. The roomy L-shaped kitchen
features a breakfast nook and an over-the-sink window.
Upstairs, two secondary bedrooms share a full bath with
a double vanity. The master bedroom is on this floor as
well. Its private bath contains access to attic storage. An
additional storage area over the garage can become a
bedroom, an office, or a study in the future.

Design by
Home Planners

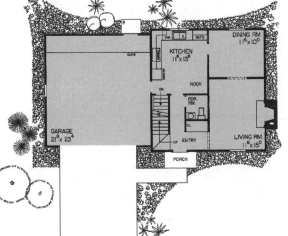

Width 46'
Depth 26'

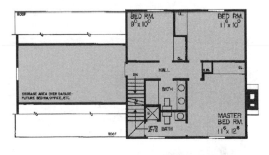

Design 2585

First Floor: 990 square feet
Second Floor: 1,011 square feet
Total: 2,001 square feet

L **D**

● An elegant Colonial, this home features an exterior highlighted with seven large-pane glass windows, shutters and front-porch pillars. The second floor overhangs in the front to extend the size of the master bedroom. The front entrance opens on the left to the formal living and dining rooms and on the right to a hearth-warmed family room. The U-shaped kitchen serves a breakfast nook enhanced by sliding glass doors to the rear terrace and the formal dining room. Upstairs are four bedrooms. The master suite contains a double closet and bath with twin vanities. The three family bedrooms share a full bath with linen storage nearby.

Design by
Home Planners

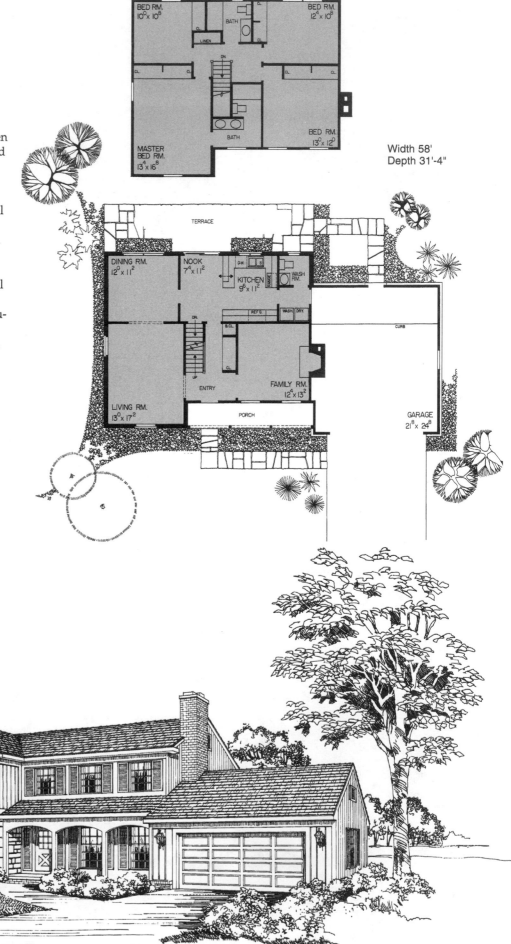

Width 58'
Depth 31'-4"

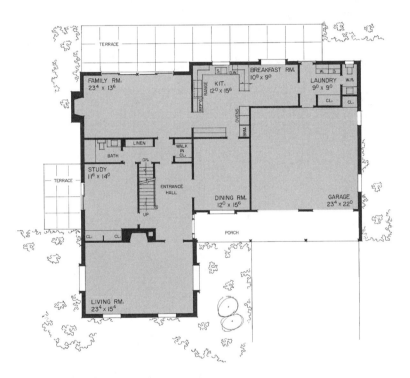

Width 60'-10"
Depth 54'-10"

Design 1728

First Floor: 1,942 square feet
Second Floor: 2,224 square feet
Total: 4,166 square feet

● Amenities abound in this L-shaped Colonial. From the grand entrance hall all of the living zones are readily accessible. To the left is the formal living room graced by a warming fireplace, to the right is the family room with yet another fireplace and access to the rear terrace. The U-shaped kitchen is convenient to both the formal dining room and to the cozy breakfast room. A quiet study is made extra special with sliding glass doors to its own private terrace. Upstairs, six bedrooms include a deluxe guest suite with its own balcony, four family bedrooms and a luxurious master suite complete with a private study. Two full baths with twin vanities service the family bedrooms and the guest suite while the master bedroom has its own pampering bath.

Design by
Home Planners

Design 1868

First Floor: 1,190 square feet
Second Floor: 1,300 square feet
Total: 2,490 square feet

● A five-bedroom farmhouse adaptation that is truly a home for family living. Flanking the foyer is the formal living room which opens to the formal dining room, making entertaining a breeze. To the rear of the plan is the big sunken family room with a fireplace to warm casual gatherings and sliding glass doors for outdoor livability. The U-shaped kitchen serves both the formal dining room and the breakfast room with ease. Four family bedrooms on the second floor fulfill the family's needs very well. One bedroom has its own bath and could be used as a guest suite. Note the grand master bedroom suite with a large walk-in closet and pampering bath, located over the garage.

Design by
Home Planners

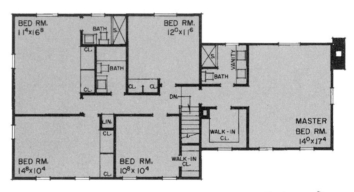

Width 54'-5"
Depth 34'-10"

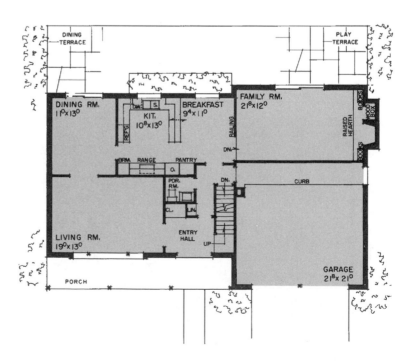

Design 1956

First Floor: 990 square feet
Second Floor: 728 square feet
Total: 1,718 square feet

D

● Loaded with Colonial appeal, this versatile two-story plan features the finest in family floor plans. The entry foyer holds a powder room and a staircase to the second floor. A formal living area connects to the dining room, allowing adequate space for entertaining in style. The U-shaped kitchen features a pass-through counter to the breakfast room. The family room is sunken slightly and is enhanced by a beam ceiling, a raised-hearth fireplace, and built-in bookshelves. Two plans are available for the second floor: one with three bedrooms and one with four. Either option allows for a master bedroom with a private bath.

Width 48'
Depth 34'-10"

3-Bedroom Plan

4-Bedroom Plan

Design by
Home Planners

QUOTE ONE®
Cost to build? See page 374
to order complete cost estimate
to build this house in your area!

Design 1715

First Floor: 1,276 square feet
Second Floor: 1,064 square feet
Total: 2,340 square feet

L **D**

● Three different facades give this house plenty of flexibility and attractiveness. A fine design for the growing family, this Colonial has lots of charm. Formal gatherings will be a pleasure with the size and convenience of the living and dining rooms. For those casual times, the beam-ceilinged family room with its warming fireplace will be ideal. Upstairs, three family bedrooms share a full bath while a master bedroom offers its own luxurious bath and a walk-in closet.

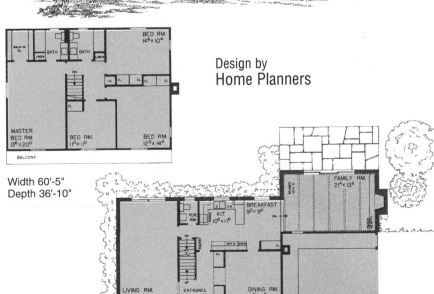

Design by
Home Planners

Width 60'-5"
Depth 36'-10"

Design 2733

First Floor: 1,177 square feet
Second Floor: 1,003 square feet
Total: 2,180 square feet

L **D**

● This is definitely a four-bedroom Colonial with charm galore. The kitchen features an island range and other built-ins. All will enjoy the sunken family room with its fireplace and sliding glass doors leading to the terrace. A basement provides room for recreational activities while the laundry remains on the first floor for extra convenience. Four bedrooms on the second floor include a master bedroom with its own bath.

Design by
Home Planners

QUOTE ONE®

Cost to build? See page 374
to order complete cost estimate
to build this house in your area!

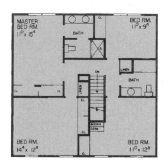

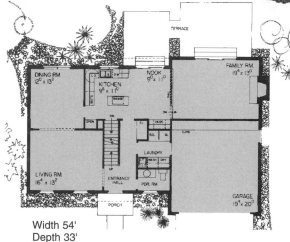

Width 54'
Depth 33'

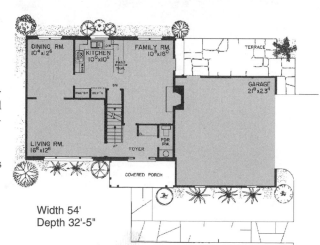

Design 1318

First Floor: 854 square feet
Second Floor: 896 square feet
Total: 1,750 square feet

● Multi-pane windows, shutters and a covered porch combine to give this warm Colonial a welcoming appeal. The huge formal living room is just off the foyer and connects to the formal dining room for ease in entertaining. The U-shaped kitchen works well with the large family room via a pass-through. Upstairs, four family bedrooms share a full hall bath and a linen closet. The master suite offers its own bath for privacy.

Width 54'
Depth 32'-5"

Design by
Home Planners

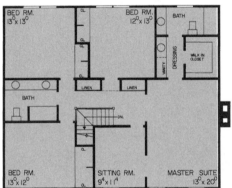

BED RM. 13⁰ x 13⁰   BED RM. 12⁰ x 13⁰   BATH

DRESSING   WALK-IN CLOSET

LINEN   LINEN

BATH

DN.

BED RM. 13⁰ x 12⁰   SITTING RM. 9⁴ x 11⁴   MASTER SUITE 13⁰ x 20⁰

Width 62'
Depth 32'-4"

Design 2540

First Floor: 1,306 square feet
Second Floor: 1,360 square feet
Total: 2,666 square feet

L **D**

● This comfortable Colonial home puts a good foot forward in family living. The entry hall is wide and gracious to receive guests (and comes complete with a powder room for convenience). Flanking it are the family room with fireplace and the formal living room. A dining room has sliding glass doors to a rear terrace and leads directly to the L-shaped kitchen with island range. A handy utility area features washer/dryer space and storage and has an exterior door to the two-car garage. Upstairs are four bedrooms with two full baths. The master bedroom has a sitting room, dressing area, walk-in closet and bath with dual vanities.

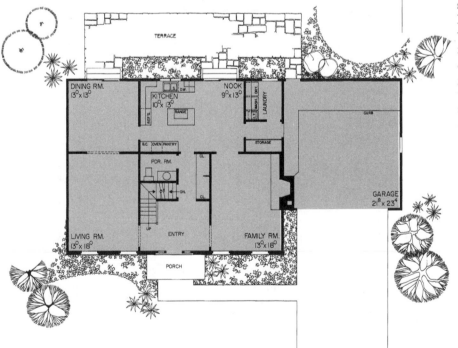

TERRACE

DINING RM. 13⁰ x 13⁰   KITCHEN 10⁰ x 13⁰   NOOK 9⁰ x 13⁰   WASH'L DRY. LAUNDRY

RANGE

CURB

B.C. OVEN PANTRY

STORAGE

PDR. RM.

DN.

UP   ENTRY

GARAGE 21⁸ x 23⁴

LIVING RM. 13⁰ x 18⁰   FAMILY RM. 13⁰ x 18⁰

PORCH

Design by
Home Planners

Design 9239

First Floor: 998 square feet
Second Floor: 1,206 square feet
Total: 2,204 square feet

● The bright entry of this two-story home opens to the formal living and dining space. To the back is the more informal family room with a fireplace and built-in bookshelves. An island kitchen features a corner sink, pantry and convenient planning desk. Upstairs, the master bedroom has a vaulted ceiling and a sumptuous master bath with a skylit dressing area, a whirlpool tub and a walk-in closet. Three family bedrooms and a full bath round out sleeping accommodations. A laundry room is located conveniently on the second floor as well.

Design by
Design Basics, Inc.

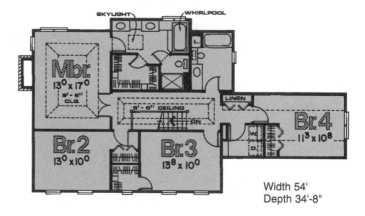

Width 54'
Depth 34'-8"

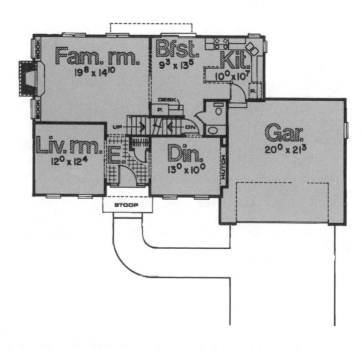

Design 9344

First Floor: 1,000 square feet
Second Floor: 1,345 square feet
Total: 2,345 square feet

● Repeating window detailing, an arched entry and a brick facade highlight the exterior of this two-story Colonial home. The dining room is served by a convenient passageway for quick kitchen service while bright windows and French doors add appeal to the living room. A relaxing family room has a bayed conversation area and a clear view through the dinette into the gourmet kitchen. Upstairs, a U-shaped hall offers separation to all four bedrooms. Homeowners will love the expansive master retreat. This oasis features a private sitting room, two walk-in closets, compartmented bath, separate vanities and a whirlpool tub.

Width 57'-4"
Depth 30'

Design by
Design
Basics,
Inc.

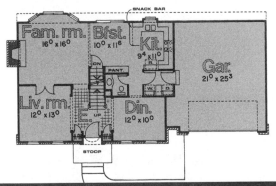

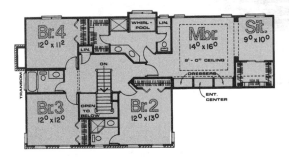

Design 9343

First Floor: 1,000 square feet
Second Floor: 993 square feet
Total: 1,993 square feet

● This plan captures the heritage and romance of an authentic Colonial home. A central hall leads to the formal rooms at the front where showpiece furnishings can be displayed. For daily living, the informal rooms can't be beat. A bookcase and large linen cabinet are thoughtful touches upstairs. Further evidence of tasteful design is shown in the master suite. A volume ceiling, large walk-in closet and whirlpool tub await the fortunate homeowner. Each secondary bedroom has bright windows to add natural lighting and comfort.

Design by
Design
Basics,
Inc.

Quote One®
Cost to build? See page 374
to order complete cost estimate
to build this house in your area!

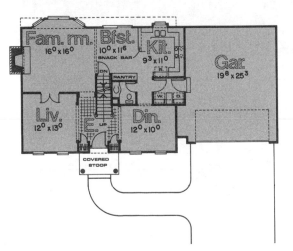

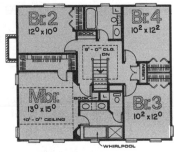

Width 56'
Depth 30'

Design 9299

First Floor: 2,063 square feet
Second Floor: 894 square feet
Total: 2,957 square feet

● An elegant brick elevation and rows of shuttered windows lend timeless beauty to this 1½-story Colonial design. The volume entry surveys formal dining and living rooms and the magnificent great room. Sparkling floor-to-ceiling windows flank the fireplace in the great room with a cathedral ceiling. French doors, bayed windows and a decorative ceiling, plus a wet bar highlight the private den. Special lifestyle amenities in the kitchen and bayed breakfast area include a built-in desk, wrapping counters and an island. A boxed ceiling adds elegance to the master suite. In the master bath/dressing area, note the large walk-in closet, built-in dresser, His and Hers vanities, oval whirlpool and plant shelves. Each secondary bedroom upstairs has a roomy closet and private bath.

Design by
Design
Basics,
Inc.

Cost to build? See page 374
to order complete cost estimate
to build this house in your area!

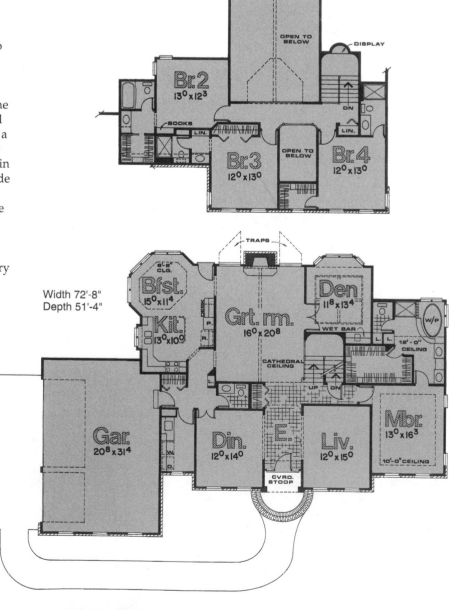

Width 72'-8"
Depth 51'-4"

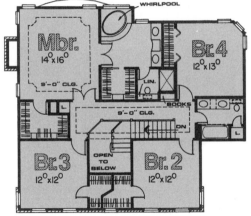

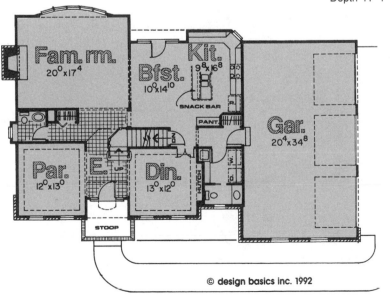

Width 61'-4"
Depth 41'-4"

Design 9389

First Floor: 1,362 square feet
Second Floor: 1,223 square feet
Total: 2,585 square feet

● Gracing the elevation of this captivating Colonial are decorative windows and brick detailing. Inside, the dining room is complemented by French doors, a distinctive ceiling treatment and space to accommodate a buffet or hutch. A formal parlor provides a place for quiet relaxation. The family room, with a fireplace, is brightened by an airy, bowed window. The spacious kitchen provides a large pantry, a snack bar and an abundant food preparation surface area. Half baths are placed conveniently near the family room and laundry. On the second floor, a resplendent master suite filled with the most desirable amenities is joined by three family bedrooms. The side-load garage accommodates three cars.

Design 9364

First Floor: 1,717 square feet
Second Floor: 1,518 square feet
Total: 3,235 square feet

● Stately columns highlight the facade of this home. The open entry allows for views into formal areas and up the tapering staircase. Alcoves flank the staircase in the entry. The dining room with hutch space accesses the kitchen through double doors. The living room accesses the sunken family room through pocket doors. Step down into the huge family room to find large windows, a fireplace, a built-in entertainment center and bookcases. The kitchen adjoins the sunny, semi-gazebo breakfast area. Secondary bedrooms make use of two full baths. The private master suite features a tiered ceiling, two walk-in closets and a roomy, bayed sitting area.

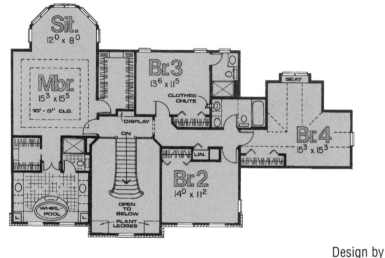

Design by
Design Basics, Inc.

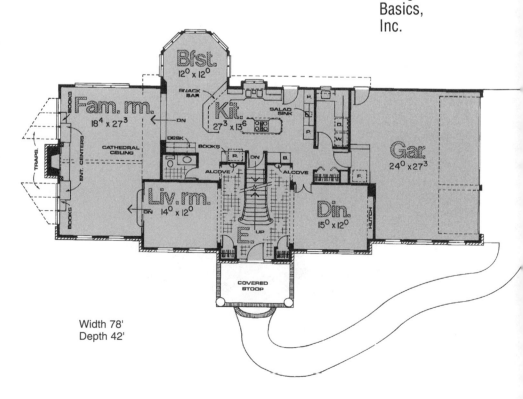

Width 78'
Depth 42'

QUOTE ONE®
Cost to build? See page 374
to order complete cost estimate
to build this house in your area!

Design 9858

First Floor: 1,570 square feet
Second Floor: 1,630 square feet
Total: 3,200 square feet

● This classic Americana design employs wood siding, a variety of window styles and a detailed front porch. Upon entry, the large two-story foyer flows into the formal dining room, with arched window accents, and the combination study/living room with a large bay window. A short passage with a wet bar accesses the family room with a wall of windows, French doors and a fireplace. The large breakfast area and open kitchen with cooking island are spacious and airy as well as efficient. The walk-in pantry, laundry and entry to the two-car garage complete this level. Upstairs, the master suite's sleeping and sitting rooms feature architectural details including columns, tray ceilings and a fireplace. The elegant master bath contains a raised oval tub, dual vanities and separate shower. Generous His and Hers closets are located beyond the bath. Additional bedrooms are complete with closets and a variety of bath combinations. This home is designed with a basement foundation.

Design by
Design Traditions

Width 59'-10"
Depth 43'-4"

Design 9913

First Floor: 1,625 square feet
Second Floor: 1,750 square feet
Total: 3,375 square feet

● This American Country home, with its clapboard siding, covered balcony and shuttered windows, echoes images of traditional small-town living. Opening to the foyer are the dining room and formal living room. The two-story great room includes a fireplace, bookcases and a window wall. Adjacent to the great room are the spacious kitchen and bayed breakfast area. A back staircase is included for easy access to upstairs bedrooms. The second floor provides three bedrooms with various bath combinations. A balcony provides a breathtaking view of the great room and foyer below. The master suite features a tray ceiling and sitting area warmed by sunlight from an angled window combination. The enormous master bath area includes a tray ceiling and His and Hers vanities and closets. This home is designed with a basement foundation.

Design by
Design Traditions

Width 63'-10"
Depth 48'-6"

Rear Elevation

Design 9823

First Floor: 1,960 square feet
Second Floor: 905 square feet
Total: 2,865 square feet

● The classical styling of this Colonial home will be appreciated by traditionalists. The foyer opens to both a banquet-sized dining room and formal living room with fireplace. Just beyond is the two-story great room. The entire right side of the main level is taken up by the master suite. The other side of the main level includes a large kitchen and breakfast room just steps away from the detached garage. Upstairs, each bedroom features ample closet space and direct access to bathrooms. The detached garage features an unfinished office or studio on its second level. This home is designed with a basement foundation.

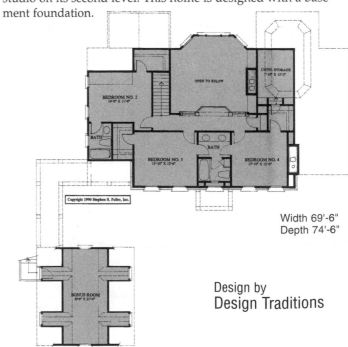

Width 69'-6"
Depth 74'-6"

Design by
Design Traditions

123

Design 8654

First Floor: 2,212 square feet
Second Floor: 874 square feet
Total: 3,086 square feet

● From the moment you see this beautiful period home, you'll be reminded of the style and grace of the South. While keeping traditional design basics intact, the home is designed for today's lifestyles. The master suite is on the first floor and boasts a coffered-ceiling bed chamber. A bayed sitting area off the walk-in closet is perfect for morning coffee. The living and family areas are beautifully intermingled with double pocket doors into both spaces. The family room features French doors leading to the patio. Note the lavatory off the rear yard and the generous laundry room. Three bedrooms upstairs are perfect for family and guests.

Design by
Home Design
Services, Inc.

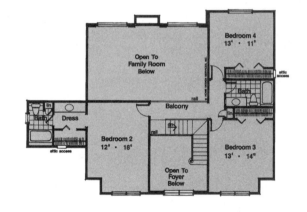

Width 87'
Depth 51'

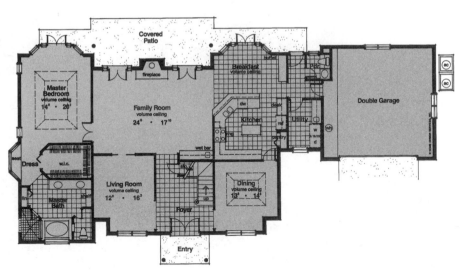

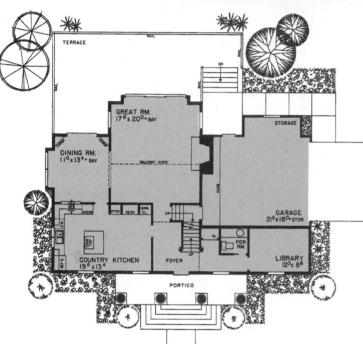

Design 2668

First Floor: 1,206 square feet
Second Floor: 1,254 square feet
Total: 2,460 square feet

L

● This elegant exterior houses a very livable plan. Every bit of space has been put to good use. The front country kitchen is a good place to begin. It is efficiently planned with its island cooktop, built-ins and pass-through to the dining room. The large great room will be the center of all family activities. Quiet times can be enjoyed in the front library. The second floor contains the sleeping zone made up of three family bedrooms and a grand master suite.

Width 52'
Depth 42'

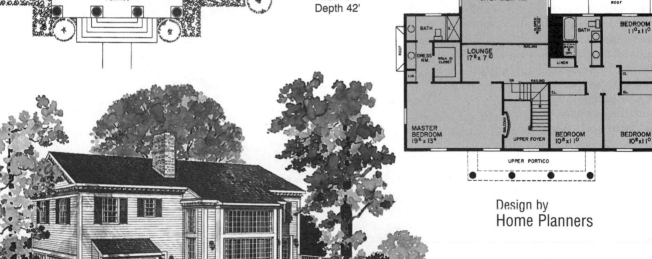

Design by
Home Planners

QUOTE ONE®

Cost to build? See page 374
to order complete cost estimate
to build this house in your area!

Design 3337

First Floor: 2,167 square feet
Second Floor: 1,992 square feet
Total: 4,159 square feet

L

● The elegant facade of this design
with its columned portico, fanlights
and dormers houses an amenity-
filled interior. The gathering room,
study and dining room, each with a
fireplace, provide plenty of room
for relaxing and entertaining. A
large work area contains a kitchen
with a breakfast room, a snack bar,
a laundry room and a pantry. The
four-bedroom upstairs includes a
master suite with a sumptuous bath
and an exercise room.

Design by
Home Planners

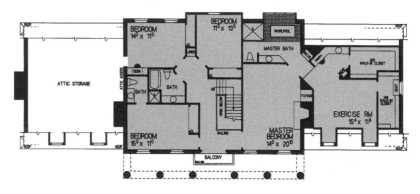

Width 94'-4"
Depth 42'-9"

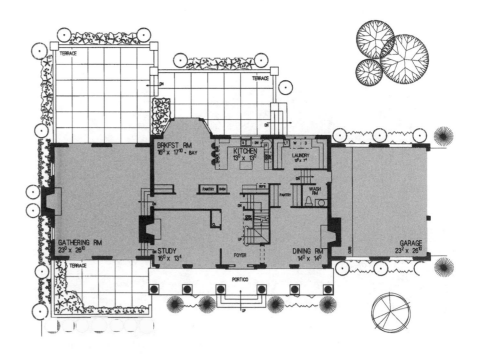

Width 70'-6"
Depth 54'-5"

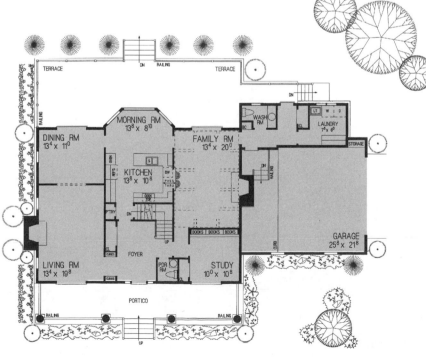

Design 3333

First Floor: 1,584 square feet
Second Floor: 1,344 square feet
Total: 2,928 square feet

L

● This Southern Colonial adaptation
boasts an up-to-date floor plan which
caters to the needs of today's families.
The entrance hall is flanked by formal
and informal living areas: to the left a
spacious living room and connecting
dining room, to the right a cozy study
and family room. A large kitchen with
a bay-windowed morning room is
convenient to both the dining and
family rooms. The upstairs sleeping
arrangements include three family
bedrooms and a sumptuous master
suite complete with a deluxe bath and
an exercise room.

Design by
Home Planners

Cost to build? See page 374
to order complete cost estimate
to build this house in your area!

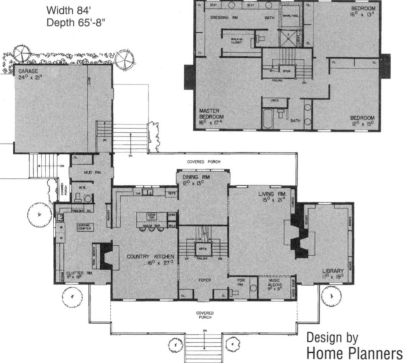

Width 84'
Depth 65'-8"

Design by
Home Planners

Design 2694

First Floor: 2,026 square feet
Second Floor: 1,386 square feet
Total: 3,412 square feet

L

● This two-story design faithfully recalls the 18th-Century homestead of Secretary of Foreign Affairs John Jay. First-floor livability includes a grand living room with a fireplace and a music alcove, a library with another fireplace and built-in bookshelves, a light-filled dining room, a large country kitchen with still another fireplace and a snack bar and a handy clutter room adjacent to the mud room. Three upstairs bedrooms include a large master suite with a walk-in closet, vanity seating and double sinks. Each of the family bedrooms contains a double closet.

QUOTE ONE®

Cost to build? See page 374 to order complete cost estimate to build this house in your area!

Width 72'
Depth 57'

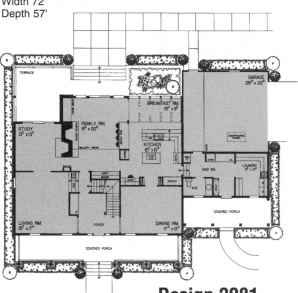

Design 2981

First Floor: 2,104 square feet
Second Floor: 2,015 square feet
Total: 4,119 square feet

L

Design by
Home Planners

● This formal two-story recalls a Louisiana plantation house, Land's End, built in 1857. The Ionic columns of the front porch and the pediment gable echo the Greek Revival style. Highlighting the interior is the bright and cheerful spaciousness of the informal family-room area. It features a wall of glass stretching to the second-story, sloping ceiling. Enhancing the drama of this area is the adjacent glass area of the breakfast room. Note the His and Hers areas of the master bedroom.

Design 3518

First Floor: 1,877 square feet
Second Floor: 1,877 square feet
Total: 3,754 square feet

L D

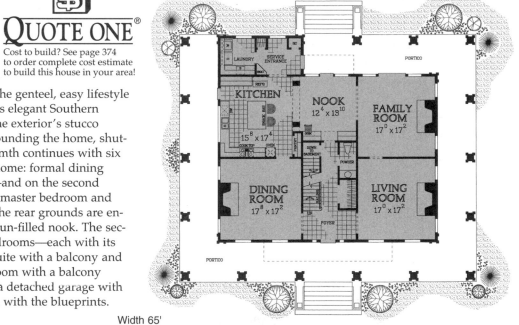

QUOTE ONE®

Cost to build? See page 374
to order complete cost estimate
to build this house in your area!

● The gracious hospitality and the genteel, easy lifestyle of the South are personified in this elegant Southern Colonial home. Contributing to the exterior's stucco warmth are square columns surrounding the home, shutters and a cupola. Inside, the warmth continues with six fireplaces found throughout the home: formal dining room, living room, family room—and on the second floor—family bedroom, romantic master bedroom and master bath. First-floor views of the rear grounds are enjoyed from the family room and sun-filled nook. The second floor contains two family bedrooms—each with its own bath—and a lavish master suite with a balcony and a pampering bath. A study/bedroom with a balcony completes the upstairs. Plans for a detached garage with an enclosed lap pool are included with the blueprints.

Width 65'
Depth 53'

Design by
Home Planners

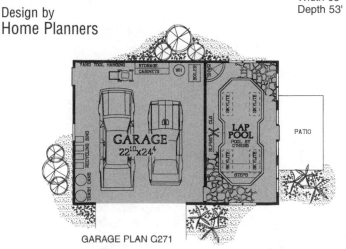

GARAGE PLAN G271

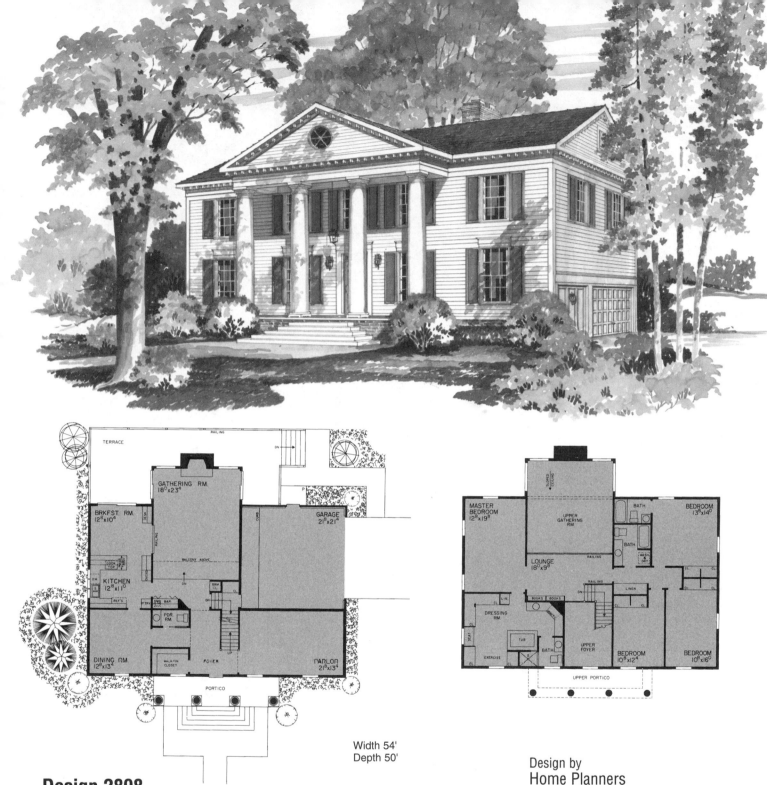

Width 54'
Depth 50'

Design by
Home Planners

Design 2898
First Floor: 1,619 square feet
Second Floor: 1,723 square feet
Total: 3,342 square feet

● Four soaring Doric columns highlight the exterior of this Greek Revival dwelling. The elevation reflects a balanced design that incorporates four bedrooms and a two-car garage in one central unit. The stylish heart of this dwelling is a two-story gathering room. A balcony lounge on the second floor offers a quiet aerie overlooking this living area. Both of these areas will have sunlight streaming through the high windows. A second living area is the parlor. It could serve as the formal area whereas the gathering room could be considered informal. Entrance to all of these areas will be through the foyer. It has an adjacent power room and spacious walk-in closet. The U-shaped kitchen will conveniently serve the breakfast and dining rooms. Second floor livability is outstanding. Study all of the features in the master bedroom: dressing room, tub and shower, large vanity and exercise area. Three more bedrooms, and another has a private bath with would make it an ideal guest room.

Design 2686

Width 73'-10"
Depth 53'-2"

First Floor: 1,683 square feet
Second Floor: 1,541 square feet
Total: 3,224 square feet

L D

● This design has its roots in the South and is referred to as a raised cottage. This adaptation has front and rear covered porches whose columns reflect a modified Greek Revival style. Flanking the center foyer are the formal living areas of the living room and library and the informal country kitchen. Upstairs, two large family bedrooms share a full hall bath while the master bedroom offers a pampering bath complete with a whirlpool tub, a separate shower, twin vanities and a walk-in closet.

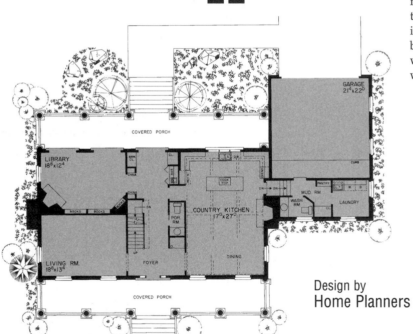

Design by
Home Planners

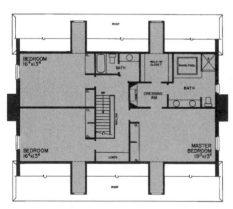

Design 3566

First Floor: 1,635 square feet
Second Floor: 586 square feet
Total: 2,221 square feet
Bonus Room: 321 square feet

L D

● Don't be fooled by the humbled appearance of this farmhouse. All the amenities abound. A grand front entrance opens into living and dining rooms. The family will surely enjoy the ambience of the keeping room with its fireplace and beamed ceiling. A service entry, with laundry nearby, separates the garage from the main house. An over-the-garage bonus room allows for room to grow or a nice study. Two quaint bedrooms and a full bath make up the second floor.

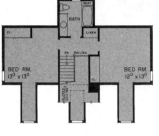

Width 76'
Depth 48'

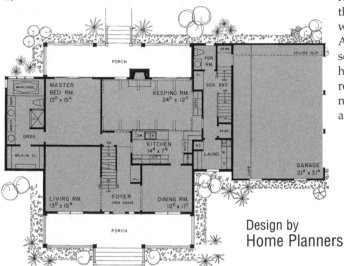

Design by
Home Planners

QUOTE ONE®
Cost to build? See page 374
to order complete cost estimate
to build this house in your area!

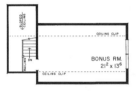

Width 50'-4"
Depth 64'-4"

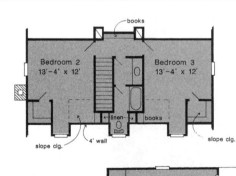

Design 9121

First Floor: 1,266 square feet
Second Floor: 639 square feet
Total: 1,905 square feet

Design by
Larry W. Garnett & Associates, Inc.

QUOTE ONE®
Cost to build? See page 374
to order complete cost estimate
to build this house in your area!

● Complete with dormers and a covered front porch, the facade details of this home are repeated at the side-load garage, making it a perfectly charming plan from any angle. From the raised foyer, step down into the living room. This area opens to a dining room which has a French door to the rear yard. Close by is a kitchen with a pantry and access to a utility room and the garage. The master suite is on the first floor for convenience and offers two large walk-in closets. Upstairs there are two secondary bedrooms and a full compartmented bath. An entry near the garage leads to a staircase to an optional storage room.

Design 2889

First Floor: 2,349 square feet
Second Floor: 1,918 square feet
Total: 4,267 square feet

● This classic Georgian design contains a variety of features that makes it outstanding: a pediment gable with cornice work and dentils, beautifully proportioned columns, and distinct window treatment. The first floor contains some special appointments: a fireplace in the living room, a wet bar in the gathering room and sliding glass doors from the study to the rear terrace. Upstairs, an extension over the garage allows for a huge walk-in closet in the deluxe master suite and a full bath with tub in the left front bedroom. Two other family bedrooms share a full bath.

California Engineered Plans and California Stock Plans are available for this home. Call 1-800-521-6797 for more information.

Cost to build? See page 374 to order complete cost estimate to build this house in your area!

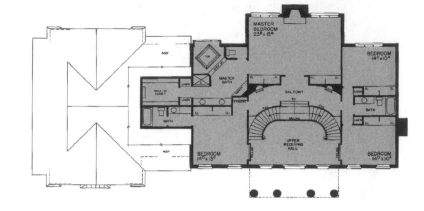

Width 90'-4"
Depth 44'-8"

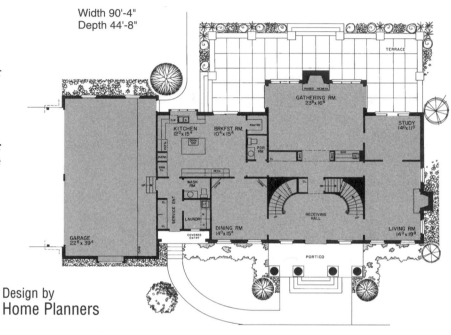

Design by
Home Planners

Design 2667

First Floor: 1,827 square feet
Second Floor: 697 square feet
Total: 2,524 square feet

● Two one-story wings flank the two-story center section of this design which echoes the architectural forms of 18th-Century Tidewater Virginia. The left wing is a huge living room; the right, the master bedroom suite, service area and garage. Kitchen, dining room and family room are centrally located. Upstairs, three family bedrooms share a full hall bath with twin vanities.

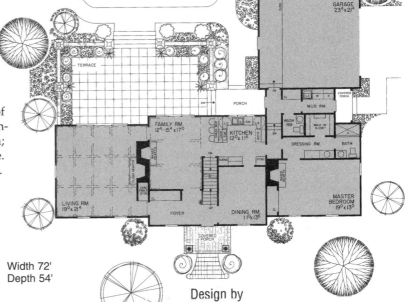

Width 72'
Depth 54'

Design by
Home Planners

Design 9125

First Floor: 1,858 square feet
Second Floor: 1,976 square feet
Total: 3,834 square feet

● Elaborate dentil molding, shuttered windows and a Palladian window over the front entry are architectural elements typical of the Gerogian style. A central foyer opens to a large receiving hall with an elegantly curving staircase and guest powder room in this plan. The formal living and dining rooms flank the entry, while the family room is to the rear. Note French doors here to a porch. The kitchen, breakfast room and family room are open to each other, creating a feeling of spaciousness. The kitchen features an island cooktop and a walk-in pantry, ideal for the serious cook. A rear staircase leads from the breakfast area to the second-floor game room, which has a 10' vaulted ceiling, built-ins and a wet bar. Also upstairs are four bedrooms and two baths, including a luxurious master suite.

Design by
Larry W.
Garnett &
Associates, Inc.

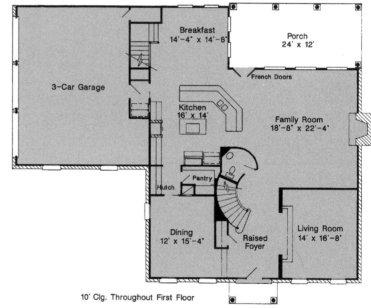

10' Clg. Throughout First Floor

Width 67'-8"
Depth 58'-8"

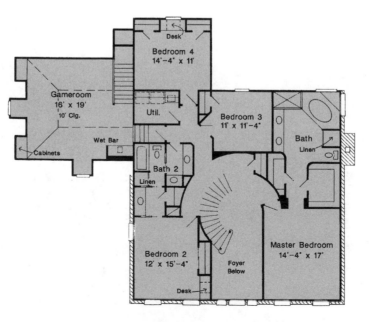

136

Design 9126

First Floor: 2,157 square feet
Second Floor: 1,346 square feet
Total: 3,503 square feet

● Traditional styling at its best—this plan is a true work of art. The entry foyer contains a curved staircase to the second floor and is open to the formal dining room. The living room has a fireplace as does the family room. A quiet study features built-in shelves and is tucked away to the rear of the plan.

Note the master bedroom on the first floor. It boasts a double walk-in closet, corner shower and large tub. Four bedrooms upstairs revolve around a game room with vaulted ceiling. Bedroom 5 has a window seat and double closets.

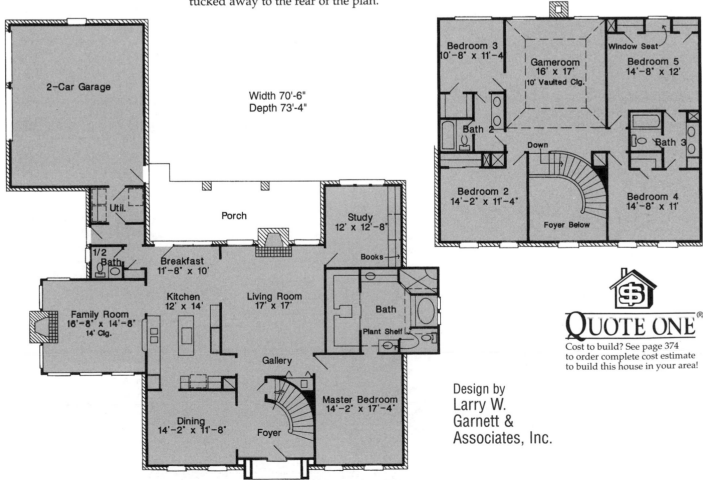

Width 70'-6"
Depth 73'-4"

Design by
Larry W.
Garnett &
Associates, Inc.

QUOTE ONE®
Cost to build? See page 374
to order complete cost estimate
to build this house in your area!

Photo by Laszlo Regos

Design by
Home Planners

Width 92'
Depth 32'-8"

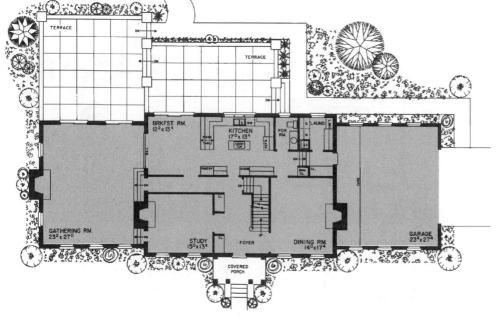

Design 2683

First Floor: 2,126 square feet
Second Floor: 1,882 square feet
Total: 4,008 square feet

L **D**

● This historical Georgian home has its roots in the 18th-Century. The full two-story center section is delightfully complemented by the 1½-story wings. An elegant gathering room, three steps down from the rest of the house, has ample space for entertaining on a grand scale. Guests and family alike will enjoy the two rooms flanking the foyer, the study and the formal dining room. Each of these rooms has a fireplace as its highlight. The breakfast room, the kitchen, the powder room and the laundry are arranged for maximum efficiency. The second floor houses the family bedrooms. Take special note of the spacious master bedroom suite. It has a deluxe bath, a fireplace, a sunken lounge with a dressing room and a walk-in closet.

QUOTE ONE®

Cost to build? See page 374
to order complete cost estimate
to build this house in your area!

Design 8139

First Floor: 1,713 square feet
Second Floor: 1,430 square feet
Total: 3,143 square feet

● This classic Georgian facade is complemented by an up-to-date floor plan with all the
extras. The lovely curved porch opens to a two-
story foyer with the formal dining room with a
fireplace on the right. To the left, the large living room features double French doors which
provide access to the covered porch beyond. A
charming sunroom is situated off the living
room and porch, providing a bright area for informal entertaining. The kitchen features a
large work island and a small morning nook
perfect for a table for two. The master suite includes a large bedroom and a His and Hers
master bath complete with separate closets,
vanities and commodes. Two family bedrooms
share a full bath with private vanity areas.
Please specify crawlspace or slab foundation
when ordering.

Design by
**Larry E. Belk
Designs**

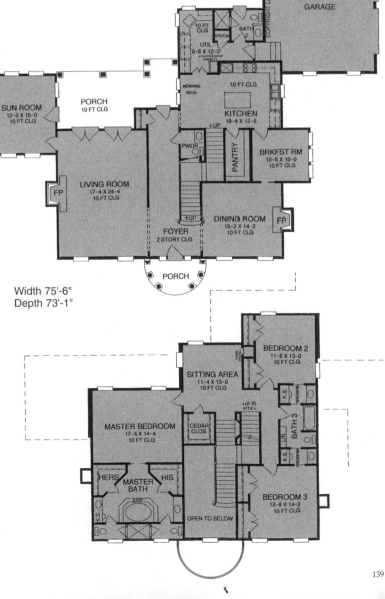

Width 75'-6"
Depth 73'-1"

Design 7208

First Floor: 1,675 square feet
Second Floor: 1,605 square feet
Total: 3,280 square feet

● A grand and glorious split staircase makes a lasting first impression in this stately two-story home. The impressive family room is lit by a beveled wall of windows—while a wet bar, built-in book cases and entertainment center provide the finishing touches. The spacious kitchen is sure to please, featuring an island cooktop with a snack bar, a planning desk and a sunny bayed breakfast area. Upstairs, each secondary bedroom enjoys a walk-in closet. Two bedrooms share a hollywood bath while a third enjoys a private bath. The master suite offers uncommon elegance with French doors opening into the master bedroom with a tray ceiling, gazebo sitting area and a separate off-season closet. Enter the master bath through French doors and enjoy its relaxing whirlpool tub, an open shower and built-in dressers in the large walk-in closet.

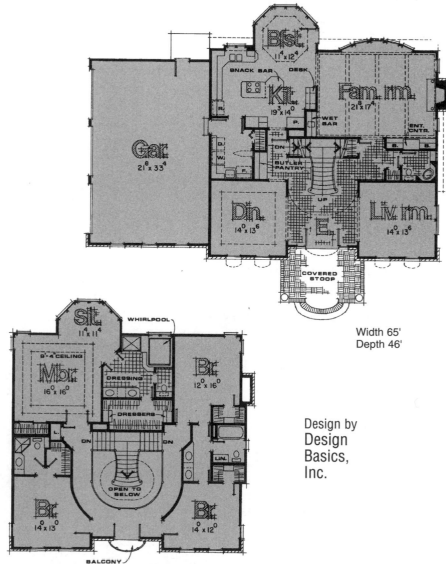

Width 65'
Depth 46'

Design by
Design
Basics,
Inc.

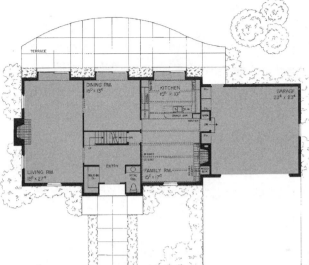

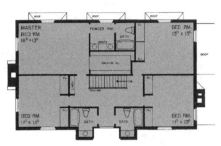

Design by
Home Planners

Width 74'
Depth 33'-1"

Design 2250

First Floor: 1,442 square feet
Second Floor: 1,404 square feet
Total: 2,846 square feet

● This stately home, which has roots that go back to an earlier period in American architecture, will forever retain its aura of distinction. The spacious front entry effectively separates the formal and informal living zones. A large country kitchen will satisfy even the pickiest gourmet and is open to the beam-ceilinged family room. Three family bedrooms on the second floor share two full hall baths while the deluxe master bedroom revels in its own private bath.

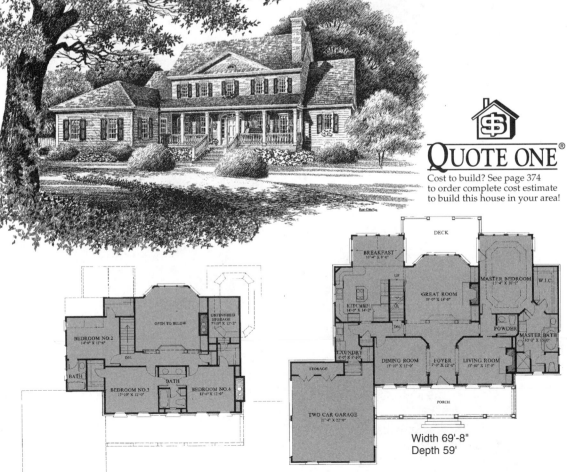

QUOTE ONE®

Cost to build? See page 374 to order complete cost estimate to build this house in your area!

Width 69'-8"
Depth 59'

Design 9850

First Floor: 1,960 square feet
Second Floor: 905 square feet
Total: 2,865 square feet

● Georgian symmetry balances the living room and dining room to the right and left of the foyer. Both are framed by columns. The main level continues into the two-story great room with built-in cabinetry, a fireplace and a large bay window. A dramatic tray ceiling, a wall of glass and access to the rear deck complete the master bedroom. The master bath features separate vanities and a large walk-in closet. Left of the great room, the main level includes a large kitchen that opens to the breakfast area. Upstairs, each bedroom features ample closet space and direct access to a bathroom. This home is designed with a basement foundation.

Design by
Design Traditions

141

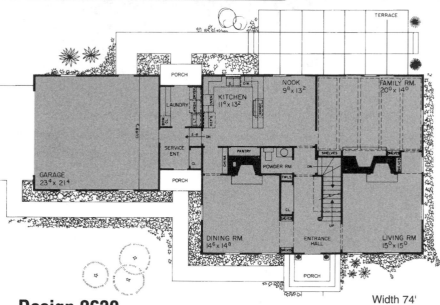

TERRACE

PORCH

KITCHEN
11⁴ x 13²

NOOK
9⁸ x 13²

FAMILY RM.
20⁰ x 14⁰

LAUNDRY

SERVICE ENT.

PANTRY

POWDER RM.

SHELVES

GARAGE
23⁴ x 21⁴

PORCH

DINING RM.
14⁶ x 14⁸

ENTRANCE HALL

LIVING RM.
15⁰ x 15⁰

UP

PORCH

● Here is a New England Georgian adaptation with an elevated doorway highlighted by pilasters and a pediment. It gives way to a second-story Palladian window, capped by a pediment projecting from the hipped roof. Inside, both the formal living room and the formal dining room are warmed by fireplaces. Openness is the key to the layout of the U-shaped kitchen, breakfast nook and family room. Upstairs, three family bedrooms share a full hall bath, while the master bedroom suite pampers with its own private bath.

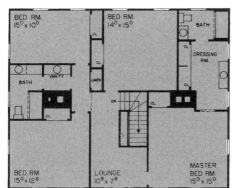

BED. RM.
15⁰ x 10⁰

BED. RM.
14⁰ x 15⁰

BATH

DRESSING RM.

BATH

VANITY

LINEN

DN

BED. RM.
15⁰ x 12⁸

LOUNGE
10⁸ x 7⁸

MASTER BED RM.
15⁰ x 15⁰

Design 2639

First Floor: 1,556 square feet
Second Floor: 1,428 square feet
Total: 2,984 square feet

L **D**

Design by
Home Planners

Width 74'
Depth 34'

● This Cape Cod Georgian recalls the Julia Wood House built approximately 1790 in Falmouth, Mass. Such homes generally featured a balustraded roof deck or "widow's walk" where wives of captains looked to sea for signs of returning ships. Our updated floor plans come with four bedrooms including a deluxe master suite on the second floor and a country kitchen, a study, a classy dining room and a cozy living room on the first floor. A third floor makes a fine studio, with a ladder leading up to the widow's walk.

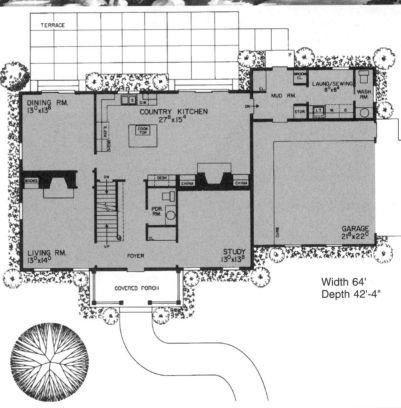

Width 64'
Depth 42'-4"

Design by
Home Planners

Design 2690

First Floor: 1,559 square feet
Second Floor: 1,344 square feet
Third Floor: 176 square feet
Total: 3,079 square feet

143

Design 9828

First Floor: 1,455 square feet
Second Floor: 1,649 square feet
Total: 3,104 square feet

● The double wings, twin chimneys and center portico of this home work in concert to create a classic architectural statement. The two-story foyer is flanked by the spacious dining room and formal living room, each containing its own fireplace. A large family room with a full wall of glass beckons the outside in while it opens conveniently onto the sunlit kitchen and breakfast room. The master suite features a tray ceiling and French doors that open onto a covered porch. A grand master bath with all the amenities, including a garden tub and huge closet, completes the master suite. Two other bedrooms share a bath while another has its own private bath. The fourth bedroom also features a sunny nook for sitting or reading. This home is designed with a basement foundation.

Design by
Design Traditions

Width 53'
Depth 46'

Cost to build? See page 374 to order complete cost estimate to build this house in your area!

Design 9886

First Floor: 1,165 square feet
Second Floor: 1,050 square feet
Total: 2,215 square feet

● Classic design knows no boundaries in this gracious two-story home. From the formal living and dining areas to the more casual family room, it handles any occasion with ease. Of special note on the first floor are the L-shaped kitchen with attached breakfast area and the guest-pampering half bath. Upstairs are three bedrooms including a master suite with a fine bath and a walk-in closet. A fourth bedroom can be developed in bonus space as needed. This home is designed with a basement foundation.

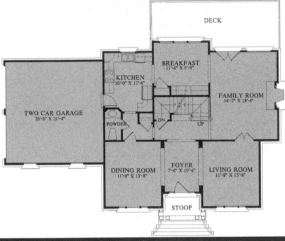

Width 58'
Depth 36'

Design by
Design Traditions

Design 9842

First Floor: 1,053 square feet
Second Floor: 1,053 square feet
Total: 2,106 square feet
Bonus Room: 212 square feet

● Brick takes a bold stand in grand traditional style in this treasured design. The front study has a nearby full bath, making it a handy guest bedroom. The family room with fireplace opens to a cozy breakfast area. For more formal entertaining there's a dining room just off the entry. The kitchen features a prep island and huge pantry. Upstairs, the master bedroom has its own sitting room and a giant-sized closet. Two family bedrooms share a full bath. This home is designed with a basement foundation.

Design by
Design Traditions

Width 52'
Depth 34'

145

Copyright 1992 Stephen S. Fuller, Inc.

W.I.C.

MASTER BATH

COVERED PORCH

BREAKFAST
11'-4" X 10'-8"

TWO STORY
FAMILY ROOM
15'-0" X 19'-0"

MASTER BEDROOM
14'-4" X 13'-0"

UP —DN.

KITCHEN
11'-4" X 12'-4"

POWDER

TWO CAR GARAGE
21'-8" X 21'-4"

LAUNDRY

LIVING ROOM
14'-4" X 11'-8"

TWO STORY
FOYER
7'-0" X 11'-4"

DINING ROOM
11'-4" X 14'-0"

STOOP

Width 64'
Depth 48'-6"

OPEN TO BELOW

BEDROOM
NO. 3
11'-4" X 14'-0"

BATH

FUTURE
BEDROOM
NO. 4
10'-6" X 14'-0"

DN.

W.I.C.

W.I.C.

OPEN TO
BELOW

BEDROOM
NO. 2
11'-4" X 14'-0"

BATH

FUTURE
W.I.C.

Design 9877

First Floor: 1,660 square feet
Second Floor: 665 square feet
Total: 2,325 square feet

● This stately two-story Georgian home echoes tradition with the use of brick and jack-arch detailing. Once inside, the foyer is flanked by a spacious dining room to the right and living room on the left; with the addition of French doors this room can also function as a guest room, if needed. Beyond the foyer lies a two-story family room accented by a warming fireplace and open railing staircase. This room flows casually into the spacious breakfast room and well-planned kitchen with access to the laundry room and garage. The secluded master bedroom with a tray ceiling and master bath including His and Hers vanities, a garden tub and walk-in closet, completes the main level of this home. Upstairs, three additional bedrooms with roomy closets and two baths combine to finish this traditional country home. This home is designed with a basement foundation.

Quote One®

Cost to build? See page 374
to order complete cost estimate
to build this house in your area!

Design by
Design Traditions

Design by
Design Traditions

colonnade detail, the living and dining rooms are perfect for entertaining. The great room features a fireplace on the outside wall. This room opens to the breakfast room and angled kitchen with plenty of cabinets and counter space. Upstairs is a guest room, a children's den area, two family bedrooms and master suite. Look for the cozy fireplace, tray ceiling and sumptuous bath in the master suite. This home is designed with a basement foundation.

Design 9814

First Floor: 1,370 square feet
Second Floor: 1,673 square feet
Total: 3,043 square feet

Width 73'-6"
Depth 49'

● This English Georgian home features a dramatic brick exterior. The series of windows and Jack-arch detailing are second only to the drama created by the porte cochere. The detached garage allows the home to stretch to the gardens. Enter into the two-story foyer—the unusually shaped staircase and balcony overlook create a tremendous first impression. Separated only by a classical

QUOTE ONE®

Cost to build? See page 374 to order complete cost estimate to build this house in your area!

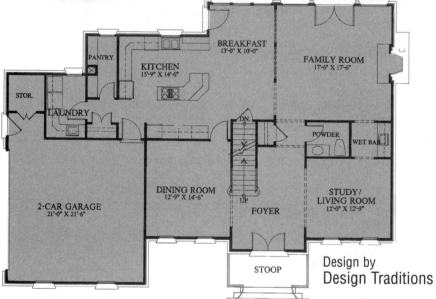

PANTRY

KITCHEN

BREAKFAST
13'-0" X 10'-0"

FAMILY ROOM
17'-6" X 17'-6"

STOR.

LAUNDRY

DN.

POWDER

WET BAR

2-CAR GARAGE
21'-0" X 21'-6"

DINING ROOM
12'-9" X 14'-6"

UP

FOYER

**STUDY/
LIVING ROOM**
12'-0" X 12'-9"

STOOP

Design by
Design Traditions

Design 9899

First Floor: 1,554 square feet
Second Floor: 1,648 square feet
Total: 3,202 square feet

● The classic styling of this brick American traditional will be respected for years to come. The formidable double-door entry with transom and a Palladian window reveals the shining foyer within. It is flanked by the spacious dining room and the formal study or parlor. A large family room with a full wall of glass conveniently opens to the breakfast room and kitchen. The master suite features a spacious sitting area with its own fireplace and tray ceiling. Two additional bedrooms share a bath, while a fourth bedroom has its own private bath. This home is designed with a basement foundation.

QUOTE ONE®

Cost to build? See page 374
to order complete cost estimate
to build this house in your area!

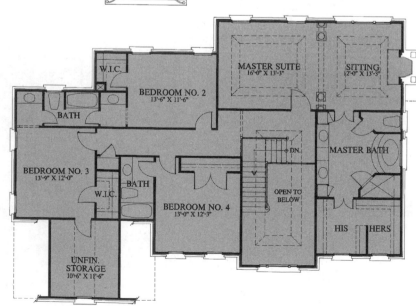

W.I.C.

BATH

BEDROOM NO. 2
13'-6" X 11'-6"

MASTER SUITE
16'-0" X 13'-3"

SITTING
12'-0" X 13'-3"

BEDROOM NO. 3
13'-9" X 12'-0"

W.I.C.

BATH

BEDROOM NO. 4
13'-0" X 12'-3"

DN.

**OPEN TO
BELOW**

MASTER BATH

HIS   **HERS**

Width 60'
Depth 43'

**UNFIN.
STORAGE**
10'-6" X 11'-6"

Design 9829

First Floor: 1,581 square feet
Second Floor: 1,415 square feet
Total: 2,996 square feet

● Classical details and a stately brick exterior accentuate the grace and timeless elegance of this home. Inside the foyer opens up to a large banquet-sized dining room with an adjacent formal living room. A central staircase, positioned for common access from all areas of the home, accents the foyer. Just beyond, the two-story great room awaits, featuring a wet bar and warming fireplace. To the left is the sunlit breakfast room and functional kitchen with breakfast bar. A large covered porch off the kitchen completes the family center. Upstairs, the master suite features an unusual bay window design and private sundeck. The accompanying bath features His and Hers closets. Two bedrooms with a connecting bath complete the rooms on the second floor. This home is designed with a basement foundation.

Width 55'
Depth 52'

Design by
Design Traditions

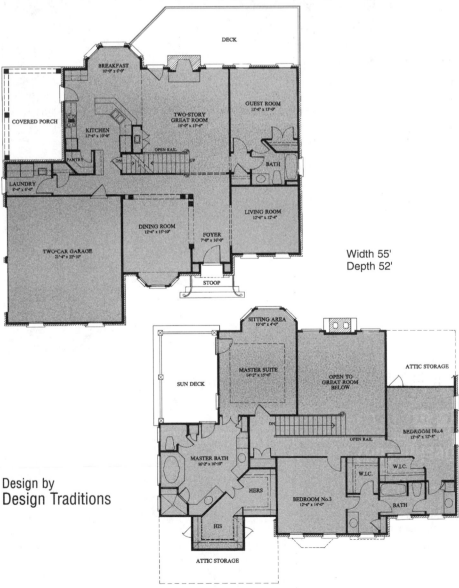

Design 3517

First Floor: 1,536 square feet
Second Floor: 679 square feet
Total: 2,215 square feet

L D

● There is more to this Early American home than a warm, inviting exterior. Inside, fireplaces warm each of the first-floor rooms—living room, country kitchen and master bedroom. To the right of the foyer is the private master suite enhanced by a walk-in closet and a pampering bath that includes a soothing whirlpool tub, twin vanities and a bath seat. To the rear of the plan an L-shaped food preparation area conveniently connects via an island snack bar to a large country kitchen that's perfect for informal gatherings. The formal living room and the laundry room complete this level. The second floor holds two secondary bedrooms, a full bath and a lounge/study with a built-in desk.

Design by
Home Planners

Width 53'
Depth 44'

QUOTE ONE®
Cost to build? See page 374
to order complete cost estimate
to build this house in your area!

Design 2870

First Floor: 900 square feet
Second Floor-Right Suite: 493 square feet
Second Floor-Left Suite: 467 square feet
Total: 1,860 square feet

● This Colonial home was designe to provide comfortable living space for two families. The first floor is the common living space. To the left of the foyer, a spacious living room wit a cheery fireplace offers a warm wel come. The adjacent dining room is drenched in sunlight from bowed windows. Thoughtful planning mak its way to the breakfast area, combined with an efficient kitchen featu ing a window above the sink and a snack bar. A handy powder room and a quiet study complete this floor. The second floor has two double-bedroom-one-bath suites. Built-ins are featured in the two bedrooms located to the rear.

Design by
Home Planners

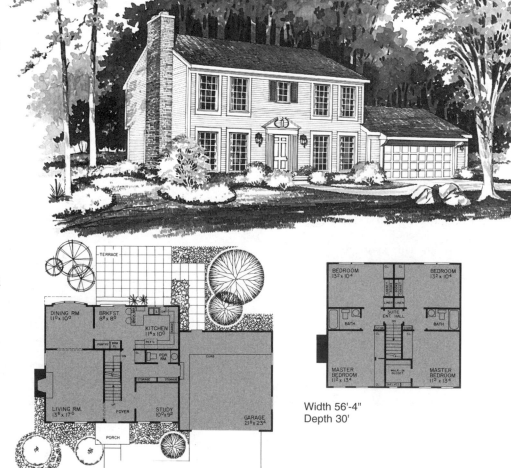

Width 56'-4"
Depth 30'

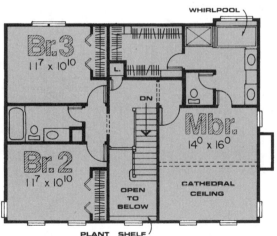

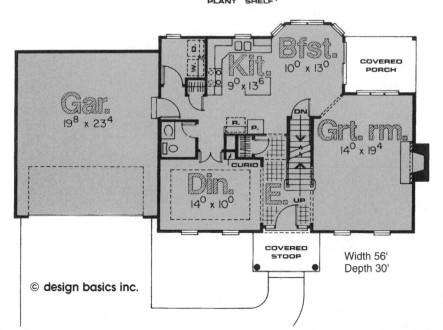

© design basics inc.

Design 7255

First Floor: 941 square feet
Second Floor: 920 square feet
Total: 1,861 square feet

● Colonial charm is abundantly displayed in this gracious two-story home. The great room, located to the right of the entry, offers views to the covered porch and multi-windowed breakfast area. To the left, a formal dining room provides a special place for dinner parties. An island kitchen with a pantry and Lazy Susan has convenient access to all areas. A powder room completes the first floor. The second floor is reserved for restful relaxation. It contains two family bedrooms, a full bath and the master suite. A cathedral ceiling graces the master bedroom. The master bath has a whirlpool tub, a walk-in shower and generous walk-in closet.

Design by
Design Basics, Inc.

Width 56'
Depth 30'

151

Design 3349

First Floor: 2,807 square feet
Second Floor: 1,363 square feet
Total: 4,170 square feet

L D

● Grand traditional design comes to the forefront in this elegant two-story. From the dramatic front entry with curving double stairs to the less formal gathering room with a fireplace and terrace access, this plan accommodates family lifestyles. Notice the split-bedroom plan with the master suite, complete with a separate study, His and Hers walk-in closets and a lavish bath, on the first floor and four family bedrooms, sharing two full baths, upstairs. A four-car garage handles the largest of family fleets.

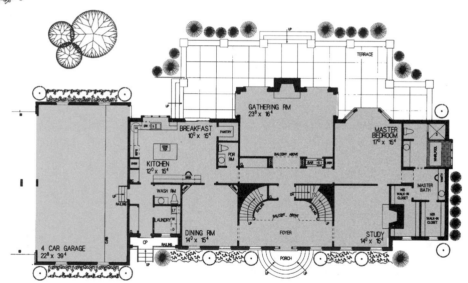

Width 109'-4"
Depth 47'

Design by
Home Planners

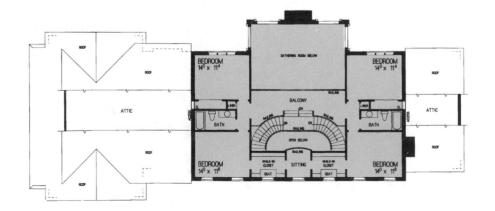

Cost to build? See page 374
to order complete cost estimate
to build this house in your area!

Design 2662

First Floor: 1,735 square feet
Second Floor: 1,075 square feet
Third Floor: 746 square feet
Total: 3,556 square feet

 L

● Influences from Georgian and Federal architecture blend harmoniously to bring out the best in this gracious home. Formal rooms with entertaining in mind come to the forefront with an elegant parlor to the left of the foyer and a grand dining room to the right. The U-shaped kitchen connects with the beam-ceilinged gathering room for informal times. Two attractive wings on opposite ends of the plan—one a study, the other a breakfast room—create symmetry. The second floor contains two family bedrooms, a full bath and a master bedroom suite. Two additional bedrooms and a shared bath comprise the third floor.

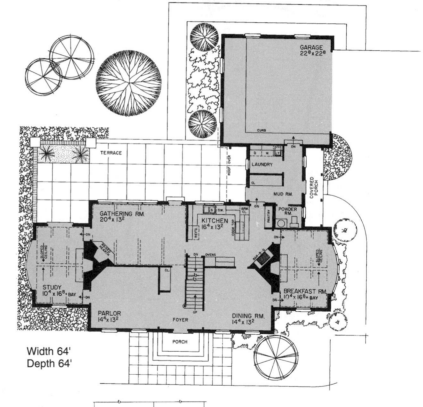

Width 64'
Depth 64'

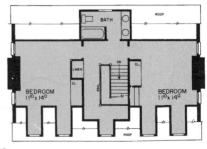

Design by
Home Planners

Design 3506

First Floor: 1,609 square feet
Second Floor: 1,633 square feet
Total: 3,242 square feet

L **D**

● Historic touches on this home include a panelled front door with carriage lamps on each side and a rear salt-box roof. The central foyer is flanked by formal living and dining rooms complete with a butler's pantry between the dining room and kitchen. The spacious kitchen includes an island work counter and space for informal eating. The family room features a beamed ceiling and centered fireplace which can be enjoyed from the kitchen also. A significant highlight is the first-floor guest bedroom. It is accompanied by a full bath and wardrobe closet, making it ideal for a family with a grandparent or two. The upstairs holds four large bedrooms and three baths. The master suite is truly exceptional, including a sitting room (with adjacent outdoor balcony) which looks over a railing and down to the sunken master bedroom. The master bath includes a walk in closet, two lavatories and a whirlpool bath.

Cost to build? See page 374 to order complete cost estimate to build this house in your area!

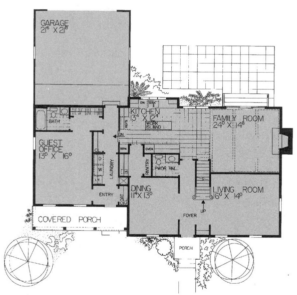

Design by
Home Planners

Width 57'-8"
Depth 52'

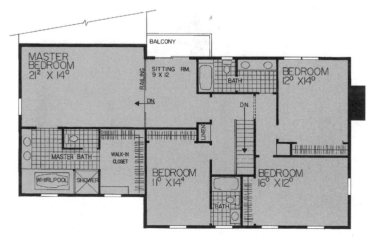

Design 2188

First Floor: 1,440 square feet
Second Floor: 1,280 square feet
Total: 2,720 square feet

● This design is characteristic of early America, however it will be right at home wherever it is located. Along with exterior charm, this design has outstanding livability. The first floor contains formal and informal areas plus convenient work centers. Built-in book shelves are the feature of both the family room and the study/bedroom. The second floor consists of the master suite, three bedrooms and a full bath. Folding stairs are in the upstairs hall for easy access to the attic.

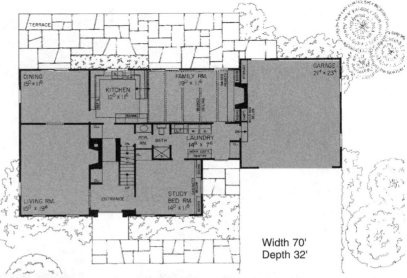

Width 70'
Depth 32'

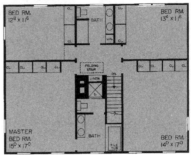

Design by
Home Planners

Design 2610

First Floor: 1,505 square feet
Second Floor: 1,344 square feet
Total: 2,849 square feet

L **D**

● This two-story traditional home strongly recalls images of a New England of yesteryear. The center entrance hall is large with a handy powder room nearby. The study has built-in bookshelves and offers a full measure of privacy. The interior kitchen has a pass-through to the family room and enjoys natural light from the bay window of the nook. A beam ceiling, a fireplace and sliding glass doors are features of the family room. The mud room highlights a closet, laundry equipment and an extra washroom. The second floor contains three family bedrooms, the master suite, two baths and plenty of closets.

Width 66'
Depth 36'

Design by
Home Planners

Cost to build? See page 374
to order complete cost estimate
to build this house in your area!

155

Design 2687 First Floor: 1,819 square feet
Second Floor: 1,431 square feet; Total: 3,250 square feet

L **D**

● Exterior styling of this home is reminiscent of the past but its floor plan is as up-to-date as it can get. Its many unique features include: a greenhouse—78 square feet—off the country kitchen, a media room for all the modern electronic equipment, a hobby/laundry room with a washroom and a bayed formal dining room. The formal living room is further enhanced by a warming fireplace. Upstairs three family bedrooms share a full hall bath with twin vanities, while the master bedroom enjoys a private master bath.

Design by
Home Planners

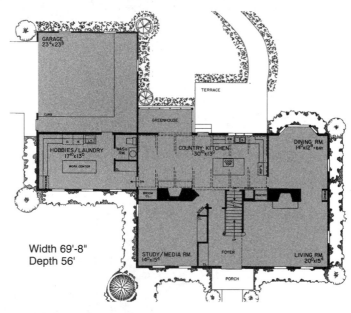

Width 69'-8"
Depth 56'

Cape Cod Cavalcade:

Designs with a New England flavor

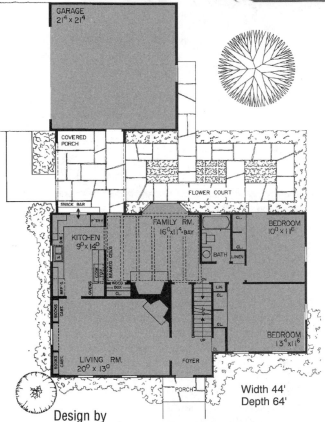

Design by
Home Planners

Width 44'
Depth 64'

Design 2145

First Floor: 1,182 square feet
Second Floor: 708 square feet
Total: 1,890 square feet

L

QUOTE ONE®
Cost to build? See page 374
to order complete cost estimate
to build this house in your area!

● Historically referred to as a "half house," this authentic adaptation has it roots in the heritage of New England. With completion of the second floor, the growing family doubles their sleeping capacity. A fireplace warms the living room while a large hearth dominates the beam-ceiling family room. A deluxe master bedroom is located upstairs and offers built-ins and a walk-in closet. Take note of the covered porch leading to the garage and the flower court.

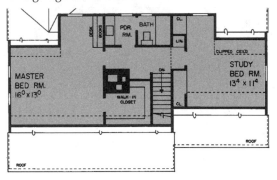

Design 3680

First Floor: 1,093 square feet

Second Floor: 580 square feet

Total: 1,673 square feet

L **D**

Width 36'
Depth 52'

Design by
Home Planners

● Brackets and balustrades on front and rear covered porches spell old-fashioned country charm on this rustic retreat. Warm evenings will invite family and guests outdoors for watching sunsets and stars. In cooler weather, the raised-hearth fireplace will make the great room a cozy place to gather. The nearby well-appointed kitchen serves both snack bar and breakfast nook. Two family bedrooms and a full bath complete the main level. Upstairs, a master bedroom with sloped ceiling offers a secluded window seat and a complete bath with garden tub, separate shower and twin lavatories. The adjacent loft/study overlooks the great room and shares the glow of the fireplace.

Design 9586

First Floor: 1,108 square feet

Second Floor: 798 square feet

Total: 1,906 square feet

Bonus Room: 262 square feet

● This charming Cape Cod, with its three dormers and covered porch, welcomes both family and visitor alike. The formal living and dining rooms both have sunny bay windows. At the rear of the plan the U-shaped kitchen works well with the nook and the family room. Upstairs, two family bedrooms share a full hall bath. The master suite features a walk-in closet, spa tub and separate shower. A bonus room located over the garage can be developed into a study, mother-in-law suite or game room.

Design by
**Alan Mascord
Design Associates, Inc.**

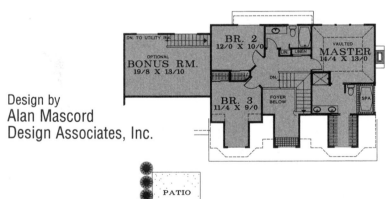

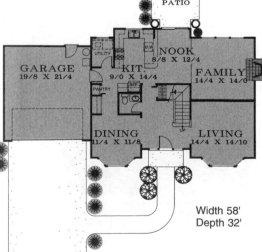

Width 58'
Depth 32'

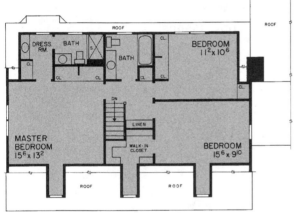

Width 60'
Depth 34'

Design 1791

First Floor: 1,157 square feet
Second Floor: 875 square feet
Total: 2,032 square feet

L D

● Cape Cods are among the most popular designs of all time. This moderately sized two-story plan is symmetrically beautiful. The traditional central foyer leads to a formal living area on the left and a study (or additional bedroom) on the right. A bay-windowed dining room is located between the spacious kitchen and the living room. A family room with a beam ceiling and raised-hearth fireplace offers access to the rear terrace through sliding glass doors. Dormer windows grace two of the three bedrooms on the second floor. The family bedrooms share a full bath. The master bedroom contains a private bath with a dressing area.

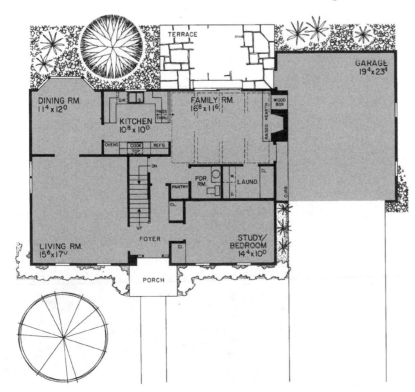

Design by
Home Planners,

Cost to build? See page 374
to order complete cost estimate
to build this house in your area!

Design 2520

First Floor: 1,419 square feet
Second Floor: 1,040 square feet
Total: 2,459 square feet

L **D**

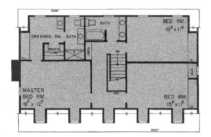

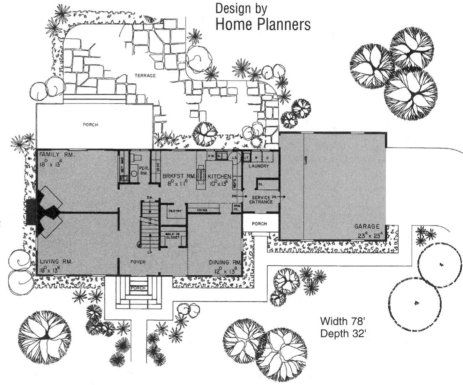

Design by
Home Planners

Width 78'
Depth 32'

● From Tidewater Virginia comes this historic adaptation, a positive reminder of the charm of Early American architecture. Note how the center entrance leads to the formal areas at the front of the plan. Both the formal living room and the cozy family room have fireplaces. The U-shaped kitchen is convenient to both the formal dining room and the breakfast room. A large utility room is located nearby. The sleeping zone is located upstairs for privacy. Three bedrooms include two secondary bedrooms and a lavish master suite.

Width 48'
Depth 32'

Design by
Home Planners

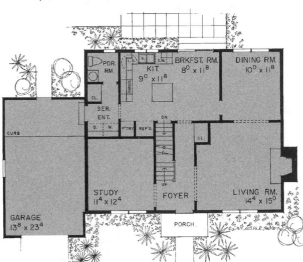

Design 3571

First Floor: 964 square feet
Second Floor: 783 square feet
Total: 1,747 square feet

L **D**

● For those interested in both traditional charm and modern convenience, this Cape Cod fits the bill. Enter the foyer and find a quiet study to the left and a living room with a fireplace to the right. Straight ahead: the kitchen and breakfast room. The island countertop affords lots of room for meal preparation. The service entry introduces a laundry and powder room. Look for three bedrooms upstairs and a pampering master bath: whirlpool, shower, double vanity and walk-in closet.

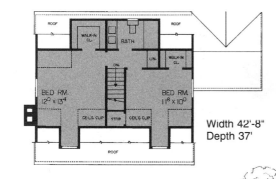

Width 42'-8"
Depth 37'

Design 2162

First Floor: 741 square feet
Second Floor: 504 square feet
Total: 1,245 square feet

L **D**

Design by
Home Planners

● This economical design delivers great exterior appeal and fine livability. In addition to kitchen eating space, there is a separate dining room with access to the rear terrace. The living room features a central fireplace. A powder room serves the first-floor bedroom or study. Two bedrooms with walk-in closets and a full bath with a double-bowl vanity occupy the second floor. A garage shelters the rear terrace.

Design 2699

First Floor: 2,188 square feet
Second Floor: 858 square feet
Total: 3,046 square feet

L

● This handsome Cape Cod offers lots of room for the family to grow. To the left of the foyer, a spacious master suite invites relaxation with its pampering master bath and an adjacent study which could easily convert into a nursery. A large living room with access to the rear terrace is warmed in the winter by a cheerful fireplace. The right side of the plan is comprised of a media room, a dining room and a country kitchen that is a cook's delight. A conveniently located mud room and laundry room complete the first floor. The second floor contains two secondary bedrooms, each with its own full bath, and a spacious lounge.

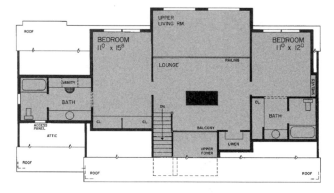

Design by
Home Planners

Quote One®
Cost to build? See page 374
to order complete cost estimate
to build this house in your area!

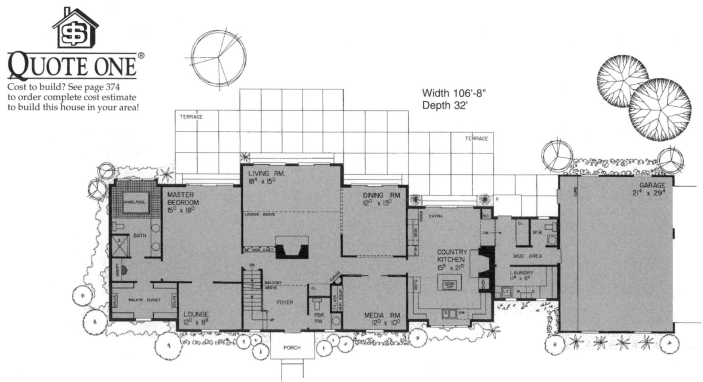

Width 106'-8"
Depth 32'

Design 2563

First Floor: 1,500 square feet
Second Floor: 690 square feet
Total: 2,190 square feet

L D

● This charming Cape Cod will capture your heart with its warm appeal. From the large living room with a fireplace and adjacent dining room to the farm kitchen with an additional fireplace, the plan works toward livability. The first-floor laundry and walk-in pantry further aid in the efficiency of this plan. The master bedroom is located on this level for privacy and is highlighted by a luxurious bath and sliding glass doors to the rear terrace. A front study might be used as a guest bedroom or a library. Upstairs there are two bedrooms and a sitting room plus a full bath to accommodate the needs of family members. Both bedrooms have access to the attic. A three-car garage allows plenty of room for vehicles and storage space.

Width 80'
Depth 32'

Design by
Home Planners

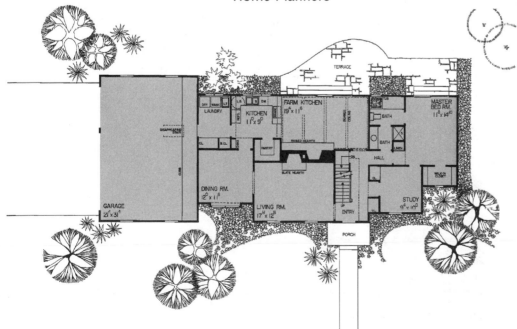

QUOTE ONE®

Cost to build? See page 374
to order complete cost estimate
to build this house in your area!

Design 2661

First Floor: 1,020 square feet
Second Floor: 777 square feet
Total: 1,797 square feet

L **D**

● It would be difficult to find a starter or retirement home with more charm than this. Inside, it contains a very livable floor plan. An outstanding first floor centers around the huge country kitchen which includes a beam ceiling, a raised-hearth fireplace, a window seat and rear-yard access. The living room with its warming corner fireplace and private study are to the front of the plan. Upstairs are three bedrooms and two full baths. Built-in shelves and a linen closet in the upstairs hallway provide excellent storage.

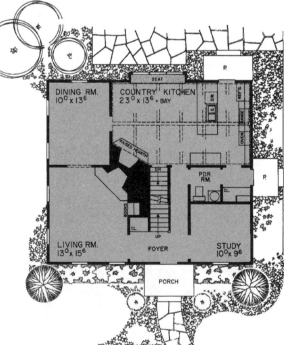

QUOTE ONE®

Cost to build? See page 374 to order complete cost estimate to build this house in your area!

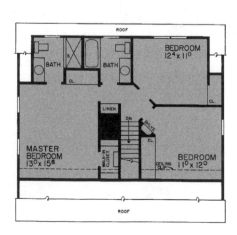

Width 34'
Depth 30'

Design by
Home Planners

Design 3511

First Floor: 1,064 square feet
Second Floor: 582 square feet
Total: 1,646 square feet

● This charming Cape Cod maximizes style and use of space. The living room features a corner fireplace and a built-in curio cabinet. Nearby, the dining room is highlighted with a built-in china closet and access to the rear grounds. A warming fireplace shares space with the efficient kitchen and dining area.

First-floor master suites are rarely found in Cape Cod style homes, and this one is exceptional. The master suite combines with a master bath including a whirlpool tub, a separate shower and a walk-in closet. The second floor is comprised of two family bedrooms sharing a full bath.

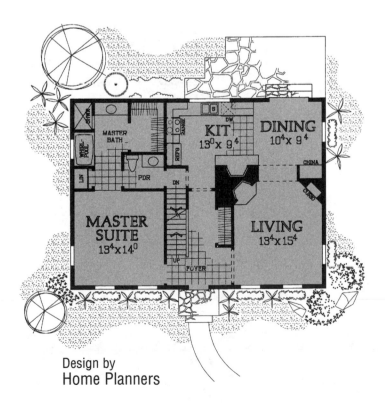

Design by
Home Planners

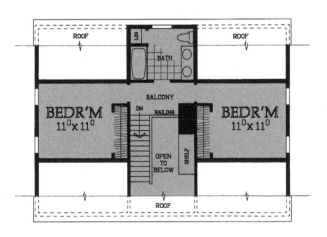

Width 38'
Depth 28'

Cost to build? See page 374
to order complete cost estimate
to build this house in your area!

Design 2682

First Floor (Basic Plan): 976 square feet
First Floor (Expanded Plan): 1,230 square feet
Second Floor (Both Plans): 744 square feet
Total (Basic Plan): 1,720 square feet
Total (Expanded Plan): 1,974 square feet

L **D**

● Here is an expandable Colonial with a full
measure of Cape Cod charm. For those who wish
to build the basic house, there is an abundance of
low-budget livability. Twin fireplaces serve the
formal living room and the informal country
kitchen. Note the spaciousness of both areas. A
dining room and a powder room are also on the
first floor of this basic plan. Upstairs are three
bedrooms and two full baths.

Design by
Home Planners

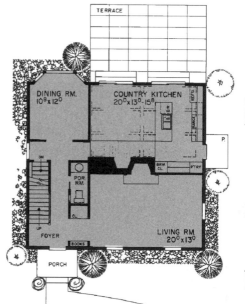

Width 32'
Depth 32'

QUOTE ONE®

Cost to build? See page 374
to order complete cost estimate
to build this house in your area!

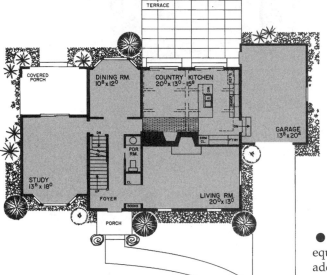

Width 60'
Depth 35'

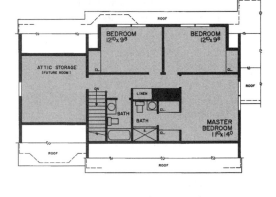

Design by
Home Planners

● This expanded version of the basic house on the opposite page is equally as reminiscent of Cape Cod. Common in the 17th-Century was the addition of appendages to the main structure. This occurred as family size increased or finances improved. This version provides for the addition of wings to accommodate a large study and a garage. Utilizing the alcove behind the study results in a big, covered porch. Certainly a charming design whichever version you decide to build for your family.

Design 2571

First Floor: 1,137 square feet
Second Floor: 795 square feet
Total: 1,932 square feet

● This cozy Cape has an efficient plan that's long on affordable livability. The multi-pane windows and mock shutters give the facade a welcoming appearance. Inside, to the right of the two-story foyer, the comfortable family room, which has both a fireplace and snack bar, is sure to be a favorite gathering area for casual occasions. The separate dining room has a gorgeous bay window and is just steps away from the efficient L-shaped kitchen. In the formal living room abundant blank wall space makes furniture arranging easy. A full bath is down next to a study that could also be a fourth bedroom. Upstairs are two family bedrooms sharing a full bath, and a deluxe master suite with a walk-in closet and private bath.

Design by
Home Planners

Width 40'
Depth 28'

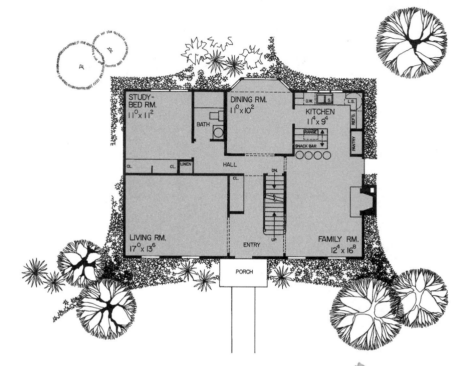

A Bunch of Bungalows:
Space-saving cottage designs

BATH

LINEN CL

GUEST
BEDROOM
13⁶ X 11⁸

Alternate 1st floor plan

Design 3318
First Floor: 1,557 square feet
Second Floor: 540 square feet
Total: 2,097 square feet

L **D**

● Details make the difference in this darling two-bedroom (or three-bedroom if you choose) bungalow. From covered front porch to covered rear porch, there's a fine floor plan. Living areas are to the rear: a gathering room with through-fireplace and pass-through counter to the kitchen and a formal dining room with porch access. To the front of the plan are a family bedroom and bath and a study. The study can also be planned as a guest bedroom with bath. Upstairs is the master bedroom with through-fireplace to the bath and a gigantic walk-in closet.

Width 48'
Depth 43'-8"

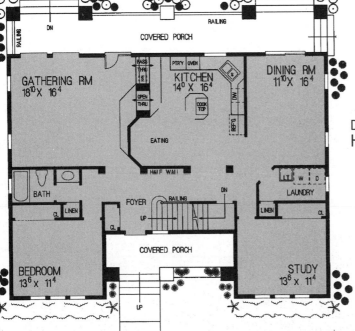

Design by
Home Planners

Cost to build? See page 374
to order complete cost estimate
to build this house in your area!

Design 3316

First Floor: 1,111 square feet
Second Floor: 886 square feet
Total: 1,997 square feet

● Don't be fooled by a small-looking exterior. This plan offers three bedrooms and plenty of living space. Notice that the screened porch leads to a rear terrace with access to the breakfast room. A living room/dining room combination adds spaciousness to the floor plan. Other welcome amenities include: boxed-bay windows in the breakfast room and dining room, fireplace in the living room, planning desk and pass-through snack bar in the kitchen, whirlpool tub in the master bath, and an open two-story foyer. The thoughtfully placed flower box, outside the kitchen window above the sink, adds a homespun touch to this already comfortable design.

Cost to build? See page 374
to order complete cost estimate
to build this house in your area!

Width 34'-1"
Depth 50'

Design by
Home Planners

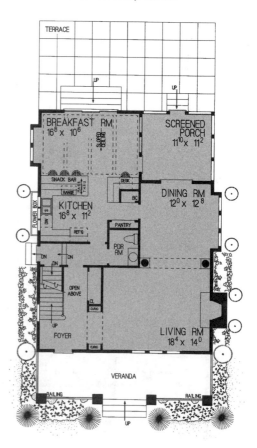

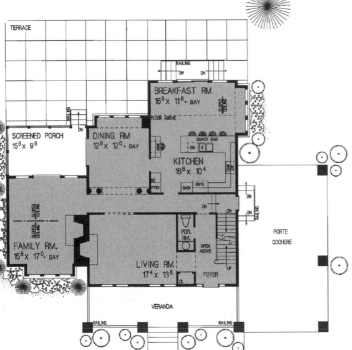

Design 3313
First Floor: 1,482 square feet
Second Floor: 885 square feet
Total: 2,367 square feet

L

● Cozy living abounds in this comfortable two-story bungalow. Enter the foyer and find a spacious living room with a fireplace to the left. Straight ahead is a U-shaped kitchen with a snack bar, a planning desk and easy access to the formal dining room. The bayed family room features a fireplace and entry to a screened porch. Upstairs, secondary bedrooms offer ample closet space and direct access to a shared bath. The master suite contains a large walk-in closet, a double-bowl vanity and compartmented shower and toilet.

Width 64'
Depth 50'

Quote One®
Cost to build? See page 374 to order complete cost estimate to build this house in your area!

Design by
Home Planners

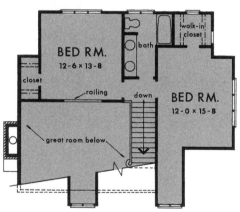

Width 37'-9"
Depth 44'-8"

Design 9697

First Floor: 1,039 square feet
Second Floor: 583 square feet
Total: 1,622 square feet

● Charming and compact, this delightful two-story plan fits primary and secondary living needs. For the small family or empty-nester, it has all the room necessary for day-to-day activities. For the vacation home builder, it functions as a cozy retreat with a fireplace and outdoor living spaces. Note that the master suite is on the first floor, away from two secondary bedrooms. The kitchen area has an island and attached dining area with boxed window. A two-story great room allows plenty of room for entertaining and relaxing.

Design by
Donald A.
Gardner,
Architects, Inc.

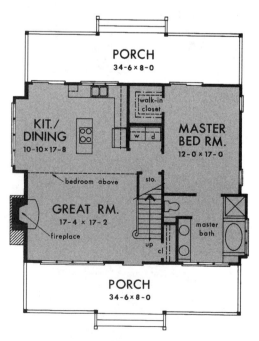

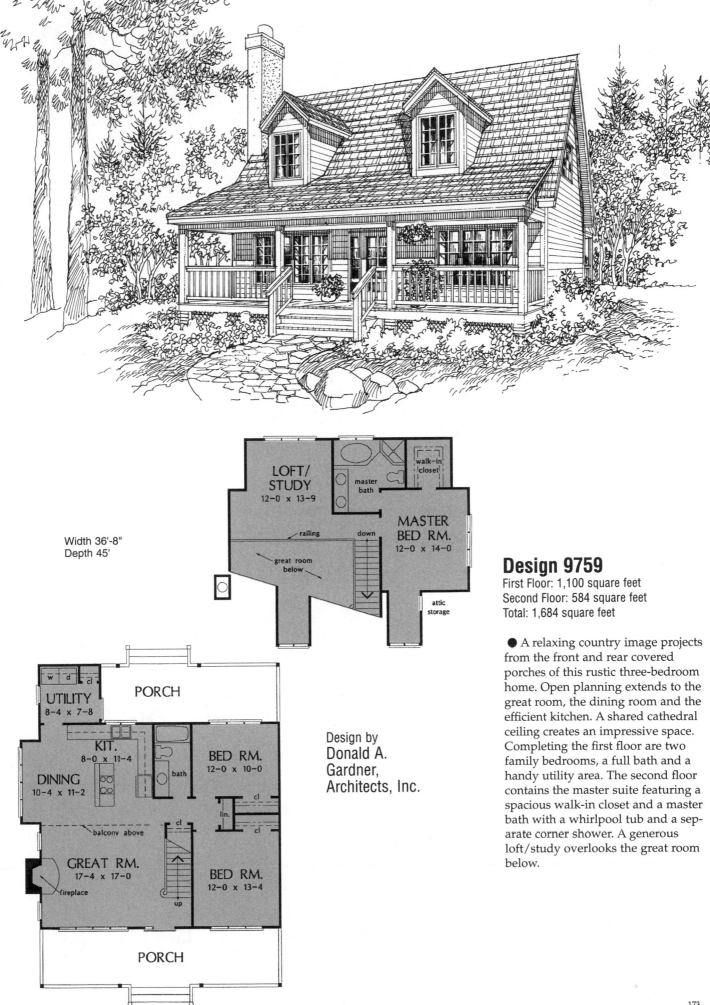

Width 36'-8"
Depth 45'

LOFT/ STUDY
12-0 x 13-9

master bath

walk-in closet

railing

down

great room below

MASTER BED RM.
12-0 x 14-0

attic storage

Design 9759

First Floor: 1,100 square feet
Second Floor: 584 square feet
Total: 1,684 square feet

● A relaxing country image projects from the front and rear covered porches of this rustic three-bedroom home. Open planning extends to the great room, the dining room and the efficient kitchen. A shared cathedral ceiling creates an impressive space. Completing the first floor are two family bedrooms, a full bath and a handy utility area. The second floor contains the master suite featuring a spacious walk-in closet and a master bath with a whirlpool tub and a separate corner shower. A generous loft/study overlooks the great room below.

w d cl.

PORCH

UTILITY
8-4 x 7-8

KIT.
8-0 x 11-4

bath

BED RM.
12-0 x 10-0

DINING
10-4 x 11-2

cl

lin.

cl

balcony above

Design by
Donald A. Gardner, Architects, Inc.

GREAT RM.
17-4 x 17-0

fireplace

up

BED RM.
12-0 x 13-4

PORCH

173

Design 9663

First Floor: 1,002 square feet
Second Floor: 336 square feet
Total: 1,338 square feet

● A mountain retreat, this rustic home features covered porches front and rear. Open living is enjoyed in a great room and kitchen/dining room combination. The cathedral ceiling gives an open, inviting sense of space. Two bedrooms and a full bath on the first level are complemented by a master suite on the second level which includes a walk-in closet and deluxe bath. There is also attic storage on the second level. Please specify basement or crawlspace foundation when ordering.

Design by
Donald A.
Gardner,
Architects, Inc.

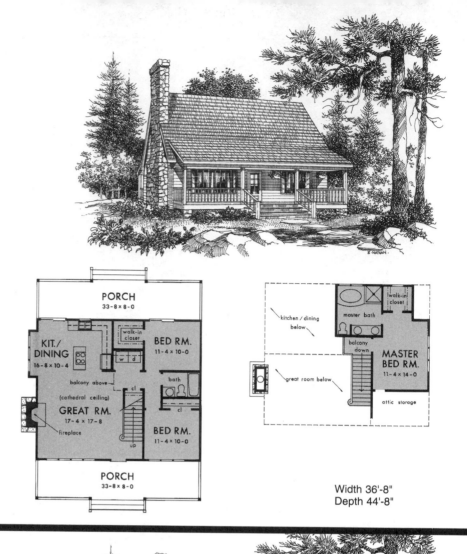

Width 36'-8"
Depth 44'-8"

Design 9666

First Floor: 1,027 square feet
Second Floor: 580 square feet
Total: 1,607 square feet

● This economical, rustic three-bedroom plan sports a relaxing country image with both front and back covered porches. The openness of the great room to kitchen/dining areas and loft/study area is reinforced with a shared cathedral ceiling. The first level allows for two bedrooms, a full bath and a utility area. The master suite on the second level has a walk-in closet and a master bath with whirlpool tub, shower and double-bowl vanity.

Design by
Donald A.
Gardner,
Architects, Inc.

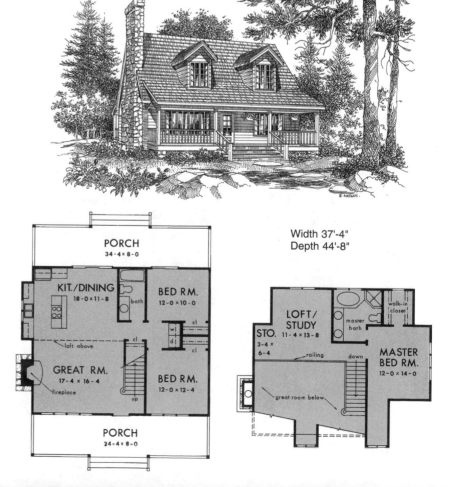

Width 37'-4"
Depth 44'-8"

QUOTE ONE®

Cost to build? See page 374 to order complete cost estimate to build this house in your area!

KOIZUMI/BUTLER

Design 3675

First Floor: 1,093 square feet
Second Floor: 580 square feet
Total: 1,673 square feet

L **D**

● Comfortable covered porches lead you into a home that is tailor-made for casual living. The foyer offers access to a front-facing great room with a raised-hearth fireplace. The great room then flows into the breakfast nook, with outdoor access, and on to the efficient kitchen. Two family bedrooms and a shared bath complete the first floor. Curved stairs lead you to the upstairs master bedroom with its amenity-filled bath and attic access and to a loft/study, also with attic access.

COVERED PORCH

RAILING

NOOK
9⁴ x 12⁴

KIT
9⁴ x 9⁸

SNACK BAR

RANGE

REFG

W.H.

FURN

UTILITY

W

D

BEDRM
10⁰ x 10⁸

STORAGE

LINE OF FLOOR ABOVE

LIN

BATH

RAILING

GREAT RM
12¹⁰ x 16¹⁰
SLOPING CLG

RAISED HEARTH

FOYER

BEDRM
12⁴ x 10²

COVERED PORCH

RAILING

Width 46'
Depth 52'

Design by
Home Planners

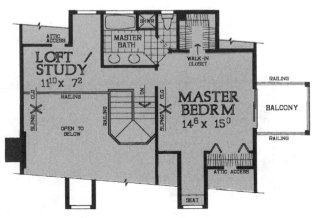

ATTIC ACCESS

MASTER BATH

SHWR

LOFT / STUDY
11¹⁰ x 7²

WALK-IN CLOSET

RAILING

MASTER BEDRM
14⁶ x 15⁰

BALCONY

RAILING

RAILING

OPEN TO BELOW

DN

SLPNG CLG

SLPNG CLG

ATTIC ACCESS

SEAT

Design 1482

First Floor: 1,008 square feet
Second Floor: 637 square feet
Total: 1,645

● Here is a chalet right from the pages of travel folders. In addition to the big bedrooms on the first floor, there are three more upstairs. The large master bedroom hasa a balcony which overlooks the lower wood deck. There are two full baths. The first floor is directly accessible from the outdoors. Note the snack bar and the panty. A laundry area is adjacent to the side entry.

Design by
Home Planners

Width 28'
Depth 48'

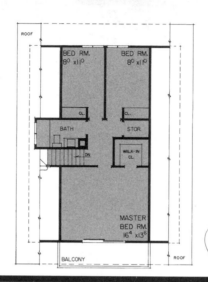

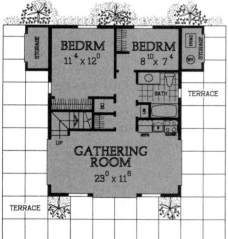

Width 32'
Depth 30'

Design 3658

First Floor: 784 square feet
Second Floor: 275 square feet
Total: 1,059

L D

Design by
Home Planners

● This chalet-type vacation home is designed to be completely livable whether it's the season for swimming or skiing. The dormitory on the upper level sleeps many vacationers, while the two bedrooms on the first floor provide the more conventional sleeping facilities. The upper level overlooks the beam-ceilinged living and dining area. With a wraparound terrace and plenty of storage space, what more could you ask for?

Design 2427

First Floor: 784 square feet
Second Floor: 504 square feet
Total: 1,288 square feet

Design by
Home Planners

● Make your vacation dreams a reality with this fabulous chalet. The most carefree characteristic is the second-floor master bedroom balcony which looks down onto the wood deck. Also on the second floor is the three-bunk dormitory. Panels through the knee walls give access to an abundant storage area—perfect for all of your seasonal storage needs. Downstairs, the kitchen utilizes a dining area and an efficient layout and has direct access to the outside. A large living room offers a grand view to a fantastic deck and has a warming fireplace. A first-floor bedroom enjoys the use of a full hall bath.

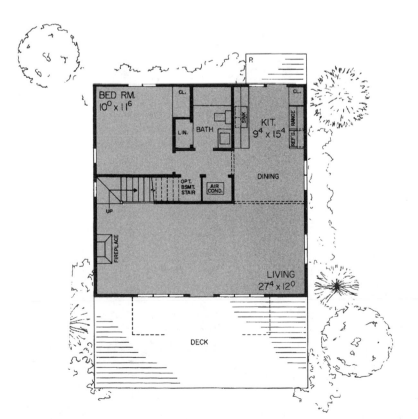

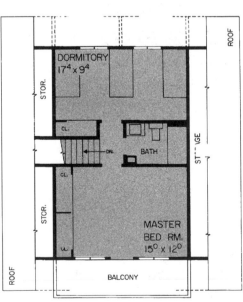

Width 28'
Depth 44'

Design 8956

First Floor: 845 square feet
Second Floor: 845 square feet
Total: 1,690 square feet

● An angled foyer and staircase lends diversity to this three-bedroom plan. The large living room, with a front-facing sitting area, affords amenities such as a fireplace and lots of wall space for various furniture arrangements. The dining room is bright and sunny and offers access outside via a French door. The U-shaped kitchen enjoys a built-in pantry, plenty of counter and cabinet space and convenience to the nearby utility room. The second floor offers two family bedrooms that share a full bath, and a master bedroom that boasts a fine angled bath.

Design by
Larry W.
Garnett &
Associates, Inc.

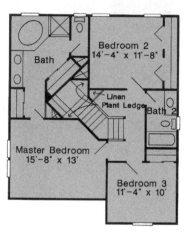

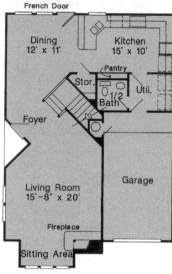

Bath

Bedroom 2
14'-4" x 11'-8"

Linen
Plant Ledge

Bath 2

Master Bedroom
15'-8" x 13'

Bedroom 3
11'-4" x 10'

Width 28'
Depth 42'-4"

French Door

Dining
12' x 11'

Kitchen
15' x 10'

Pantry

Stor.

1/2
Bath

Util.

Foyer

Living Room
15'-8" x 20'

Garage

Fireplace

Sitting Area

Design 9148

First Floor: 838 square feet
Second Floor: 453 square feet
Total: 1,291 square feet

● Small but exceedingly comfortable, this two-story, split-bedroom plan works well for families and empty-nesters alike. The open living/dining area is complemented by a U-shaped kitchen. A warming fireplace in the living room is flanked by bright windows. The master bedroom is found on the first floor and has its own bath plus plenty of closet space and a ten-foot ceiling. Upstairs there are two additional bedrooms and a full bath. Space is available for a fourth bedroom, adding 164 square feet to the plan.

QUOTE ONE®

Cost to build? See page 374 to order complete cost estimate to build this house in your area!

Design by
Larry W.
Garnett &
Associates, Inc.

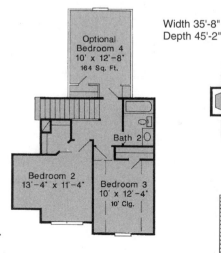

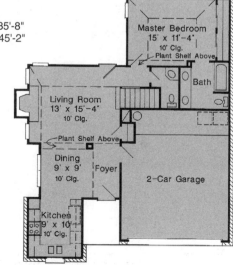

Optional
Bedroom 4
10' x 12'-8"
164 Sq. Ft.

Bath 2

Bedroom 2
13'-4" x 11'-4"

Bedroom 3
10' x 12'-4"
10' Clg.

Width 35'-8"
Depth 45'-2"

Master Bedroom
15' x 11'-4"
10' Clg.
Plant Shelf Above

Bath

Living Room
13' x 15'-4"
10' Clg.

Plant Shelf Above

Dining
9' x 9'
10' Clg.

Foyer

Kitchen
9' x 10'
10' Clg.

2-Car Garage

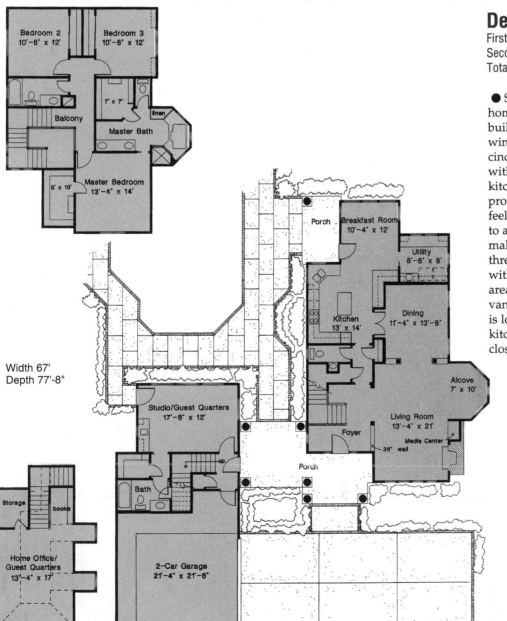

Bedroom 2
10'-8" x 12'

Bedroom 3
10'-8" x 12'

Balcony

7' x 7'

linen

Master Bath

5' x 10'

Master Bedroom
13'-4" x 14'

Width 67'
Depth 77'-8"

Porch

Breakfast Room
10'-4" x 12'

Utility
8'-8" x 8'

Kitchen
13' x 14'

Dining
11'-4" x 13'-8'

Studio/Guest Quarters
17'-8" x 12'

Alcove
7' x 10'

Bath

up

Foyer

Living Room
13'-4" x 21'

Porch

Media Center
36" wall

Storage

books

Home Office/
Guest Quarters
13'-4" x 17'

2-Car Garage
21'-4" x 21'-8'

Design 9190

First Floor: 1,213 square feet
Second Floor: 932 square feet
Total: 2,145 square feet

● Step into the foyer of this delightful home and find a living room with a built-in media center and an adjacent windowed alcove. Entertaining's a cinch in the columned dining room with double doors leading to the kitchen. Here, an island work space provides an extra amount of custom feel. The breakfast room enjoys access to an airy back porch. A utility room makes chores less tedious. Upstairs, three bedrooms include a master suite with a beautiful bayed tub and shower area, two walk-in closets and twin vanities. A deluxe studio or guest suite is located off the two-car garage. A kitchenette, a full bath and a walk-in closet are found here.

Design by
Larry W.
Garnett &
Associates, Inc.

Design 8922

First Floor: 2,242 square feet
Second Floor: 507 square feet
Total: 2,749 square feet

● Inspired by the turn-of-the-century homes along the Atlantic Coast, this design features finely detailed brickwork which is accented with shingle siding. The formal dining room is separated from traffic by three-foot walls. The grand two-story living room includes a sloped ceiling, a media center, a fireplace and circular stairs to the second floor. The gourmet kitchen overlooks the living area, breakfast room and a large covered porch. Three bedrooms include a master suite with spacious bath. The second floor offers a gameroom and a cozy study with dormer windows, a sloped ceiling and a built-in bookcase.

Design by
Larry W.
Garnett &
Associates, Inc.

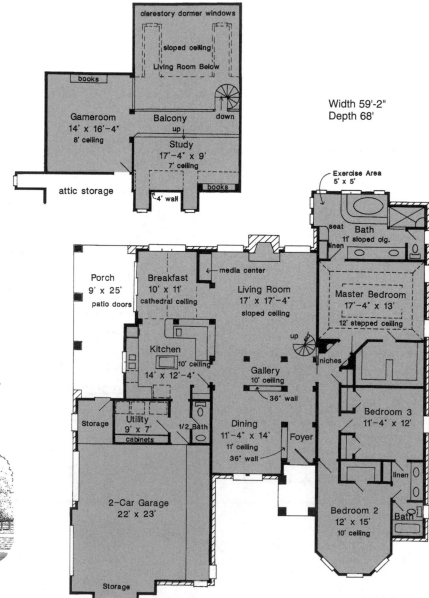

clerestory dormer windows

sloped ceiling

Living Room Below

books

Gameroom
14' x 16'-4"
8' ceiling

Balcony

down

up

Study
17'-4" x 9'
7' ceiling

attic storage

books

4' wall

Width 59'-2"
Depth 68'

Exercise Area
5' x 5'

seat

Bath
11' sloped clg.

linen

media center

Porch
9' x 25'

patio doors

Breakfast
10' x 11'
cathedral ceiling

Living Room
17' x 17'-4"
sloped ceiling

Master Bedroom
17'-4" x 13'
12' stepped ceiling

Kitchen
14' x 12'-4"
10' ceiling

up

niches

Gallery
10' ceiling

36' wall

Bedroom 3
11'-4" x 12'

Storage

Utility
9' x 7'
cabinets

1/2 Bath

Dining
11'-4" x 14'
11' ceiling
36' wall

Foyer

linen

2-Car Garage
22' x 23'

Bedroom 2
12' x 15'
10' ceiling

Bath

Storage

REAR VIEW

180

Design 9055

First Floor: 997 square feet
Second Floor: 1,069 square feet
Total: 2,066 square feet

● With its exceptional detail and proportions, this home is reminiscent of the Queen Anne Style. The foyer opens to a living area with a bay-windowed alcove and a fireplace with flanking bookshelves. A full-length bay window and a French door fill the breakfast area with natural light. Upstairs, the master bedroom offers unsurpassed elegance and convenience. The sitting area has an eleven-foot ceiling with arch-top windows. The bath area features a large walk-in closet, His and Hers sinks and plenty of linen storage. Plans for a two-car detached garage are included.

Quote One®

Cost to build? See page 374 to order complete cost estimate to build this house in your area!

Design by
Larry W.
Garnett &
Associates, Inc.

Width 39'-8"
Depth 39'-2"

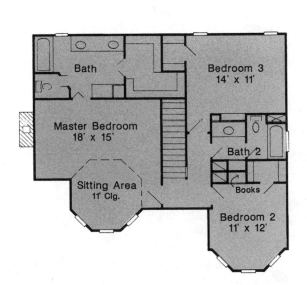

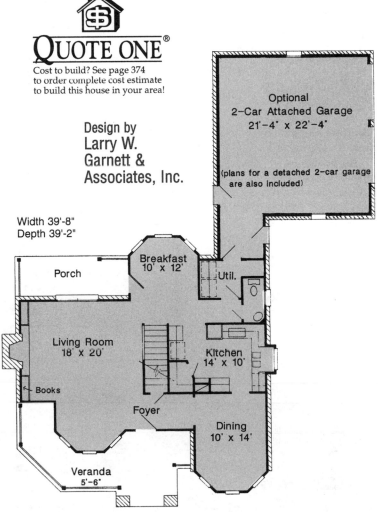

Design 9060

First Floor: 1,326 square feet
Second Floor: 1,086 square feet
Total: 2,412 square feet

● The oval-glass front door of this elegant Queen Anne home opens into the foyer, which showcases the bannistered stairs. The spacious family room enjoys a bay-windowed alcove and a fireplace. French doors lead to the game room, which can easily become guest quarters with a private bath. The kitchen offers a walk-in pantry and abundant cabinet and counter space. Adjacent to the bay-windowed breakfast room is a utility area with room for a washer, a dryer, a freezer and a small counter top with cabinets above. A door from this area can provide access to the two-car, detached garage for which plans are included. Upstairs, Bedrooms 2 and 3 each feature walk-in closets, along with built-in bookcases. The master area, with its sitting alcove and special bath, is the perfect retreat.

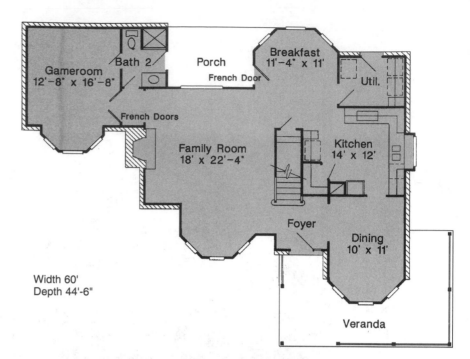

Width 60'
Depth 44'-6"

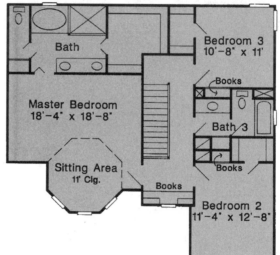

Design by
Larry W. Garnett & Associates, Inc.

Design 2973

First Floor: 1,269 square feet
Second Floor: 1,227 square feet
Total: 2,496 square feet

L

● The two finely detailed outdoor living spaces found on this Victorian home add much to formal and informal entertaining options. Living and dining areas include a formal living room and dining room, a family room with fireplace, a study, and a kitchen with an attached breakfast nook. The second floor has three family bedrooms and a luxurious master bedroom with whirlpool spa and His and Hers walk-in closets.

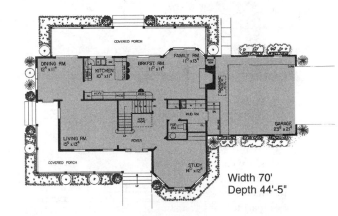

Width 70'
Depth 44'-5"

Design by
Home Planners

QUOTE ONE

Cost to build? See page 374
to order complete cost estimate
to build this house in your area!

Design 9058

First Floor: 1,348 square feet
Second Floor: 1,058 square feet
Total: 2,406 square feet

● This Queen Anne-style home offers not only an octagon-shaped tower, but also ornate bay windows and decorative gable shingles. Inside, a two-way fireplace is functional in both the living room and the family area. Highlights of the kitchen include a walk-in pantry, a center work island, and a box window at the sink. The utility room leads to a detached, two-car garage, for which the plans are included. Upstairs, the master bedroom is accented with a sitting area. Two additional bedrooms share a dressing area and a bath.

Design by
Larry W. Garnett & Associates, Inc.

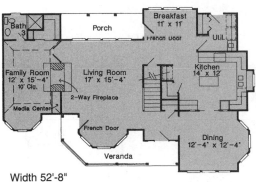

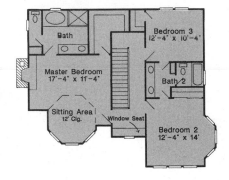

Width 52'-8"
Depth 33'-4"

Design 9699

First Floor: 1,519 square feet
Second Floor: 792 square feet
Total: 2,311 square feet

Design 9698

First Floor: 1,790 square feet
Second Floor: 792 square feet
Total: 2,582 square feet

Design by
Donald A.
Gardner,
Architects, Inc.

● Within one great exterior lies two floor plans—choose the one that best suits your lifestyle. Notice that the second floor is the same for both plans—the difference lies only in the first-floor layout. It features a great room and formal dining room on Design 9699; a formal living room, dining room and family room on Design 9698. The master bedroom on the first level has a walk-in closet and master bath with double-bowl vanity, shower and garden tub. The second-level consists of three bedrooms: one has a private bath while the other two share a full bath. A separate garage is connected to the house with a covered breezeway for convenience. Order Design 9698 for living room option; order Design 9699 for great room option.

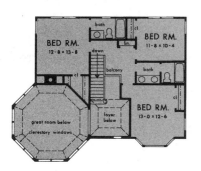

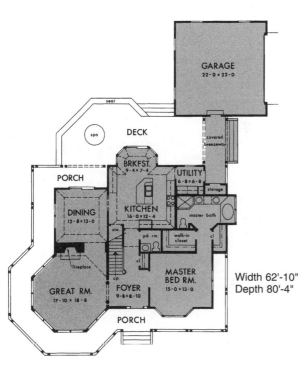

Width 62'-10"
Depth 80'-4"

Width 63'
Depth 80'-4"

Design by Larry W. Garnett & Associates, Inc.

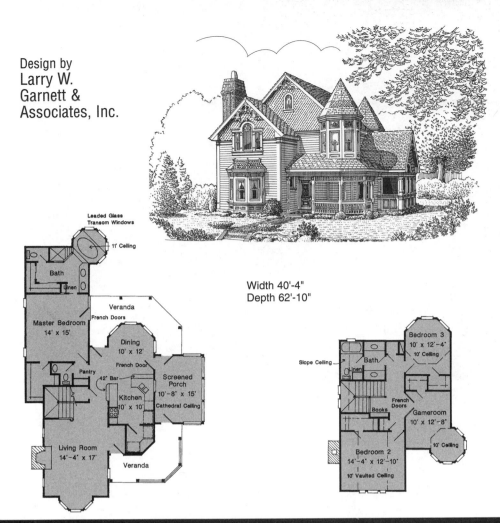

Width 40'-4"
Depth 62'-10"

Leaded Glass Transom Windows

11' Ceiling

Bath

Linen

Veranda

French Doors

Master Bedroom
14' x 15'

Dining
10' x 12'

French Door

Pantry

42" Bar

Kitchen
10' x 10'

Screened Porch
10'-8" x 15'
Cathedral Ceiling

Living Room
14'-4" x 17'

Veranda

Slope Ceiling

Bath

Linen

Bedroom 3
10' x 12'-4"
10' Ceiling

French Doors

Books

Gameroom
10' x 12'-8"

10' Ceiling

Bedroom 2
14'-4" x 12'-10"
10' Vaulted Ceiling

Design 9063

First Floor: 1,236 square feet
Second Floor: 835 square feet
Total: 2,071 square feet

● The living area of this spectacular Queen Anne style home features a fireplace and a bay-windowed alcove. The centrally located kitchen overlooks a dining area with full-length windows and a French door. The master bedroom features a large walk-in closet and French doors opening to the rear veranda. Upstairs, French doors open into a game room. Bedroom 2 offers a walk-in closet and a ten-foot sloped ceiling. Bedroom 3 also provides a walk-in closet and a raised octagon-shaped ceiling. Plans are included for a detached two-car garage and an optional screened porch.

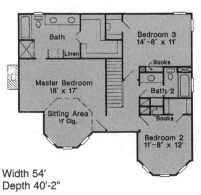

QUOTE ONE®
Cost to build? See page 374 to order complete cost estimate to build this house in your area!

Design 9059

First Floor: 1,299 square feet
Second Floor: 1,069 square feet
Total: 2,368 square feet

● With a veranda wrapping around an octagon-shaped turret, this home recalls the grand Queen Anne-style designs of the late 19th Century. The foyer offers access to both the bay-windowed dining room and the living area. French doors lead from the living area to a game room, which can easily become a guest room with a private bath. The second floor features two children's bedrooms, each with a walk-in closet and a built-in bookcase. The master bedroom features a sitting area with an 11'-high, octagon-shaped ceiling. Plans are included for a detached, two-car garage.

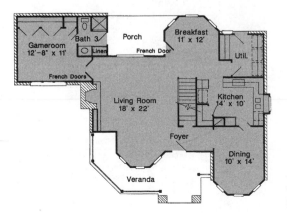

Gameroom
12'-8" x 11'

Bath 3

Linen

Porch

French Door

Breakfast
11' x 12'

Util.

French Doors

Living Room
18' x 22'

Kitchen
14' x 10'

Foyer

Dining
10' x 14'

Veranda

Bath

Linen

Books

Bedroom 3
14'-8" x 11'

Master Bedroom
18' x 17'

Bath 2

Books

Sitting Area
11' Clg.

Bedroom 2
11'-8" x 12'

Width 54'
Depth 40'-2"

Design by Larry W. Garnett & Associates, Inc.

Design 9061

First Floor: 2,087 square feet
Second Floor: 1,150 square feet
Total: 3,237 square feet

● Reminiscent of the grand, brick Victorians of the late 19th-Century, this design features a raised, octagon-shaped turret with a wrap-around veranda and patterned shingle siding at the gables. The large, two-story living room is perfect for formal or family entertaining, with the breakfast area and kitchen close by. A study with built-in bookcases is perfect for a home office or a relaxing reading area. The master suite features a sitting area and a luxurious bath with a glass-enclosed shower, linen storage and a walk-in closet with full-length mirrored doors. Each of the three upstairs bedrooms enjoys a private lavatory area and ample closet space. The large game room features a cathedral ceiling and a balcony railing overlooking the living room.

Design by
Larry W.
Garnett &
Associates, Inc.

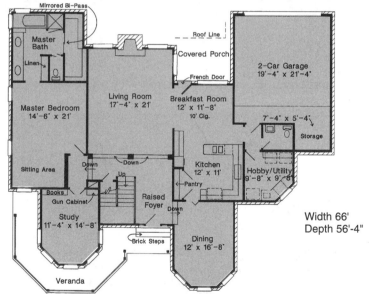

Width 66'
Depth 56'-4"

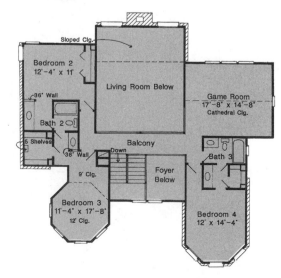

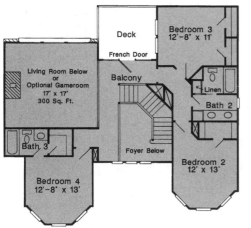

Deck

French Door

Bedroom 3
12'-8" x 11'

Living Room Below
or
Optional Gameroom
17' x 17'
300 Sq. Ft.

Balcony

Linen

Bath 2

Foyer Below

Bath 3

Bedroom 2
12' x 13'

Bedroom 4
12'-8" x 13'

Design by
Larry W.
Garnett &
Associates, Inc.

Design 9062

First Floor: 2,254 square feet
Second Floor: 1,228 square feet
Total: 3,482 square feet

● Decorative shingle siding and a dominant front veranda create a charming turn-of-the-century exterior. The magnificent foyer offers a view of the two-story living area with floor-to-ceiling glass at the rear. A raised walkway provides a dramatic entry to the master suite with a cozy sitting area. The kitchen features a walk-in pantry and a boxed-out window at the sink. The family room offers a bay-window area and French doors opening to the covered porch. There is also a garage, for which plans are included. Upstairs, a balcony walkway leads to Bedroom 4 with a private bath. Bedrooms 2 and 3 showcase ample closet space and a shared bath with separate dressing areas. The plans offer an optional 17' x 17' game area above the living room.

Width 62'-6"
Depth 65'-4"

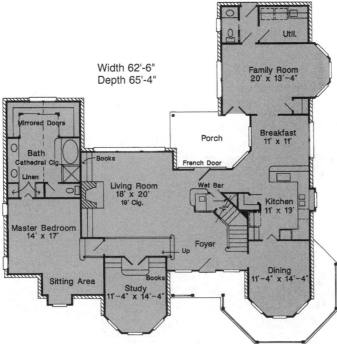

Util.

Family Room
20' x 13'-4"

Mirrored Doors

Bath
Cathedral Clg.

Books

Linen

Porch

Breakfast
11' x 11'

French Door

Living Room
18' x 20'
19' Clg.

Wet Bar

Kitchen
11' x 13'

Master Bedroom
14' x 17'

Foyer

Up

Sitting Area

Books

Study
11'-4" x 14'-4"

Dining
11'-4" x 14'-4"

QUOTE ONE®

Cost to build? See page 374 to order complete cost estimate to build this house in your area!

Design 9014

First floor: 1,565 square feet
Second floor: 1,598 square feet
Total: 3,163 square feet

● The angled entry of this Victorian home opens to a grand foyer and a formal parlor with expansive windows and a French door leading to the side yard. The formal dining area features a built-in hutch. Double French doors open from the foyer to the large study with bookcases and full-length windows. The spacious family room with a fireplace and wet bar is a superb entertainment area. The kitchen with its work island and abundant cabinet space overlooks the octagon-shaped breakfast room. Upstairs, the master bedroom has French doors which open onto a rear deck, and an oversized walk-in closet. The distinctive bath features a bay windowed tub area and glass-enclosed shower. Three additional bedrooms each have walk-in closets. Plans for a two-car detached garage are included.

Design by
Larry W.
Garnett &
Associates, Inc.

Width 47'-10"
Depth 59'-2"

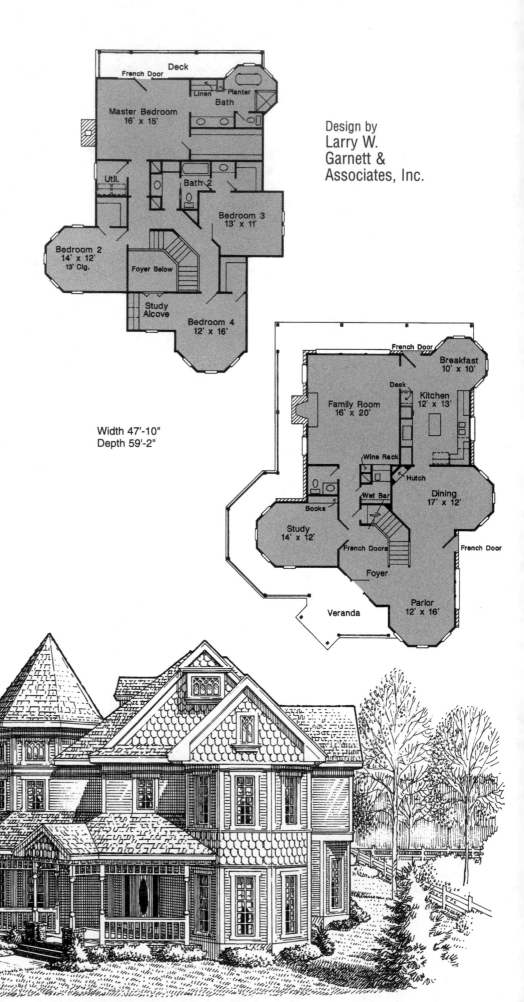

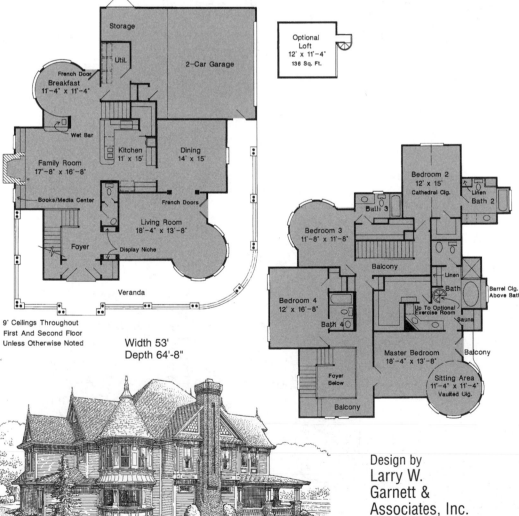

Storage

2-Car Garage

Util.

French Door
Breakfast
11'-4" x 11'-4"

Wet Bar

Kitchen
11' x 15'

Dining
14' x 15'

Family Room
17'-8" x 16'-8"

Books/Media Center

French Doors

Foyer

Living Room
18'-4" x 13'-8"

Display Niche

Veranda

9' Ceilings Throughout
First And Second Floor
Unless Otherwise Noted

Width 53'
Depth 64'-8"

Optional
Loft
12' x 11'-4"
136 Sq. Ft.

Bedroom 2
12' x 15'
Cathedral Clg.

Linen

Bath 2

Bath 3

Bedroom 3
11'-8" x 11'-8"

Balcony

Linen

Bath

Barrel Clg.
Above Bath

Bedroom 4
12' x 16'-8"

Up To Optional
Exercise Room

Sauna

Bath 4

Master Bedroom
18'-4" x 13'-8"

Balcony

Foyer
Below

Sitting Area
11'-4" x 11'-4"
Vaulted Clg.

Balcony

Design by
Larry W.
Garnett &
Associates, Inc.

SIDE

Design 9017

First Floor: 1,617 square feet
Second Floor: 1,818 square feet
Total: 3,435 square feet
Optional Loft: 136 square feet

● With its cantilevered gable
sloping with a gentle curve to the
first floor and a raised turret, this
design is representative of late
19th-Century style. The entry
foyer overlooks the living and
dining rooms, both with expansive
windows and coffered ceilings.
An open serving bar provides the
kitchen with a full view of the
family area, with its massive fireplace. The second-floor master
suite offers a sitting area with a
vaulted ceiling. A glass-block
shower and a whirlpool tub
beneath expansive casement windows are part of the exquisite
bath. Three additional bedrooms
boast private baths and walk-ins,
along with special features.

Quote One®
Cost to build? See page 374
to order complete cost estimate
to build this house in your area!

189

Design by
Larry W.
Garnett &
Associates, Inc.

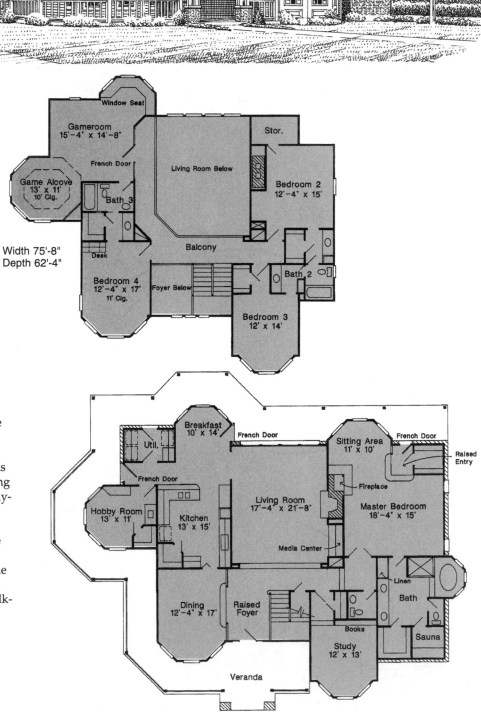

Window Seat

Gameroom
15'-4" x 14'-8"

Stor.

French Door

Living Room Below

Game Alcove
13' x 11'
10' Clg.

Bath 3

Bedroom 2
12'-4" x 15'

Width 75'-8"
Depth 62'-4"

Desk

Balcony

Bedroom 4
12'-4" x 17'
11' Clg.

Foyer Below

Bath 2

Bedroom 3
12' x 14'

Design 9071

First Floor: 2,524 square feet
Second Floor: 1,529 square feet
Total: 4,053 square feet

● This lovely Queen Anne-style design has all the amenities you would expect in such a grand home. The raised foyer overlooks the formal dining room and living area, and provides access to a bay-windowed study and secluded master suite with a sitting area and a fireplace. Next to the large kitchen and breakfast area is a laundry room and a special home office or hobby room. Upstairs, Bedrooms 2 and 3 each have walk-in closets and separate dressing areas. A French door leads to a large gameroom with a built-in window seat and an octagonal games area. Plans for a two-car, detached garage are included.

Breakfast
10' x 14'

Util.

French Door

Sitting Area
11' x 10'

French Door

Raised Entry

French Door

Fireplace

Hobby Room
13' x 11'

Kitchen
13' x 15'

Living Room
17'-4" x 21'-8"

Master Bedroom
18'-4" x 15'

Media Center

Linen

Bath

Dining
12'-4" x 17'

Raised Foyer

Books

Sauna

Study
12' x 13'

Veranda

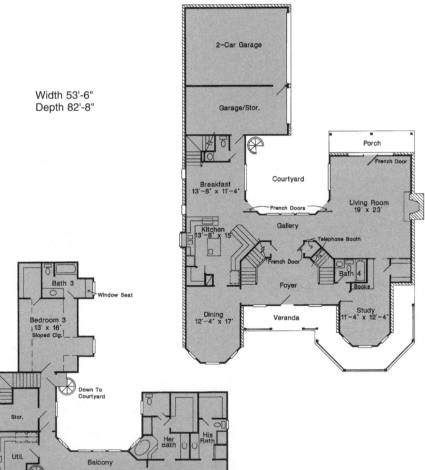

Width 53'-6"
Depth 82'-8"

2-Car Garage

Garage/Stor.

Breakfast
13'-8" x 11'-4"

Courtyard

Porch

French Door

Kitchen
13'-8" x 15'

Gallery

Living Room
19' x 23'

Telephone Booth

French Door

Bath 4

Foyer

Books

Dining
12'-4" x 17'

Veranda

Study
11'-4" x 12'-4"

Bath 3

Window Seat

Bedroom 3
13' x 16'
Sloped Clg.

Down To
Courtyard

Stor.

Util.

Balcony

Her Bath

His Bath

Up To
Attic

Bath 2

Master Bedroom
18' x 13'
10' Step-Up Clg.

Foyer Below

Bedroom 2
13'-8" x 14'

Sitting Area
11' x 14'

Design 9072

First Floor: 1,920 square feet
Second Floor: 1,898 square feet
Total: 3,818 square feet

● Balance, symmetry and elaborate gingerbread detailing highlight this Queen Anne-style home. Inside, the living room, kitchen and breakfast area are ideal for relaxing or entertaining. Accessible from the foyer and living room, the study (or guest room) includes a walk-in storage area and built-in bookcases. From the breakfast area, rear stairs lead to the second floor. Bedroom 3 can be secluded as area for an older child. Leading to the private master suite is a balcony that overlooks the dramatic foyer and stairs on one side and the courtyard on the other.

Design by
Larry W.
Garnett &
Associates, Inc.

Design 9012

First Floor: 1,357 square feet
Second Floor: 1,079 square feet
Total: 2,436 square feet

● An inviting wraparound veranda with delicate spindlework and a raised turret with leaded-glass windows recall the grand Queen Anne-style Victorians of the late 1880s. Double doors open from the dramatic two-story foyer to a private study with built-in bookcases and a bay window. French doors open from the living room to the front veranda and to the screened porch. A fireplace adds warmth to the breakfast area and the island kitchen. Above the two-car garage is an optional area that is perfect for a home office or guest quarters. Upstairs, the balcony, with built-in bookcases and window seat, overlooks the foyer below. A twelve-foot octagon-shaped ceiling and leaded-glass windows define a cozy sitting area in the master suite. A raised alcove in the master bath contains a garden tub and glass-enclosed shower. An optional exercise loft and plant shelves complete this elegant master bath. Two additional bedrooms, one with a private deck, and the other with a cathedral ceiling, share a dressing area and bath.

QUOTE ONE®

Cost to build? See page 374 to order complete cost estimate to build this house in your area!

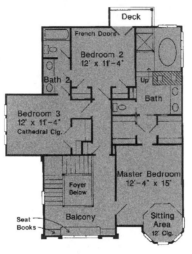

Deck

French Doors

Bedroom 2
12' x 11'-4"

Bath 2

Up

Bath

Bedroom 3
12' x 11'-4"
Cathedral Clg.

Foyer Below

Master Bedroom
12'-4" x 15'

Seat
Books

Balcony

Sitting Area
12' Clg.

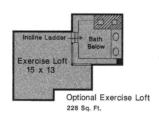

Incline Ladder → Bath Below

Exercise Loft
15 x 13

Optional Exercise Loft
228 Sq. Ft.

Office
16'-4" x 17'

Optional Second Floor
At Garage
167 Sq. Ft.

Design by
Larry W. Garnett & Associates, Inc.

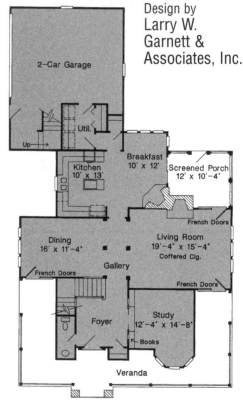

2-Car Garage

Util.

Up

Kitchen
10' x 13'

Breakfast
10' x 12'

Screened Porch
12' x 10'-4"

French Doors

Dining
16' x 11'-4"

Living Room
19'-4" x 15'-4"
Coffered Clg.

Gallery

French Doors

French Doors

Foyer

Study
12'-4" x 14'-8"

Books

Veranda

Width 42'-8"
Depth 75'

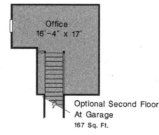

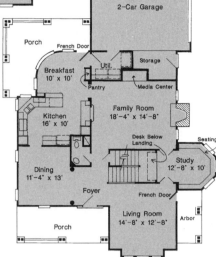

Design by
Larry W.
Garnett &
Associates, Inc.

Width 46'-6"
Depth 65'-8"

Design 9056

First Floor: 1,354 square feet
Second Floor: 1,418 square feet
Total: 2,772 square feet

QUOTE ONE®

Cost to build? See page 374
to order complete cost estimate
to build this house in your area!

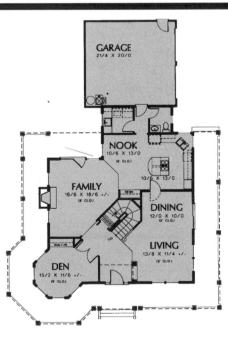

● Inside this charming turn-of-the-century design, classical columns separate the foyer and dining room. A French door opens from the living room to a lattice-covered side arbor. Double doors in both the living and family rooms provide access to a bay-windowed study with built-in bookcases and a desk. Upstairs, the master suite features an elegant bath with a garden tub inset in a bay window and a walk-in closet. Bedrooms 3 and 4 share a bath, while Bedroom 2 has a private bath and a bay windowed alcove.

Design 9585

First Floor: 1,337 square feet
Second Floor: 1,025 square feet
Total: 2,362 square feet

● An octagonal tower, a wraparound porch and amenities galore all combine to give this house tons of appeal. The tower is occupied by a sunny den on the first floor and a delightful bedroom on the second floor. A large efficient kitchen easily serves both the formal dining room and the cheerful nook. Upstairs, two bedrooms share a full hall bath while the master bedroom revels in its luxurious private bath.

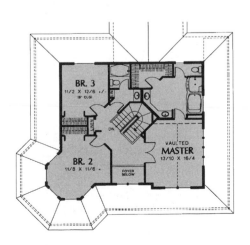

Width 50'-6"
Depth 72'-6"

Design by
Alan Mascord
Design Associates, Inc.

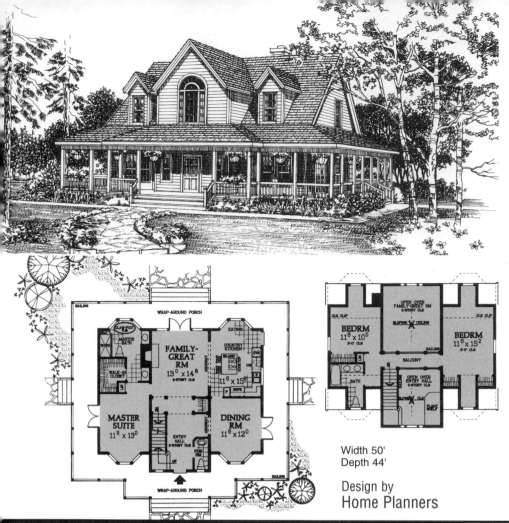

Design 3619

First Floor: 1,171 square feet
Second Floor: 600 square feet
Total: 1,771 square feet

L **D**

● Enjoy gracious living in this Southern-style farmhouse. From the wraparound porch, the two-story entry hall opens through an archway to a formal dining room. The efficient country kitchen shares space with a bay-windowed eating area. The two-story family/great room is warmed by a fireplace in winter and open to the outdoors in summer through double French doors. The master suite offers a bay window, porch access, a huge walk-in closet and a private bath. The second floor holds two family bedrooms and a full bath. Plans for an optional indoor swimming pool/spa and detached garage are included.

Width 50'
Depth 44'

Design by
Home Planners

Quote One®

Cost to build? See page 374 to order complete cost estimate to build this house in your area!

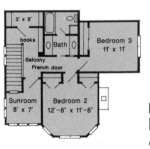

Garage Width 20'
Garage Depth 24'

Design by
Larry W. Garnett & Associates, Inc.

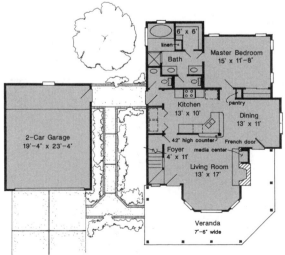

Width 30'-10"
Depth 51'

Design 8959

First Floor: 1,051 square feet
Second Floor: 631 square feet
Total: 1,682 square feet

● This charming farmhouse, with its wide, wraparound veranda supplies all the space needed for whittling and listening to cricket songs. Once inside, the charm continues with a foyer that opens to a bay-windowed living room with a fireplace and a media center. The thoughtfully designed kitchen furnishes a step-saving layout, and a nearby formal dining room opens to the veranda through a French door. Privacy is paramount in the master bedroom located at the rear of the first floor. A large walk-in closet, dual vanities, a separate tub and shower and a compartmented toilet are contained in the private bath. The second floor holds two secondary bedrooms, a full bath, a sunroom, a built-in bookcase and a large storage space.

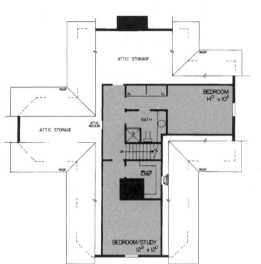

Design 2970

First Floor: 1,538 square feet
Second Floor: 1,526 square feet
Third Floor: 658 square feet
Total: 3,722 square feet

L

● This charming Victorian features a covered outdoor living area on all four sides! It even ends at a screened porch which features a sun deck above. This interesting plan offers three floors of livability. And what livability it is! Plenty of formal and informal living facilities to go along with the potential of five bedrooms. The master suite is just fantastic. It is adjacent to a wonderful sitting room and offers a sun deck and lavish bath/personal care facilities. The third floor will make a wonderful haven for the family's student members.

Design by
Home Planners

Width 67'
Depth 66'

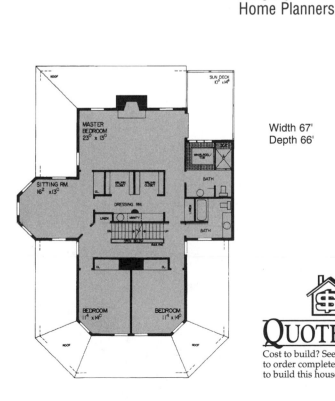

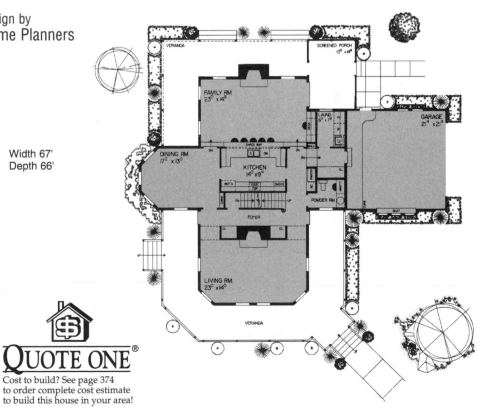

Quote One®

Cost to build? See page 374
to order complete cost estimate
to build this house in your area!

Design by
Larry W.
Garnett &
Associates, Inc.

Design 9068

First Floor: 1,879 square feet
Second Floor: 848 square feet
Total: 2,727 square feet

● A raised turret and front gable with decorative shingle siding dominate the facade of this Queen Anne home. The library alcove that is situated at the front of the living room offers built-in bookcases. The country-style kitchen opens directly to the breakfast area. The secluded master bedroom features a master bath with His and Hers walk-in closets, a custom tub and separate shower. Upstairs, three bedrooms share a large, well-planned bathroom. Plans for a detached garage are included.

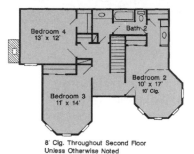

Bedroom 4
13' x 12'

Bath 2

Bedroom 2
10' x 17'
10' Clg.

Bedroom 3
11' x 14'

8' Clg. Throughout Second Floor
Unless Otherwise Noted

Width 59'-8"
Depth 57'-8"

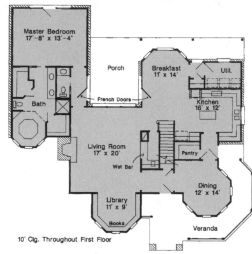

Master Bedroom
17'-8" x 13'-4"

Porch

Breakfast
11' x 14'

Util.

French Doors

Bath

Kitchen
16' x 12'

Living Room
17' x 20'

Pantry

Wet Bar

Dining
12' x 14'

Library
11' x 9'

Books

Veranda

10' Clg. Throughout First Floor

Design 9678

First Floor: 1,393 square feet
Second Floor: 1,195 square feet
Total: 2,588 square feet

● This elegant Victorian features an exterior of distinctive decorative detailing, yet offers an interior plan that satisfies today's standards. A spacious living room incorporates a large bay-windowed area and a fireplace. The generous kitchen with island counter is centrally located to the dining and family rooms and to the sun room. On the second level, the master suite has a fireplace, walk-in closet and bay-windowed area which can serve as a study. Of the three additional bedrooms, one enjoys a private bath; the others share a full bath. Plans for a separate garage are available if specified.

BED RM.
11-4 x 11-6

BED RM.
11-0 x 13-0

BED RM.
11-0 x 13-0

bath

bath

fireplace

MASTER
BED RM.
13-4 x 18-0

down

study

master bath

Design by
Donald A.
Gardner,
Architects, Inc.

Width 44'
Depth 50'-8"

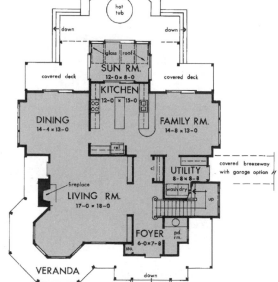

seat

DECK

hot tub

down

down

glass roof

SUN RM.
12-0 x 8-0

covered deck

covered deck

KITCHEN
12-0 x 15-0

DINING
14-4 x 13-0

FAMILY RM.
14-8 x 13-0

ref

covered breezeway
with garage option

UTILITY
8-8 x 8-8

fireplace

wash dry

LIVING RM.
17-0 x 18-0

up

FOYER
6-0 x 7-8

pd. rm.

sto.

VERANDA

down

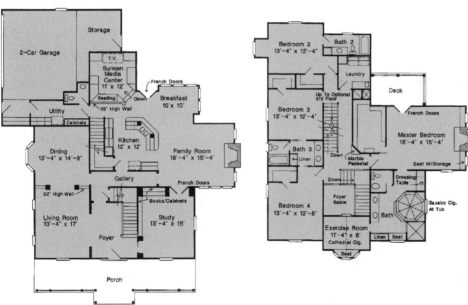

Width 59'-4"
Depth 72'-8"

Floor Plan Labels (First Floor)

Storage
2-Car Garage
T.V.
Sunken Media Center 11' x 12'
French Doors
Seating
28" High Wall
Breakfast 10' x 10'
Utility
Cabinets
Dining 13'-4" x 14'-8"
Kitchen 12' x 12'
Family Room 18'-4" x 15'-4'
32" High Wall
Gallery
French Doors
Living Room 13'-4" x 17'
Books/Cabinets
Study 13'-4" x 15'
Foyer
Porch

Floor Plan Labels (Second Floor)

Bedroom 2 13'-4" x 12'-4"
Bath 2
Laundry
Deck
Up To Optional 3rd Floor
Bedroom 3 13'-4" x 12'-4'
French Doors
Master Bedroom 18'-4" x 15'-4"
Down
Bath 3
Linen
Marble Pedestal
Seat W/Storage
Bedroom 4 13'-4" x 12'-8'
Down
Foyer Below
Dressing Table
Gazebo Clg. At Tub
Bath
Exercise Room 11'-4" x 8'
Cathedral Clg.
Linen Seat
Seat

Design by
Larry W.
Garnett &
Associates, Inc.

Design 9015

First Floor: 1,948 square feet
Second Floor: 1,891 square feet
Total: 3,839 square feet

● As authentic as the exterior of this design is, the interior offers all the luxury and elegance that today's homeowners could desire. The formal living and dining rooms are separated by detailed wood columns. Built-in bookcases and cabinets highlight the block-paneled study. The centrally located kitchen becomes the focal point of a truly outstanding family living center which includes a sunken media area, breakfast alcove and a family room with a fireplace. Adjacent to the kitchen is a large hobby room with a built-in desk, a space for a freezer and generous cabinet storage. The secluded master suite is beyond compare, with such extras as a fireplace with flanking window seats and cabinets, an enormous walk-in closet and a private deck. The luxurious bath features a dressing table, a whirlpool tub with a gazebo-shaped ceiling above and an oversized shower. Finally, there is a private exercise room with a bay-window seat. Three additional bedrooms and a laundry room complete the second floor. A staircase leads to an optional third floor area.

Design 9270

First Floor: 1,113 square feet
Second Floor: 965 square feet
Total: 2,078 square feet

● Elegant detail, a charming veranda and the tall brick chimney create a pleasing facade on this four-bedroom Victorian home. Yesterday's simpler lifestyle is reflected throughout this plan. A large bayed parlor with sloped ceiling is visible from the entry. Step down to enter the gathering room with a fireplace and plenty of windows. Note the pantry cabinet and built-in desk in the kitchen and breakfast area. The formal dining room opens to the parlor for entertaining ease. The second-floor master suite is segregated for privacy and provides a dressing and bath area with double lavatories, skylight and whirlpool tub.

Width 46'
Depth 41'-5"

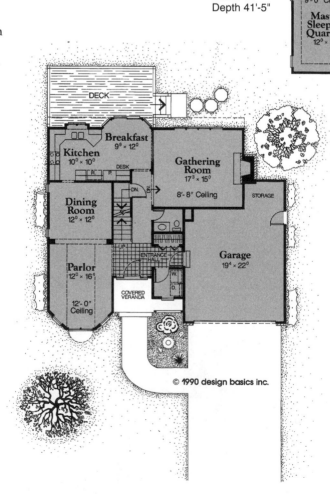

© 1990 design basics inc.

Design by
Design
Basics,
Inc.

Design 9269

First Floor: 1,081 square feet
Second Floor: 1,136 square feet
Total: 2,217 square feet

● Victorian charm and detailing radiate from this design. Inside, formal living spaces begin in a dining room with hutch space and a parlor highlighted by a bayed window. The T-shaped staircase allows quick access to the informal spaces at the rear, such as the comfortable gathering room with a fireplace, built-in bookcase and many windows. Upstairs, a compartmented bath is shared by the secondary sleeping quarters. Gracing the master sleeping quarters is a private dressing/bath area offering an oval whirlpool, angled vanity and walk-in wardrobe.

Design by
Design Basics, Inc.

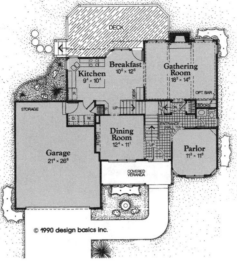

Width 53'
Depth 42'

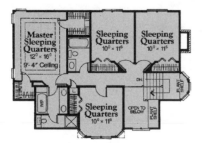

Design 9271

First Floor: 919 square feet
Second Floor: 923 square feet
Total: 1,842 square feet

● Victorian accents such as the wrap-around veranda and the repeating fan detail add distinction to this four-bedroom, two-story home. From the entry, enjoy the clear view to the sunny great room with a fireplace, perfect for daily living. Upstairs, the staircase with bright windows and decorator plant shelf leads to secondary sleeping quarters. Master sleeping quarters are graced by a tiered ceiling, His and Hers wardrobes and a private master bath.

Width 46'
Depth 40'

Design by
Design Basics, Inc.

Design 8970

First Floor: 1,213 square feet
Second Floor: 535 square feet
Total: 1,748 square feet

● This charming Folk Victorian home may start as a small cottage, but if all expansion options are used, it grows to a sizable 2,166-square-foot home. The basic plan is well-designed and provides fine livability with a living room, dining room, kitchen, three bedrooms and two baths. Of special note is the private master suite which invites relaxation with a pampering tub, a separate shower and a compart-mented toilet, accessible from the hall-way as well. Plenty of storage is avail-able in the huge walk in closet. The addition of the sunlit morning room is a welcome space for casual dining, while the guest room with a private bath enhances livability and offers room to stretch. A two-car garage may be completed at the same time or completed later if you prefer.

Design by
Larry W.
Garnett &
Associates, Inc.

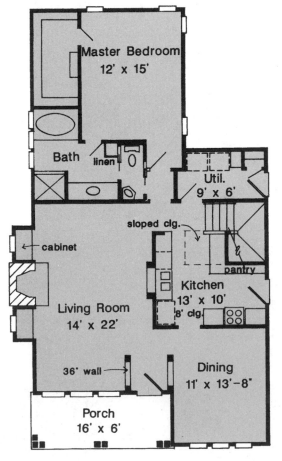

Master Bedroom
12' x 15'

Bath

linen

cabinet

Util.
9' x 6'

sloped clg.

pantry

Kitchen
13' x 10'

8' clg.

Living Room
14' x 22'

36" wall

Dining
11' x 13'-8"

Porch
16' x 6'

Width 30'-8"
Depth 51'-8"

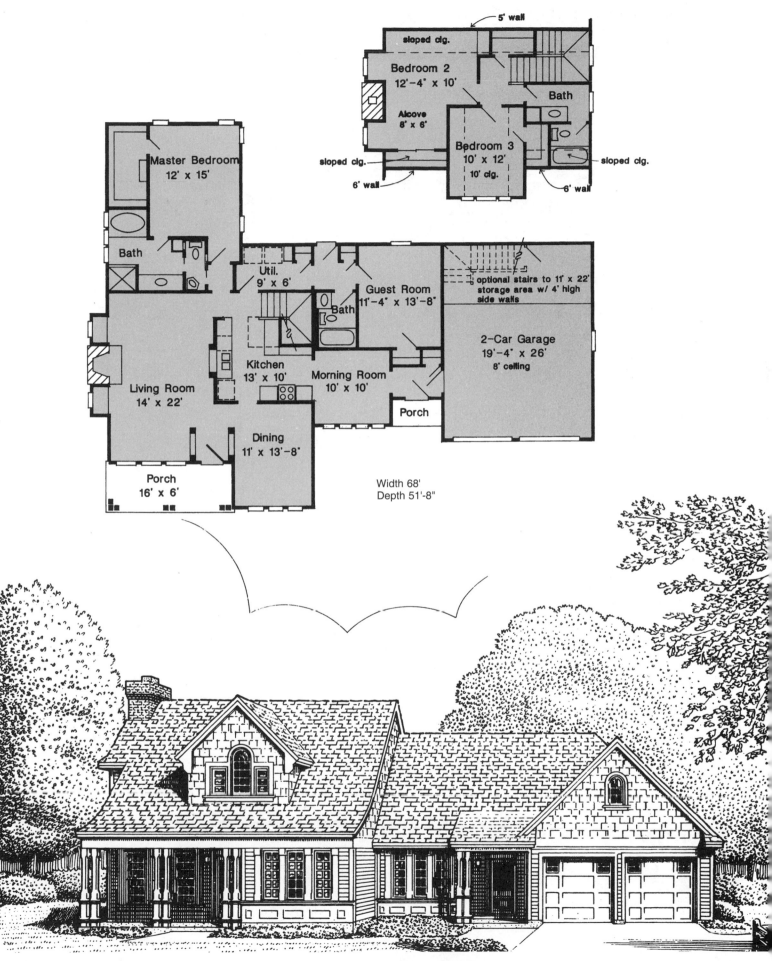

sloped clg.

5' wall

Bedroom 2
12'-4" x 10'

Alcove
8' x 6'

Bath

sloped clg.

Bedroom 3
10' x 12'
10' clg.

sloped clg.

6' wall

6' wall

Master Bedroom
12' x 15'

Bath

Util.
9' x 6'

Guest Room
11'-4" x 13'-8"

optional stairs to 11' x 22'
storage area w/ 4' high
side walls

2-Car Garage
19'-4" x 26'
8' ceiling

Living Room
14' x 22'

Bath

Kitchen
13' x 10'

Morning Room
10' x 10'

Porch

Dining
11' x 13'-8"

Width 68'
Depth 51'-8"

Porch
16' x 6'

Design 9067

First Floor: 1,999 square feet
Second Floor: 933 square feet
Total: 2,932 square feet

● The wraparound veranda and simple lines give this home an unassuming elegance that is characteristic of its Folk Victorian heritage. Opening directly to the formal dining room, the two-story foyer offers extra space for large dinner parties. Double French doors lead to the study with raised paneling and a cozy fireplace. Built-in bookcases conceal a hidden security vault. The private master suite features a corner garden tub, glass enclosed shower and a walk-in closet. Overlooking the family room and built-in breakfast nook is the central kitchen. A rear staircase provides convenient access to the second floor from the family room. The balcony provides a view of the foyer below and the Palladian window. Three additional bedrooms complete this exquisite home.

Design by
Larry W.
Garnett &
Associates, Inc.

Cost to build? See page 374 to order complete cost estimate to build this house in your area!

Width 79'-8"
Depth 59'

REAR

Design 9131

First floor: 978 square feet
Second floor: 464 square feet
Total: 1,442 square feet

● From the covered front veranda to the second-story Palladian window, this home exudes warmth and grace. The living area is complemented by a cozy corner fireplace and is attached to a dining area with French doors to a screened porch and the front veranda. The galley-style kitchen is the central hub of the first floor. A large bedroom on this floor has an attached full bath and serves equally well as guest bedroom or master bedroom. The second floor holds two bedrooms and another full bath.

Width 35'-8"
Depth 44'-8"

Design by
Larry W.
Garnett &
Associates, Inc.

Quote One®

Cost to build? See page 374
to order complete cost estimate
to build this house in your area!

Design 9009

First floor: 1,351 square feet
Second floor: 862 square feet
Total: 2,213 square feet

Design by
Larry W.
Garnett &
Associates, Inc.

● The most distinctive characteristic of the Queen Anne style, the steeply pitched hipped central roof with cross gables, is evident on this design. Extending beyond the veranda is a lattice-covered arbor, ideal for outdoor entertaining. The dining room has French doors that open to both the rear yard and the front veranda. A breakfast alcove with expansive windows is part of the efficient kitchen. French doors and a bay window provide a comfortable retreat in the secluded master suite. Upstairs, three additional bedrooms each have large walk-in closets and special window treatments. The attached two-car garage is quite flexible in that the door can be located at either side or at the rear.

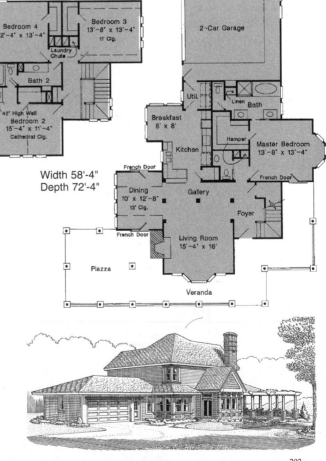

Width 58'-4"
Depth 72'-4"

● Covered porches front and rear are the first signal that this is a fine example of Folk Victorian styling. Complementing the exterior is a grand plan for family living. A formal living room and attached dining room provide space for entertaining guests. The large family room with fireplace is a gathering room for everyday. Both areas have access to outdoor spaces. Four bedrooms occupy the second floor. The master suite features two lavatories, a window seat and three closets. One of the family bedrooms has its own private balcony and could be used as a study. Note the open staircase and convenient linen storage.

Design 3385

First Floor: 1,096 square feet
Second Floor: 900 square feet
Total: 1,996 square feet

L **D**

Quote One®

Cost to build? See page 374 to order complete cost estimate to build this house in your area!

Width 56'
Depth 44'

Design by
Home Planners

Photo by Andrew D. Lautman

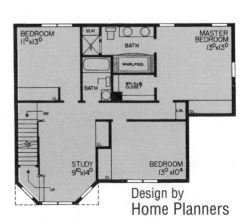

Design 3309

First Floor: 1,375 square feet
Second Floor: 1,016 square feet
Total 2,391 square feet

L

● Covered porches, front and back, are a fine preview to the livable nature of this Victorian. Living areas are defined in a family room with a fireplace, formal living and dining rooms and a kitchen with a breakfast room. Note the sliding glass doors from the breakfast room to the rear veranda. An ample laundry room, a garage with storage area and a powder room round out the first floor. Three second-floor bedrooms are joined by a study and two full baths. The master suite on this floor has two closets (one a convenient walk-in), a double vanity, a whirlpool tub and a separate shower.

Quote One®

Cost to build? See page 374 to order complete cost estimate to build this house in your area!

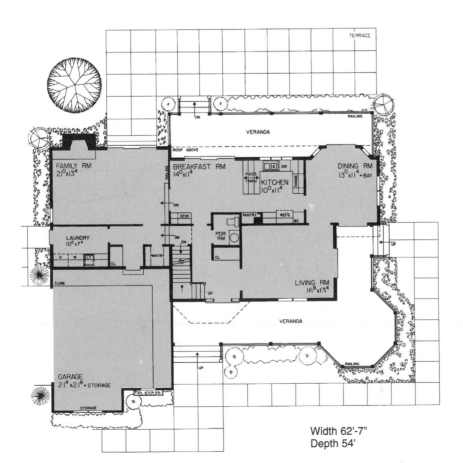

Width 62'-7"
Depth 54'

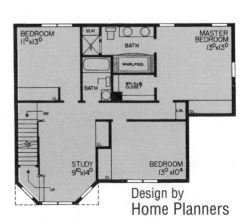

Design by
Home Planners

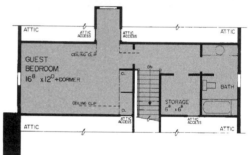

Design by
Home Planners

Design 2969
First Floor: 1,618 square feet
Second Floor: 1,315 square feet
Third Floor: 477 square feet
Total: 3,410 square feet

L **D**

Width 71'-8"
Depth 48'-4"

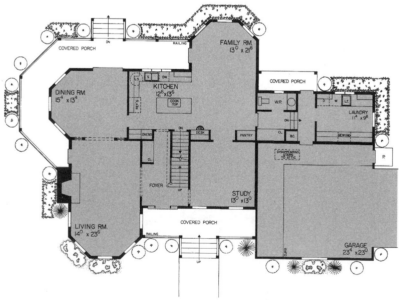

● What could beat the charm of a turreted Victorian with covered porches to the front, side and rear? This delicately detailed exterior houses an outstanding family-oriented floor plan. Projecting bays make their contribution to the exterior styling. In addition, they provide an extra measure of livability to the living, dining and family rooms, plus two of the bedrooms. The efficient kitchen, with its island cooking station, functions well with the dining and family rooms. A study provides a quiet first-floor haven for the family's less active pursuits. Upstairs, there are three big bedrooms and a fine master bath. The third floor provides a guest suite and huge bulk storage area (make it a cedar closet if you wish). This house has a basement for the development of further recreational and storage facilities. Note the two fireplaces, large laundry and attached two-car garage.

Tudor Traditions:
Homes with English accents

Design by
Home Planners

QUOTE ONE®
Cost to build? See page 374
to order complete cost estimate
to build this house in your area!

Design 3331
First Floor: 1,115 square feet
Second Floor: 690 square feet
Total: 1,805 square feet

L

● Who could guess that this compact design contains three bedrooms and two full baths? The kitchen works well with the nearby dining room which offers outdoor dining via a sunny deck. A fireplace in the two-story gathering room welcomes company. The first-floor master bedroom is sure to please with its large private bath. Upstairs, two bedrooms share a full hall bath and access to an open lounge with a balcony.

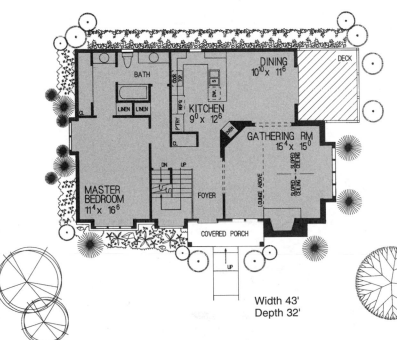

Width 43'
Depth 32'

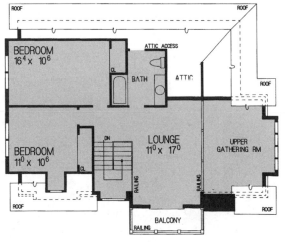

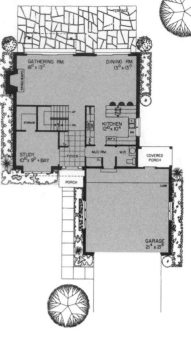

Width 43'
Depth 52'-8"

Design 2959

First Floor: 1,003 square feet
Second Floor: 1,056 square feet
Total: 2,059 square feet

● Here the stateliness of Tudor styling is captured in a design suited for a narrow building site. This two-story has all the livability found in many much larger homes. The 29-foot living/dining area stretches across the entire rear of the house and opens to a large terrace. The efficient U-shaped kitchen is found near the mud room with adjacent wash room. Enhancing first-floor livability is the study with a huge walk-in closet. Upstairs are three bedrooms, two baths and an outdoor balcony.

Design by
Home Planners

Quote One®

Cost to build? See page 374
to order complete cost estimate
to build this house in your area!

Design 2964

First Floor: 1,441 square feet
Second Floor: 621 square feet
Total: 2,062 square feet

● Tudor houses have their own unique exterior features. This outstanding two-story has a first-floor master bedroom plus two bedrooms with a lounge upstairs. The living room is dramatically spacious. It has a two-story sloping ceiling and large glass areas across the back. The open staircase to the upstairs has plenty of natural light as does the stairway to the basement recreation area.

Design by
Home Planners

Width 55'
Depth 59'-8"

Quote One®

Cost to build? See page 374
to order complete cost estimate
to build this house in your area!

Photo by Nick Kelsh

Quote One®

Cost to build? See page 374
to order complete cost estimate
to build this house in your area!

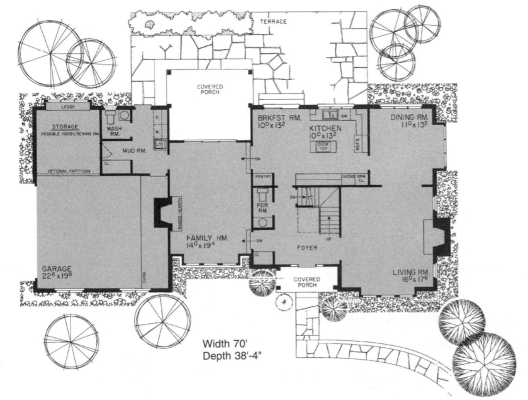

Width 70'
Depth 38'-4"

Design 2855

First Floor: 1,372 square feet
Second Floor: 1,245 square feet
Total: 2,617 square feet

L **D**

● This elegant Tudor house is
perfect for the family who wants
to move up in living area, style
and luxury. As you enter this
home you will find a large living
room with a fireplace on your
right. Adjacent, the formal dining
room has easy access to both the
living room and the kitchen. The
kitchen/breakfast room has an
open plan and access to the rear
terrace. Sunken a few steps, the
spacious family room is highlighted with a fireplace and access
to the rear covered porch. Note
the optional planning of the
garage storage area. Plan this area
according to the needs of your
family. Upstairs, your family will
enjoy three bedrooms and a full
bath, along with a spacious master
bedroom suite, complete with a
window seat, two closets and a
lavish bath.

Design by
Home Planners

209

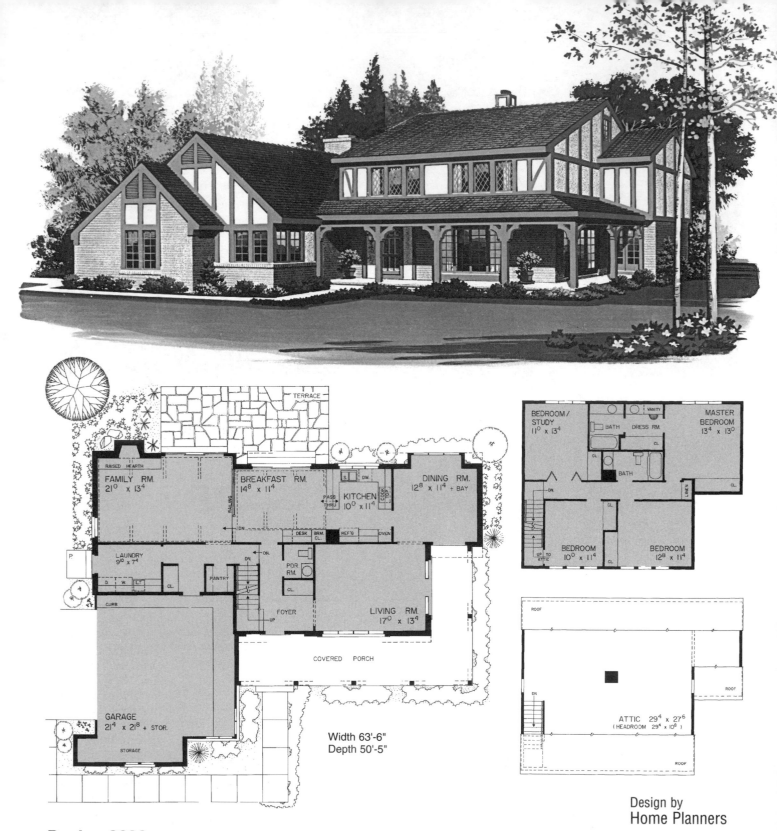

Width 63'-6"
Depth 50'-5"

Design by
Home Planners

Design 2939 First Floor: 1,409 square feet; Second Floor: 1,020 square feet; Total: 2,429 square feet

D

● Here's a Tudor adaptation with plenty of warmth and comfort for the entire family! Start with the big wrap-around covered porch in front. Then there's a large attic with headroom, a bonus for bulk storage and even possible expansion. An efficient U-shaped kitchen features many built-ins and a pass-through to a beam-ceilinged breakfast room. Sliding glass doors to a terrace are highlights in both the sunken family room and the breakfast room. A service entrance to the garage has a storage closet on each side, plus a secondary entrance through the laundry area. Recreational activities and hobbies can be enjoyed in the basement area. There are four bedrooms plus two baths upstairs, isolated from household noise and activity. A quiet corner living room opens to a sizable formal dining room. This room enjoys natural light from a bay window that overlooks the backyard.

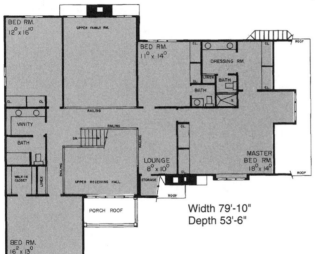

BED RM.
12⁰ x 16⁰

UPPER FAMILY RM.

BED RM.
11⁰ x 14⁰

DRESSING RM.

LINEN
BATH

BATH

VANITY

BATH

RAILING

WALK-IN CLOSET

LINEN

LOUNGE
8⁰ x 10⁰

UPPER RECEIVING HALL

STORAGE

MASTER BED RM.
18⁰ x 14⁰

ROOF

PORCH ROOF

BED RM.
16² x 13⁰

Width 79'-10"
Depth 53'-6"

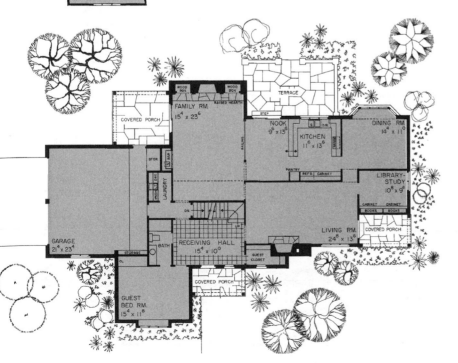

COVERED PORCH

FAMILY RM.
15⁴ x 23⁶

WOOD BOX   WOOD BOX
RAISED HEARTH

TERRACE

STEP

NOOK
9⁰ x 13⁵

KITCHEN
11⁶ x 13⁶

DINING RM.
14⁴ x 11⁰

STOR.

LAUNDRY

PANTRY
REFG.   CABINET

LIBRARY-STUDY
10⁸ x 9⁰

GARAGE
21⁴ x 23⁴

STORAGE

BATH

RECEIVING HALL
15⁴ x 10⁰

GUEST CLOSET

GABINET   GABINET
BOOKS   BOOKS

LIVING RM.
24⁹ x 13⁶

COVERED PORCH

COVERED PORCH

GUEST BED RM.
15⁴ x 11⁸

Design 2356

First Floor: 1,969 square feet
Second Floor: 1,702 square feet
Total: 3,671 square feet

L **D**

● Here is truly an exquisite Tudor adaptation. The exterior, with its interesting roof lines, window treatment, stately chimney and its appealing use of brick and stucco, could hardly be more dramatic. Inside, the delightfully large receiving hall has a two-story ceiling and controls the flexible traffic patterns. The living and dining rooms, with the library nearby, will cater to formal living pursuits. The guest room offers another haven for the enjoyment of peace and quiet. Observe the adjacent full bath. For the family's informal activities there are the interactions of the family room—covered porch—nook—kitchen zone. Notice the raised-hearth fireplace, the wood boxes, the sliding glass doors, built-in bar and the kitchen pass-through. Adding to the charm of the family room is its high ceiling. The second floor offers three family bedrooms, a lounge and a deluxe master suite.

Design by
Home Planners

Design 3554

First Floor: 3,275 square feet
Second Floor: 2,363 square feet
Total: 5,638 square feet

L D

● A splendid garden entry greets visitors to this regal Tudor home. Past the double doors is a two-story foyer that leads to the various living areas of the home. A quiet library is secluded directly off the foyer and has a box-bay window, private powder room and sloped ceiling. Formal living takes place to the right of the foyer—an attached garden room shares a through-fireplace with this area. Formal dining is found to the left of the foyer, accessed from the kitchen via a butler's pantry. The gathering room handles casual occasions and is just across the hall from the wet bar. Upstairs there is a grand master suite with a lavish bath and a sitting room and three secondary bedrooms, each with a private bath.

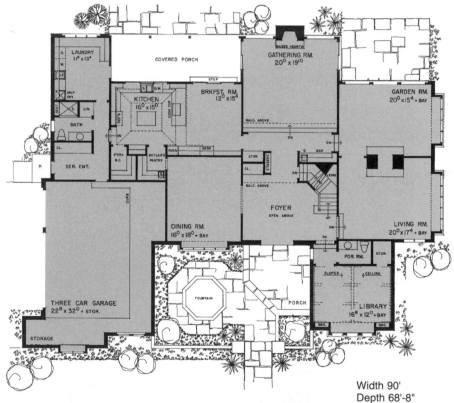

Width 90'
Depth 68'-8"

Design by
Home Planners

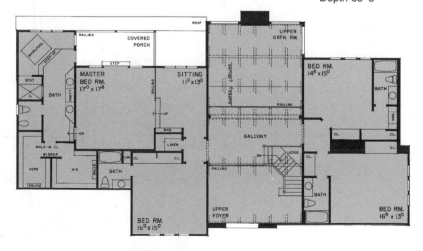

Design by
Home Planners

Width 60'
Depth 72'

QUOTE ONE ®
Cost to build? See page 374
to order complete cost estimate
to build this house in your area!

Design 3360
First Floor: 2,673 square feet
Lower Floor: 1,389 square feet
Total: 4,062 square feet

● This plan has the best of both worlds—a traditional exterior and a modern, multi-level floor plan. The raised, central foyer routes traffic effectively to all areas: the kitchen, gathering room, sleeping area and media room. The lower level includes space for a summer kitchen, an activities room with a fireplace and access to a rear terrace and a bedroom with full bath. On the first level, the master suite features a luxurious bath and His and Hers walk-in closets, while a large family bedroom has access to a full hall bath.

Design 3555

First Floor: 1,930 square feet
Second Floor: 1,676 square feet
Total: 3,606 square feet

L **D**

● Round-top windows add elegance to the interior and exterior of this traditional home. Large gathering areas on the first floor flow together for ease in entertaining. The sunken gathering room stretches from the front of the house to the back, with a terrace at each end and a fireplace in the middle. Another fireplace is found in the conversation area adjoining the kitchen. The formal dining room features a bay window. Sleeping areas upstairs include a master bedroom with a spacious bath and a huge walk-in closet, three family bedrooms and two full baths.

Design by
Home Planners

Width 68'
Depth 57'-8"

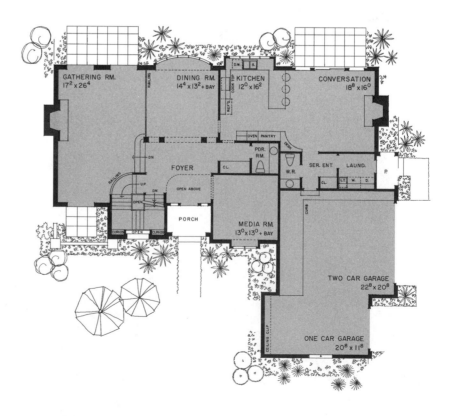

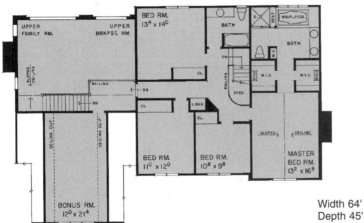

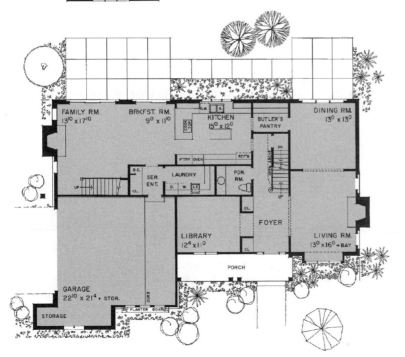

Width 64'
Depth 45'

Design 3551

First Floor: 1,575 square feet
Second Floor: 1,501 square feet
Total: 3,076 square feet

L **D**

● Efficient floor planning provides a spacious, yet economical Tudor home. The large kitchen adjoins a breakfast/family room combination with fireplace. A butler's pantry connects the kitchen to the formal dining room with terrace access. A second fireplace is found in the living room. Also on the first floor: a library and convenient powder room. The master bedroom features His and Hers walk-in closets and a grand bath with whirlpool tub. The bedroom next door would make a fine nursery or office. A large bonus room over the garage offers many optional uses.

Design by
Home Planners

Cost to build? See page 374 to order complete cost estimate to build this house in your area!

Design 2967

First Floor: 1,877 square feet
Second Floor: 467 square feet
Total: 2,344 square feet

● Special interior amenities abound in this unique 1½-story Tudor. Living areas include an open gathering room/dining room area with fireplace and pass-through to the breakfast room. Quiet time can be spent in a sloped-ceiling study. Look for plenty of workspace in the island kitchen and workshop/storage area. Sleeping areas are separated for utmost privacy: an elegant master suite on the first floor, two bedrooms and a full bath on the second. Note the unusual curved balcony seat in the stairwell and the second floor ledge—a perfect spot for displaying plants or collectibles.

Design by
Home Planners

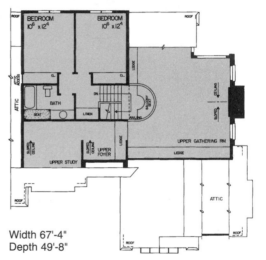

Width 67'-4"
Depth 49'-8"

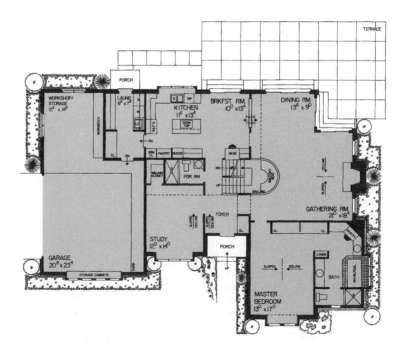

Design 3342

First Floor: 1,467 square feet
Second Floor: 715 square feet
Total: 2,182 square feet

L

● Just the right amount of living space is contained in this charming traditional Tudor house and it is arranged in a great floor plan. The split bedroom configuration, with two bedrooms (or optional study) on the first floor and the master suite on the second floor with its own studio, assures complete privacy. The living room has a second-floor balcony overlook and a warming fireplace. The full-width terrace in back is reached through sliding glass doors in each room at the rear of the house.

Design by
Home Planners

Width 55'-8"
Depth 55'

QUOTE ONE®

Cost to build? See page 374
to order complete cost estimate
to build this house in your area!

Design 2854

First Floor: 1,261 square feet
Second Floor: 950 square feet
Total: 2,211 square feet

L **D**

QUOTE ONE®

Cost to build? See page 374
to order complete cost estimate
to build this house in your area!

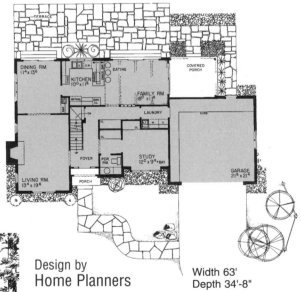

● Though technically a story and a half, the second floor has so much livability, it's more like a two-story plan. In addition to a large master suite, two kids' rooms and a second full bath, the second floor has a cozy spot that could serve as a lounge, nursery or play area. The first floor is solidly utilitarian: living room with fireplace, large separate dining room, family room, efficient U-shaped kitchen, study with nifty bay window and covered porch.

Design by
Home Planners

Width 63'
Depth 34'-8"

Design by
Home Planners

Design 3366

Main Floor: 1,638 square feet
Upper Floor: 650 square feet
Lower Floor: 934 square feet
Total: 3,222 square feet

L

● There is much more to this design than meets the eye. While it may look like a 1½-story plan, bonus recreation and hobby space in the walk-out basement adds almost 1,000 square feet. The first floor holds living and dining areas as well as the deluxe master bedroom suite. Two family bedrooms share a full bath on the second floor and are connected by a balcony that overlooks the gathering room below. Notice the covered porch beyond the breakfast and dining rooms.

Width 57'
Depth 51'-8"

QUOTE ONE®

Cost to build? See page 374 to order complete cost estimate to build this house in your area!

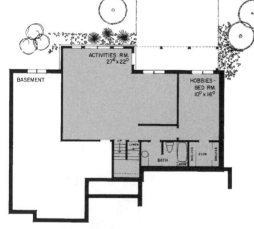

Design by
Home Planners

Design 2927

First Floor: 1,425 square feet
Second Floor: 704 square feet
Total: 2,129 square feet

D

● This charming Tudor adaptation features a complete second-floor master bedroom suite with a balcony overlooking the living room, plus a studio and the master bathroom. The first floor contains a convenient kitchen with a pass-through to the breakfast room. There's also a formal dining room just steps away. An adjacent rear living room enjoys its own fireplace. Other features include a rear media room or optional third bedroom. A downstairs bedroom enjoys an excellent front view.

Width 55'-4"
Depth 52'-4"

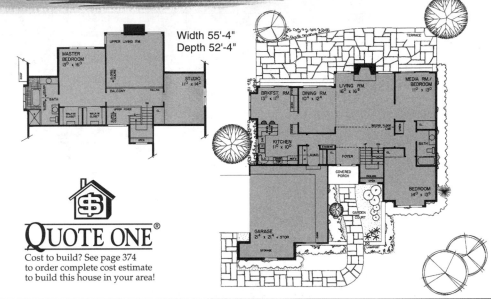

QUOTE ONE®

Cost to build? See page 374 to order complete cost estimate to build this house in your area!

QUOTE ONE®

Cost to build? See page 374 to order complete cost estimate to build this house in your area!

Width 90'
Depth 37'-4"

Design by
Home Planners

Design 3351

First Floor: 1,794 square feet
Second Floor: 887 square feet
Total: 2,681 square feet

L **D**

● Home-grown comfort is the key to the appeal of this traditionally Tudor-styled home. From the kitchen with attached family room to the living room with a fireplace and attached formal dining room, this plan has it all. Notice the first-floor master bedroom with a whirlpool tub and an adjacent study. On the second floor are three more bedrooms with ample closet space and a full bath.

Design 9819

Width 50'
Depth 50'-6"

First Floor: 1,678 square feet
Second Floor: 1,677 square feet
Total: 3,355 square feet

Design by
Design Traditions

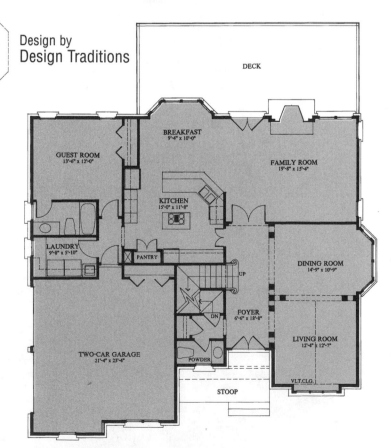

● This English Manor home features a dramatic brick and stucco exterior accented by a gabled roofline and artful half-timbering. Inside, the foyer opens to the formal living room accented with a vaulted ceiling and boxed bay window. The dining room flows directly off the living room and features its own angled bay window. Through the double doors lies the center of family activity. An entire wall of glass, accented by a central fireplace, spans from the family room through to the breakfast area and kitchen. For your guests, a bedroom and bath are located on the main level. The second floor provides two additional bedrooms and a bath for children. The master suite—with its tray ceiling, fireplace and private study—is a pleasant retreat. This home is designed with a basement foundation.

European Elegance:
Designs with Old-World influence

Design 9834
First Floor: 1,355 square feet
Second Floor: 1,360 square feet
Total: 2,715 square feet

● The appeal of this home is definitely European and its interior is open and inviting. The formal living room and dining room are separated only by decorative columns. To the left of the foyer is the comfortable family room with a large fireplace and open rail detailing, allowing access to the breakfast room and kitchen. An open staircase to the gallery above leads to a grand master suite with a tray ceiling and a luxurious master bath with a whirlpool tub, His and Hers vanities and a large, walk-in closet. Two bedrooms with a connecting bath and a third bedroom with a private bath complete the room arrangements. This home is designed with a basement foundation.

Width 52'
Depth 49'

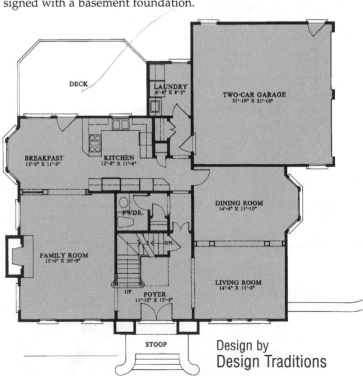

Design by
Design Traditions

Design 9563

First Floor: 1,509 square feet
Second Floor: 1,286 square feet
Total: 2,795 square feet
Bonus Room: 538 square feet

● Classic French style brings a touch of joie de vivre to this exquisite two-story home. Space for formal entertaining is shared by the parlor with its warming fireplace and the baronial dining room. An adjacent gourmet kitchen serves the dining room and breakfast nook with equal ease. The family room features a fireplace, a corner media center, unobstructed views and access to the rear grounds. The second floor contains four bedrooms, including the grand master suite. Here, steps away, is the master bath with a spa that invites relaxation. A large bonus room provides additional space for expansion as it is needed.

Design by
Alan Mascord
Design Associates, Inc.

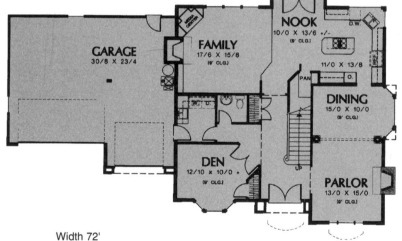

Width 72'
Depth 42'

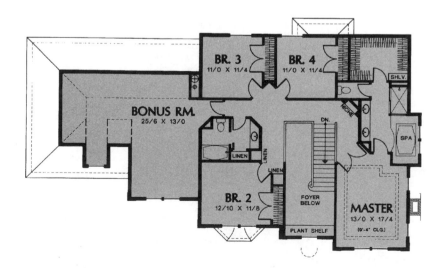

Design by
Design Traditions

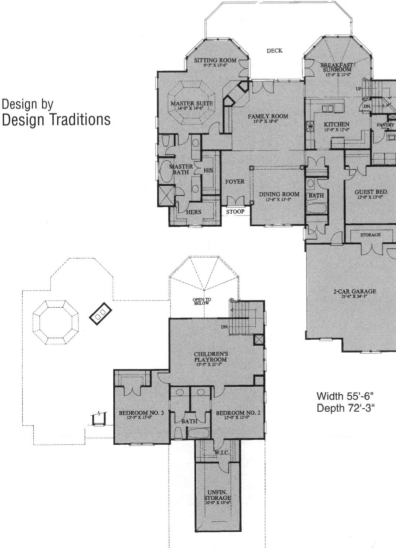

Width 55'-6"
Depth 72'-3"

Design 9825

First Floor: 2,129 square feet
Second Floor: 895 square feet
Total: 3,024 square feet

● Reminiscent of country estates in Europe, this stucco-exterior home makes a grand statement of architectural excitement. The foyer offers an impressive view of the dining room, family room and through to the back of the house—all from one breath-taking perspective. The master suite promises privacy and comfort with its lovely sitting room, awash in bright sunlight from its many windows. French doors leading to the back deck complete this ideal private retreat. The kitchen, with its vaulted breakfast/sunroom area, allows easy maneuverability. All guests will enjoy maximum comfort with the downstairs guest room. Upstairs are two more bedrooms, plus storage space, and a large, sunny playroom overlooking the breakfast area below. This home is designed with a basement foundation.

Design 9906

First Floor: 1,270 square feet
Second Floor: 1,070 square feet
Total: 2,340 square feet

● This elegant European-styled house easily accommodates formal entertaining, with a foyer that opens into a living room on the left, a dining room on the right. Introduce your guests to the warmth of the family room with its fireplace and expansive views. This area dissolves into a breakfast nook and a large kitchen. The first floor also makes room for a guest bedroom and a full bath. The second floor holds three additional bedrooms. The master suite, with His and Hers closets and a private bath, is sure to delight. Bedrooms 3 and 4 share a full bath. This home is designed with a basement foundation.

Design by
Design Traditions

Width 50'
Depth 44'

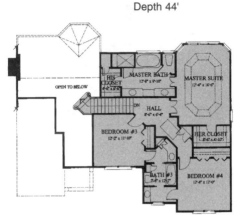

Design 9893

First Floor: 1,660 square feet
Second Floor: 665 square feet
Total: 2,325 square feet

● This European design is filled with space for formal and informal occasions. Informal areas include an open kitchen, breakfast room and family room. Formal rooms surround the foyer, with the living room on the left and dining room on the right. The master suite, located on the first floor, includes a gorgeous master bath and a walk-in closet. Each of the family bedrooms upstairs also features a walk-in closet and access to a full bath. A fourth bedroom, not included in the square footage, is optional. This home is designed with a basement foundation.

Width 64'
Depth 48'-6"

Design by
Design Traditions

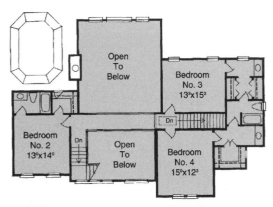

Width 84'-4"
Depth 63'

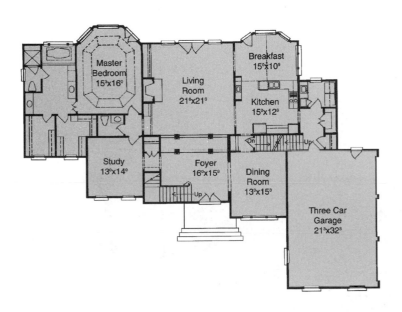

Design 9919

First Floor: 2,461 square feet
Second Floor: 1,114 square feet
Total: 3,575 square feet

● A myriad of glass and ornamental stucco detailing complement the asymmetrical facade of this two-story home. Inside, the striking two-story foyer provides a dramatic entrance, accented by the sweeping balustered stair and bathed in sunlight from the large triple-arched windows. To the right, the formal dining room resides. An efficient L-shaped kitchen and bayed breakfast nook are conveniently located to the dining area. The living room, with its welcoming fireplace, opens through double doors to the rear terrace. The private master suite provides access to the rear terrace and adjacent study. The master bath is sure to please with its relaxing garden tub, separate shower, grand His and Hers walk-in closets and a compartmented toilet. The second floor contains three large bedrooms, one with a private bath, while the others share a bath. This home is designed with a basement foundation.

Design by
Design Traditions

Design 9932

First Floor: 2,420 square feet
Second Floor: 1,146 square feet
Total: 3,566 square feet

● Multi-pane glass windows, double French doors and ornamental stucco detailing are complementary elements on the facade of this home. An impressive two-story foyer opens to the formal living and dining rooms. Natural light is available through the attractive windows in each room. The kitchen features a pass-through to the two-story family room and an adjoining sky-lit breakfast room. The first-floor master suite offers an elegant vaulted bedroom ceiling, a bath with twin vanities, a separate shower and tub, and two spacious walk-in closets. Upstairs, Bedroom 2 has its own bath and can be used as a guest suite. Two other bedrooms share a large bath with twin vanities. This home is designed with a basement foundation.

Design by
Design Traditions

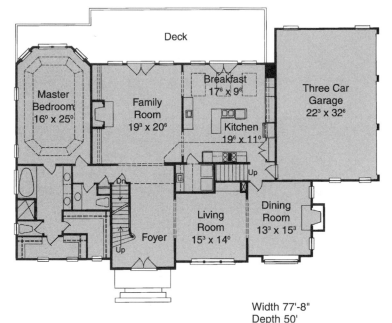

Width 77'-8"
Depth 50'

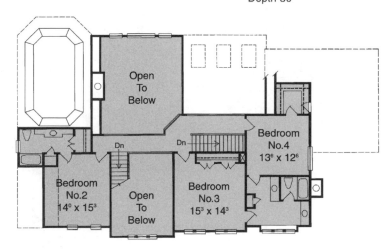

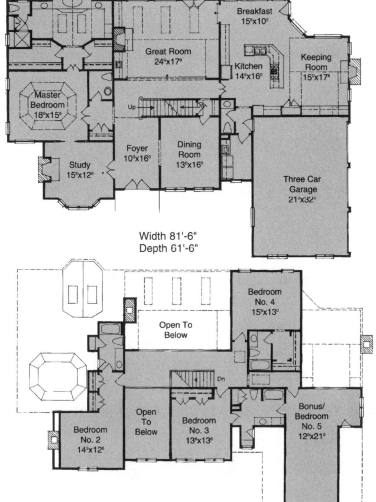

Width 81'-6"
Depth 61'-6"

Design 9921

First Floor: 2,832 square feet
Second Floor: 1,394 square feet
Total: 4,226 square feet
Bonus/Bedroom #5: 425 square feet

● Arched windows and a sculpted bay window provide personality and charm to this lovely French estate. Inside, the arrangement of rooms is well-suited for a variety of lifestyles. The large dining room and study off the foyer provide the opportunity for formal receiving and entertaining Access from the dining room to the kitchen is provided through a service alcove. For informal gatherings, look to the spacious kitchen, the multi-windowed breakfast room or the cozy keeping room with its welcoming fireplace. The great room provides opportunities for either formal or informal gatherings. Conveniently, yet privately located, the master suite is designed to take full advantage of the adjacent study and family area. A vaulted master bath and His and Hers walk-in closets highlight this impressive suite. The second floor contains three bedrooms, three full baths and a bonus room that also functions as Bedroom 5. This home is designed with a basement foundation.

Design by
Design Traditions

Design 9813

First Floor: 1,724 square feet
Second Floor: 700 square feet
Total: 2,424 square feet

● All the charm of gables, stonework and multi-level roof lines combine to create this home. To the left of the foyer you will see the dining room, highlighted by a tray ceiling and expansive windows with transoms. This room and the living room flow together to form one large entertainment area. In the gourmet kitchen is a work island, oversized pantry and an adjoining octagonal breakfast room. The great room features a pass-through wet bar, fireplace and bookcases. The master suite enjoys privacy at the rear of the home. An open-rail loft above the foyer leads to two additional bedrooms with walk-in closets, private vanities and a shared bath. This home is designed with a basement foundation.

QUOTE ONE®

Cost to build? See page 374
to order complete cost estimate
to build this house in your area!

Design by
Design Traditions

Width 47'-10"
Depth 63'-10"

Design 9849

First Floor: 780 square feet
Second Floor: 915 square feet
Total: 1,695 square feet

● The lines of this home are traditional and formal, with classical architectural detailing that describes an elegant style. To the right of the foyer is a formal dining room with passage to the kitchen, which is open to the breakfast area and great room. The large fireplace is framed by glass and light. The second-floor master suite's double-door entrance and fireplace are of special interest. The adjoining master bath and walk-in closet complement this area well. Bedrooms 2 and 3 complete this level with a shared bath. This home is designed with a basement foundation.

Design by
Design Traditions

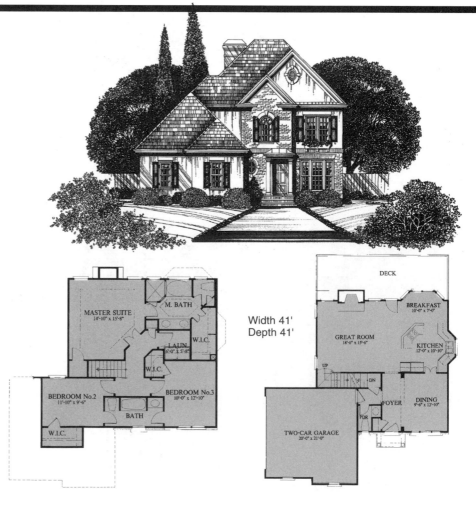

Width 41'
Depth 41'

Design 9802

First Floor: 1,811 square feet
Second Floor: 1,437 square feet
Total: 3,248 square feet

● The exterior of this home is decidedly European inspired. Surrounding the arched entry are windows with arched transoms, which admit outside light to enhance the magnificence of the two-story foyer. The formal atmosphere of the living and dining rooms is brought together by a central, dual-opening fireplace. Generously sized windows in these rooms allow unhindered views of outside living areas or children's play areas.

An additional fireplace can be found in the corner of the keeping room, adjacent to the enormous kitchen and the breakfast area which is set in a bay window. Upstairs, the master suite features an expansive master bath with His and Hers closet space. Also on this level, two bedrooms have their own baths. Bedroom 3 offers access to a huge unfinished storage room. This home is designed with a basement foundation.

Design by
Design Traditions

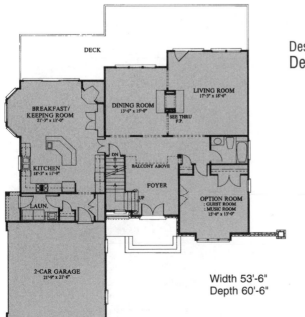

Width 53'-6"
Depth 60'-6"

Design 9916

First Floor: 1,165 square feet
Second Floor: 1,050 square feet
Total: 2,215 square feet

● This beautiful European-styled stucco home puts luxury features into only 2,215 square feet. The main living areas are found on the first floor: formal living and dining rooms flanking the entry foyer; family room with a fireplace; and an L-shaped kitchen with an attached breakfast room. The second-floor master bedroom is a real treat with a tray ceiling and a thoughtfully appointed bath. Bedrooms 2 and 3 share a full bath with a double-bowl vanity. This home is designed with a basement foundation.

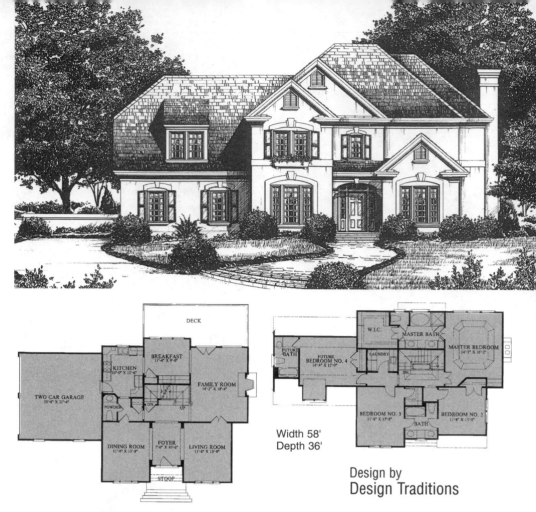

Width 58'
Depth 36'

Design by
Design Traditions

Design 9907

First Floor: 1,720 square feet
Second Floor: 545 square feet
Total: 2,265 square feet

● This French Country Cottage is a charming example of European architecture. A two-story foyer opens to a two-story family room with a fireplace. To the right, the formal living and dining rooms are separated by columns. The island kitchen is adjoined by a breakfast room with a bay window. A large master bedroom is located on the first floor, while the second floor provides two bedrooms and a full bath, as well as an optional fourth bedroom with an attached bath. This home is designed with a basement foundation.

Design by
Design Traditions

Width 50'
Depth 53'-6"

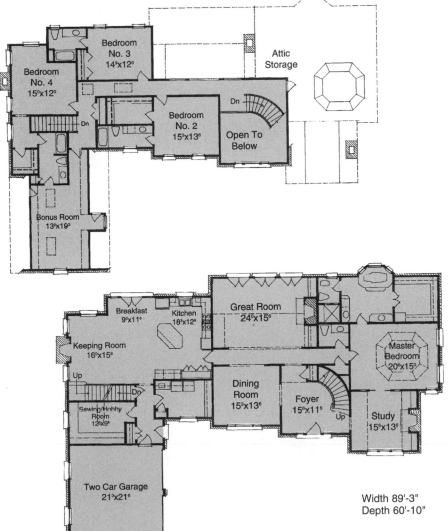

Design 9922

First Floor: 3,030 square feet
Second Floor: 1,510 square feet
Total: 4,540 square feet
Bonus Room: 324 square feet

● Brick details, casement windows and large expanses of glass add an Old World touch of glamour to this gracious two-story home. Inside, asymmetrical shapes create an interesting twist to this functional floor plan. Sunlight floods the two-story foyer, highlighted by the sweeping curves of the balustrade. For formal occasions, look to the spacious dining room, the inviting study and the vaulted great room. The master suite provides a quiet retreat with access to the study through paneled pocket doors. Luxury abounds in the spacious master bedroom and sumptuous master bath complete with a garden tub and a huge walk-in closet. The kitchen, breakfast room and keeping room provide a well-designed family living area. Three private secondary bedrooms with full baths are contained on the second floor. A bonus room is also featured on the second floor. This home is designed with a basement foundation.

Width 89'-3"
Depth 60'-10"

Design by
Design Traditions

Design 8186

First Floor: 1,919 square feet
Second Floor: 1,190 square feet
Total: 3,109 square feet

● The beautiful entrance is framed by huge columns topped by elegant arches and welcomes you into this classic European home. Inside, the formal dining room to the right of the foyer is defined by yet another set of columns and arches. The appealing living room offers access to the rear yard via two sets of double French doors. A gourmet kitchen is conveniently located near the dining room and a sunny breakfast room. An inviting family room with a fireplace and access to a rear porch is also nearby. The deluxe master suite, with lavish bath and His and Hers walk-in closets, completes this level. Upstairs, a large bedroom has its own full bath and may be used as a guest suite. Two other bedrooms share a full bath and access to a huge game room. Please specify crawlspace or slab foundation when ordering.

Design by
Larry E. Belk
Designs

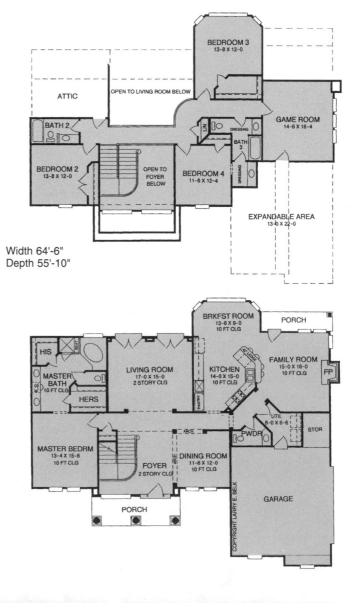

Width 64'-6"
Depth 55'-10"

DECK

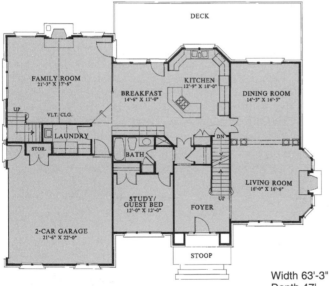

FAMILY ROOM
21'-3" X 17'-6"

KITCHEN
12'-9" X 18'-0"

BREAKFAST
14'-6" X 11'-0"

DINING ROOM
14'-3" X 16'-3"

UP

VLT. CLG.

LAUNDRY

DN

STOR.

BATH

LIVING ROOM
16'-0" X 16'-6"

STUDY/
GUEST BED
12'-0" X 12'-0"

FOYER

UP

2-CAR GARAGE
21'-6" X 22'-0"

STOOP

Width 63'-3"
Depth 47'

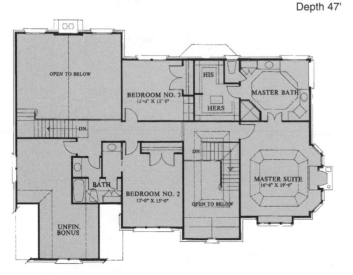

OPEN TO BELOW

HIS

BEDROOM NO. 3
13'-0" X 11'-0"

MASTER BATH

HERS

DN

BATH

DN

BEDROOM NO. 2
12'-0" X 15'-0"

OPEN TO BELOW

MASTER SUITE
16'-6" X 19'-6"

UNFIN.
BONUS

Design by
Design Traditions

Design 9837

First Floor: 1,847 square feet
Second Floor: 1,453 square feet
Total: 3,300 square feet

● To suit those who favor Classic European styling,
this English Manor home features a dramatic brick
exterior which is further emphasized by the varied
roofline and the finial atop the uppermost gable.
The main level opens with a two-story foyer and
formal rooms on the right. The living room contains
a fireplace set in a bay window. The dining room is
separated from the living room by a symmetrical
column arrangement. The more casual family room
is to the rear. For guests, a bedroom and bath are located on the main level. The second floor provides
additional bedrooms and baths for family as well as
a magnificent master suite. This home is designed
with a basement foundation.

Design 9930

First Floor: 2,346 square feet
Second Floor: 1,260 square feet
Total: 3,606 square feet

● The European character of this home is enhanced through the use of stucco and stone on the elevation, giving this Country French estate home its charm and beauty. Inside the home is a setting created for convenient yet private living. The foyer has access to the dining room and study/living room. The master bedroom suite is privately located on the right side of the home with an optional entry to the study, a large garden bath and a view

to a private deck area at the rear. The two-story family room is positioned for convenient access to the back staircase, the kitchen, the wet bar and the deck area. Upstairs are three more large bedrooms; two have a shared bath and private vanities and one has a full private bath. All bedrooms have convenient access to the back staircase and open-rail views to the family room below. This home is designed with a basement foundation.

Design by
Design Traditions

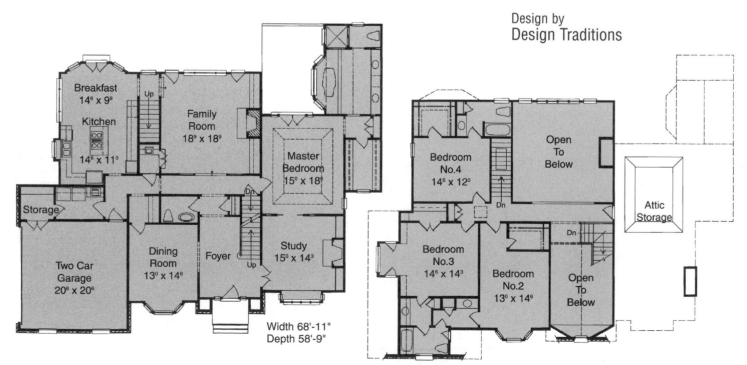

Width 68'-11"
Depth 58'-9"

Design 9931

First Floor: 2,161 square feet
Second Floor: 2,110 square feet
Total: 4,271 square feet

● A blend of stucco and stone create the charm in this Country French estate home. The asymmetric design and arched glass windows add to the European character. Inside, the plan offers a unique arrangement of rooms conducive to today's lifestyles. The foyer makes an impression with a staircase neatly tucked inside an octagonal bay, well-lit by a series of arched glass windows. The large open-rail galley above is an interesting addition. A living room and a dining room flank the foyer, creating a functional formal area. The large den or family room is positioned at the rear of the home with convenient access to the kitchen, patio and covered arbor. Equally accessible to the arbor and patio are the kitchen and breakfast/sitting area. A large butler's pantry is located near the kitchen and dining room. Upstairs, the vaulted master suite and two large bedrooms provide private retreats. This home is designed with a basement foundation.

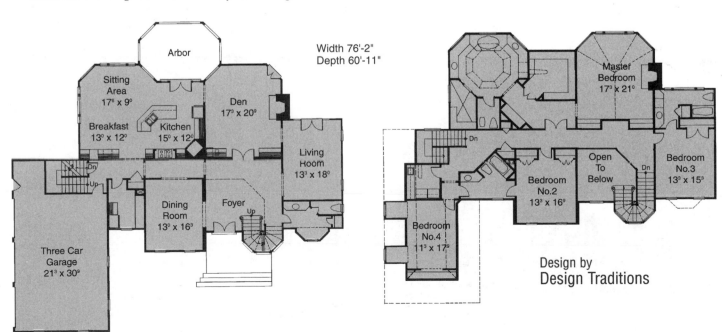

Width 76'-2"
Depth 60'-11"

Design by
Design Traditions

Design 8651

First Floor: 1,624 square feet
Second Floor: 1,167 square feet
Total: 2,791 square feet

● Much of the architecture in the elevation of this home is reflective of 1930s style residential architecture. Upon entering the foyer, visitors are treated to a view of the outdoor herb gardens and the stone fountain. The formal living room, with its traditional bay-windowed wall and French doors to the patio, is timeless. The formal dining room boasts columns and traditional window treatments, all authentically 1930s period design. This home welcomes family living with the trilogy of family room, nook and kitchen all sharing one space. The three bedrooms on the second level make maximum use of space and vistas. The master suite offers a deck, a bay window, a walk-in closet and a spacious bath with a see-through fireplace at the tub.

Design by
**Home Design
Services, Inc.**

Width 55'
Depth 68'

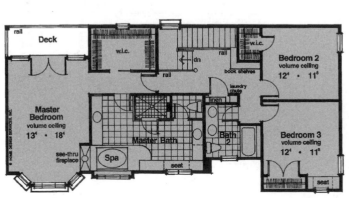

Design 8023

First Floor: 2,109 square feet
Second Floor: 1,060 square feet
Total: 3,169 square feet

● Old-world charm blends a warm, inviting exterior with a traditional, efficient floor plan. From the foyer, note the curved wall that rises with the staircase. The kitchen is a delight with its large cooktop island, walk-in pantry and its sunlit sink with a corner grouping of windows. The pampering master suite offers access through French doors to a covered patio and includes a relaxing master bath with His and Hers walk-in clos-

ets, a corner whirlpool tub surrounded by windows and dual vanities. Bedroom 4 may be used as a study or would be ideal used as an office. Upstairs, a curved balcony overlooks the two-story living room. Bedroom 2 features a full bath, a walk-in closet and access to an upper deck. Bedroom 3 has access to its own full bath. A game room with French doors opening to an upper deck completes the second floor.

Width 61'-11"
Depth 67'-7"

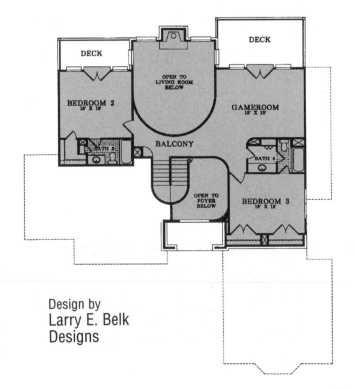

Design by
Larry E. Belk
Designs

Design 8034

First Floor: 2,639 square feet
Second Floor: 1,625 square feet
Total: 4,264 square feet

● European traditional style is the hallmark of this best-selling plan. The stucco finish provides an elegant look to a home that is as beautiful from the rear as it appears from the front curb. Available in a 3,800-square-foot version as well, this home is a perfect blend of charm and practicality. The two-story foyer is graced by a lovely staircase and a Romeo balcony overlook from upstairs. Two columns flank the entry to the great room notable for its beautiful window-wall facing the rear grounds. Two-story double bays on the rear of the home form the keeping room and the breakfast room on one side and the master bedroom and its sitting area on the other. A huge walk-in pantry and an adjacent butler's pantry connect the dining room to the kitchen. Rear stairs from the kitchen join the family gathering area with the three bedrooms and game room upstairs. With a large study downstairs and walk-in attic storage available for expansion upstairs, this home provides all the amenities needed for today's busy family.

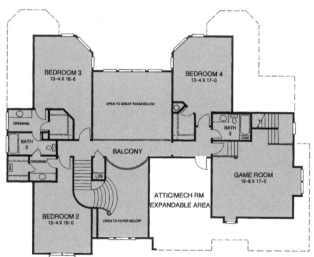

Width 73'-8"
Depth 58'-6"

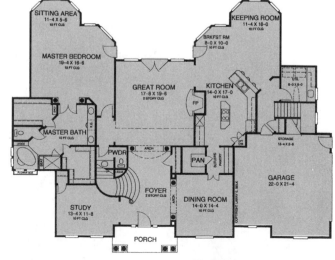

Design by
Larry E. Belk
Designs

REAR

Width 67'-8"
Depth 77'-2"

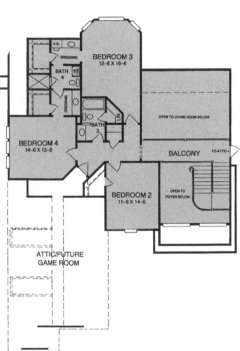

Design by
Larry E. Belk
Designs

Design 8103

First Floor: 2,547 square feet
Second Floor: 1,128 square feet
Total: 3,675 square feet

● An imposing entrance with massive columns connected by twin arches is the focal point for this European traditional design. A two-story foyer and living room give the home an elegant, open feel. The kitchen and breakfast room are open to a large family room—a great place for informal gatherings. The large utility room and the three-car garage are situated nearby. The master suite and the study are located on the opposite side of the home and provide a private retreat for the owner. Three bedrooms and two baths are located upstairs. Bath 4 features two dressing areas for privacy. All the bedrooms are designed with large walk-in closets. Walk-in access is available to the attic, and the large area over the garage can be finished for a game room or an in-home office. Please specify crawlspace or slab foundation when ordering.

COPYRIGHT 1993 LARRY E. BELK

Design by
Larry E. Belk
Designs

Width 67'-8"
Depth 74'-2"

Design 8048

First Floor: 2,469 square feet
Second Floor: 1,025 square feet
Total: 3,494 square feet

Quote One®

Cost to build? See page 374
to order complete cost estimate
to build this house in your area!

● An arresting double arch gives this European style home a commanding presence. Once inside, a two-story foyer provides an open view directly through the formal living room to the rear grounds beyond. The use of square columns defining the formal dining room adds an air of elegance to the home. A spacious kitchen with a prep island and bayed breakfast area share space with the family room. A welcoming fireplace is visible to all areas and creates an area for family and informal gatherings. The private master suite features dual lavs,

His and Hers walk-in closets, a corner garden tub and a separate shower. A second bedroom, which doubles as a nursery or a study, and a full bath are located nearby. Two bedrooms and a bath, which includes two dressing areas, are located on the second floor. A large game room completes this wonderful family home. Additional expandable area is available over the three-car garage. Please specify crawlspace or slab foundation when ordering.

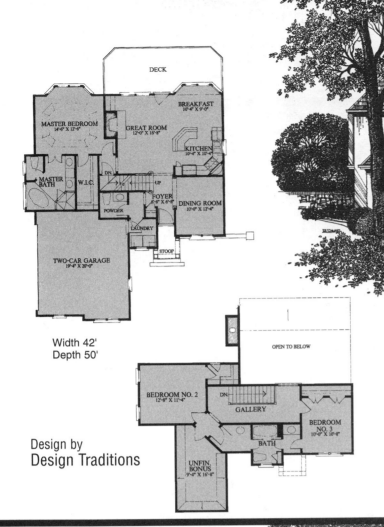

Width 42'
Depth 50'

Design by
Design Traditions

DECK

MASTER BEDROOM
14'-6" X 12'-6"

GREAT ROOM
12'-0" X 16'-8"

BREAKFAST
10'-4" X 9'-0"

KITCHEN
10'-4" X 10'-4"

MASTER
BATH

W.I.C.

DN

UP

FOYER
8'-8" X 6'-0"

DINING ROOM
10'-0" X 12'-0"

POWDER

LAUNDRY

STOOP

TWO-CAR GARAGE
19'-4" X 20'-0"

OPEN TO BELOW

BEDROOM NO. 2
12'-8" X 11'-4"

DN

GALLERY

BEDROOM
NO. 3
10'-0" X 10'-8"

BATH

UNFIN.
BONUS
9'-4" X 16'-8"

Design 9847

First Floor: 1,225 square feet
Second Floor: 565 square feet
Total: 1,790 square feet

● A combination of materials and shapes is reminiscent of an English country home. Beyond the columned entry is a classic raised foyer which leads to a sunken dining room and great room. The openness of the plan is evident in the kitchen and breakfast areas. The master bedroom boasts a tray ceiling, fireplace and bay window. The open gallery staircase overlooks the great room and provides entry to two more bedrooms as well as an unfinished bonus room. This home is designed with a basement foundation.

Design 9900

First Floor: 1,103 square feet
Second Floor: 1,103 square feet
Total: 2,206 square feet
Bonus Room: 212 square feet

● A stucco exterior provides a European appeal for this family home. An expansive family room provides space for entertaining. The formal dining room is just off the foyer. Upstairs, the master suite includes a sitting area and an enormous bath with a dual vanity, a whirlpool tub, a separate shower and a walk-in closet. Two family bedrooms share a full bath with a dual vanity. The bonus room makes a great home office. This home is designed with a basement foundation.

Copyright 1992 Stephen S. Fuller, Inc.

DECK

Width 52'
Depth 34'

BREAKFAST
9'-6" x 9'-0"

KITCHEN
10'-0" x 12'-6"

PANTRY

LAUNDRY
8'-0" X 5'-6"

FAMILY ROOM
13'-6"x 14'-6"

BATH

FOYER
7'-0" x 11'-0"

DINING ROOM
12'-0" x 11'-0"

TWO-CAR GARAGE
20'-0" x 22'-0"

GUEST ROOM/
STUDY
11'-6"x 11'-0"

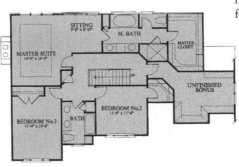

SITTING
9'-0" x 8'-10"

M. BATH

MASTER
CLOSET

MASTER SUITE
14'-0" x 14'-0"

DN

UNFINISHED
BONUS

BEDROOM No.3
11'-6" x 14'-6"

BATH

BEDROOM No.2
11'-6" x 11'-0"

Design by
Design Traditions

241

COPYRIGHT 1991 LARRY E. BELK

Design 8026

First Floor: 2,188 square feet
Second Floor: 1,110 square feet
Total: 3,298 square feet

● This brick-and-stucco home with European
style showcases an arched entry and presents a
commanding presence from the curb. Inside, the
living room, the dining room and the family room
are located at the rear of the home to provide
wide open views of the rear grounds beyond. A
colonnade with connecting arches defines the
space for a living room with a fireplace and the
dining room. The spacious master suite features a
relaxing sitting area, His and Hers closets and an
extravagant master bath. Take special note of the
private His and Hers bathrooms. On the second
floor, three bedrooms, two baths and a game room
complete the home.

Design by
Larry E. Belk
Designs

Cost to build? See page 374
to order complete cost estimate
to build this house in your area!

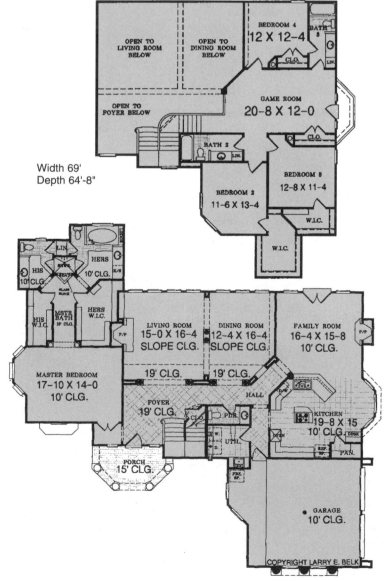

Width 69'
Depth 64'-8"

242

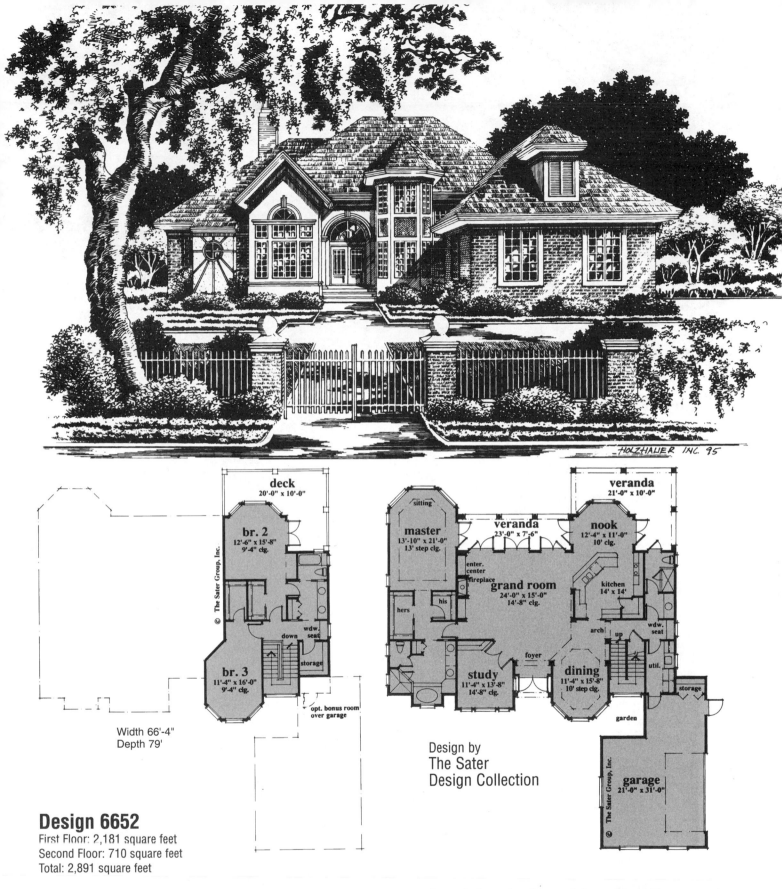

deck
20'-0" x 10'-0"

br. 2
12'-6" x 15'-8"
9'-4" clg.

br. 3
11'-4" x 16'-0"
9'-4" clg.

down

wdw. seat

storage

opt. bonus room over garage

Width 66'-4"
Depth 79'

© The Sater Group, Inc.

sitting

master
13'-10" x 21'-0"
13' step clg.

enter. center fireplace

his

hers

veranda
23'-0" x 7'-6"

grand room
24'-0" x 15'-0"
14'-8" clg.

study
11'-4" x 13'-8"
14'-8" clg.

foyer

dining
11'-4" x 15'-8"
10' step clg.

veranda
21'-0" x 10'-0"

nook
12'-4" x 11'-0"
10' clg.

kitchen
14' x 14'

arch

up

wdw. seat

util.

storage

garden

garage
21'-0" x 31'-0"

© The Sater Group, Inc.

Design by
**The Sater
Design Collection**

Design 6652

First Floor: 2,181 square feet
Second Floor: 710 square feet
Total: 2,891 square feet

● An arched, covered porch presents fine double doors leading to a spacious foyer in this decidedly European home. A two-story bay windowed tower contains an elegant formal dining room on the first floor and a spacious bedroom on the second floor. The grand room is aptly named, with a fireplace, three sets of doors opening onto a roofed veranda, and a built-in entertainment center. A large kitchen is ready to please the gourmet of the family with a big walk-in pantry for storage. A sunny, bay windowed eating nook is nearby and has access to a second covered veranda. The secluded master suite is luxury in itself. A bay-windowed sitting area, access to the rear veranda, His and Hers walk-in closets and a lavish bath are all set to pamper you. Upstairs, two bedrooms, both with walk-in closets, share a full hall bath with twin vanities. Bedroom 2 has its own private deck. Please specify basement or slab foundation when ordering.

Design 8182

First Floor: 2,200 square feet
Second Floor: 889 square feet
Total: 3,089 square feet

● Multi-pane windows, varied roof lines and a stucco facade combine to give this home a wonderful European flavor. A two-story foyer ushers you into the formal areas of the living room and dining room. The large kitchen works well with the cozy family room and sunny breakfast room, with a pass-through to the family room. A nearby bedroom has access to a full bath and can be used as a guest suite. The luxurious master bedroom with its lavish bath and His and Hers walk-in closets rounds out this level. Dominating the second floor, the large game room is accessible to the two family bedrooms. Each bedroom has a walk-in closet and a shared full bath. Please specify crawlspace or slab foundation when ordering.

Design by
Larry E. Belk
Designs

Width 60'-6"
Depth 68'

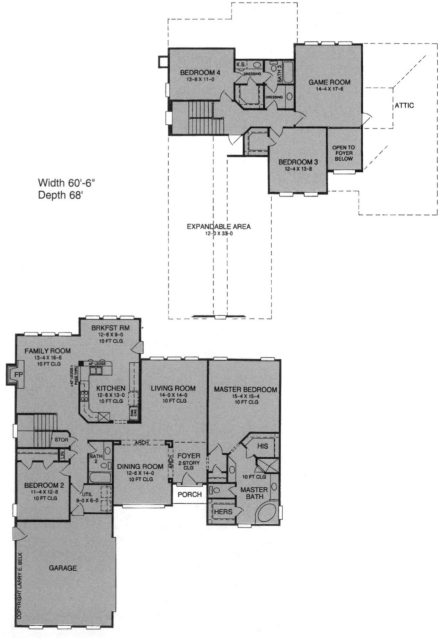

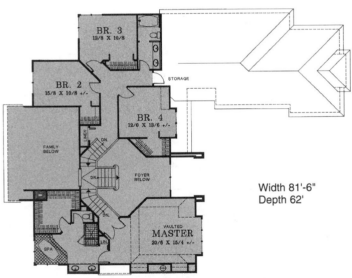

Width 81'-6"
Depth 62'

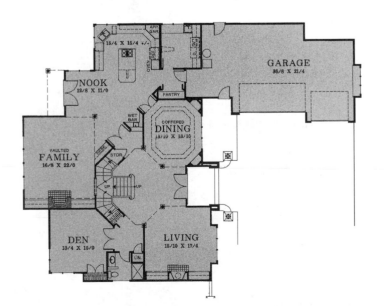

Design 9434

First Floor: 2,226 square feet
Second Floor: 1,444 square feet
Total: 3,670 square feet

● European styling takes center stage in this beautiful two-story home. The interior allows for a variety of lifestyle options. For example, the den on the main floor can be used as a convenient guest bedroom because of its adjacent full bath. Formal living and dining rooms flank the entry and both feature their share of treasured amenities. The oversized family room provides a fireplace and is adjacent to the breakfast nook and island kitchen. Upstairs are four bedrooms, including a spectacular master suite overlooking the front courtyard. A three-car garage easily accommodates the family fleet.

Design by
Alan Mascord
Design Associates, Inc.

Design 8179

First Floor: 1,966 square feet
Second Floor: 872 square feet
Total: 2,838 square feet

● The grand, two-story foyer of this European-style home leads you into the formal dining room defined by pillars. A deluxe master bedroom suite is full of amenities including His and Hers walk-in closets, a corner garden tub, twin vanities and access to a private covered porch. A study/bedroom and a full bath help complete this floor. Upstairs, three bedrooms, each with walk-in closets, share a full hall bath. Please specify crawlspace or slab foundation when ordering.

Width 63'-10"
Depth 79'-10"

Design by
Larry E. Belk
Designs

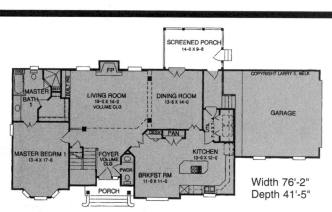

Width 76'-2"
Depth 41'-5"

Design by
Larry E. Belk
Designs

Design 8132

First Floor: 1,581 square feet
Second Floor: 1,079 square feet
Total: 2,660 square feet

● A gracefully covered porch leads to a volume foyer in this French flavored home. Directly ahead of the foyer is the elegant living room, graced by a fireplace. The first of two master bedroom suites is located on the first floor for complete privacy and offers a deluxe master bath and large walk-in closet. Upstairs, a balcony leads to two family bedrooms, each with a walk-in closet. Bedroom 3 is graced by a private deck and access to attic storage. The second master suite mirrors the first with its luxurious bath and sunny bay window. Please specify crawlspace or slab foundation when ordering.

Design 8030

First Floor: 2,528 square feet
Second Floor: 1,067 square feet
Total: 3,595 square feet

● The massive entry to this beautiful home insures that
all who pass will take note of this imposing elevation.
Upon entering, one steps into a two-story foyer with a
gallery effect created by oversized columns and connecting arches. A graceful curved staircase rises from the foyer
to the second floor. The dining room is showcased off the
foyer. Situated with views to the side and rear of the
home, the great room is designed with an offset perfect for
a grand piano or a game table. The kitchen and breakfast
room are centrally located for access to the rear yard. The
master suite features a sitting area and a luxury bath with
a see-through fireplace. The second floor completes the
home with three bedrooms, two baths and a game room.

REAR

Design by
Larry E. Belk
Designs

Width 69'-2"
Depth 73'-10"

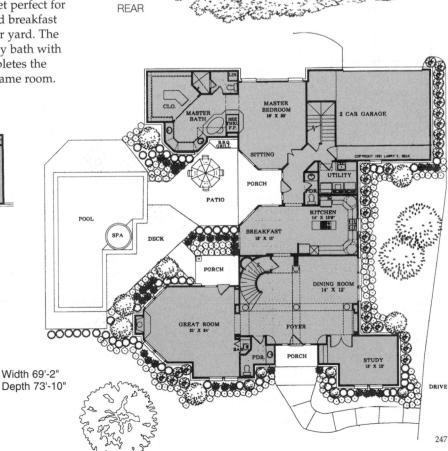

Design 9224

First Floor: 1,583 square feet
Second Floor: 1,442 square feet
Total: 3,025 square feet

● The stately exterior of this home will be a welcome addition to any neighborhood. The front entry, with its gracefully curving staircase, is flanked by the formal dining room with detailed ceiling and a cozy library with arched window. To the rear, the beam-ceilinged family room provides both formal and informal living space. Note the bay window and through-fireplace to the kitchen. The hearth area of the kitchen makes an inviting spot for the family to gather. The four-bedroom sleeping area is highlighted by the master suite which features a unique ceiling, walk-in closet and luxurious bath.

Design by
Design Basics, Inc.

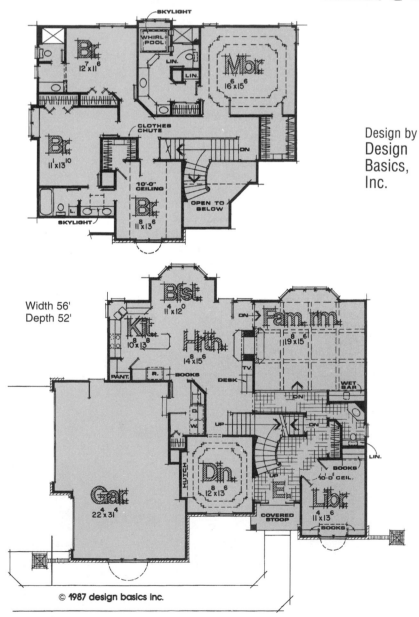

Width 56'
Depth 52'

© 1987 design basics inc.

248

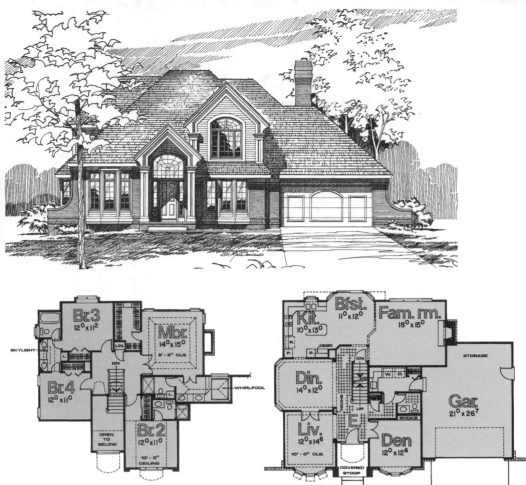

Design 9254

First Floor: 1,392 square feet
Second Floor: 1,153 square feet
Total: 2,545 square feet

● From the volume entry of this traditionally styled home radiate spacious living areas, both formal and informal. The living room and den both sport bay windows while the casual family room has a cozy fireplace and large windows overlooking the rear yard. The kitchen features a center island counter and work desk near the attached breakfast room. Upstairs there are four bedrooms—three family bedrooms and a master suite. Bedrooms 3 and 4 share a full bath, while Bedroom 2 has its own private bath. The master bath has double vanities and a whirlpool tub.

Design by
Design
Basics,
Inc.

Width 56'
Depth 43'-4"

Design 9369

First Floor: 1,369 square feet
Second Floor: 1,111 square feet
Total: 2,480 square feet

● Combined dining and living areas provide abundant space for formal entertaining. Or if preferred, escape to the den for quiet time with a book—built-in bookshelves fill out one wall of this room. The kitchen makes use of island counter space and breakfast nook. The family room with fireplace, a laundry and a powder room round out the first floor. The master bedroom—with tiered ceiling and bath with a whirlpool—highlights the second floor. Three additional bedrooms and another full bath complete the design.

Design by
Design
Basics,
Inc.

Width 64'
Depth 46'

Design 9195

First Floor: 1,872 square feet
Second Floor: 724 square feet
Total: 2,596 square feet

● Open floor planning is the key to the spacious combination of formal and informal areas. Blended for convenience is the formal dining room, a gallery, a living room with a fireplace and a home theater, a breakfast area with porch access and an efficient L-shaped kitchen. Guest quarters tucked behind the two-car garage provide an extra measure of privacy. Pamper yourself in the relaxing master bath which is highlighted by a separate tub and shower. Bedrooms 2 and 3 share a full bath.

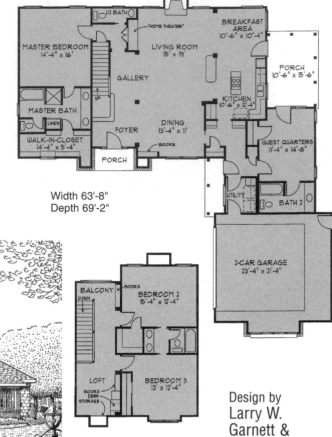

Width 63'-8"
Depth 69'-2"

Design by
Larry W.
Garnett &
Associates, Inc.

Design 9029

First Floor: 1,208 square feet
Second Floor: 1,066 square feet
Total: 2,274 square feet

● This quaint little plan works so well on narrow lots that you might never suspect all the livability that can be found inside. From the front foyer turn right to a living room that has as its focus an open hearth through to the rear family room. A left turn from the foyer leads to a formal dining room with bay window. Another bay window can be found in the breakfast room which is next to an efficient L-shaped kitchen. Upstairs are three lovely bedrooms. The master suite contains a sitting room, double walk-in closet and separate tub and shower.

Design by
Larry W.
Garnett &
Associates, Inc.

Width 60'
Depth 36'-8"

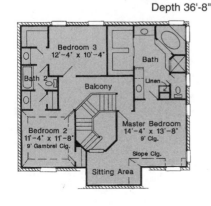

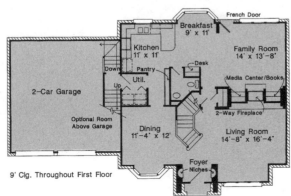

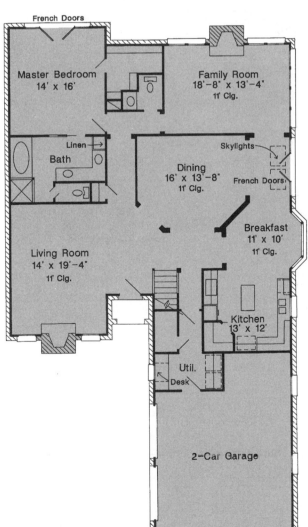

Design 9172

First Floor: 2,066 square feet
Second Floor: 601 square feet
Total: 2,667 square feet

● A family room backs up the first floor of this plan and delights with its abundant windows and central fireplace. There's also a living room with a fireplace that shares an interesting formal relationship with the dining room. The kitchen expands into a breakfast room. Locate your washer and dryer in the utility room off the garage. Sleeping accommodations excel with an excellent master suite situated at the rear of the first floor. Upstairs, two bedrooms offer plenty of room for creative furniture arrangements.

Width 44'-8"
Depth 77'-4"

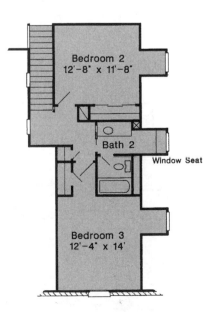

Design by
Larry W.
Garnett &
Associates, Inc.

Design 9902

First Floor: 830 square feet
Second Floor: 1,060 square feet
Total: 1,890 square feet

● The pleasing character of this house does not stop behind its facade. The foyer opens up into a large space encompassing the great room with fireplace and the kitchen/breakfast room. Stairs lead from the great room to the second floor—and here's where you'll find the laundry! The master suite spares none of the amenities: full bath with double vanity, shower, tub and walk-in closet. Bedrooms 2 and 3 share a full bath. This home is designed with a basement foundation.

Design by
Design Traditions

Width 41'
Depth 40'-6"

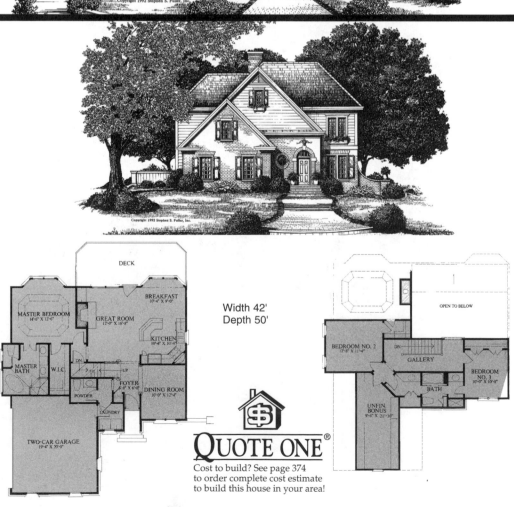

Design 9896

First Floor: 1,225 square feet
Second Floor: 563 square feet
Total: 1,788 square feet

● A 1½-story home with mixed exterior materials is hard to beat. Both casual and formal occasions are accommodated from the great room with a fireplace to the formal dining room. An informal breakfast room complements the gourmet kitchen; its bay window makes family dining a treat. The master suite is found on the first floor. It features a huge walk-in closet, corner tub, separate shower and compartmented toilet. There are two family bedrooms on the second floor. Unfinished space on the second floor can function as storage or be developed into a fourth bedroom if needed. This home is designed with a basement foundation.

Design by
Design Traditions

Width 42'
Depth 50'

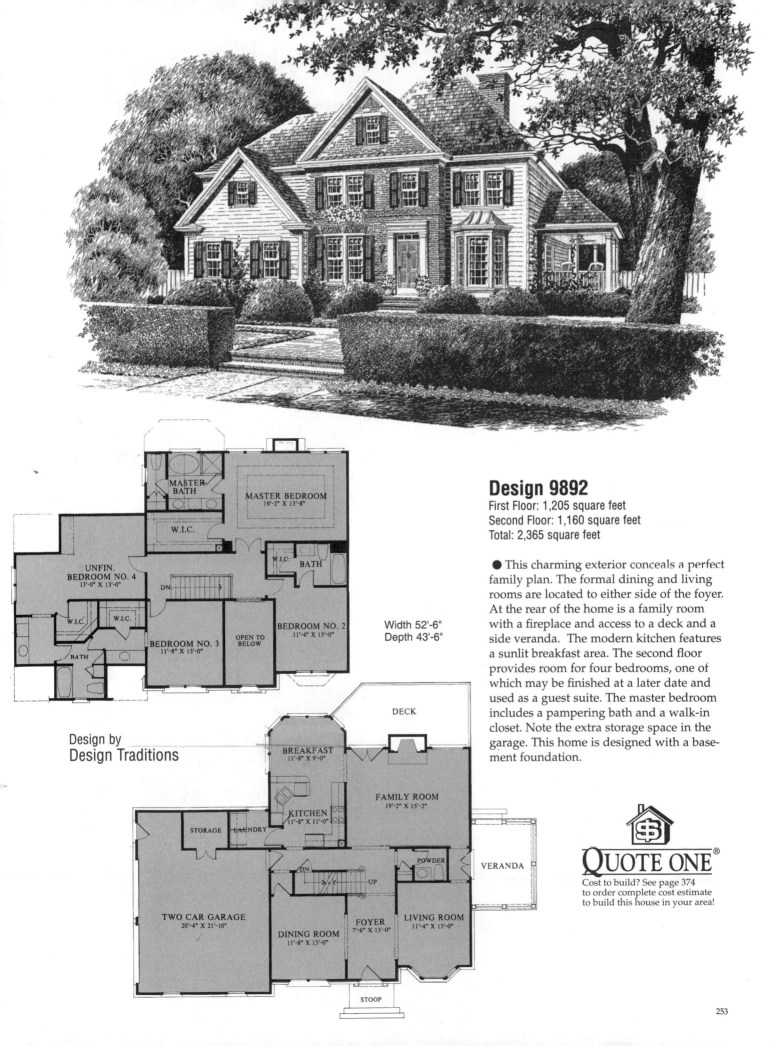

Design 9892

First Floor: 1,205 square feet
Second Floor: 1,160 square feet
Total: 2,365 square feet

● This charming exterior conceals a perfect family plan. The formal dining and living rooms are located to either side of the foyer. At the rear of the home is a family room with a fireplace and access to a deck and a side veranda. The modern kitchen features a sunlit breakfast area. The second floor provides room for four bedrooms, one of which may be finished at a later date and used as a guest suite. The master bedroom includes a pampering bath and a walk-in closet. Note the extra storage space in the garage. This home is designed with a basement foundation.

Width 52'-6"
Depth 43'-6"

Design by
Design Traditions

Quote One®
Cost to build? See page 374
to order complete cost estimate
to build this house in your area!

Second Floor Plan

MASTER BATH

MASTER BEDROOM
19'-2" X 13'-8"

W.I.C.

UNFIN. BEDROOM NO. 4
13'-0" X 13'-0"

W.I.C.

BATH

W.I.C.

DN

W.I.C.

BATH

BEDROOM NO. 3
11'-8" X 13'-0"

OPEN TO BELOW

BEDROOM NO. 2
11'-4" X 13'-0"

First Floor Plan

DECK

BREAKFAST
11'-8" X 9'-0"

FAMILY ROOM
19'-2" X 15'-2"

KITCHEN
11'-8" X 11'-0"

STORAGE

LAUNDRY

POWDER

VERANDA

TWO CAR GARAGE
20'-4" X 21'-10"

DN

UP

FOYER
7'-6" X 13'-0"

LIVING ROOM
11'-4" X 13'-0"

DINING ROOM
11'-8" X 13'-0"

STOOP

Design 9410

First Floor: 1,484 square feet
Second Floor: 1,402 square feet
Bonus Room: 430 square feet
Total: 3,316 square feet

● This impressive Tudor is designed for lots that slope up slightly from the street—the garage is five feet below the main floor. Just to the right of the entry, the den is arranged to work well as an office. Formal living areas include a living room with fireplace and an elegant dining room. The family room also has a fireplace and is close to the bumped-out nook—a great casual dining area. All the bedrooms are generously sized, especially the master bedroom with plenty of amenities and a huge walk-in closet. A large vaulted bonus room features convenient access from both the family room and the upper hallway.

Design by
Alan Mascord
Design Associates, Inc.

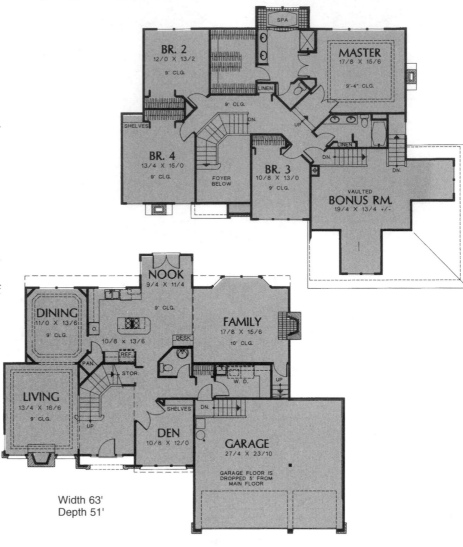

Width 63'
Depth 51'

254

Design 9555

First Floor: 1,304 square feet
Second Floor: 1,190 square feet
Total: 2,494 square feet

● This darling European home exhibits a floor plan that will accommodate the growing family. Living and dining areas and a curved staircase open off the foyer. An expansive kitchen easily serves a breakfast room, which has French doors leading to the rear yard. In the family room, a fireplace and triple windows create a comfortable atmosphere. A handy utility room accesses the three-car garage. The second-floor master suite is special with a sitting area and a bath that features dual lavatories, a garden tub, a separate shower and a toilet compartment. Three family bedrooms each have a spacious closet; all share a full bath.

Design by
Alan Mascord
Design Associates, Inc.

NOOK
11/0 X 15/8

FAMILY RM.
18/4 X 14/6
(9' CLG.)

10/0 X 16/0

DINING
13/0 X 11/0

GARAGE
10/0 X 19/4   19/4 X 21/0

LIVING
13/0 X 13/8 +/-

UP

QUOTE ONE®
Cost to build? See page 374
to order complete cost estimate
to build this house in your area!

Width 50'
Depth 48'

BR. 2
12/0 X 11/0

MASTER
20/0 X 15/0 +/-
(8'-8" CLG.)

LIN

DN.

BR. 3
11/10 X 10/4

BR. 4
13/0 X 12/0

Design 9871

First Floor: 2,208 square feet
Second Floor: 1,250 square feet
Total: 3,458 square feet

● Quaint, yet as majestic as a country manor on the Rhine, this European-styled stucco home enjoys the enchantment of arched windows and finials to underscore its charm. The two-story foyer leads through French doors to the study with its own hearth and English-coffered ceiling. Coupling with this cozy refuge is the master suite with tray ceiling and large accommodating bath and closet. The large, sunken great room is highlighted by a fireplace, bookcases, lots of glass and easy access to a back stair and large gourmet kitchen. Upstairs are two bedrooms which share a connecting bath. A third, more spacious bedroom gives guests the ultimate in convenience with a private bath and a walk-in closet. This home is designed with a basement foundation.

QUOTE ONE®

Cost to build? See page 374
to order complete cost estimate
to build this house in your area!

Design by
Design Traditions

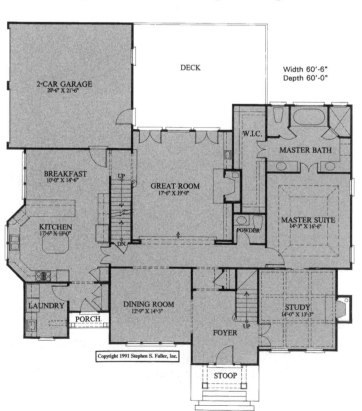

Width 60'-6"
Depth 60'-0"

Copyright 1991 Stephen S. Fuller, Inc.

Width 60'-6"
Depth 60'

Design 9864

First Floor: 1,395 square feet
Second Floor: 1,210 square feet
Total: 2,605 square feet

QUOTE ONE®

Cost to build? See page 374
to order complete cost estimate
to build this house in your area!

● The well-balanced use of stucco and stone combined with box-bay window treatments and a covered entry make this English country home especially inviting. The two-story foyer opens on the right to the attractive living and dining rooms with large windows. The step-saving kitchen and breakfast areas flow easily into the two-story great room and a media room with a see-through fireplace. The second floor offers a pleasing combination of open design and privacy. The master bedroom has a modified tray ceiling and is complete with a sitting area. The master bath with a double vanity, separate shower and water closet leads to a large walk-in closet. Double vanities are also found in the full bath off the hall. Bedrooms 2 and 3 are ample in size and feature walk-in closets. This home is designed with a basement foundation.

Design by Design Traditions

Second Floor

BEDROOM NO. 2
12'-0" X 12'-0"

SITTING

OPEN TO BELOW

MASTER BEDROOM
19'-8" X 13'-6"

BALCONY

W.I.C.   W.I.C.

MASTER BATH

DN

BATH

BEDROOM NO. 3
12'-0" X 12'-6"

OPEN TO BELOW

W.I.C.

UNFIN. BONUS
12'-0" X 11'-4"

First Floor

DECK

TWO STORY GREAT ROOM
14'-0" X 18'-0"

BREAKFAST
10'-0" X 10'-0"

MEDIA ROOM
12'-0" X 15'-6"

KITCHEN
12'-6" X 11'-6"

LAUNDRY   POWDER

UP   DN.   UP

DINING ROOM
12'-0" X 11'-6"

TWO STORY FOYER
10'-6" X 10'-8"

LIVING ROOM
13'-4" X 10'-6"

TWO CAR GARAGE
21'-10" X 22'-6"

STOOP

Width 47'
Depth 47'-6"

REAR

Design 8089

First Floor: 1,471 square feet
Second Floor: 1,040 square feet
Total: 2,511 square feet

● Three arched windows dominate the entrance to this elegant original. The dining room and great room are located at the rear of the home and are separated by a graceful arched opening flanked by columns. A roomy breakfast area opens off the kitchen and features a bay window. The master suite includes a bath with a whirlpool tub, a shower and a large walk-in closet. The upstairs offers two options: three bedrooms and 1½ baths; or three bedrooms and two baths. Please specify crawlspace or slab foundation when ordering.

Width 56'-10"
Depth 55'-9"

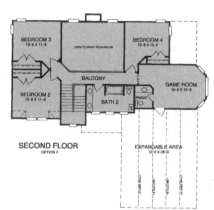

SECOND FLOOR
OPTION 2

EXPANDABLE AREA
12-0 X 28-0

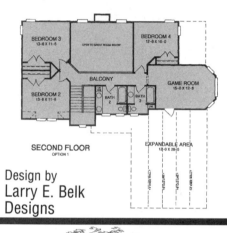

SECOND FLOOR
OPTION 1

EXPANDABLE AREA
12-0 X 28-0

Design by
Larry E. Belk
Designs

Design 8093

First Floor: 1,635 square feet
Second Floor: 844 square feet
Total: 2,479 square feet

● Twin gables and classic porch details give this home a look that is distinguished, yet warmly inviting. Inside, a large great room is conveniently located near the kitchen and breakfast room. The kitchen features an abundance of cabinets and a large work island. The master suite is located downstairs for privacy and features amenities such as the corner whirlpool tub, a separate shower and a huge walk-in closet. Upstairs, three additional bedrooms share a full hall bath. Please specify crawlspace or slab foundation when ordering.

Design by
Larry E. Belk
Designs

Width 58'-10"
Depth 59'-10"

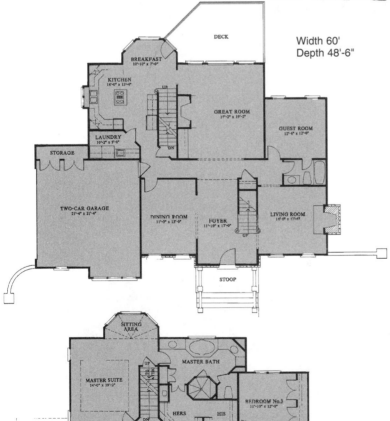

Width 60'
Depth 48'-6"

Design 9833

First Floor: 1,683 square feet
Second Floor: 1,544 square feet
Total: 3,227 square feet
Bonus Room: 176 square feet

● Handsomely arranged, this country cottage possesses an inviting quality. The stucco exterior, mixed with stone and shingles, creates a warmth that is accented with a fan-light transom and a pendant door frame. The formal two-story foyer opens onto all the drama of the staircase and then flows easily into the dining room, living room and great room. The great room features a fireplace and bookcases on the side wall and opens to a well-lit breakfast and kitchen area. To complete the main level of this home, a guest room or office is planned, offering visitors the utmost in privacy. Provided upstairs are three additional bedrooms and space for a bonus or play room. The master suite features a tray ceiling and adjoining sitting area with special ceiling treatment. The master bath offers a large garden tub with separate vanities, His and Hers closets and an octagonal glass shower. This home is designed with a basement foundation.

Design by
Design Traditions

Design 9821

First Floor: 2,070 square feet
Second Floor: 790 square feet
Total: 2,860 square feet

Quote One®

Cost to build? See page 374
to order complete cost estimate
to build this house in your area!

● The striking combination of wood frame, shingles and glass
create the exterior of this classic cottage. The foyer opens to the
main level layout. To the left of the foyer is a study with a warming hearth and a vaulted ceiling. To the right is the formal dining
room. A great room with an attached breakfast area is near the
kitchen. A guest room is nestled in the rear of the plan for privacy.
The master suite provides an expansive tray ceiling, a glass sitting
area and easy passage to the outside deck. Upstairs, two bedrooms are accompanied by a sunken loft for a quiet getaway. This
home is designed with a basement foundation.

Rear Elevation

Design by
Design Traditions

Width 58'-4"
Depth 54'-10"

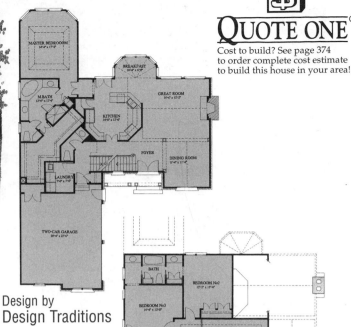

Design 9812

First Floor: 1,580 square feet
Second Floor: 595 square feet
Total: 2,175 square feet
Bonus Room: 290 square feet

Design by
Design Traditions

Width 48'-6"
Depth 70'-11"

● This home features a front porch which warmly welcomes family and visitors, as well as protecting them from the weather. Inside, the spacious foyer leads directly to a large, vaulted great room with massive fireplace. The grand kitchen offers both storage and large work areas opening up to the breakfast room. In the privacy and quiet of the rear of the home is the master suite with its garden bath, His and Hers vanities and oversized closet. The second floor provides two additional bedrooms with a shared bath along with a balcony overlook to the foyer below. This home is designed with a basement foundation.

Width 54'
Depth 39'-5"

Design 9857

First Floor: 1,156 square feet
Second Floor: 1,239 square feet
Total: 2,395 square feet

Design by
Design Traditions

● This traditional home combines an attractive, classic exterior with an open and sophisticated interior design. To the right of the foyer reside both the living and dining rooms with their individual window treatments. Entering the kitchen from the dining room is a corner butler pantry for added convenience while entertaining. The open design flows from the breakfast area to family room. The open foyer staircase leads to the upper level, beginning with the master suite. The master bath contains a luxurious tub, separate shower and dual vanities, as well as a large linen closet. A large, walk-in master closet completes the suite. Bedroom two is inviting with its bay window and large closet. All three secondary bedrooms share a hall bath with a separate vanity and bathing area. This home is designed with a basement foundation.

Design 9918

First Floor: 1,710 square feet
Second Floor: 1,470 square feet
Total: 3,180 square feet

● Many generously sized, shuttered windows flood this stunning home with the clear, warming light of outdoors—captivating with its classic styling. The two-story foyer with its tray ceiling makes a dramatic entrance. To the right, a banquet-sized dining room offers space for a buffet, while the large kitchen allows easy access to the bay-windowed breakfast room.

To the left is a versatile room which can serve as a living room, study or guest room. Beyond the foyer is the great room, which sports a cheerful fireplace flanked by bookcases. An open-railed stairway leads to three bedrooms on the second floor. The exquisite master suite is truly a room to live in, with its stylish tray ceiling and warming fireplace. Its elegance is intensified right down to the bay window and huge walk-in closet with a built-in dressing table. This home is designed with a basement foundation.

Design by
Design Traditions

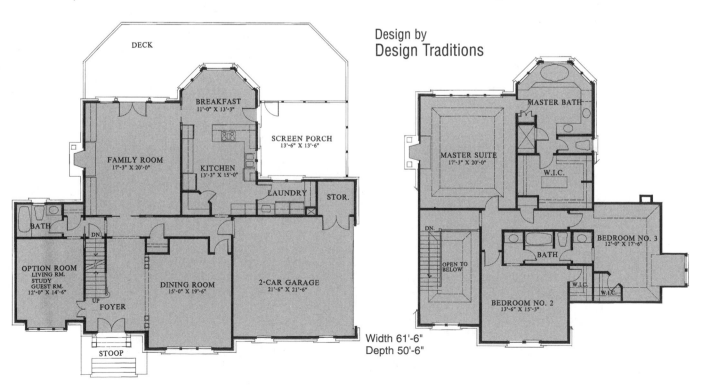

Width 61'-6"
Depth 50'-6"

Design 9869

First Floor: 1,475 square feet
Second Floor: 1,460 square feet
Total: 2,935 square feet

Rear Elevation

Design by
Design Traditions

● Through this home's columned entry, the two-story foyer opens to the living room with wet bar. The media room features a fireplace and is accessed from both the main hall and great room. The two-story great room with fireplace is open to the breakfast area, kitchen and rear staircase, making entertaining a pleasure. The kitchen design is ideal with breakfast bar and preparation island and is conveniently located near the laundry room. The dining room is ideal for formal entertaining. The upper level begins with the balcony landing overlooking the great room. The master bedroom features a bay-windowed sitting area and a tray ceiling. The master bath has dual vanities, a corner garden tub, a separate shower, a large walk-in closet and an optional secret room. Across the balcony, Bedrooms 2 and 3 share a bath. Bedroom 4 has its own private bath. This home is designed with a basement foundation.

QUOTE ONE®

Cost to build? See page 374 to order complete cost estimate to build this house in your area!

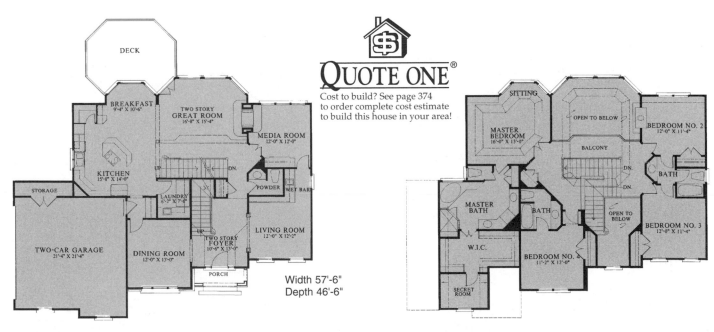

Width 57'-6"
Depth 46'-6"

Design 9809

First Floor: 1,870 square feet
Second Floor: 1,030 square feet
Total: 2,900 square feet

● This home, in the grandest tradition, features brick detailing that frames its arched double door and windows. Dormer windows and a roof of multiple levels infuse a definite drama and soft charm in this stately design. The two-story foyer opens into the great room with its fireplace and French doors that lead to the terrace. The open plan of the kitchen is a favorite and cheery arrangement with its contemporary angles which provide maximum convenience as well as easy access to both the dining room and breakfast area. A vaulted tray ceiling marks the master suite with distinction. Its vaulted bath area is set in an intimate bay window, overlooking the back terrace for privacy. Three other generously sized bedrooms are upstairs, as well as a bonus room, a large storage area and a loft which overlooks the dramatic foyer below. This home is designed with a basement foundation.

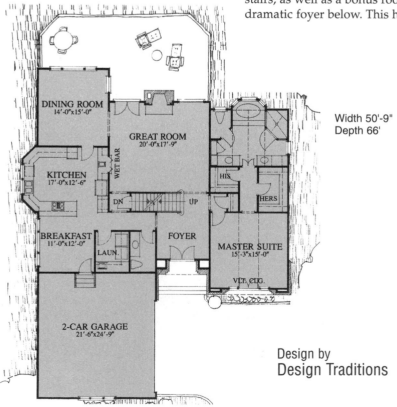

Width 50'-9"
Depth 66'

Design by
Design Traditions

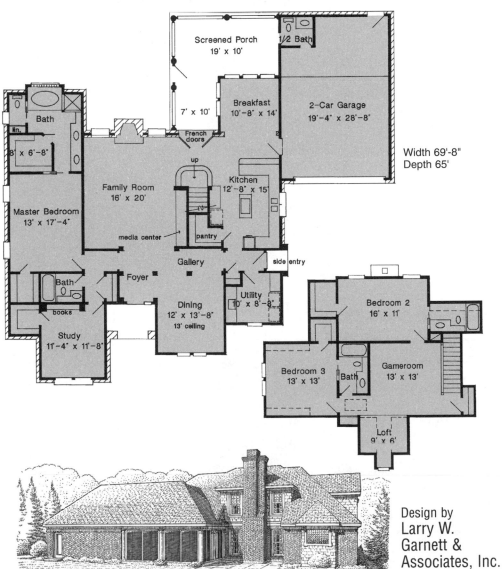

Screened Porch
19' x 10'

1/2 Bath

7' x 10'

French doors

Breakfast
10'-8" x 14'

2-Car Garage
19'-4" x 28'-8"

Width 69'-8"
Depth 65'

Bath

8' x 6'-8"

Master Bedroom
13' x 17'-4"

Family Room
16' x 20'

up

Kitchen
12'-8" x 15'

media center

pantry

Gallery

side entry

Bath

Foyer

books

Dining
12' x 13'-8"
13' ceiling

Utility
10' x 8'-8"

Study
11'-4" x 11'-8"

Bedroom 2
16' x 11'

Bedroom 3
13' x 13'

Bath

Gameroom
13' x 13'

Loft
9' x 6'

Design by
Larry W.
Garnett &
Associates, Inc.

Rear

Design 9183

First Floor: 2,138 square feet
Second Floor: 842 square feet
Total: 2,980 square feet

● This plan abounds with all the amenities, starting with a columned foyer that leads to a spacious dining room and an even bigger family room. A study located at the front of the house will convert to the ideal guest room with its walk-in closet and nearby full bath. In the kitchen, an island cooktop sets the pace—along with an immense walk-in pantry. Off the breakfast area, a screened porch wraps around to the back of the house and even gains access to a wash room that connects to the garage. A utility room enjoys its own sunny spot as well as a helpful countertop. Three bedrooms include a first-floor master suite with two walk-in closets and a fabulous private bath. The family bedrooms on the second floor each feature walk-in closets and their own full bathrooms. A gameroom on this floor further enhances the plan.

Design 2543

First Floor: 2,345 square feet
Second Floor: 1,687 square feet
Total: 4,032 square feet

L **D**

● This best-selling French adaptation is highlighted by effective window treatment, delicate cornice detailing, appealing brick quoins and excellent proportion. Inside, a large, two-story foyer leads under the arch of a dual staircase to a gathering room graced by a central fireplace and access to the rear terrace. The formal living and dining rooms flank the foyer and work well together for entertaining. The gourmet kitchen offers a work island, has an attached breakfast room with access to the terrace and offers a huge walk-in pantry. Upstairs a deluxe master bedroom suite is lavish in its efforts to pamper you. Three secondary bedrooms share this level, one with its own bath and a walk-in closet while two others share a full hall bath.

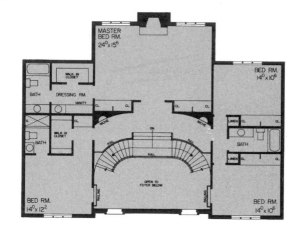

Width 90'-4"
Depth 44'

Design by
Home Planners

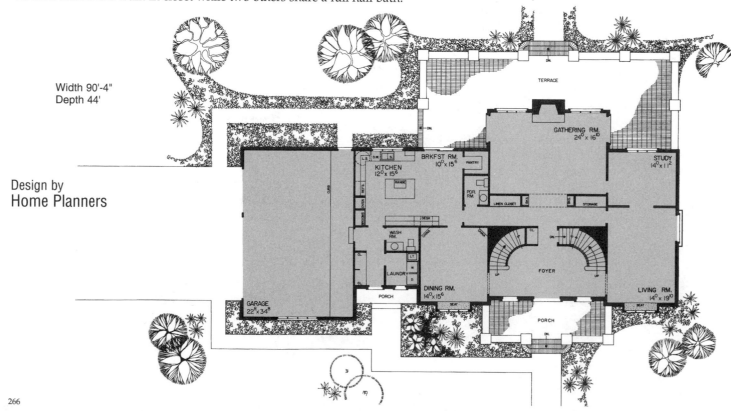

A Legacy Of Luxury:
Homes to pamper

Design 9934

First Floor: 3,568 square feet
Second Floor: 1,667 square feet
Total: 5,235 square feet

Design by
Design Traditions

● The ornamental stucco detailing on this home creates an Old-World Mediterranean charm and complements its strength and prominence. The two-story foyer with a sweeping curved stair opens to the large formal dining room and study. The master suite, offering convenient access to the study, is complete with a fireplace, His and Hers walk-in closets, a bath with twin vanities and a separate shower and tub. The two-story great room overlooks the rear patio. A large kitchen with an island workstation opens to an octagonal-shaped breakfast room and the family room. A staircase located off the family room provides additional access to the three second-floor bedrooms that offer walk-in closets and plenty of storage. This home is designed with a basement foundation.

Width 86'-8"
Depth 79'

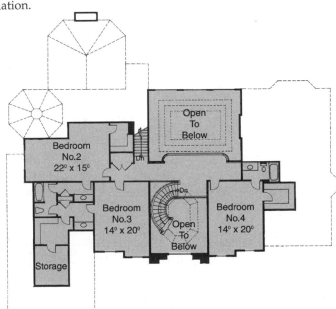

Family Room 20⁰ x 18⁰

Breakfast 14⁰ x 14⁰

Kitchen 18⁰ x 16⁰

Great Room 26⁰ x 18⁰

Master Bedroom 20⁰ x 19⁰

Dining Room 16⁰ x 18⁰

Foyer

Study 15⁰ x 18⁰

Three Car Garage 22⁰ x 30⁰

Bedroom No. 2 22⁰ x 15⁰

Open To Below

Bedroom No. 3 14⁰ x 20⁰

Bedroom No. 4 14⁰ x 20⁰

Open To Below

Storage

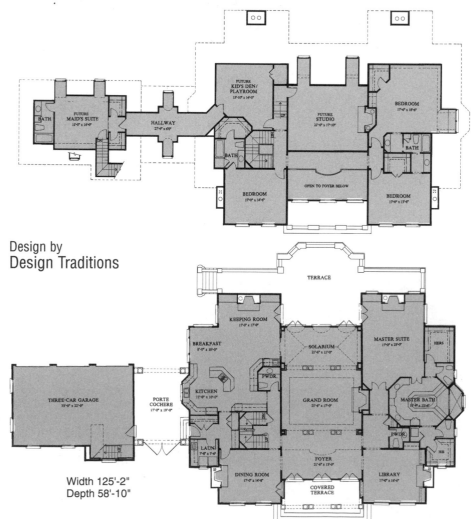

Design by
Design Traditions

Width 125'-2"
Depth 58'-10"

Design 9937

First Floor: 3,703 square feet
Second Floor: 1,427 square feet
Total: 5,130 square feet

● This magnificent estate is detailed with exterior charm: a porte cochere connecting the detached garage to the house, a covered terrace and oval windows. The first floor consists of a lavish master suite, a cozy library with a fireplace, an absolutely stupendous grand room/solarium combination, an elegantly formal dining room with another fireplace and a kitchen/breakfast room/keeping room that will delight everyone in the family. The second floor is equally impressive. Three large bedrooms dominate this level, each with a walk-in closet. For the kids there is a play room/kid's den and up another flight of stairs is a room for future expansion into a deluxe studio with a fireplace. Over the three-car garage and attached to the second floor via the roof of the porte cochere, there is a room for a future mother-in-law suite or maid's suite. This home is designed with a basement foundation.

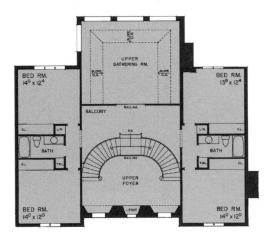

Design 3380

First Floor: 3,350 square feet
Second Floor: 1,203 square feet
Total: 4,553 square feet

● Reminiscent of a Mediterranean villa, this grand manor is a show-stopper on the outside and a comfortable residence on the inside. An elegant receiving hall boasts a double staircase and is flanked by the formal dining room and the library. A huge gathering room is found to the back and is graced by a fireplace and a wall of sliding glass doors to the rear terrace. The master bedroom is found on the first floor for privacy. With a lavish bath to pamper you, and His and Hers walk-in closets, this suite will be a delight to retire to each evening. Upstairs are four additional bedrooms with ample storage space, a large balcony overlooking the gathering room and two full baths.

Width 97'
Depth 74'-4"

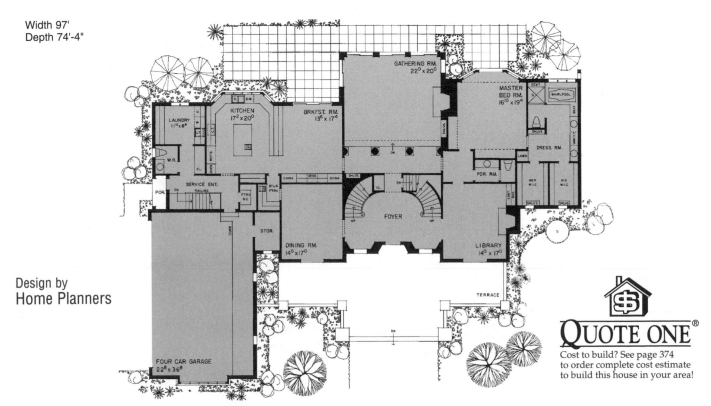

Design by
Home Planners

Quote One®
Cost to build? See page 374
to order complete cost estimate
to build this house in your area!

© 1991 The Sater Group, Inc.

Design 6635

First Floor: 4,760 square feet
Second Floor: 1,552 square feet
Total: 6,312 square feet

● As beautiful from the rear as from the front, this home features a spectacular blend of arch-top windows, French doors and balusters. Dramatic two-story ceilings and tray details add custom spaciousness. An impressive, informal leisure room has a sixteen-foot-high tray ceiling, an entertainment center and a grand ale bar. The large, gourmet kitchen is well appointed and easily serves the nook and formal dining room. The master suite has a large bedroom and a bayed sitting area. His and Hers vanities and walk-in closets and a curved, glass-block shower are highlights in the bath. The staircase leads to the deluxe secondary guest suites, two of which have observation decks to the rear and each with their own full baths.

Design by
**The Sater
Design Collection**

QUOTE ONE®

Cost to build? See page 374
to order complete cost estimate
to build this house in your area!

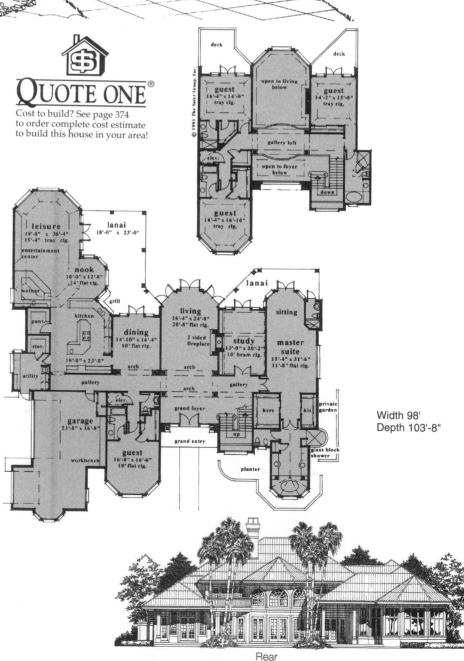

Width 98'
Depth 103'-8"

Rear

HOLZHAUER INC. 95

Design 6651

First Floor: 3,546 square feet
Second Floor: 1,213 square feet
Total: 4,759 square feet

● A marvelously arched entry welcomes and encourages you to call this beautiful mansion home. Inside, the two-story foyer leads under the second floor bridge into the lavish living room which is grace by a through-fireplace to the study and three sets of double French doors to the rear terrace. A huge octagonal leisure room at the back of the plan offers a built-in entertainment center and mirrors the living room's three sets of double French doors. A large kitchen with a cooktop island easily serves both the formal dining room and the sunny breakfast nook. The

master suite, located at the far right of the plan, is luxury defined. The master bedroom is lit by natural light from the bay window and has access to a rear veranda. Large His and Hers walk-in closets will fulfill all your storage needs and a sumptuous master bath is designed to pamper. Upstairs, three family bedrooms each have walk-in closets. Two share a full bath with twin vanities while the third has a private bath. A three-car garage will easily handle the family fleet. Please specify basement or slab foundation when ordering.

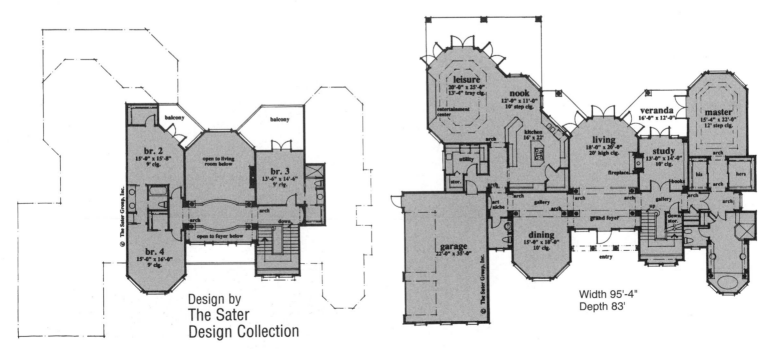

Design by
The Sater
Design Collection

Width 95'-4"
Depth 83'

Design 9564

First Floor: 2,290 square feet
Second Floor: 2,142 square feet
Total: 4,432 square feet

● An impressive entry opens onto a
two-story foyer with a magnificent staircase. Formal living comes to the forefront with a columned dining room on
the right and an inviting living room to
the left. The kitchen is a connoisseurs
delight, complete with a large pantry
and a nook that contains a computer
center. The two-story family room is the
center of attention with its unique wall
of bow windows and a cheerful fireplace. A den and powder room complete
the first floor. The second floor holds
three secondary bedrooms, two full
baths, a media room and an elegant
master suite with a private deck and a
deluxe master bath.

Design by
Alan Mascord
Design Associates, Inc.

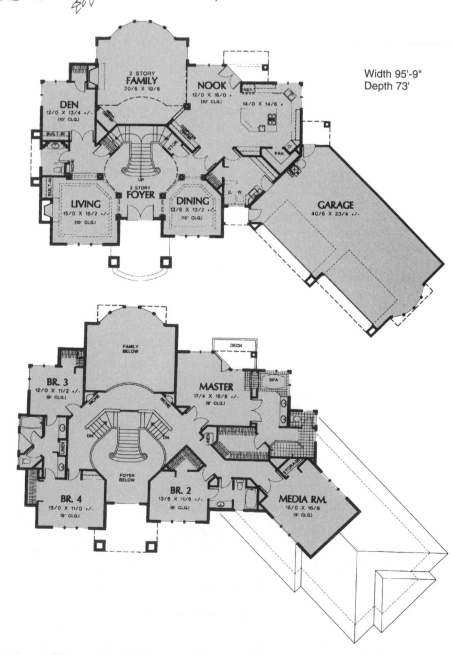

Width 95'-9"
Depth 73'

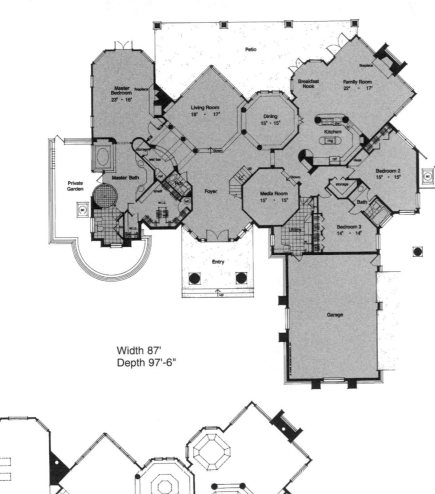

Width 87'
Depth 97'-6"

Design by
**Home Design
Services, Inc.**

Design 8628

First Floor: 3,770 square feet
Second Floor: 634 square feet
Total: 4,404 square feet

● This fresh and innovative design creates unbeatable ambience. Octagon shaped rooms, columns and flowing spaces will delight all. The breakfast nook and family room both open onto a patio—a perfect arrangement for informal entertaining. The dining room is sure to please with elegant pillars separating it from the sunken living room. A media room delights both with its shape and by being convenient to the nearby kitchen—perfect for snack runs. A private garden surrounds the master bath, with its spa tub and enormous walk-in closet. The master bedroom is enchanting with a fireplace and access to the outdoors. Additional family bedrooms come in a variety of different shapes and sizes; Bedroom 4 reigns over the second floor and features its own full bath.

© The Sater Group, Inc.

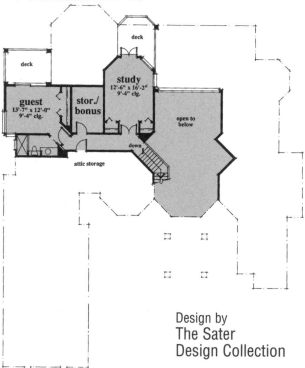

Design by
**The Sater
Design Collection**

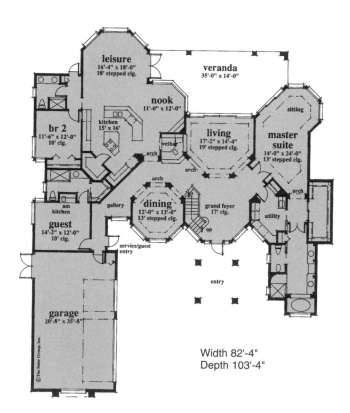

Width 82'-4"
Depth 103'-4"

Design 6650

First Floor: 3,092 square feet
Second Floor: 656 square feet
Total: 3,748 square feet

● Luxury is paramount in this four-bedroom traditional home. A columned entry leads to the grand foyer. The exclusive master suite is split from the two secondary bedrooms, residing to the right of the plan, and has a private entrance to the lanai. An arched entry provides access to large His and Hers closets and an extravagant master bath featuring a whirlpool tub and a separate shower. The central portion of the first floor contains the living area. The living room and adjacent dining room provide space for formal entertaining. For the best in casual living, the spacious kitchen, multi-windowed nook and leisure room are combined. The second floor contains a comfortable guest suite with a full bath and a bay-windowed study. Both enjoy private decks.

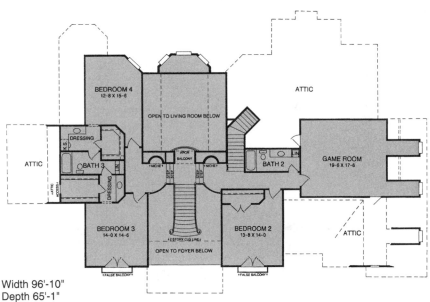

Width 96'-10"
Depth 65'-1"

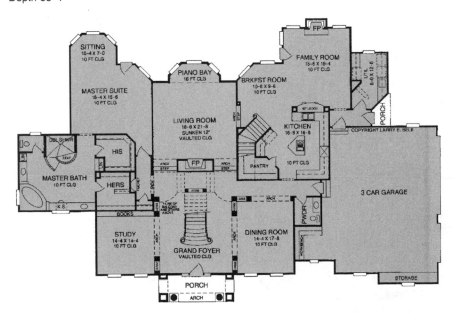

Design 8185

First Floor: 3,264 square feet
Second Floor: 1,671 square feet
Total: 4,935 square feet

● An impressive entry, multi-pane
windows and mock balconies combine
to give this facade an elegance of which
to be proud. The grand foyer showcases
a stunning staircase and is flanked by a
formal dining room to the right and a
cozy study to the left. The elegant
sunken living room is graced by a fireplace, a wondrous piano bay and a
vaulted ceiling. The openness of the
sunny breakfast room and the family
room make casual entertaining a breeze.
Located on the first floor for privacy,
the master bedroom suite is lavish with
its luxuries. A bayed sitting area encourages early morning repose, while
the bath revels in pampering you. Upstairs, three bedrooms share two full
baths and have access to a large game
room over the three-car garage. Please
specify crawlspace or slab foundation
when ordering.

Design by
Larry E. Belk
Designs

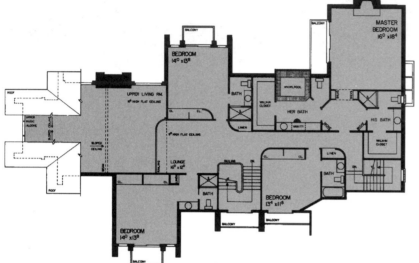

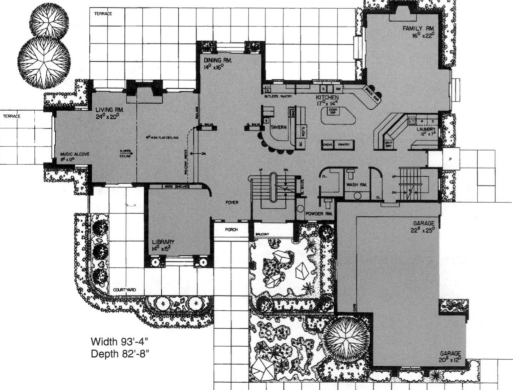

Design 2952

First Floor: 2,870 square feet
Second Floor: 2,222 square feet
Total: 5,092 square feet

● Semi-circular arches complement the strong linear roof lines and balconies of this exciting contemporary. The first floor is filled with well-planned amenities for entertaining and relaxing. The foyer opens to a step-down living room with a dramatic sloped ceiling, a fireplace and three sliding glass doors that access the front courtyard and terrace. A tavern with built-in wine rack and an adjacent butler's pantry are ideal for entertaining. The family room features a fireplace, sliding glass door and a handy snack bar. The kitchen allows meal preparation, cooking and storage within a step of the central work island. Three second-floor bedrooms, each with a private bath and balcony, are reached by either of two staircases. The master suite, with His and Hers baths and walk-in closets, whirlpool and fireplace, adds the finishing touch to this memorable home.

Width 93'-4"
Depth 82'-8"

Design by
Home Planners

Design 8626

First Floor: 3,236 square feet
Second Floor: 494 square feet
Total: 3,730 square feet

● If you want to build a home that is light years ahead of most other designs, non-traditional, yet addresses every need for your family, this showcase home is for you. From the moment you walk into this home you are confronted with wonderful interior architecture that reflects modern, yet refined taste. The exterior says European Villa; the interior creates special excitement. Note the special rounded corners found throughout the home and the many amenities. The master suite is especially appealing with fireplace and grand bath. Upstairs are a library/sitting room and a very private den or guest bedroom.

Design by
Home Design
Services, Inc.

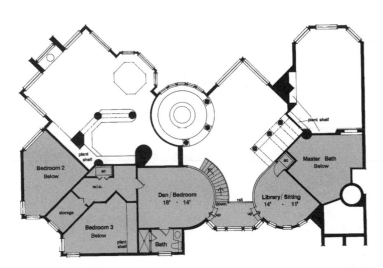

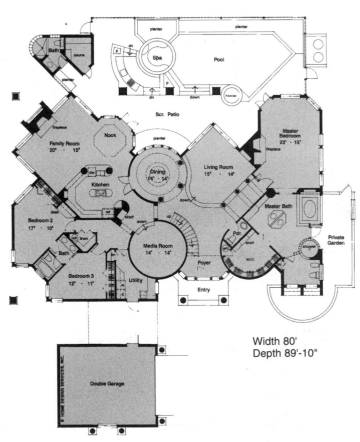

Width 80'
Depth 89'-10"

Design 8657

First Floor: 2,422 square feet
Second Floor: 971 square feet
Total: 3,393 square feet

● The word tradition epitomizes what this design is all about, except for one thing: this design fully utilizes modern livability. Formal dining and living areas, both with bay windows, flank the front entry; the family room opens up into fireplace and back-yard views. The U-shaped kitchen has a work island and a pass-through to the outside. Nearby, the spacious breakfast room provides access to the covered porch—you'll find this same access in the bedroom/den. The master bedroom, entered through double doors, is situated on the other side of the house and comes complete with a spa tub, a walk-in closet and a solarium. Upstairs, greet the kids with three bedrooms and their own personal living space. There's even an upstairs deck!

Design by
Home Design
Services, Inc.

Width 77'-8"
Depth 64'-8"

Design 3509

Main Level: 2,434 square feet
Lower Level: 2,434 square feet
Total: 4,868 square feet

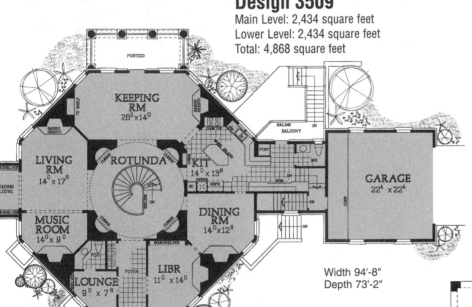

PORTICO

KEEPING RM
26² x 14⁰

LIVING RM
14⁰ x 17⁶

ROTUNDA

KIT
14⁰ x 19⁸

BOOKSHELVES
READING ALCOVE
BOOKSHELVES

MUSIC ROOM
14⁰ x 9⁰

DINING RM
14⁰ x 12⁸

RAILING BALCONY

GARAGE
22⁴ x 22⁴

LOUNGE
9⁰ x 7⁸

LIBR
11⁰ x 14⁰

FOYER

PORTICO

UP

Width 94'-8"
Depth 73'-2"

Design by
Home Planners

● If you're looking to do something a little different for your home building experience, this adaptation of Jefferson's "Poplar Forest" home may be just the ticket. Originally built in the hills around Lynchburg, Virginia, Poplar Forest served Jefferson as a retreat from the hustle and bustle of a new country. Now, equipped with modern amenities, this home will be your perfect retreat. The entry gives way to a sitting or receiving area on the left and a library on the right. Fireplaces adorn all of the major living areas upstairs: dining room, keeping room, living room and library. Downstairs bedrooms include a master suite with a fireplace and a private luxury bath.

COVERED PORCH

STUDY
11⁰ x 12⁸

BEDRM
11⁰ x 12⁸

TERRACE

BALCONY ABOVE

BATH

MASTER SUITE
14⁰ x 18⁴

LAUNDRY ROOM

SITTING AREA

HALLWAY

STORAGE

OPEN ABOVE

BEDRM
13¹⁰ x 12⁴

HER WALK-IN CLOSET

MASTER BATH

HIS WALK-IN CLOSET

MECH & STORAGE

QUOTE ONE®

Cost to build? See page 374
to order complete cost estimate
to build this house in your area!

REAR

Design 9936

First Floor: 3,902 square feet
Second Floor: 2,159 square feet
Total: 6,061 square feet

Design by
Design Traditions

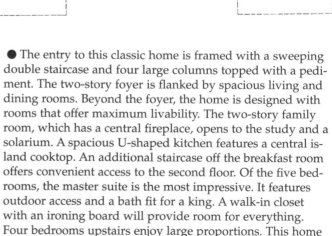

Bedroom No.5 18⁰ x 15⁰

Open To Below

Bedroom No.2 15⁶ x 15⁰

Bedroom No.4 14⁰ x 19³

Open To Below

Bedroom No.3 14⁰ x 18⁰

Attic Storage

Dn   Dn

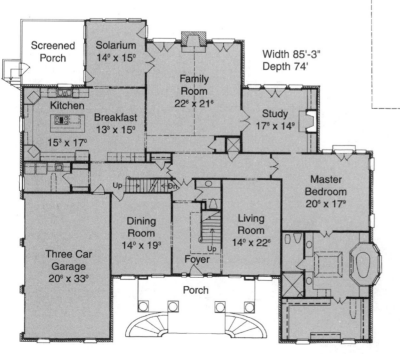

Screened Porch

Solarium 14⁰ x 15⁰

Family Room 22⁶ x 21⁶

Width 85'-3"
Depth 74'

Kitchen 15³ x 17⁰

Breakfast 13³ x 15⁰

Study 17⁶ x 14⁹

Up

Dn

Master Bedroom 20⁶ x 17⁹

Three Car Garage 20⁶ x 33⁰

Dining Room 14⁰ x 19³

Living Room 14⁰ x 22⁶

Up

Foyer

Porch

● The entry to this classic home is framed with a sweeping double staircase and four large columns topped with a pediment. The two-story foyer is flanked by spacious living and dining rooms. Beyond the foyer, the home is designed with rooms that offer maximum livability. The two-story family room, which has a central fireplace, opens to the study and a solarium. A spacious U-shaped kitchen features a central island cooktop. An additional staircase off the breakfast room offers convenient access to the second floor. Of the five bedrooms, the master suite is the most impressive. It features outdoor access and a bath fit for a king. A walk-in closet with an ironing board will provide room for everything. Four bedrooms upstairs enjoy large proportions. This home is designed with a basement foundation.

Design 2984

First Floor: 3,116 square feet
Second Floor: 1,997 square feet
Total: 5,113 square feet

L

● An echo of Whitehall, built in 1765 in Anne Arundel County, Maryland, resounds in this home. Its classic symmetry and columned facade herald a grand interior. There's no lack of space whether entertaining formally or just enjoying a family get-together, and all are kept cozy with fireplaces in the gathering room, study and family room. An island kitchen with attached breakfast room handily serves the nearby dining room. Four second-floor bedrooms include a large master suite with another fireplace, a whirlpool tub and His and Hers closets in the bath. Three more full baths are found on this floor.

Design by
Home Planners

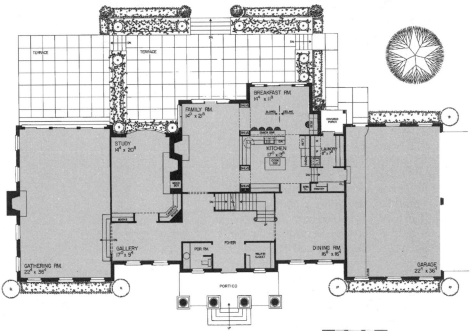

Width 104'
Depth 54'-8"

REAR

Design 9575

Main Level: 1,887 square feet
Upper Level: 1,382 square feet
Lower Level: 906 square feet
Total: 4,175 square feet

● Graceful curves and ceiling treatments are showcased in this hillside home. Double front doors give passage to the airy foyer. An octagonal library impresses with its double-door entry and built-ins. The living and dining rooms remain open to each other, guaranteeing good flow for entertaining. The exceptional kitchen caters to family activities with a nook and a family room with a fireplace located nearby. The master suite provides a getaway with its elegant styling and planning. This suite offers a pampering bath containing a walk-in closet, a spa tub and separate shower and a double-bowl vanity. Three other bedrooms are on the second floor and share a full hall bath. The walk-out basement contains a games room and a guest bedroom next to a full bath. A three-car garage accommodates the family fleet.

Design by
Alan Mascord
Design Associates, Inc.

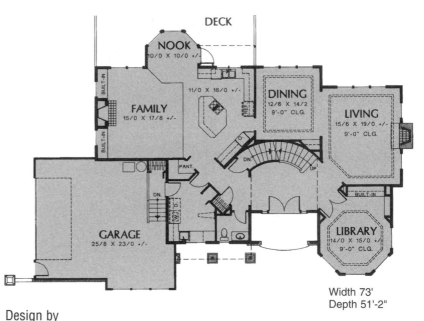

Width 73'
Depth 51'-2"

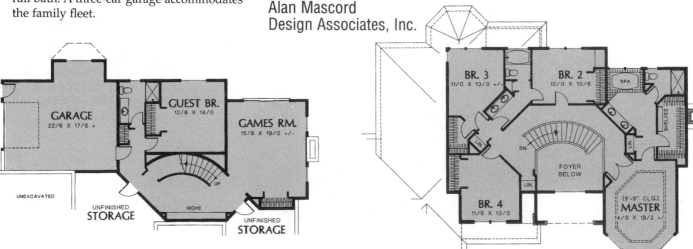

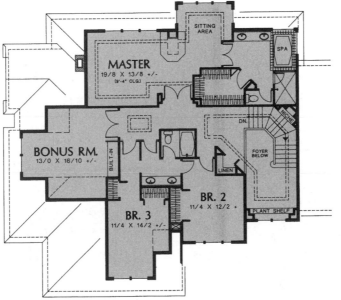

Design 9550

First Floor: 1,779 square feet
Second Floor: 1,335 square feet
Total: 3,114 square feet
Bonus Room: 479 square feet

● This traditional home has more to offer than a fine looking exterior. Tucked behind the three-car garage is an office with access from the outside as well as the inside, making this ideal for a home-based business. The foyer leads to the bay-windowed library on the left and the formal living and dining rooms on the right. The sunny eating nook also offers a bay window and combines with a spacious kitchen featuring a walk-in pantry and an angled cooktop island. Nearby you will find the family room with built-ins flanking both sides of the fireplace and access to the back yard. The second floor contains the sleeping area. The elaborate master suite boasts a restful sitting area and a luxurious bath with a spa and a walk-in closet. Two family bedrooms share a full bath. A large bonus room could be developed into a study or children's media room.

Width 68'
Depth 53'-6"

Design by
Alan Mascord
Design Associates, Inc.

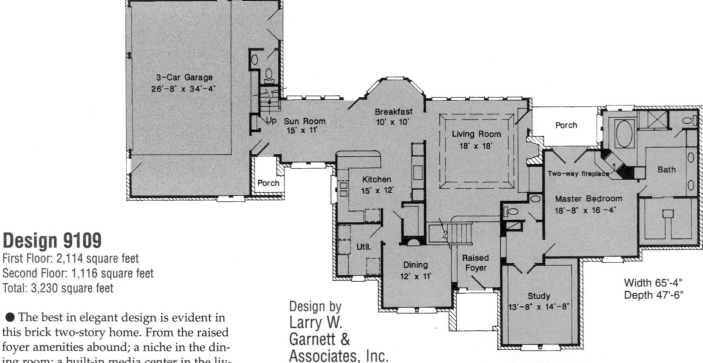

3-Car Garage
26'-8" x 34'-4"

Up Sun Room
15' x 11'

Breakfast
10' x 10'

Living Room
18' x 18'

Porch

Two-way fireplace

Bath

Master Bedroom
18'-8" x 16-4"

Kitchen
15' x 12'

Porch

Util.

Dining
12' x 11'

Raised
Foyer

Study
13'-8" x 14'-8"

Width 65'-4"
Depth 47'-6"

Design 9109

First Floor: 2,114 square feet
Second Floor: 1,116 square feet
Total: 3,230 square feet

● The best in elegant design is evident in this brick two-story home. From the raised foyer amenities abound; a niche in the dining room; a built-in media center in the living room and built-in bookcases in the study. A two-way fireplace, French doors to a rear covered porch, a huge walk-in closet and a pampering bath all grace the master suite. Even the U-shaped kitchen has built-in hutch space and its attached breakfast area has French doors to a covered porch. The vaulted living room offers a wall of windows, a central fireplace and a French door to the rear porch. The second floor holds three bedrooms and a gameroom. Eleven-foot ceilings are the rule in all but one of these rooms.

Design by
Larry W.
Garnett &
Associates, Inc.

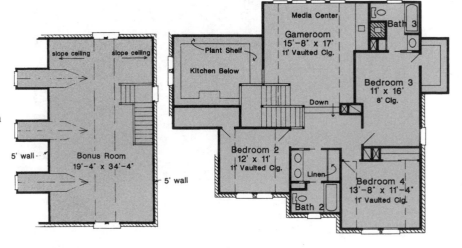

slope ceiling slope ceiling

5' wall

Bonus Room
19'-4" x 34'-4"

5' wall

Media Center

Gameroom
15'-8" x 17'
11' Vaulted Clg.

Plant Shelf

Kitchen Below

Bath 3

Bedroom 3
11' x 16'
8' Clg.

Down

Bedroom 2
12' x 11'
11' Vaulted Clg.

Linen

Bedroom 4
13'-8" x 11'-4"
11' Vaulted Clg.

Bath 2

284

Design by
**Design
Basics,
Inc.**

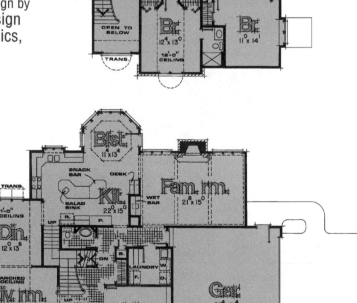

Design 9229

First Floor: 1,709 square feet
Second Floor: 1,597 square feet
Total: 3,306 square feet

● An attractive facade and amenity-filled interior make this home a showplace both outside and in. Immediately off the two-story foyer is the living room and connecting formal dining room, both with interesting ceilings, and the quiet library with built-in bookcases. The enormous gourmet kitchen features a large island work counter/snack bar, a pantry, a desk and a gazebo breakfast area. Just steps away is the spacious family room with a grand fireplace and windows overlooking the back yard. Upstairs are three family bedrooms served by two baths and a luxurious master suite with a bay-windowed sitting room, detailed ceiling and a skylit bath with a whirlpool.

Width 62'
Depth 55'-4"

Design 8909

First Floor: 2,817 square feet
Second Floor: 2,055 square feet
Total: 4,872 square feet

● Formal Renaissance detailing, distinctive dormer windows, and a massive chimney provide an exterior design that is a blend of French Eclectic and English Georgian styling. A grand foyer and a central gallery allow for easy traffic flow throughout the home. Double doors open to reveal a library and a study enhanced by built-in bookshelves and a stately fireplace. The kitchen, with its handy work island and abundant cabinet space, opens to a sunny breakfast room. Five bedrooms, including a lavish master suite, each sport a private bath. This plan also includes optional 467-square-foot guest quarters.

Width 93'-4"
Depth 82'-4"

Design by
Larry W.
Garnett &
Associates, Inc.

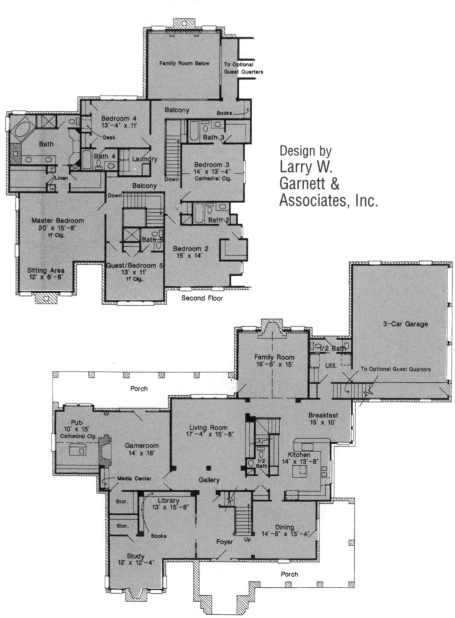

Plant Shelf

Kitchen Below

Gameroom
15'-4" x 17'
11' Clg.

Bath 2

Linen

Down

Bedroom 2
11' x 16'
8' Clg.

Bedroom 3
12' x 11'
11' Clg.

Linen

Bath 3

Bedroom 4
13'-4" x 11'-4"
11' Clg.

Design by
Larry W.
Garnett &
Associates, Inc.

Bath

Stor.

Guest Quarters
15'-4" x 18'
9' Clg.

Kitchen
12' x 12'
9' Clg.

Breakfast
10' x 13'

Kitchen
14' x 16'
Volume Clg.

Pantry

Skylights

French Door

Dining
15'-4" x 11'

1/2 Bath

Shop

Util.

3-Car Garage

Living Room
18' x 22'
11' Step-Up Clg.

Media Center

Planter

Raised Foyer

Porch

French Doors

Two-Way Fireplace

Clerestory Windows
Skylights

Bath

Linen

Master Bedroom
16'-4" x 18'-8"

1/2 Bath

French Doors

Study
13'-4" x 13'-8"

Books

Width 79'-8"
Depth 86'-6"

10' Clg. Throughout First Floor
Unless Otherwise Noted

Design 8973

First Floor: 2,381 square feet
Second Floor: 1,202 square feet
Total: 3,583 square feet
Guest Quarters: 606 square feet

● Radial-head windows and an arched, recessed entry complement the front-facing gables to create a graceful facade to this one-of-a-kind home. A built-in media center and a fireplace make the living room an ideal location for entertaining; the bookshelf-lined study offers a quiet retreat. The kitchen features a walk-in pantry, a volume ceiling that opens to the game room above, and spectacular arched windows over the sink. A gallery with skylights and French doors leads past the dining room to the service entrance where a staircase provides access to guest quarters above the garage. A two-way fireplace separates the master bedroom from the bath, where a whirlpool tub is inset perfectly in a windowed alcove.

Design 2940

First Floor: 4,786 square feet; Second Floor: 1,842 square feet; Total: 6,628 square feet

L D

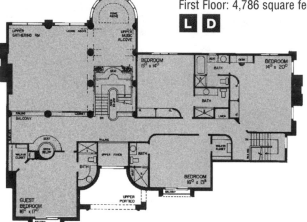

● Graceful window arches soften the massive chimneys and steeply gabled roof of this grand Norman manor. A two-story gathering room is two steps down from the adjacent lounge with impressive wet bar and semi-circular music alcove. The highly efficient galley-style kitchen overlooks the family room fireplace and spectacular windowed breakfast room. The master suite is a private retreat with a fireplace and a wood box tucked into the corner of its sitting room. Separate His and Hers baths and dressing rooms guarantee plenty of space and privacy. A large, built-in whirlpool tub adds the final touch. Upstairs, a second-floor balcony overlooks the gathering room below. There are also four additional bedrooms, each with a private bath.

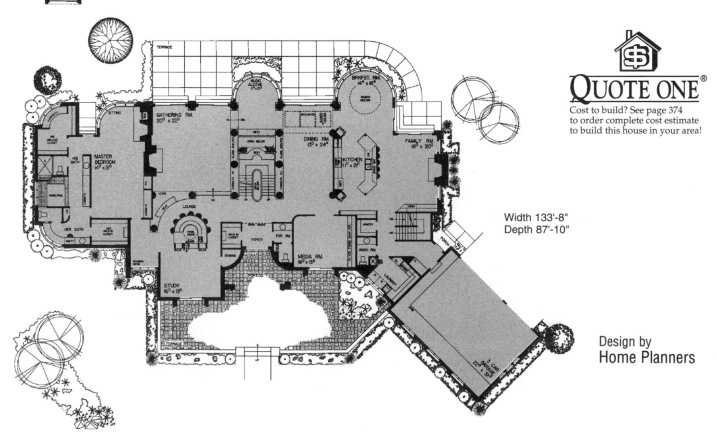

QUOTE ONE®

Cost to build? See page 374 to order complete cost estimate to build this house in your area!

Width 133'-8"
Depth 87'-10"

Design by
Home Planners

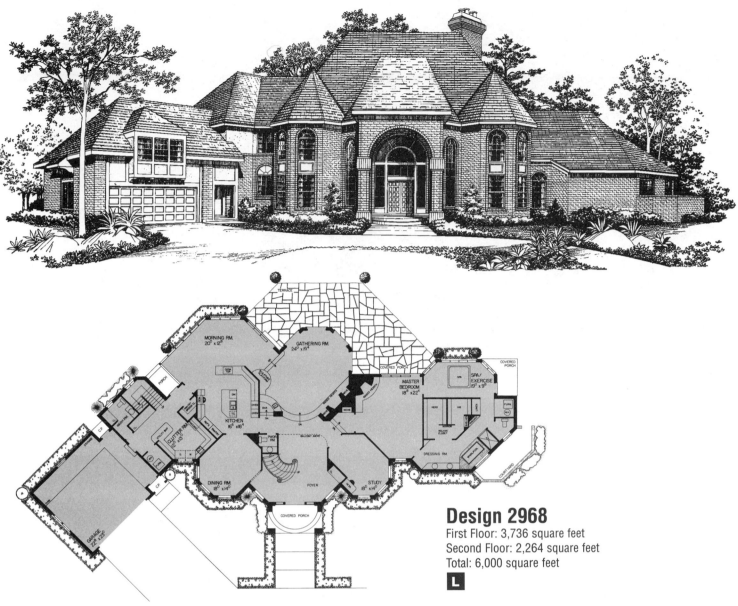

Design 2968

First Floor: 3,736 square feet
Second Floor: 2,264 square feet
Total: 6,000 square feet

L

Width 133'-4"
Depth 65'-5"

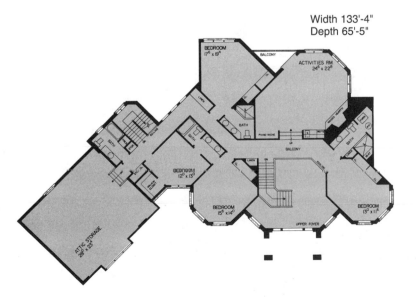

● The distinctive covered entry to this stunning manor, flanked by twin turrets, leads to a gracious foyer with impressive fan lights. The plan opens from the foyer to a formal dining room, master study and step-down gathering room. The spacious kitchen has numerous amenities including an island work station and a built-in desk. The adjacent morning room and gathering room with a wet bar and a raised-hearth fireplace are bathed in light and open to the terrace for outdoor entertaining. The luxurious master suite has a wealth of amenities as well. The second floor features four bedrooms and an oversized activities room with a fireplace and a balcony. Unfinished attic space can be completed to your specifications.

Design by
Home Planners

Design 9085

First Floor: 2,467 square feet
Second Floor: 710 square feet
Total: 3,177 square feet

● With dramatic traditional appeal this brick two-story home has a floor plan that is impressive. From the central foyer, go left to a sunken living room with a view of the formal dining room. A gameroom adjoins the U-shaped kitchen with attached breakfast nook. To the right is the master bedroom suite with a twelve-foot ceiling and a luxury bath. Note the access to the courtyard from this room as well as from the gameroom. Guest quarters lie to the rear of the first-floor plan. A curving staircase to the second floor leads to two additional bedrooms which share a full bath. The upstairs balcony overlooks the foyer and gameroom below.

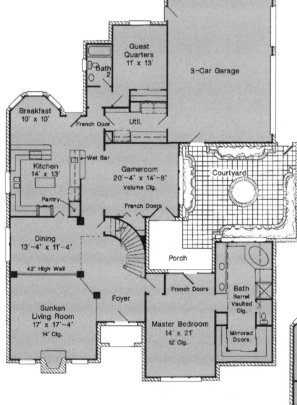

Design by
Larry W.
Garnett &
Associates, Inc.

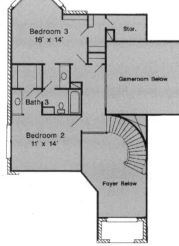

Width 55'
Depth 78'-8"

QUOTE ONE®

Cost to build? See page 374
to order complete cost estimate
to build this house in your area!

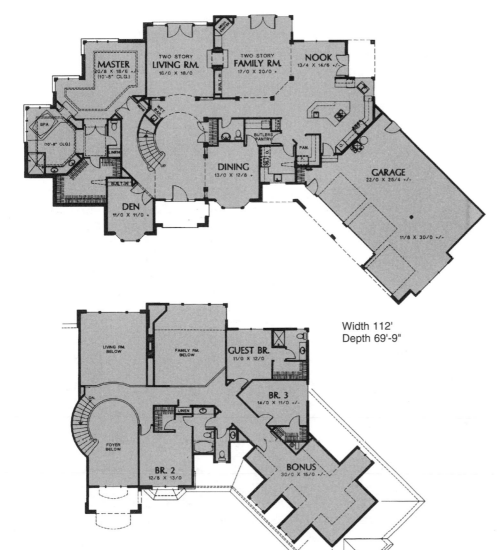

Width 112'
Depth 69'-9"

Design 9565

First Floor: 3,098 square feet
Second Floor: 1,113 square feet
Total: 4,211 square feet
Bonus Room: 567 square feet

● Ceilings soar to two-story heights in this elegant traditional home. A magnificent entry makes a grand impression, leading to the formal living room which shares a through-fireplace with the family room. The kitchen is a gourmet's delight with a center island and a walk-in pantry. An adjacent butler's pantry handily serves the columned dining room for formal entertaining. The first-floor master suite offers a relaxing private retreat. Double doors open onto a dressing area leading to a huge walk-in closet and a lavish master bath that features a soothing spa. The second floor contains three bedrooms—one a guest room with a private bath.

Design by
Alan Mascord
Design Associates, Inc.

Design by
**Larry W.
Garnett &
Associates, Inc.**

Design 9079

First Floor: 2,042 square feet
Second Floor: 900 square feet
Total: 2,942 square feet

● Outstanding exterior detail puts its mark upon this exquisite estate home. No less can be expected in its interior plan. A raised entry foyer leads to open living areas of the plan. The living room has a library area with built-in shelves and a fireplace; the dining room has a bay window and French doors to the rear porch. A U-shaped island kitchen has an attached light-filled breakfast area. Two bedrooms are found on the first floor. One is a master suite with a huge walk-in closet and clerestory windows; the other can serve as a perfect guest suite. Upstairs are two additional bedrooms, sharing a full bathroom, plus a game room with outdoor deck, and a half bath.

Width 58'
Depth 68'-8"

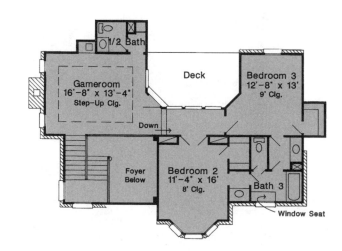

Design 9337

First Floor: 1,923 square feet
Second Floor: 1,852 square feet
Total: 3,775 square feet

● Breathtaking details and bright windows highlight this luxurious two-story home. Just off the
spectacular entry is an impressive private den. The
curved hall between the living and dining rooms
offers many formal entertaining options. Informal
gatherings will be enjoyed in the huge screened-in
porch. In the family room, three arched windows, a
built-in entertainment center and a fireplace flanked
by bookcases enhance daily comfort. Up the front
staircase and overlooking the dramatic entry, are four
large bedrooms. Three secondary bedrooms have

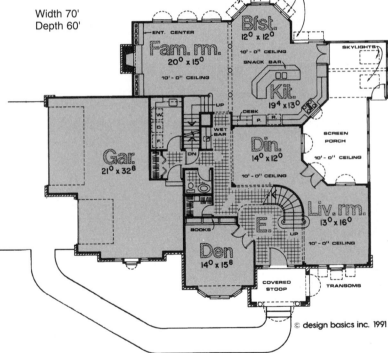

Width 70'
Depth 60'

© design basics inc. 1991

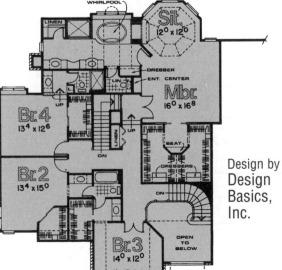

Design by
Design
Basics,
Inc.

generous closet space and private access to a bath. A sumptuous master suite awaits the home owners with its built-in entertainment center and His and Hers walk-in closets with a
built-in seat and dressers. Separated from the whirlpool bath
by a through-fireplace, the bayed gazebo sitting area adds an
elegant touch.

Design 8908

First Floor: 3,985 square feet
Second Floor: 2,278 square feet
Total: 6,263 square feet

● First-and second-story bay windows with copper roofs and detailed brick arches at the front entry and veranda recall classic estate homes of the 1920s. The magnificent foyer features an impressive staircase and balcony. The gallery offers a view into the formal living room, which has a fireplace flanked by built-in bookcases and access to the terrace via French doors. Double doors open to a private master suite with an octagonal sitting area and corner fireplace. The formal dining room shares a two-way fireplace with the pub area. Three pairs of French doors provide a view from the kitchen and breakfast area into the sun-drenched solarium/family room. Second-floor living space includes four bedrooms, a raised library/reading area and a huge game room.

Design by
Larry W.
Garnett &
Associates, Inc.

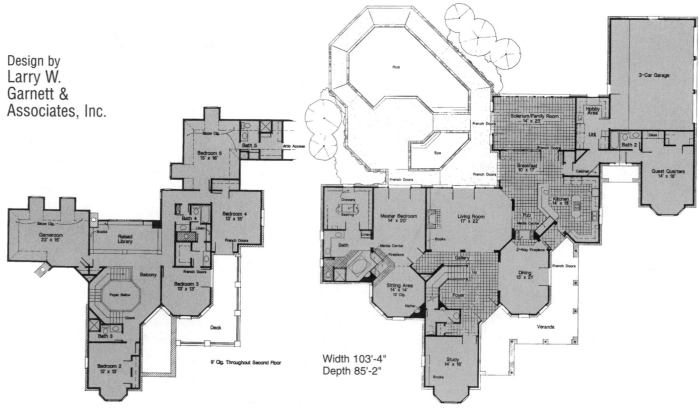

Width 103'-4"
Depth 85'-2"

Design 8079

First Floor: 3,722 square feet
Second Floor: 1,859 square feet
Total: 5,581 square feet

● Traditional in every detail, this stately brick home is finished with limestone quoins and window banding. A richly detailed limestone entrance reinforces the enduring quality of this design. Rising gracefully up from the two-story entry, the staircase is just a prelude to the great room beyond, where a fantastic window wall overlooks the rear grounds. The dining room is located off the entry and has a lovely coffered ceiling. The kitchen, breakfast room and sun room are conveniently grouped for entertaining. The elaborate master suite includes a gorgeous coffered ceiling in the master bedroom. The second story includes four bedrooms and an enormous game room.

Design by
Larry E. Belk
Designs

Width 127'-10"
Depth 83'-9"

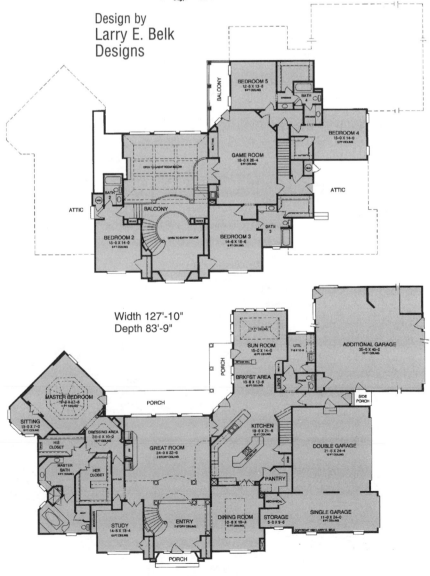

Design 9151

First Floor: 2,230 square feet
Second Floor: 1,899 square feet
Total: 4,129 square feet

● Rich with traditional detail, this elegant home will be treasured for a lifetime. The side-lit entry leads to a beautiful raised foyer from which the first floor unfolds. To the left is a bay-windowed music alcove and gallery with living room beyond. The formal dining area is to the right. At the center of the plan is an L-shaped island kitchen with corner sinks and a large walk-in pantry. A glass enhanced breakfast room contains French doors to a covered porch. A bedroom with full bath and study complete this floor. Upstairs are three additional bedrooms, each with its own bath, and a large gameroom. The master suite has double walk-in closets and a sumptuous bath.

Design by
Larry W.
Garnett &
Associates, Inc.

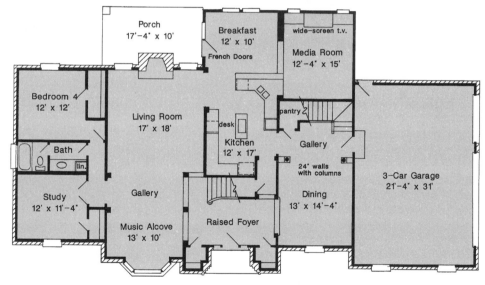

Width 82'
Depth 46'-2"

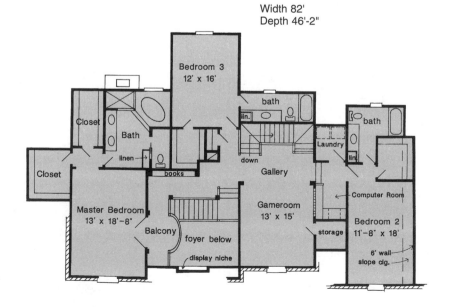

Design 8225

First Floor: 2,006 square feet
Second Floor: 1,346 square feet
Total: 3,352 square feet

● Multi-pane windows, mock-shutters and an arched entryway provide this home with a lot of curb appeal. Inside, the two-story foyer leads under the second-story balcony to a grand two-story living room where a wall of windows lets natural light flow in. An arch leads from this room into an elegant formal dining room, defined by pillars. The large efficient kitchen easily serves the bay-windowed breakfast room, the nearby family room and the formal dining room. In the family room a fireplace is flanked by built-in bookcases and another wall of windows helps to brighten family gatherings. Located on the first floor for privacy, the deluxe master bedroom suite offers many pampering amenities. From His and Hers walk-in closets to the luxurious bath, this room is sure to please. Upstairs, two bedrooms—each with a walk-in closet—share a full bath, while a third bedroom has access to a separate hall bath. A large game room is also on this level. Please specify crawlspace or slab foundation when ordering.

Design by
Larry E. Belk
Designs

Width 65'-2"
Depth 55'

Design 2955

First Floor: 3,840 square feet
Second Floor: 3,435 square feet
Total: 7,275 square feet

● Cross gables, decorative half-timbers and three massive chimneys mark the exterior of this magnificent baronial Tudor. A circular staircase housed in the turret makes an impressive opening statement in the two-story foyer. A powder room and telephone center are located off the foyer for easy use by guests. Two steps down lead to the elegant living room with a music alcove or to the sumptuous library with a wet bar. The kitchen is a chef's delight with a work island, a full cooking counter, and a butler's pantry leading to the formal dining room. The second floor features four bedrooms, two with fireplaces and each with a private bath and abundant closet space. The master suite contains an additional fireplace, His and Hers walk-in closets, a whirlpool bath and a private sitting room in a windowed alcove. Adjacent to the master suite is a nursery that would also make an ideal exercise room.

Design by
Home Planners

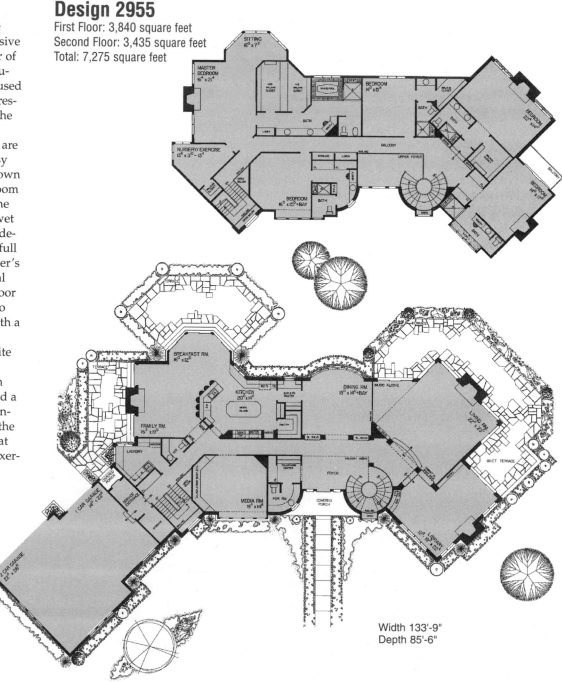

Width 133'-9"
Depth 85'-6"

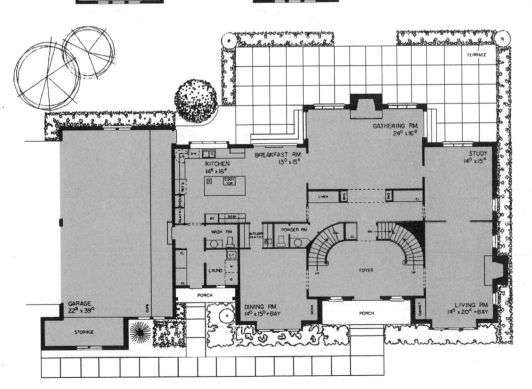

Design by
Home Planners

Width 97'-4"
Depth 53'

Design 2957

First Floor: 2,557 square feet
Second Floor: 1,939 square feet
Total: 4,496 square feet

L **D**

● The decorative half-timbers and stone wall-cladding on this manor are stately examples of Tudor architecture. A grand double staircase is the highlight of the elegant, two-story foyer that opens to each of the main living areas. The living and gathering rooms are anchored by impressive central fireplaces. Filled with amenities, the island kitchen has a nearby breakfast room for casual meals. Functioning with both the kitchen and the formal dining room is the butler's pantry. Accessible from both the gathering and living rooms is the quiet study. The outstanding master suite features a cozy bedroom fireplace, a picturesque whirlpool bath and a convenient walk-in closet. Three additional second-floor bedrooms include a guest suite with a dressing room and a walk-in closet.

Design 2954

First Floor: 3,079 square feet
Second Floor: 1,461 square feet
Total: 4,540 square feet

L

● This enchanting manor displays architectural elements typical of the Victorian Style: asymmetrical facade, decorative shingles and gables, and a covered porch. The two-story living room with fireplace and wet bar opens to the glass-enclosed rear porch with skylights. A spacious kitchen is filled with amenities including an island cooktop, built-in desk, and butler's pantry connecting to the dining room. The master suite, adjacent to the study, opens to the rear deck; a cozy fireplace keeps the room warm on chilly evenings. Separate His and Hers dressing rooms are outfitted with vanities and walk-in closets, and a luxurious whirlpool tub connects the baths. The second floor opens to a large lounge with built-in cabinets and bookshelves. Three bedrooms and two full baths complete the second-floor livability. The three-car garage contains disappearing stairs to an attic storage area.

Design by
Home Planners

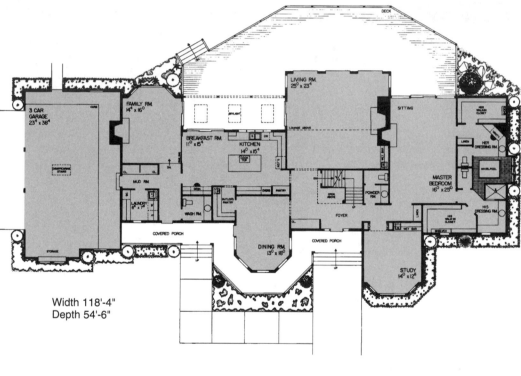

Width 118'-4"
Depth 54'-6"

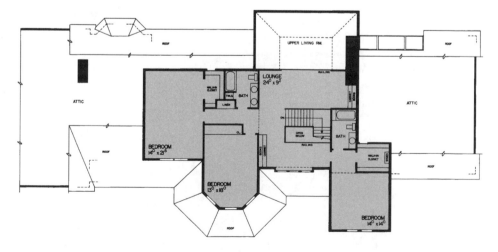

Design 2953

First Floor: 2,995 square feet
Second Floor: 1,831 square feet
Total: 4,826 square feet

L D

● A magnificent, finely wrought covered porch wraps around this impressive Victorian estate home. The gracious two-story foyer provides a direct view past the stylish bannister and into the great room with a large central fireplace. To the left of the foyer is a bookshelf-lined library and to the right is a dramatic, octagonal-shaped dining room. The island cooktop completes a convenient work triangle in the kitchen and a pass-through connects this room with the Victorian-style morning room. A butler's pantry, a walk-in closet and a broom closet offer plenty of storage space. A luxurious master suite is located on the first floor and opens to the rear covered porch. A through-fireplace warms the bedroom, sitting room, and dressing room, which includes His and Hers walk-in closets. The step-up whirlpool tub is an elegant focal point to the master bath. Four uniquely designed bedrooms, three full baths, and a restful lounge with a fireplace are located on the second floor.

Design by
Home Planners

Width 95'
Depth 99'-3"

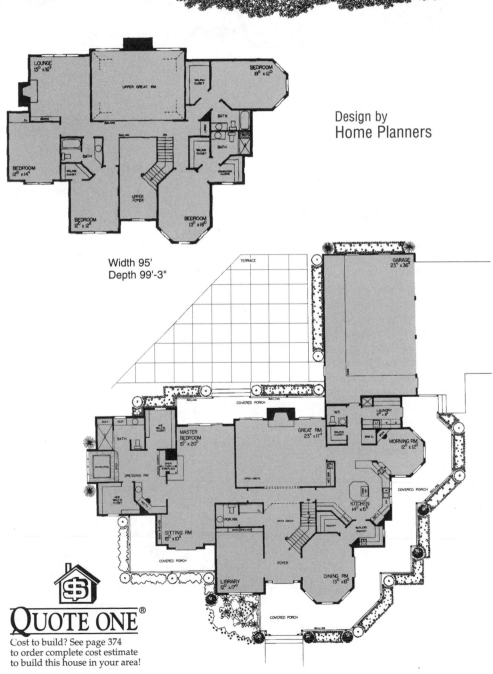

QUOTE ONE®

Cost to build? See page 374
to order complete cost estimate
to build this house in your area!

Design 8906

First Floor: 2,519 square feet
Second Floor: 787 square feet
Total: 3,306 square feet

● This comfortable farmhouse design begins with a wide veranda that wraps partially around the sides of the house. At its center is the entry leading to a central foyer bounded on the left by a formal dining room and on the right by a cozy study. The kitchen has a peninsular counter that overlooks the large family room and connects to the sunny breakfast room. Special features in these living spaces include a warming fireplace, a French door to a covered porch and built-in bookcases. The deluxe master suite is to the rear of the plan and contains its own sitting area and a grand bath. An additional bedroom is found on this floor and has a full bath and a walk-in closet. Upstairs are two more bedrooms and a full bath, plus a gameroom that everyone will enjoy.

Design by
Larry W. Garnett & Associates, Inc.

Width 67'
Depth 53'

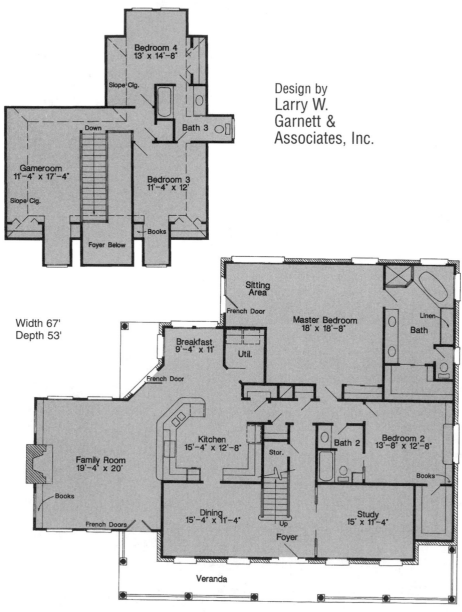

Quote One®

Cost to build? See page 374
to order complete cost estimate
to build this house in your area!

Bath

2-Way Fireplace

Master Bedroom
15'-8" x 16'

French Doors

Living Room
22'-8" x 16'-8"

Breakfast
10' x 10'

Util.

Porch

2-Car Garage

Storage

Kitchen
12'-4" x 12'

Bedroom 4
10' x 12'-8"

Foyer

Dining
16' x 13'-4"

Porch

Width 79'
Depth 60'-6"

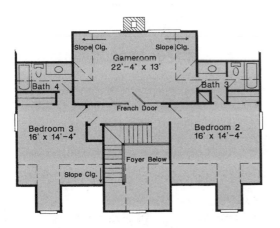

Slope Clg.   **Slope Clg.**

Gameroom
22'-4" x 13'

Bath 4

Bath 3

French Door

Bedroom 3
16' x 14'-4"

Bedroom 2
16' x 14'-4"

Foyer Below

Slope Clg.

Design by
**Larry W.
Garnett &
Associates, Inc.**

Design 9005

First Floor: 1,995 square feet
Second Floor: 1,077 square feet
Total: 3,072 square feet

● A wraparound front porch and
dormer windows give this home a
casual and comfortable appearance. A
leaded-glass transom above the front
door, along with the dormer window
in the sloped ceiling, fill the foyer
with natural light. The large living
room features French doors on each
side of an elegant fireplace, and a
built-in wet bar. An island cooktop,
along with a walk-in pantry are part
of the well-planned kitchen. The utility room, with extra work space, leads
to an attached two-car garage and
storage area. The master bedroom has
generous closet space and a two-way
fireplace opening into the master
bath. His and Hers lavatories, an
oversized tub and a glass-enclosed
shower complete this elegant master
bath. The second-floor balcony has
French doors opening into a large
game room. Bedroom 3 has a private
bath, while Bedroom 2 shares access
to a bath with the game room. Each
bedroom has a sloped ceiling and a
cozy alcove created by the dormer
window.

Width 88'-6"
Depth 50'-6"

Design 9910

First Floor: 2,565 square feet
Second Floor: 1,375 square feet
Total: 3,940 square feet

● A symmetrical facade with twin chimneys makes a grand statement. A covered porch welcomes visitors and provides a pleasant place to spend cool evenings. The entry foyer is flanked by formal living areas: a dining room and a living room, each with a fireplace. A third fireplace is the highlight of the expansive great room to the rear. An L-shaped kitchen offers a work island and a walk-in pantry for amenities and easily serves the nearby breakfast and sun rooms. The deck is accessible through the great room, the sun room or the master bedroom. The first-floor master bedroom suite is lavish in its luxuries: His and Hers walk-in closets, a sunny bay window and a sumptuous bath. The second floor offers three bedrooms, two full baths and plenty of storage space. This home is designed with a basement foundation.

Design by
Design Traditions

Design 2665

First Floor: 1,152 square feet
Second Floor: 1,152 square feet
Total: 2,304 square feet
(Excludes Guest Suite and Galleries)

● The origin of this house dates back to 1787 and George Washington's Mount Vernon. A keeping room with a pass-through to the kitchen and a fireplace with a built-in wood box, a formal dining room, a breakfast room and a formal living room with a fireplace on the first floor allow plenty of social possibilities. Separate guest quarters with a full bath, a lounge area and an upstairs studio which is connected to the main house by a gallery further enhance this home's livability. A matching gallery is located on the other side of the house and leads to the garage with a storage room or hobby room situated above. Four bedrooms with two full baths are found on the second floor, including the master suite with a fireplace. In the left wing, the guest bedroom/lounge with its upstairs study can be optionally designed as a game room with a spiral staircase and a loft area.

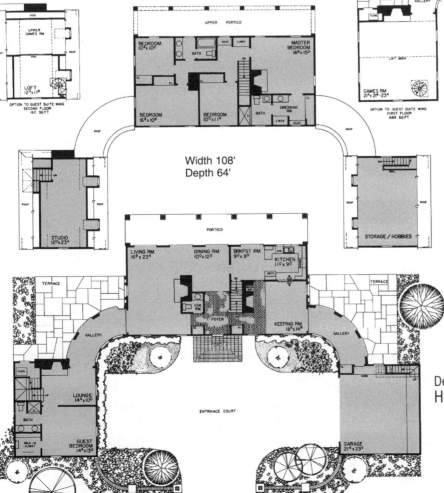

Width 108'
Depth 64'

Design by
Home Planners

Cost to build? See page 374 to order complete cost estimate to build this house in your area!

305

COPYRIGHT 1993 LARRY E. BELK

Design 8057

First Floor: 3,359 square feet
Second Floor: 2,174 square feet
Total: 5,533 square feet

● A truly unique luxury home, this farmhouse has all the amenities. The fantastic covered porch surrounds three sides of the home and provides a wonderful area for outdoor living. A two-story foyer angles to draw the eye through double arches to the elegant living room with a fireplace flanked by built-ins and an area for the grand piano. The kitchen, breakfast room and family room are grouped to provide clear views to the rear grounds. An office, with large walk-in storage, is provided off the kitchen. An enormous game room with wet bar, bath and walk-in closet is also downstairs. A study with a built-in aquarium features an adjoining utility area. Upstairs, the master bedroom with vaulted ceiling opens to a large upper sun deck. The master bath features all the extras with His and Hers vanities and walk-in closets, a separate shower and a whirlpool tub. Bedroom 4 has a private bath and can also serve as a master bedroom. Bedrooms 2 and 3 share a third bathroom.

Design by
Larry E. Belk
Designs

Width 96'-5"
Depth 85'-6"

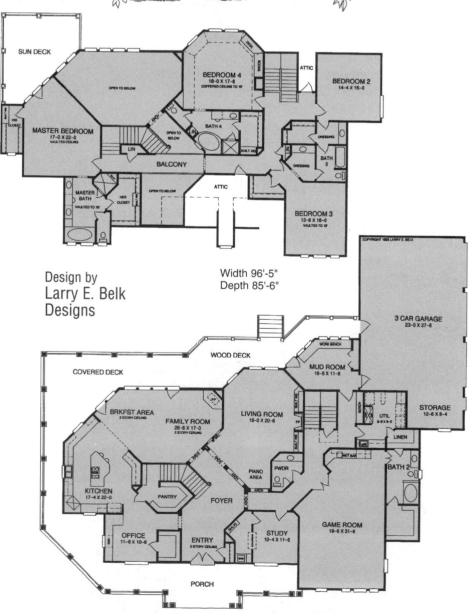

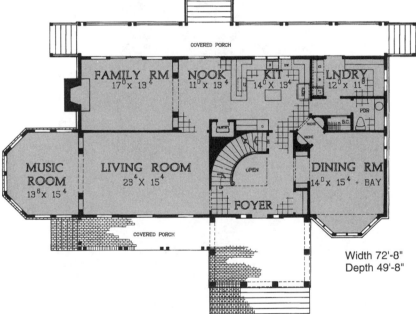

COVERED PORCH

| FAMILY RM 17⁰ x 13⁴ | NOOK 11⁰ x 13⁴ | KIT 14⁰ x 13⁴ | LNDRY 12⁰ x 11⁸ |

PANTRY

PDR

NICHE

B.C.

| MUSIC ROOM 13⁸ x 15⁴ | LIVING ROOM 23⁴ x 15⁴ | | DINING RM 14⁰ x 15⁴ + BAY |

OPEN

FOYER

COVERED PORCH

Width 72'-8"
Depth 49'-8"

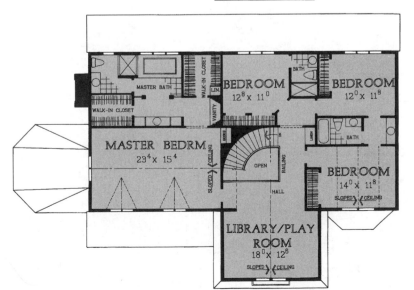

MASTER BATH

WALK-IN CLOSET

WALK-IN CLOSET

VANITY

| | BATH | |
| MASTER BEDRM 23⁴ x 15⁴ | BEDROOM 12⁸ x 11⁰ | BEDROOM 12⁰ x 11⁸ |

SLOPED CEILING

OPEN

RAILING

BATH

| | BEDROOM 14⁰ x 11⁸ |

HALL

SLOPED CEILING

LIBRARY/PLAY ROOM 18⁰ x 12⁸

SLOPED CEILING

Design 3512

First Floor: 1,983 square feet
Second Floor: 1,892 square feet
Total: 3,875 square feet

L **D**

● This home's large foyer features a dramatic curving staircase to the second floor. The center entrance floor plan offers efficient and flexible traffic patterns. Formal living areas are located to the front of the plan; informal living areas are to the rear. The formal dining room is big and has a delightful bay window. The formal living room is spacious and functions through a pleasingly detailed columned archway with the cheerful music room. The rear kitchen is U-shaped with an island work surface and a walk-in pantry. The adjacent breakfast nook functions through sliding glass doors with the porch. Four bedrooms, three baths and a huge library/playroom grace the upstairs.

Quote One®

Cost to build? See page 374
to order complete cost estimate
to build this house in your area!

Design by
Home Planners

Design 9889

First Floor: 2,161 square feet
Second Floor: 2,110 square feet
Total: 4,271 square feet

● A blend of stucco and stone create the charm in this country French estate home. The asymmetrical design and arched glass windows add to the European character. Inside, the plan offers a unique arrangement of rooms conducive to today's lifestyles. A living room and a dining room flank the foyer, creating a functional formal area. The large den or family room is positioned at the rear of the home with convenient access to the kitchen, patio and covered arbor. Equally accessible to the arbor and patio are the kitchen and breakfast/sitting area. A large butler's pantry is located near the kitchen and dining room. Upstairs, the vaulted master suite and three large bedrooms provide private retreats. This home is designed with a basement foundation.

Design by
Design Traditions

Width 76'-2"
Depth 60'-11"

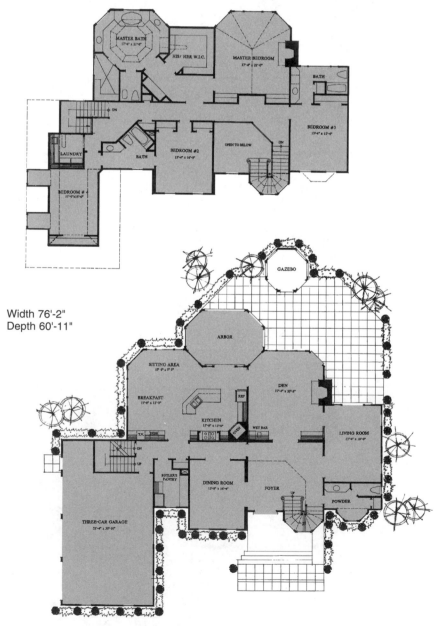

Contemporary Compositions:
An array of modern designs

Design by
Home Planners

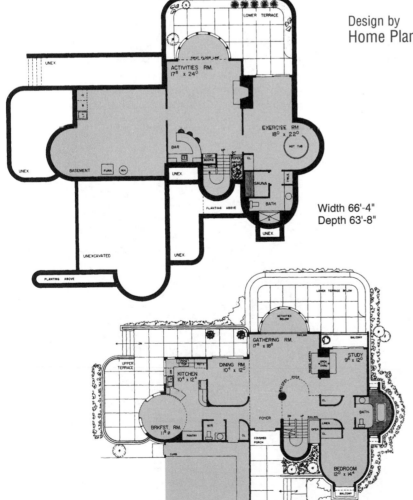

Width 66'-4"
Depth 63'-8"

Design 2926

Main Level: 1,570 square feet
Upper Level: 598 square feet
Lower Level: 1,080 square feet
Total: 3,248 square feet

● An incredible use of curving lines and circles in this ultra-modern design makes for an interesting floor plan. The dramatic use of balconies and overlooks in the plan highlights a first-floor gathering room with a fireplace open to the study, and formal dining room and kitchen with a curved breakfast room. A uniquely shaped bedroom on this floor has a balcony and full bath. Access the second floor by a curved stair to find the master suite which dominates this floor. A lower-level activities room with a bar and a fireplace, and an exercise room with an attached sauna, hot tub and bath overlook the lower terrace. Take special note of the generous use of skylights throughout.

Design 8891

First Floor: 1,689 square feet
Second Floor: 534 square feet
Total: 2,223 square feet

● Interesting lattice detail, a combination of brick and shingle siding and rounded accent walls make this home unique in appearance. Inside, smaller front living and dining rooms are augmented by larger rear-oriented family and breakfast areas. The L-shaped kitchen offers a walk-in pantry and a cooktop work island. A courtyard circled off the master bed-room focuses the start of yard development and highlights the forms of the house. The luxurious and stylish master bedroom suite has a very special bath with a platform tub divided from the glass-walled shower. Upstairs, two bed-rooms and a loft share ample proportions and a hall bath. The two-car garage connects to the laundry/mudroom.

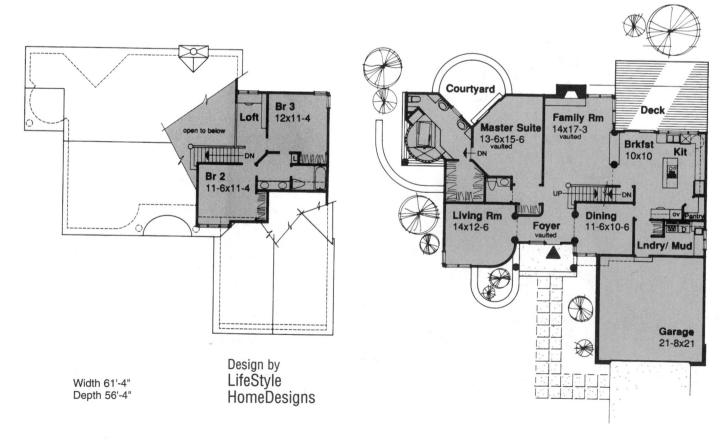

Width 61'-4"
Depth 56'-4"

Design by
LifeStyle
HomeDesigns

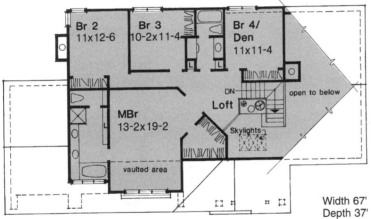

Br 2
11x12-6

Br 3
10-2x11-4

Br 4/ Den
11x11-4

DN

open to below

Loft

MBr
13-2x19-2

Skylights

vaulted area

Width 67'
Depth 37'

Design by
LifeStyle
HomeDesigns

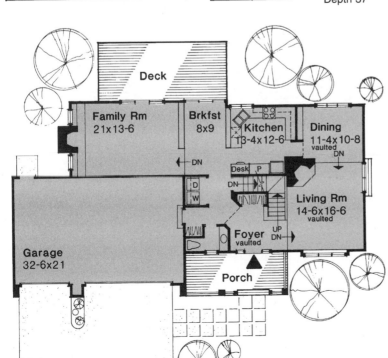

Deck

Family Rm
21x13-6

Brkfst
8x9

Kitchen
13-4x12-6

Dining
11-4x10-8
vaulted

DN

Desk P

DN

D
W

Living Rm
14-6x16-6
vaulted

Foyer
vaulted

UP
DN

Garage
32-6x21

Porch

Design 8899

First Floor: 1,290 square feet
Second Floor: 1,155 square feet
Total: 2,445 square feet

● A vaulted, skylit foyer with a dramatic staircase opens this plan. To the right, a gracious sunken living room with a fireplace opens to a dining room. The full kitchen is conveniently located between the dining room and the sunny breakfast room. The sunken family room features a central hearth and built-in cabinets. A rear deck enhances outdoor livability and is accessible from both the breakfast and family rooms. On the second floor, four bedrooms—or three and a den—include a spacious master suite. Its bath includes a separate shower and tub and dual lavatories.

Design 9572

First Floor: 1,180 square feet
Second Floor: 1,025 square feet
Total: 2,205 square feet

● For lots that slope up from the street, this plan has much to offer. A three-car garage opens to a laundry room. Through here, family living areas gain attention: a family room with a fireplace, a bayed breakfast nook and an ample kitchen setting the stage. Double doors lead to outdoor livability from the dining room. Formal areas include a front-facing living room with a bay window and a tier-ceilinged dining room. Upstairs, a spacious master bedroom enjoys a private luxury bath and a walk-in closet. Three family bedrooms include two with window seats.

Width 53'
Depth 54'

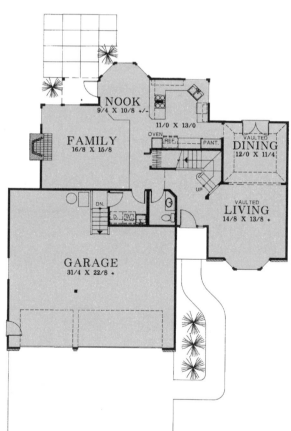

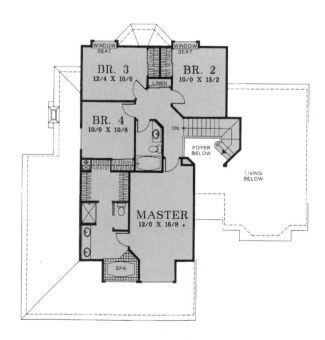

Design by
**Alan Mascord
Design Associates, Inc.**

Design 9551

First Floor: 1,682 square feet
Second Floor: 1,589 square feet
Total: 3,271 square feet
Bonus Room: 287 square feet

● Wood shingles, a double-door glass entry and varying roof lines add a special twist to this otherwise traditional home. The plan is designed for easy living. To the right of the foyer are the formal living and dining rooms. Adjacent to the dining area is an efficient, step-saving kitchen featuring a cooktop island and a walk-in pantry. The nearby breakfast nook offers dual access to the terrace and combines well with the family room for family gatherings. The second floor contains three bedrooms, a bath and the master suite. Two walk-in closets lead to the unique and luxurious master bath. A den, with a detailed ceiling and offering access to a private deck, and a bonus room complete the upstairs.

Width 49'
Depth 52'

FAMILY
21/6 X 17/4 +/-
(10' CLG.)

NOOK
12/0 X 14/6
(10' CLG.)

14/6 X 16/6

WOOD

10/10 X 8/4

DINING
13/0 X 11/0
(10' CLG.)

DESK

PAN.

UP

LIVING
13/0 X 15/2
(10' CLG.)

GARAGE
21/4 X 21/8

DECK OVER

TERRACE

DECK

BR. 3
11/0 X 15/8
(9' CLG.)

BR. 2
11/0 X 11/2
(9' CLG.)

DEN
10/8 X 11/2
(10' CLG.)

MASTER
13/0 X 16/6
(10' CLG.)

BR. 4
11/0 X 12/4
(9' CLG.)

LINEN

DN.

FOYER BELOW

DN.

(10' CLG.)

TUB

BONUS RM.
13/0 X 13/6 +
(9' CLG.)

Design by
**Alan Mascord
Design Associates, Inc.**

313

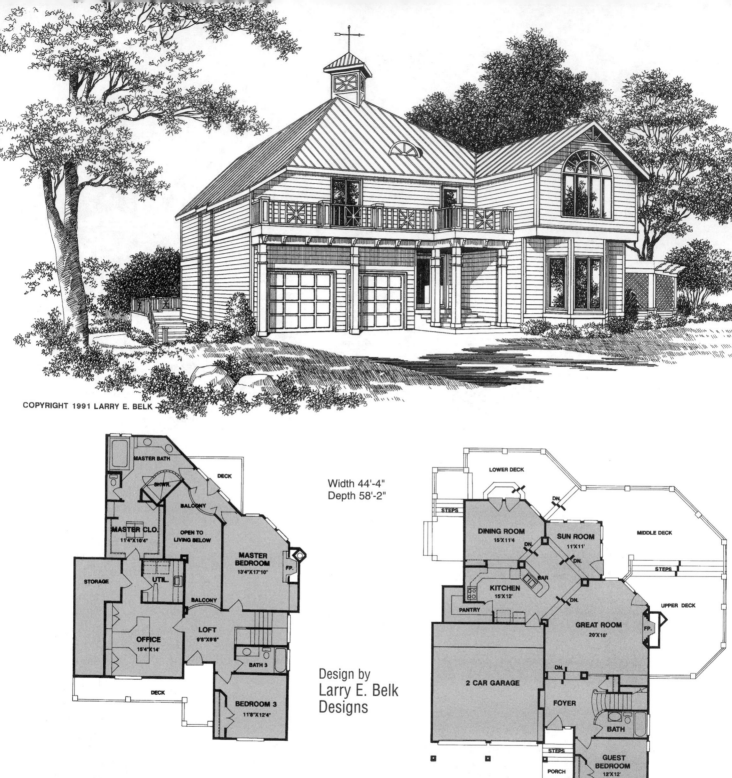

Width 44'-4"
Depth 58'-2"

Design by
Larry E. Belk
Designs

Design 8001

First Floor: 1,309 square feet
Second Floor: 1,343 square feet
Total: 2,652 square feet

● Clean, contemporary lines set this home apart and make it a stand out in any location. The metal roof and roof-top cupola rotated on a 45-degree angle add interest. Twin chimneys located on the right side of the house are constructed on a 45-degree angle to continue the theme. Stunning is the word when the front door opens on this home. Near the foyer, a 28-foot shaft opens from floor level to the top of the cupola. Remote control transoms in the cupola open automatically to increase ventilation. The great room, sun room, dining room and kitchen are all adjacent to provide areas for entertaining.

Originally designed for a sloping site, the home incorporates multiple levels inside. Additionally, there is access to a series of multi-level outside decks from the dining room, sun room and great room. All these areas have at least one glass wall overlooking the rear. The master bedroom and bath upstairs are bridged by a pipe-rail balcony that provides access to a rear outside deck. The master suite includes a huge master closet. Additional storage is located off the hallway to the office.

Design by
Home Planners

Width 65'
Depth 51'-8"

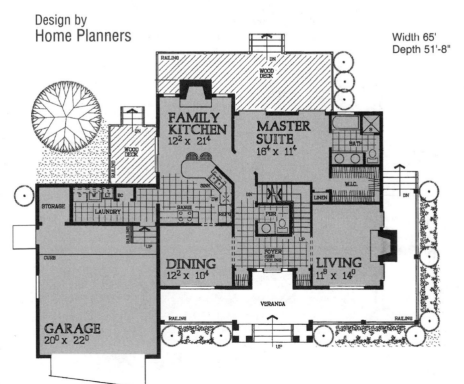

Design 3467

First Floor: 1,276 square feet
Second Floor: 658 square feet
Total: 1,934 square feet

L

● A projecting front gable supported by columns effectively frames the paneled front door of this house while creating an impressive and inviting entrance. Inside, both formal living and dining rooms flank the foyer and deliver an extra measure of livability through thoughtful traffic patterns. A fireplace in the living room is bordered by glass doors leading to a side porch. For more casual living, the kitchen opens over a snack bar to the family living area. Note the central fireplace and sliding glass doors to the raised deck outside. Located at the rear of the first floor, the master bedroom is lavish in its accommodations including a private bath and a walk-in closet. Upstairs, two family bedrooms with dormers and nearby built-in desks share a full hall bath.

QUOTE ONE®
Cost to build? See page 374
to order complete cost estimate
to build this house in your area!

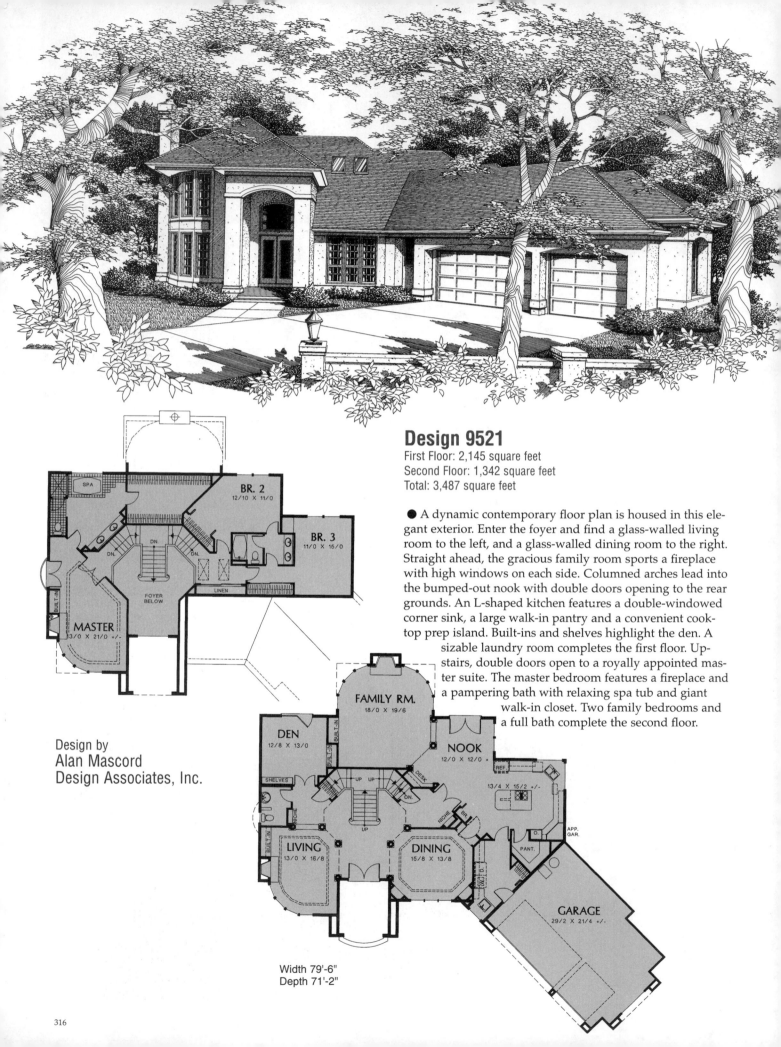

Design 9521

First Floor: 2,145 square feet
Second Floor: 1,342 square feet
Total: 3,487 square feet

● A dynamic contemporary floor plan is housed in this elegant exterior. Enter the foyer and find a glass-walled living room to the left, and a glass-walled dining room to the right. Straight ahead, the gracious family room sports a fireplace with high windows on each side. Columned arches lead into the bumped-out nook with double doors opening to the rear grounds. An L-shaped kitchen features a double-windowed corner sink, a large walk-in pantry and a convenient cook-top prep island. Built-ins and shelves highlight the den. A sizable laundry room completes the first floor. Upstairs, double doors open to a royally appointed master suite. The master bedroom features a fireplace and a pampering bath with relaxing spa tub and giant walk-in closet. Two family bedrooms and a full bath complete the second floor.

Design by
Alan Mascord
Design Associates, Inc.

Width 79'-6"
Depth 71'-2"

Design 2826 First Floor: 1,112 square feet
Second Floor: 881 square feet; Total: 1,993 square feet

D

Width 49'
Depth 54'-4"

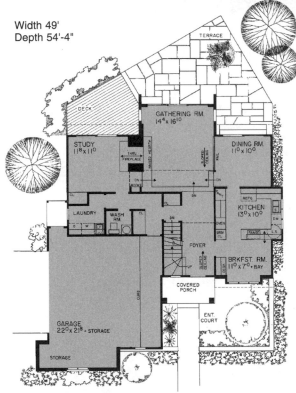

Alternate Dining Room Plan

● This is an outstanding example of the type of informal, traditional-style architecture that has captured the modern imagination. Notice the spacious sunken gathering room with sliding glass doors to the rear terrace, which shares a through-fireplace with the quiet study that offers access to a rear deck. Formal and informal dining areas are nicely separated by a roomy U-shaped kitchen. Upstairs, the master bedroom suite is sure to please, while two family bedrooms and a lounge fulfill the family's needs.

Design by
Home Planners

QUOTE ONE®
Cost to build? See page 374
to order complete cost estimate
to build this house in your area!

© The Sater Group, Inc.

Design 6649

First Floor: 3,035 square feet
Second Floor: 945 square feet
Total: 3,980 square feet

● Rich custom details in this lovely
transitional home provide luxury for
the most discriminating homeowners.
To the left of the foyer is the private
master suite. The lavish bath contains
a large walk-in closet, dual vanities
and a compartmented toilet. An adjacent study combines well with the
suite. The dining room is perfect for
formal occasions and the nearby
kitchen with its island prep center
and eating nook are ideal for casual
meals. Completing this area is a
leisure room with a built-in wet bar.
The second floor accommodates a loft,
two bedrooms with private baths, a
large deck and a sun deck.

Design by
**The Sater
Design Collection**

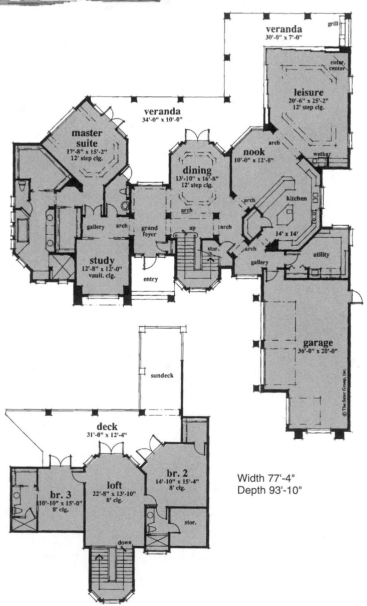

Width 77'-4"
Depth 93'-10"

HOLZHALER INC. 94

veranda
40'-0" x 9'-0"

fireplace

leisure
19'-4" x 17'-4"
10' high clg.

optional
entertainment
center

master suite
15'-0" x 18'-2"
11' step clg.

living
20'-2" x 15'-8"
2 story clg.

pantry

desk

nook
9'-0" x 11'-0"

kitchen
12' x 12'

up

utility

study
13'-4" x 12'-0"
12'-6" high clg.

foyer

dining
13'-6" x 14'-0"
vault. clg.

entry

garage
22'-4" x 42'-8"

Width 76'
Depth 90'

deck

loft
19'-8" x 14'-4"

wetbar

down

open to
living below

br. 3
16'-10" x 11'-4"
9'-4" clg.

br. 2
11'-4" x 14'-10"
9'-4" clg.

Design 6646

First Floor: 2,551 square feet
Second Floor: 1,037 square feet
Total: 3,588 square feet

● This beautiful home has many attributes. These include a bowed dining room and a living room with a fireplace and outdoor access. For family gatherings, the kitchen remains open to the living areas. A study off the foyer will be much appreciated. A full bath leads to the outdoors—perfect for poolside. The master suite enjoys its own personal luxury bath with a whirlpool tub, dual lavatories, a compartmented toilet and bidet and a separate shower. Dual walk-in closets provide ample storage space. Upstairs, two bedrooms share a full bath. A loft with a wet bar accommodates playtime. A wraparound deck is an added feature.

Design by
The Sater Design Collection

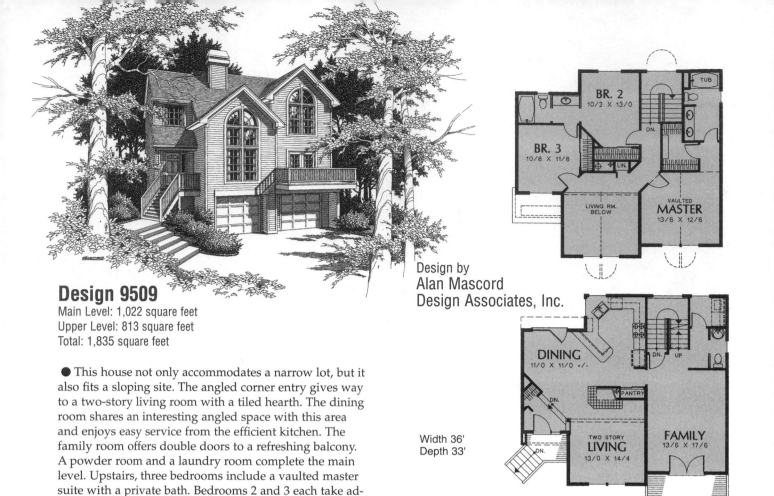

Design 9509

Main Level: 1,022 square feet
Upper Level: 813 square feet
Total: 1,835 square feet

● This house not only accommodates a narrow lot, but it also fits a sloping site. The angled corner entry gives way to a two-story living room with a tiled hearth. The dining room shares an interesting angled space with this area and enjoys easy service from the efficient kitchen. The family room offers double doors to a refreshing balcony. A powder room and a laundry room complete the main level. Upstairs, three bedrooms include a vaulted master suite with a private bath. Bedrooms 2 and 3 each take advantage of direct access to a full bath.

Design by
Alan Mascord
Design Associates, Inc.

Width 36'
Depth 33'

Design 9610

First Floor: 1,209 square feet
Second Floor: 525 square feet
Total: 1,734 square feet

● A well-proportioned, compact house such as this never feels cramped, and its special floor plan makes it seem larger than it really is. From the two-story entrance foyer move to the living/dining area with cathedral ceiling and skylights. The master suite features its own bath with double-bowl vanity, whirlpool tub and shower. Look for walk-in closets here as well as in the two family bedrooms upstairs. A large deck off the living area allows space for a hot tub.

Design by
Donald A.
Gardner,
Architects, Inc.

Width 49'
Depth 48'-6"

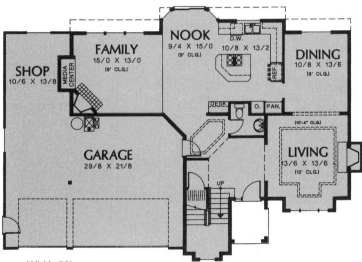

Width 58'
Depth 42'

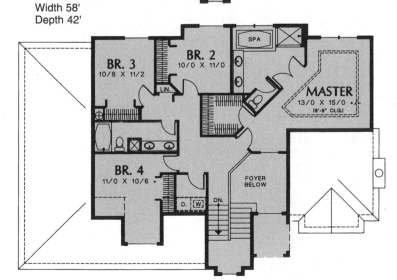

Design 9583

First Floor: 1,216 square feet
Second Floor: 1,192 square feet
Total: 2,408 square feet
Optional Office: 140 square feet

● With multiple gables, a pillared front porch and multi-pane windows, this home gives variety a good name. Inside the two-story foyer, fine traffic patterns emerge. To the right is the formal living room with a detailed ceiling and a fireplace. An L-shaped kitchen, with a cooktop work island, separates the formal dining room from the bay-windowed breakfast nook. Graced by a corner fireplace and a built-in media center, the family room is sure to please. Upstairs, three family bedrooms share a full bath with twin vanities and have easy access to the laundry room. A deluxe master bedroom suite is amenity filled. From the detailed ceiling and a walk-in closet, to double French doors leading to a lavish master bath, this room is ready to pamper you. A three-car garage will shelter the family fleet and at the back is an area that can be either a workshop or a cozy home office.

Design by
Alan Mascord
Design Associates, Inc.

Design 8674

First Floor: 1,816 square feet
Second Floor: 703 square feet
Total: 2,519 square feet

● No matter where you're building, this design offers two exteriors to heighten possibilities. The double-door entry opens to the combined formal living and dining areas. Nearby, the kitchen enjoys ample space for gourmet-meal preparations, as well as an attached breakfast nook. In the family room, a volume ceiling and a fireplace are sure to please. The master bedroom, located at the rear of the first floor, has access to the covered patio. It also sports a bath with a double-bowl lavatory, a garden tub and a large walk-in closet. On the second floor, three bedrooms enjoy peace and quiet and share a hall bath. An option for a loft is included in the set blueprints.

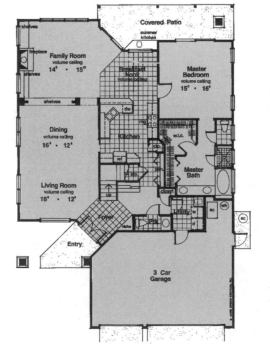

Width 45'
Depth 67'-6"

Design by
Home Design
Services, Inc.

Design 8671

First Floor: 1,657 square feet
Second Floor: 678 square feet
Total: 2,335 square feet

● Columns add the finishing touches to a home with a choice of facades. The double-door entry opens to the foyer with a front-to-back view. The adjacent vaulted living room has sliding glass doors to the covered patio. The kitchen is open to both the family room and the sunny breakfast room. Interesting angles and a volume ceiling add appeal to the formal dining room. The first-floor master bedroom features twin vanities, a separate tub and shower and a large walk-in closet. A study or bedroom completes this level. Upstairs, three additional bedrooms share a full bath with twin vanities. The plan includes both elevations.

Design by
Home Design
Services, Inc.

Width 58'-8"
Depth 56'

Alt. Elevation

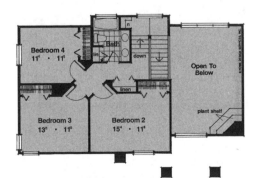

323

Design 9566

First Floor: 2,515 square feet
Second Floor: 2,131 square feet
Total: 4,646 square feet

● A reception-size foyer provides a grand entrance to this contemporary stucco home. To the left, graceful columns lead to the bayed living room and dining room, combined for the finest formal entertaining space. A quiet den with built-ins and graced with another bay window is located through double doors to the right. The rear of the first floor is designed for casual living. The family room with its warming hearth shares space with an eating nook and a spacious island kitchen. Split-bedroom planning is found on the second floor. The romantic master suite features a unique bath designed for relaxation and offers an enormous walk-in closet. Three secondary bedrooms are contained on the second floor as well as a media room for electronics buffs. Notice the ceiling detail throughout.

Design by
Alan Mascord
Design Associates, Inc.

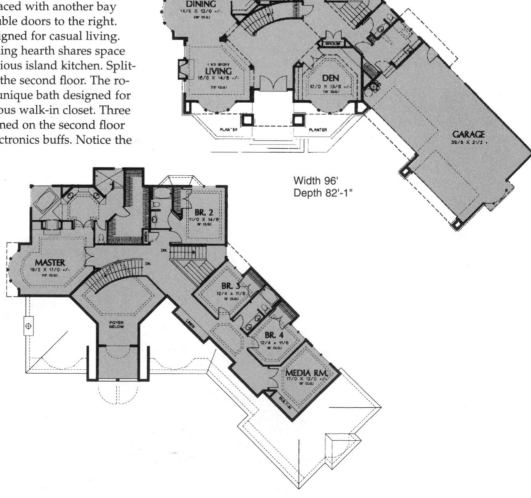

Width 96'
Depth 82'-1"

Design 3558

First Floor: 2,328 square feet
Second Floor: 603 square feet
Total: 2,931 square feet

L **D**

● This home will keep even the most active family from feeling cramped. A broad foyer opens to a living room that measures 24 feet across and features sliding glass doors to a rear terrace and a covered porch. Adjacent to the kitchen is a conversation area with additional access to the covered porch, a snack bar, fireplace and a window bay. A butler's pantry leads to the formal dining room. Placed conveniently on the first floor, the master suite features a roomy bath with a huge walk-in closet and dual vanities. A library with plenty of blank wall space for bookcases completes this level. Two large bedrooms are found on the second floor and share a full hall bath.

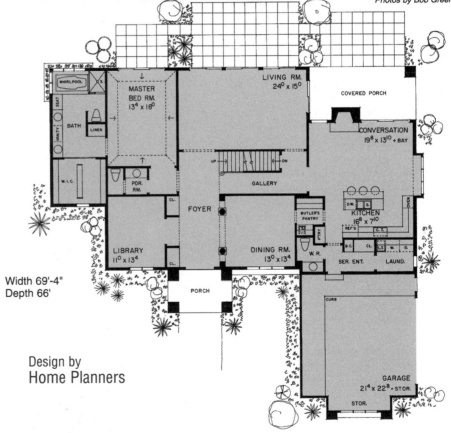

Width 69'-4"
Depth 66'

Design by
Home Planners

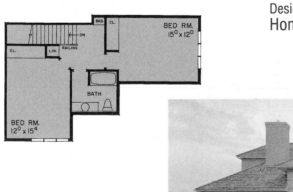

QUOTE ONE®

Cost to build? See page 374
to order complete cost estimate
to build this house in your area!

Design 9400

First Floor: 1,618 square feet
Second Floor: 1,212 square feet
Total: 2,830 square feet
Bonus Room: 376 square feet

● This attractive European-styled plan is enhanced by a stucco finish and arched windows complementing the facade. The two-story foyer, with its angled stair, opens to the dramatically vaulted living room on one side and den with French doors on the other. An efficient L-shaped island kitchen works well with the formal dining room to its left and a sunny nook to the right. A bayed family room with a warming hearth completes this floor. Upstairs a sumptuous master suite includes a spa tub, a shower, twin vanities and a large walk-in closet. Two family bedrooms share a full skylit bath with twin vanities. Over the garage is a vaulted bonus room, perfect as a game or hobby room.

Design by
**Alan Mascord
Design Associates, Inc.**

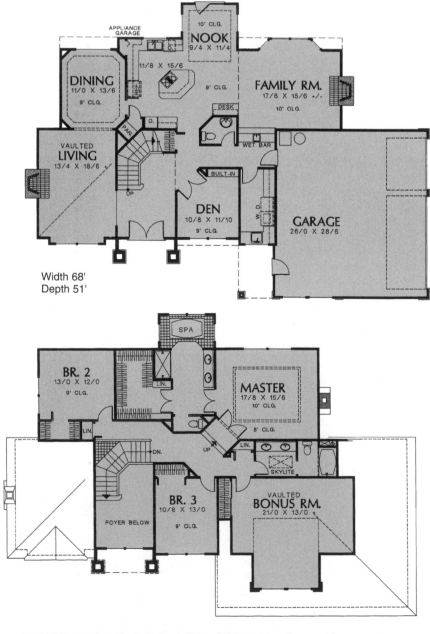

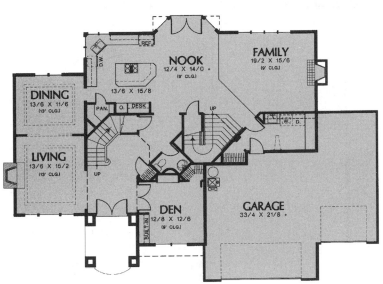

Width 72'
Depth 52'

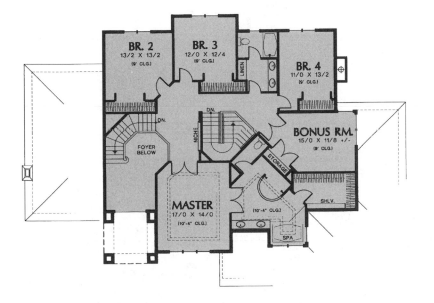

Design 9562

First Floor: 1,915 square feet
Second Floor: 1,469 square feet
Total: 3,384 square feet
Bonus Room: 202 square feet

● Reminiscent of Prairie Style or Craftsman homes from earlier in this century, this home's facade leans toward contemporary. The floor plan also is contemporary. It includes a den with built-ins and a large kitchen with a gourmet island cooktop, which leaves room for appliances aplenty. Separate formal and informal living areas accommodate all occasions. A three-car garage makes room for automobiles, bicycles, or boats. Upstairs there are four bedrooms, including a master bedroom suite. A bonus room with storage space could serve as play space for growing children.

Design by
**Alan Mascord
Design Associates, Inc.**

327

© HOME DESIGN SERVICES, INC.

J.N. HANSEN P.T.L.

Design 8659

First Floor: 1,230 square feet
Second Floor: 649 square feet
Total: 1,879 square feet

● The tiled foyer of this two-story home opens to a living/dining space with a soaring ceiling, a fireplace in the living room and access to a covered patio that invites outdoor livability. The kitchen has an oversized, sunny breakfast area with a volume ceiling. The first-floor master bedroom offers privacy with its sumptuous bath; a corner soaking tub, dual lavatories and a compartmented toilet lend character to the room. Upstairs, a loft overlooking the living spaces could become a third bedroom. One of the family bedrooms features a walk-in closet. Both bedrooms share a generous hall bath.

Design by
Home Design
Services, Inc.

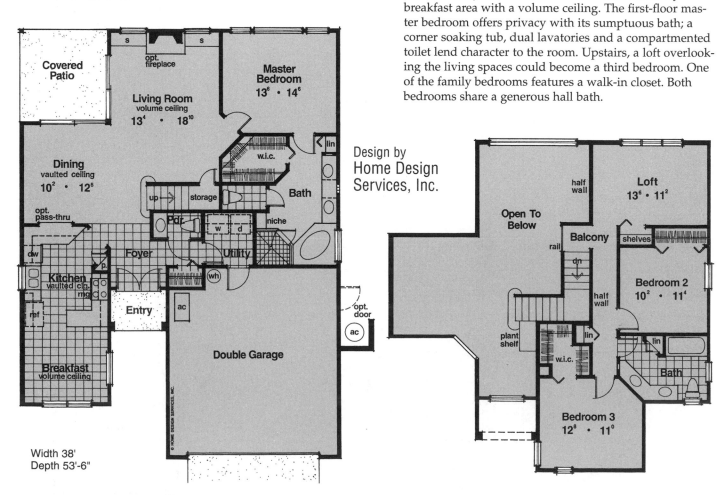

Design 8660

First Floor: 1,766 square feet
Second Floor: 880 square feet
Total: 2,646 square feet

● A striking use of keystone banding helps to create the majestic elevation of this home. Inside, versatility is the operative word for this plan and its large spaces: formal entertaining, casual family living—all take off with the expansive dining, family and game rooms. Access to the covered patio is found in the master bedroom, the game room and the breakfast area.

The master bedroom, with its vaulted ceiling, features His and Hers closets and a bath with a soaking tub and a large shower. Upstairs, three bedrooms share a loft space perfect for the kids. A cleverly arranged hall bath offers a double-bowl vanity. If desired, Bedroom 2 may support a private full bath.

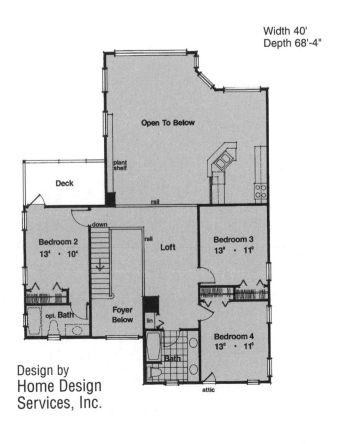

Width 40'
Depth 68'-4"

Design by
Home Design
Services, Inc.

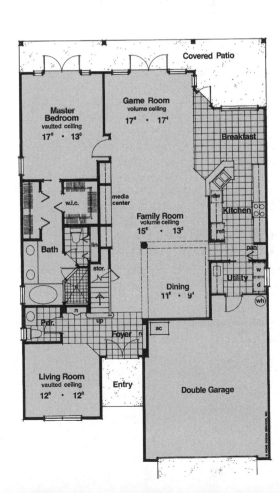

© The Sater Group, Inc.

HOLZHAUER INC. 94

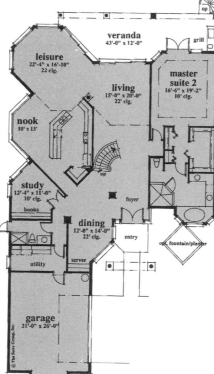

Design by
**The Sater
Design Collection**

Design 6648

First Floor: 2,618 square feet
Second Floor: 1,945 square feet
Total: 4,563 square feet

● Double doors open to a grand foyer
with a formal dining room to the left. The
nearby kitchen and nook combine with a
multi-windowed two-story leisure room
for more casual living, and an adjacent
two-story living room for more formal pursuits. The first-floor master suite features a
large walk-in closet, a luxurious bath and
access to the rear veranda. The second floor
contains a guest suite with a private bath
and balcony, a bedroom/bonus room with
its own balcony and a second master suite.
This second master bedroom is highlighted
by double doors opening onto a private
deck. A walk-in closet, a spacious bath with
a bumped-out tub and a separate shower
provide finishing touches to this private
suite.

Width 54'-8"
Depth 97'-4"

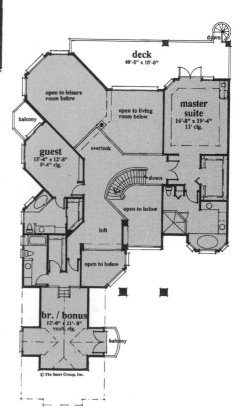

J.N. HANSEN

Design 8683

First Floor: 2,254 square feet
Second Floor: 608 square feet
Total: 2,862 square feet

● Indoor/outdoor relationships are enhanced by the beautiful courtyard that decorates the center of this home. A gallery provides views of the courtyard and leads to a kitchen featuring a center work island and an adjacent breakfast room offering easy access to the back yard. Combined with the family room, this space will be a favorite for informal gatherings. To the left, the gallery leads to the formal living room and master suite. The secluded master bedroom features a tray ceiling and double doors that lead to a covered patio. Retreat to the master bath, where a relaxing tub awaits to pamper. The second floor contains a full bath shared by Bedroom 3 and 4 and a loft with its own balcony that provides flexible space for an additional bedroom.

Covered Patio

opt.
Pool
Bath

Breakfast

Family Room
volume ceiling
17⁸ · 16⁰

fireplace

summer
kitchen

volume
ceiling

dw

Kitchen

up

Covered Patio

Courtyard

w.i.c. cl

Master
Bedroom
volume ceiling
20⁰ · 14⁰

pan

ref

Bedroom 2
volume ceiling
11⁴ · 11⁰

Bath

m

Foyer

Dining
volume ceiling
14⁴ · 11⁰

Bath

lin

Living Room
volume ceiling
15⁴ · 11⁴

Entry

Utility

w d

wh

ac

w.i.c.

Workshop

Width 66'
Depth 78'-10"

Double Garage

Balcony

Bath

opt. **Bedroom 5**
volume ceiling
13⁰ · 11⁰

Design by
**Home Design
Services, Inc.**

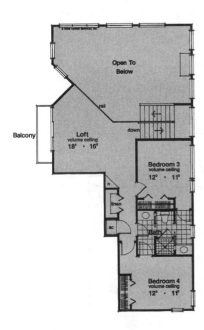

Open To
Below

rail

Balcony

Loft
volume ceiling
18⁴ · 16⁰

down

Bedroom 3
volume ceiling
12⁰ · 11⁰

linen

ac

Bath

Bedroom 4
volume ceiling
12⁴ · 11⁰

Design 9446

First floor: 1,600 square feet
Second floor: 1,123 square feet
Total: 2,723 square feet

● Beyond the contemporary facade of this home lies a highly functional floor plan. First-floor living areas include formal living and dining rooms, a private den, and a large family room that connects directly to the breakfast nook and island kitchen. The upper level contains three bedrooms, including a master suite with a nine-foot tray ceiling and a sumptuous master bath which encompasses a huge walk-in closet, a whirlpool spa and a double vanity in the bath. A fine hall bath completes this floor.

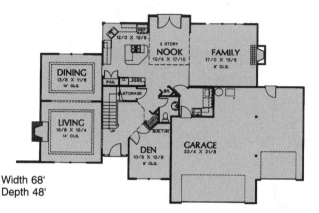

Width 68'
Depth 48'

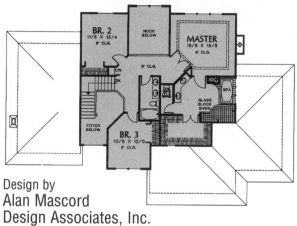

Design by
Alan Mascord
Design Associates, Inc.

Width 40'-7"
Depth 57'-8"

Design by
Home Planners

Design 3456

First Floor: 1,130 square feet
Second Floor: 1,189 square feet
Total: 2,319 square feet

L

● This volume-look home's angled entry opens to a wealth of living potential with a media room to the right and formal living and dining rooms to the left. A covered porch, accessed from both the dining and breakfast rooms, adds outdoor dining possibilities. The kitchen utilizes a built-in desk and a snack bar pass-through to the breakfast area. Upstairs, four bedrooms include a master suite with a balcony and three family bedrooms.

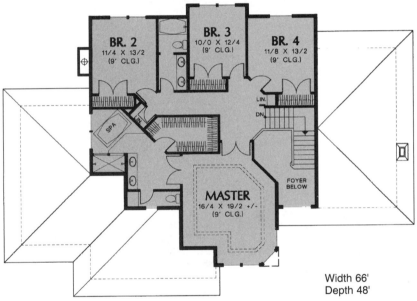

Width 66'
Depth 48'

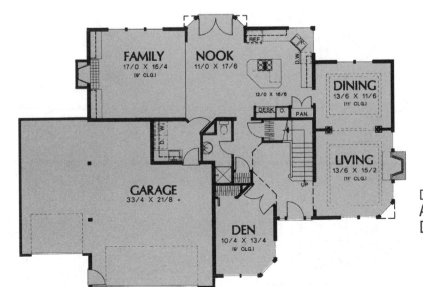

Design 9595

First Floor: 1,575 square feet
Second Floor: 1,338 square feet
Total: 2,913 square feet

● This two-story is impressive from
the first glance. A two-story bay window graces both the cozy den on the
first floor and the deluxe master suite
on the second floor. Inside, to the
right of the foyer is the formal living
room, enhanced by a warming fireplace. This room opens at the rear of
the plan into a formal dining room
which is just steps away from a large
and efficient island kitchen. Casual
living is comfortable in the attached
nook, with the nearby family room
sporting a second fireplace. Upstairs,
three family bedrooms offer plenty of
storage and share a hall bath. The
master suite is impressive with its
tray ceiling, large walk-in closet, twin
vanities and corner spa. A three-car
garage easily holds the family fleet.

Design by
Alan Mascord
Design Associates, Inc.

333

Design 8679

First Floor: 2,531 square feet
Second Floor: 669 square feet
Total: 3,200 square feet

● This exquisite brick and stucco contemporary takes its que from the tradition of Frank Lloyd Wright. The formal living and dining area combine to provide a spectacular view of the rear grounds. Unique best describes the private master suite, highlighted by a mitered bow window, a raised sitting area complete with a wet bar, oversized His and Hers walk-in closets and a lavish master bath complete with a relaxing corner tub, a separate shower and twin vanities. The family living area encompasses the left portion of the plan, featuring a spacious family room with a corner fireplace, access to the covered patio from the breakfast area and a step-saving kitchen. Bedroom 2 connects to a private bath. Upstairs, two bedrooms share a balcony, a sitting room and full bath.

Design by
Home Design
Services, Inc.

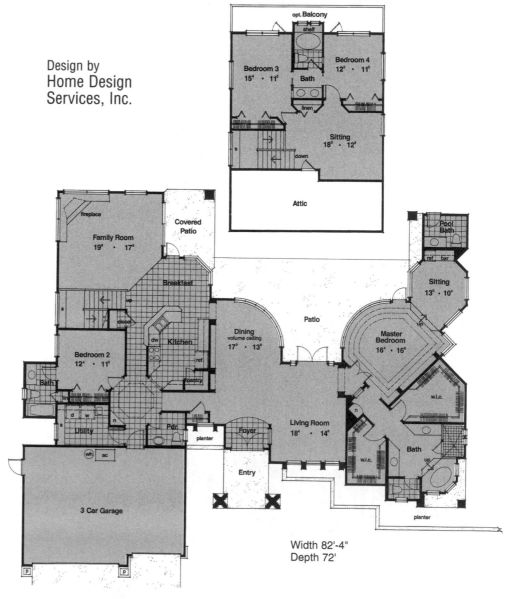

Width 82'-4"
Depth 72'

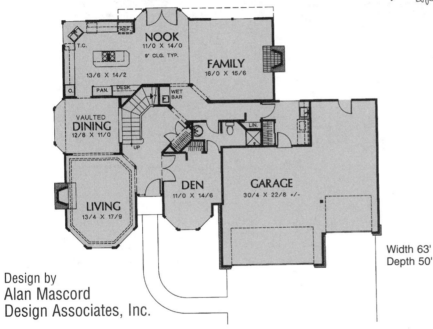

NOOK
11/0 X 14/0
9' CLG. TYP.

FAMILY
18/0 X 15/6

REF.

T.C.

13/6 X 14/2

O.

PAN. DESK

WET BAR

VAULTED
DINING
12/8 X 11/0

UP

LIN.

DEN
11/0 X 14/6

GARAGE
30/4 X 22/8 +/-

LIVING
13/4 X 17/9

Design by
Alan Mascord
Design Associates, Inc.

Width 63'
Depth 50'

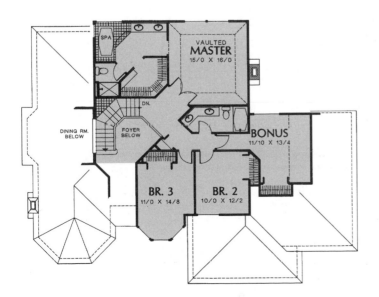

SPA

VAULTED
MASTER
15/0 X 16/0

DN.

DINING RM.
BELOW

FOYER
BELOW

BONUS
11/10 X 13/4

BR. 3
11/0 X 14/8

BR. 2
10/0 X 12/2

Design 9478

First Floor: 1,586 square feet
Second Floor: 960 square feet
Total: 2,546 square feet

● This exquisite plan features two tower structures that enhance its dramatic facade. Inside, it contains a beautifully functioning room arrangement that caters to family lifestyles. The living areas radiate around the central hallway which also contains the stairway to the second floor. The living room is large and open, convenient for both casual and formal occasions and opens onto the formal dining room which is graced by a bay window. The nearby den is further enhanced by a second bay window and an attached full bath, making the room perfect for use as a guest suite. Three bedrooms upstairs include two family bedrooms and a grand master suite with a bath fit for a king. An oversized walk-in closet and vaulted ceiling are found here. Bonus space over the garage can be developed at a later time to suit changing needs.

Design 3311

First Floor: 2,662 square feet
Lower Level: 1,548 square feet
Total: 4,210 square feet

L D

● Here's a hillside haven for family living with plenty of room to entertain in style. Enter the main level from a dramatic columned portico that leads to a large entry hall. The gathering room, graced by a fireplace and sliding glass doors to the rear deck, is straight back and adjoins a formal dining area. A true gourmet kitchen with plenty of room for casual eating and conversation is nearby. The abundantly appointed master suite on this level is complemented by a luxurious bath complete with His and Hers walk-in closets, a whirlpool tub in a bumped-out bay and a separate shower. Note the media room to the front of the house. On the lower level are two more bedrooms—each with access to the rear terrace, a full bath, a large activity area with a fireplace and a convenient summer kitchen.

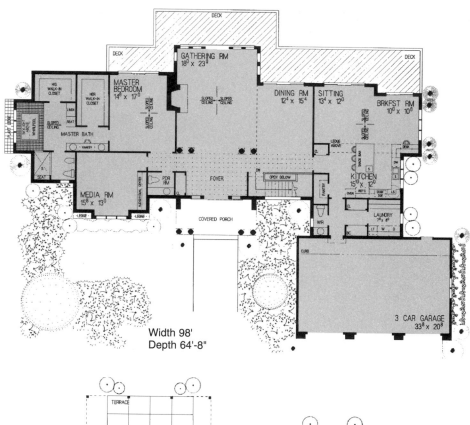

Width 98'
Depth 64'-8"

Quote One®

Cost to build? See page 374
to order complete cost estimate
to build this house in your area!

Design by
Home Planners

Design 3450

First Floor: 1,801 square feet
Second Floor: 1,086 square feet
Total: 2,887 square feet

L **D**

● The striking facade of this two-story includes multiple rooflines, arch topped windows and a covered front porch with four columns. To the left of the two-story foyer is a large gathering room with a fireplace and bay window. The adjoining dining room leads to a covered side porch. The kitchen includes a snack bar, a pantry, a desk and an eating area. The first-floor master suite provides a spacious bath with a walk-in closet, a whirlpool and a shower. Also on the first floor: a study and a garage workshop. Two family bedrooms and a lavish guest suite share the second floor.

Quote One®

Cost to build? See page 374
to order complete cost estimate
to build this house in your area!

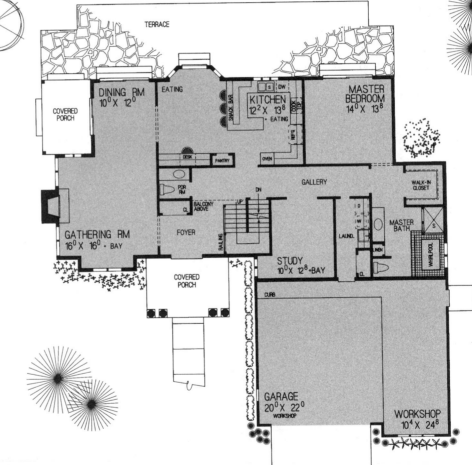

Width 65'-4"
Depth 60'

Design by
Home Planners

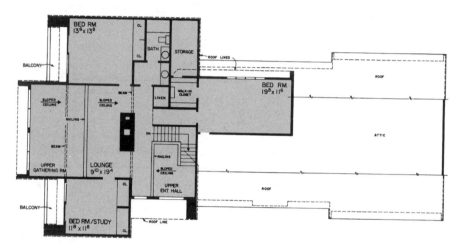

Design 2781

First Floor: 2,132 square feet
Second Floor: 1,156 square feet
Total: 3,288 square feet

L **D**

● This beautifully designed two-story
provides an eye-catching contemporary
exterior. The floor plan is a perfect complement. The front kitchen features an
island range, adjacent breakfast nook,
and pass-through to a formal dining
room. A cozy family room with sliding
glass doors to the rear terrace is also
nearby. The first-floor master suite offers a spacious walk-in closet and dressing room. The side terrace can be
reached from the master suite, the gathering room and the study. The second
floor contains three bedrooms, two with
private balconies, and storage space galore. The center lounge overlooking the
gathering room offers a sloped ceiling.

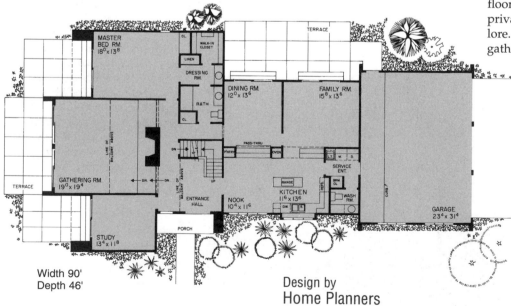

Width 90'
Depth 46'

Design by
Home Planners

Quote One®
Cost to build? See page 374
to order complete cost estimate
to build this house in your area!

Design 2920

First Floor: 3,067 square feet
Second Floor: 648 square feet
Total: 3,715 square feet

L **D**

● This contemporary design has a great deal to offer. A fireplace opens up to both the living room and country kitchen. The kitchen is a gourmet's delight, with a huge walk-in pantry and a deluxe work island which includes a snack bar and easy access to the formal dining room. A media room has plenty of storage and offers access to the rear terrace. Privacy is the key word when describing the sleeping areas. The first-floor master bedroom is away from the traffic of the house and features a dressing/exercise room, a whirlpool tub and shower and a spacious walk-in closet. Two more bedrooms and a full bath are on the second floor. The three-car garage is arranged so that the owners have use of a double-garage with an attached single on reserve for guests. The cheerful sun room adds 296 square feet to the total.

Width 97'
Depth 102'-8"

Design by
Home Planners

Cost to build? See page 374
to order complete cost estimate
to build this house in your area!

Design 2488

First Floor: 1,113 square feet
Second Floor: 543 square feet
Total: 1,656 square feet

D

● For a lakeside retreat or as a retirement haven, this charming design offers the best in livability. The gathering room with a corner fireplace, a U-shaped kitchen with an attached dining room, the lovely deck and a first-floor master suite make a complete and comfortable living space. Two bedrooms with a full bath and a balcony lounge upstairs complement the design and provide sleeping accommodations for family and guests.

Photo by Laszlo Regos

Design by
Home Planners

Width 44'
Depth 32'

Design by
Home Planners

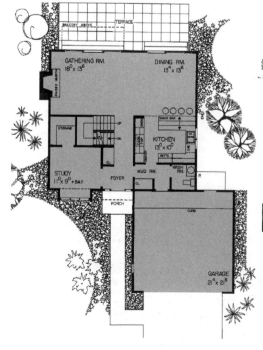

Width 40'-4"
Depth 52'

Design 2711

First Floor: 975 square feet
Second Floor: 1,024 square feet
Total: 1,999 square feet

L D

QUOTE ONE®
Cost to build? See page 374
to order complete cost estimate
to build this house in your area!

● Sleek, affordable style. The large dining area, a U-shaped kitchen, the mudroom off the garage and a spacious master bedroom are key selling points for a young family. Two other bedrooms share a full hall bath on the second floor. Also note the private balcony off the master suite, a cozy study with a box bay window and lots of storage space, a sunny terrace to the rear of the house and a sizable snack bar for the kids—and adults.

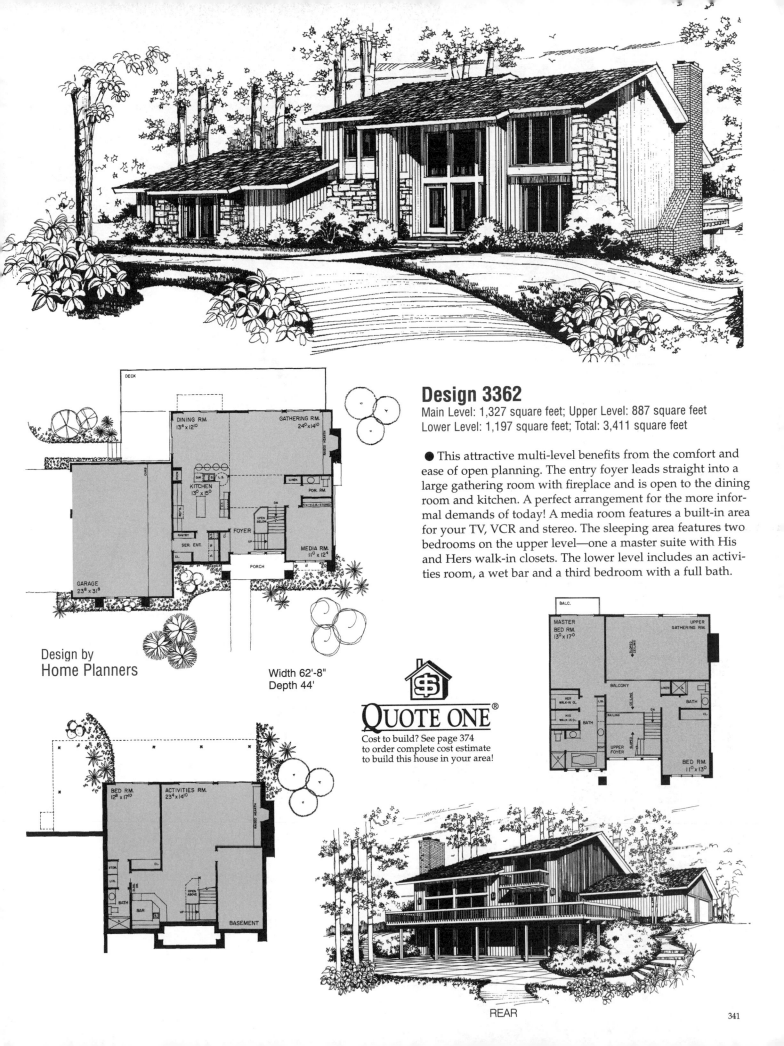

Design 3362

Main Level: 1,327 square feet; **Upper Level:** 887 square feet
Lower Level: 1,197 square feet; **Total:** 3,411 square feet

● This attractive multi-level benefits from the comfort and ease of open planning. The entry foyer leads straight into a large gathering room with fireplace and is open to the dining room and kitchen. A perfect arrangement for the more informal demands of today! A media room features a built-in area for your TV, VCR and stereo. The sleeping area features two bedrooms on the upper level—one a master suite with His and Hers walk-in closets. The lower level includes an activities room, a wet bar and a third bedroom with a full bath.

Design by
Home Planners

Width 62'-8"
Depth 44'

Quote One®

Cost to build? See page 374
to order complete cost estimate
to build this house in your area!

REAR

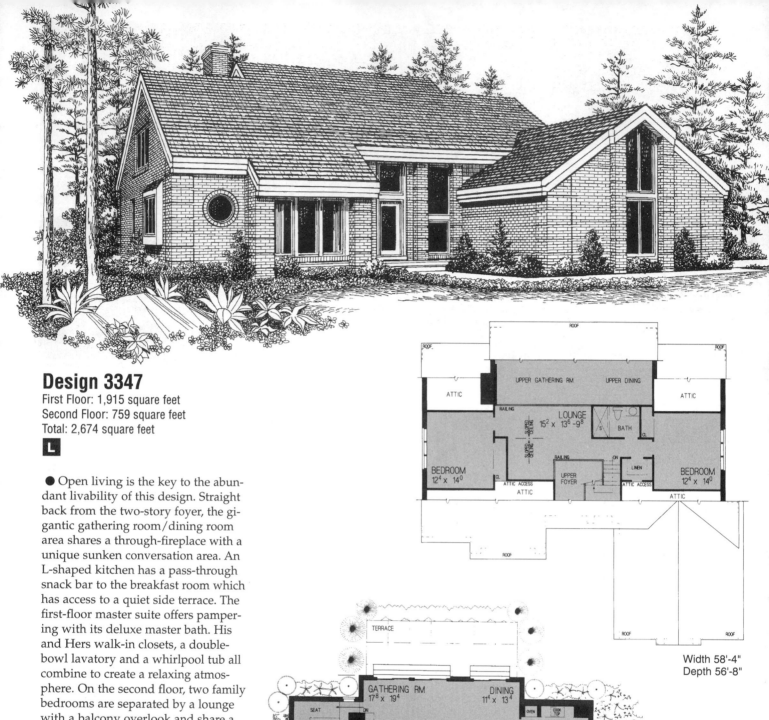

Design 3347

First Floor: 1,915 square feet
Second Floor: 759 square feet
Total: 2,674 square feet

L

● Open living is the key to the abundant livability of this design. Straight back from the two-story foyer, the gigantic gathering room/dining room area shares a through-fireplace with a unique sunken conversation area. An L-shaped kitchen has a pass-through snack bar to the breakfast room which has access to a quiet side terrace. The first-floor master suite offers pampering with its deluxe master bath. His and Hers walk-in closets, a double-bowl lavatory and a whirlpool tub all combine to create a relaxing atmosphere. On the second floor, two family bedrooms are separated by a lounge with a balcony overlook and share a full hall bath.

QUOTE ONE®

Cost to build? See page 374
to order complete cost estimate
to build this house in your area!

Width 58'-4"
Depth 56'-8"

Design by
Home Planners

Design 2490

First Floor: 1,414 square feet
Second Floor: 620 square feet
Total: 2,034 square feet

● A sloping roof and visible skylights entice you to look closer into this contemporary home. Split-bedroom planning makes the most of this plan; the first-floor master suite pampers with a lavish bath and a fireplace while two family bedrooms reside upstairs and share a full bath. The living areas are open and have easy access to the rear terrace. The U-shaped kitchen is convenient to the dining room via a casual snack bar. A fireplace brings warmth to the gathering room, making the area cheerful.

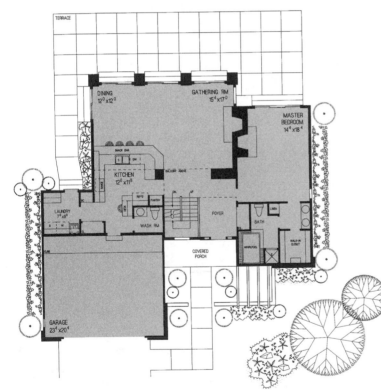

Width 53'
Depth 51'-8"

Design by
Home Planners

Quote One ®

Cost to build? See page 374
to order complete cost estimate
to build this house in your area!

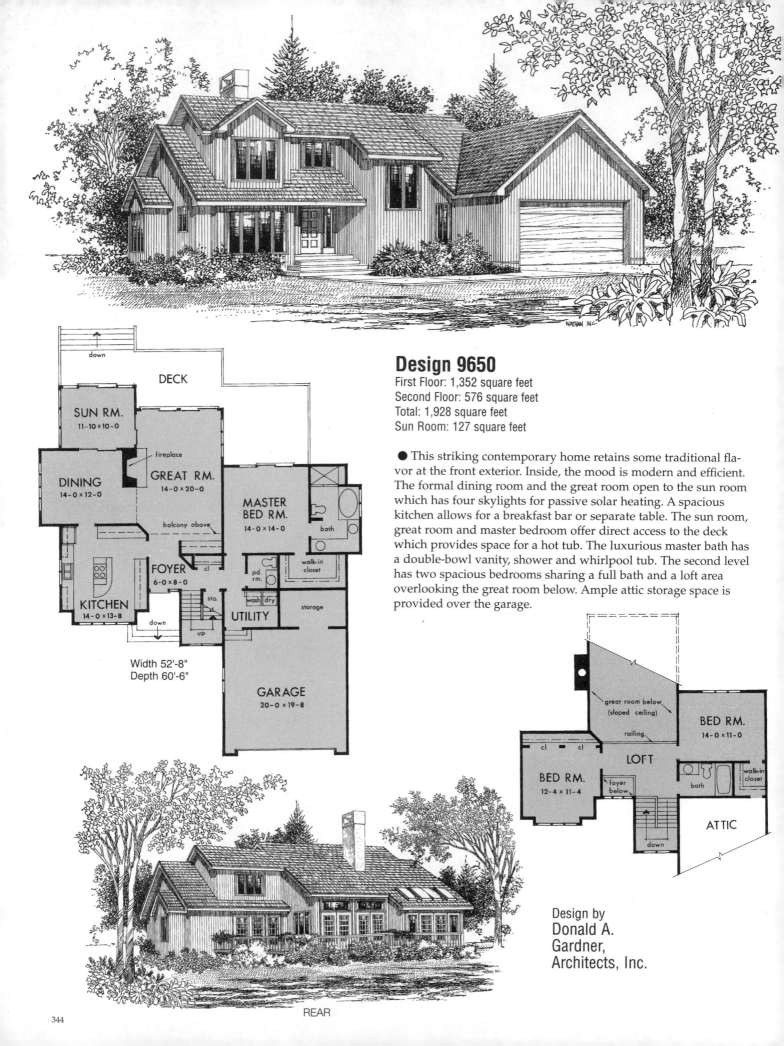

Design 9650

First Floor: 1,352 square feet
Second Floor: 576 square feet
Total: 1,928 square feet
Sun Room: 127 square feet

● This striking contemporary home retains some traditional flavor at the front exterior. Inside, the mood is modern and efficient. The formal dining room and the great room open to the sun room which has four skylights for passive solar heating. A spacious kitchen allows for a breakfast bar or separate table. The sun room, great room and master bedroom offer direct access to the deck which provides space for a hot tub. The luxurious master bath has a double-bowl vanity, shower and whirlpool tub. The second level has two spacious bedrooms sharing a full bath and a loft area overlooking the great room below. Ample attic storage space is provided over the garage.

Design by
Donald A.
Gardner,
Architects, Inc.

DECK

SUN RM.
11-10 × 10-0

fireplace

DINING
14-0 × 12-0

GREAT RM.
14-0 × 20-0

MASTER BED RM.
14-0 × 14-0

bath

balcony above

FOYER
6-0 × 8-0

cl

KITCHEN
14-0 × 13-8

pd. rm.

walk-in closet

wash dry

storage

UTILITY

sta.

down   up

GARAGE
20-0 × 19-8

Width 52'-8"
Depth 60'-6"

great room below
(sloped ceiling)

railing

BED RM.
14-0 × 11-0

cl   cl

LOFT

BED RM.
12-4 × 11-4

foyer below

bath

walk-in closet

down

ATTIC

REAR

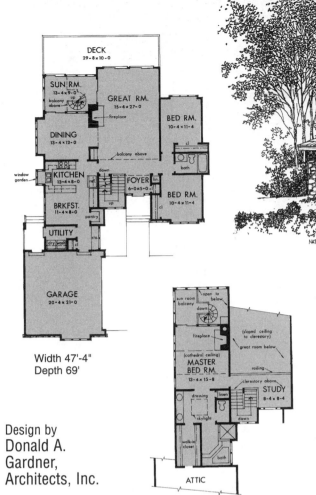

DECK
29-8 x 10-0

SUN RM.
13-4 x 9-0
balcony above

GREAT RM.
15-4 x 27-0
fireplace

BED RM.
10-4 x 11-4

DINING
13-4 x 12-0
balcony above

KITCHEN
13-4 x 8-0

FOYER
6-0 x 5-0

BED RM.
10-4 x 11-4

BRKFST.
11-4 x 8-0
pantry

UTILITY

GARAGE
20-4 x 21-0

window garden

Width 47'-4"
Depth 69'

Design by
Donald A.
Gardner,
Architects, Inc.

sun room balcony

open to below

MASTER BED RM.
13-4 x 15-8

fireplace
(cathedral ceiling)

(sloped ceiling to clerestory)

great room below

railing

clerestory above

STUDY
8-4 x 8-4

dressing
linen
skylight

walk-in closet

bath

ATTIC

Design 9646

First Floor: 1,564 square feet
Second Floor: 604 square feet
Total: 2,168 square feet

● One of the first floor's attractions, the sun room will delight all with its spiral staircase leading to a balcony and the master suite. The great room enjoys a fireplace and two sets of sliding glass doors leading to the deck. In the kitchen, a U-shape lends itself to outstanding convenience. Three bedrooms include two secondary bedrooms and a glorious master suite. Located on the second floor, the master bedroom has a fireplace, a generous dressing area with a skylight and a lavish bath. Please specify basement or crawlspace foundation when ordering.

MASTER BED RM.
13-4 x 13-4
walk-in closet
master bath

KITCHEN
13-10 x 12-0

FOYER
9-6 x 5-0

up

balcony above

DINING/GREAT RM.
24-8 x 16-8
fireplace

DECK

Width 41'-10"
Depth 61'-6"

Design 9700

First Floor: 1,150 square feet
Second Floor: 470 square feet
Total: 1,620 square feet

● This rustic three-bedroom vacation home allows for casual living both inside and out. The two-level great room offers many windows along with an impressive rock fireplace. The generous kitchen boasts a cooking island with serving counter and direct access to the deck. The master bedroom suite is located on the first floor for both convenience and privacy. Two additional bedrooms are on the second floor with plenty of storage and loft area.

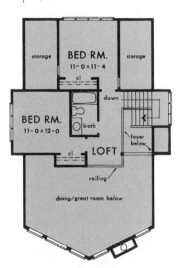

storage

BED RM.
11-0 x 11-4

storage

down

BED RM.
11-0 x 12-0

bath

LOFT

foyer below

railing

dining/great room below

Design by
Donald A.
Gardner,
Architects, Inc.

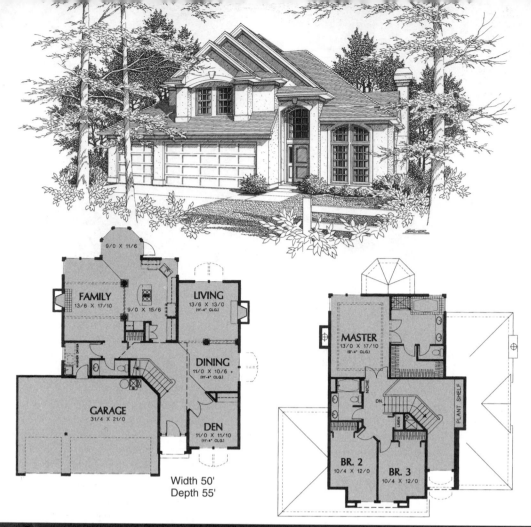

Width 50'
Depth 55'

Design by
Alan Mascord
Design Associates, Inc.

Design 9558
First Floor: 1,322 square feet
Second Floor: 1,000 square feet
Total: 2,322 square feet

● A multi-windowed breakfast nook will brighten your mornings. Columns dress up the beam-ceilinged family room and the kitchen. An island cook-top is placed in an efficient work triangle also defined by an angled double sink and a refrigerator. A den with built-ins, a dining room and a rear living room with a fireplace provide ample space for various pursuits. A three-bedroom upstairs includes two secondary bedrooms of ample proportions and a master bedroom suite that opens through double doors.

QUOTE ONE®
Cost to build? See page 374
to order complete cost estimate
to build this house in your area!

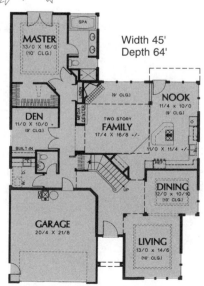

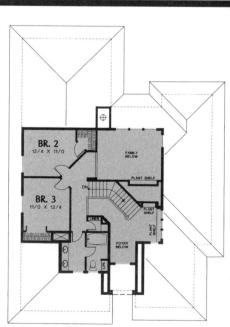

Design 9581
First Floor: 1,896 square feet
Second Floor: 568 square feet
Total: 2,464 square feet

● Inside the grand entrance of this contemporary home a large foyer offers a gracious introduction to the formal living and dining rooms. Nearby, the L-shaped island kitchen serves formal and informal areas with equal ease. A two-story family room with a built-in media center and a corner fireplace shares space with a sunny nook. The private master suite features a walk-in closet and a luxurious master bath. The second floor contains two bedrooms and a full bath.

Width 45'
Depth 64'

Design by
Alan Mascord
Design Associates, Inc.

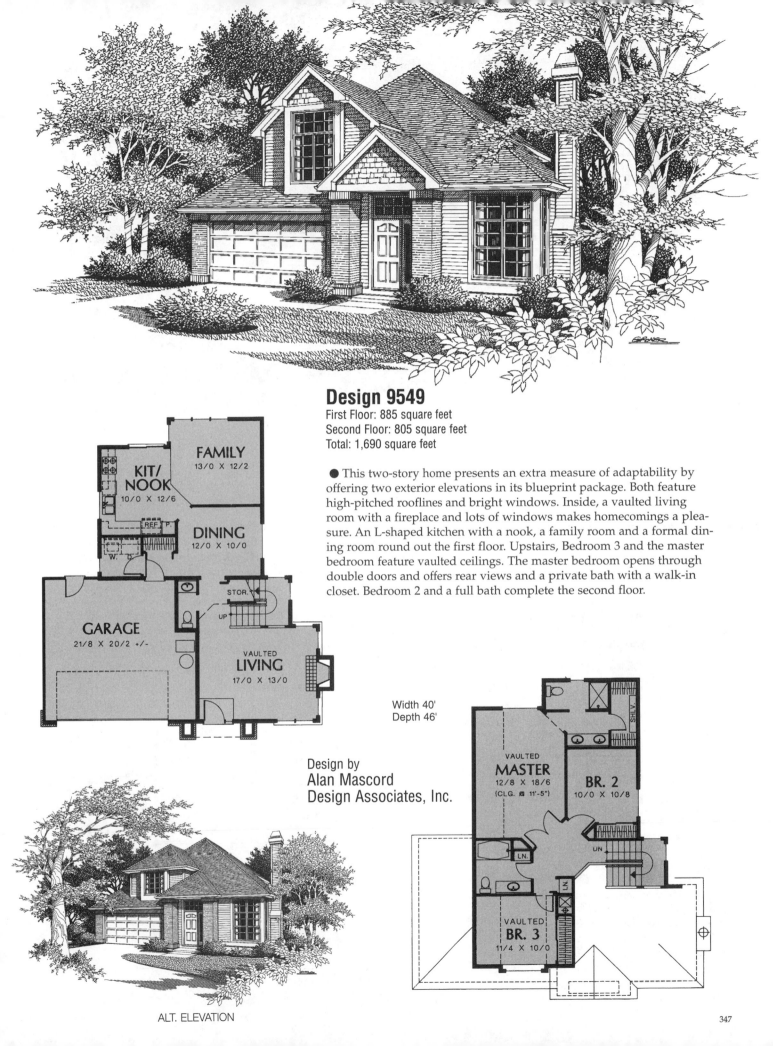

Design 9549

First Floor: 885 square feet
Second Floor: 805 square feet
Total: 1,690 square feet

● This two-story home presents an extra measure of adaptability by offering two exterior elevations in its blueprint package. Both feature high-pitched rooflines and bright windows. Inside, a vaulted living room with a fireplace and lots of windows makes homecomings a pleasure. An L-shaped kitchen with a nook, a family room and a formal dining room round out the first floor. Upstairs, Bedroom 3 and the master bedroom feature vaulted ceilings. The master bedroom opens through double doors and offers rear views and a private bath with a walk-in closet. Bedroom 2 and a full bath complete the second floor.

FAMILY
13/0 X 12/2

KIT/NOOK
10/0 X 12/6

REF. P.

DINING
12/0 X 10/0

W. D.

GARAGE
21/8 X 20/2 +/-

STOR.

UP

VAULTED
LIVING
17/0 X 13/0

Width 40'
Depth 46'

Design by
**Alan Mascord
Design Associates, Inc.**

SHLV.

VAULTED
MASTER
12/8 X 18/6
(CLG. @ 11'-5")

BR. 2
10/0 X 10/8

LN.

LN.

LN.

VAULTED
BR. 3
11/4 X 10/0

ALT. ELEVATION

Design 9635

First Floor: 1,434 square feet
Second Floor: 746 square feet
Total: 2,180 square feet
Sun Room: 130 square feet

● Bold contemporary lines strike an elegant chord in this two-story plan. The entry foyer leads to a multi-purpose great room with a fireplace and sliding glass doors to a rear deck. The formal dining room is nearby and there is a connecting sun room. A U-shaped kitchen features an attached breakfast room and large walk-in pantry. Two bedrooms on this floor share a full bath. The master suite dominates the second floor. It features a large walk-in closet, double lavatories, a corner tub, and spiral stairs from its private balcony to the sun room below. The upstairs balcony connects it to a study or optional bedroom. Please specify basement or crawlspace foundation when ordering.

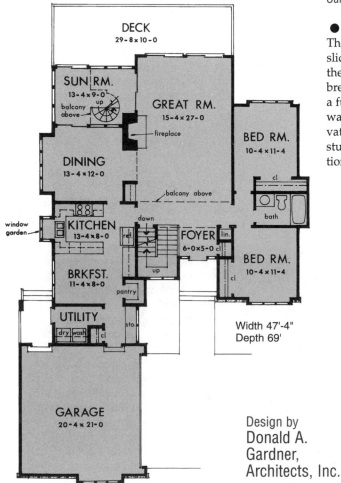

Width 47'-4"
Depth 69'

Design by
Donald A.
Gardner,
Architects, Inc.

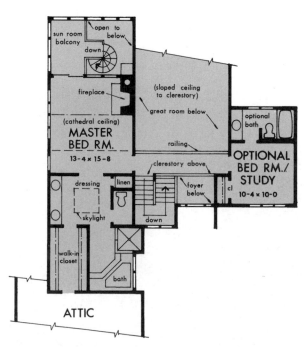

348

Striking Sun-Country:
Designs for warm climates

Photos by Allen Maertz

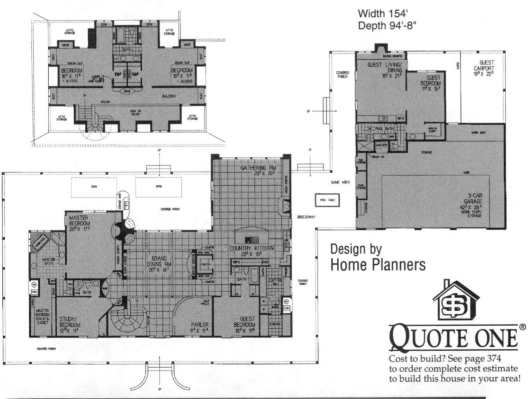

Width 154'
Depth 94'-8"

Design by
Home Planners

QUOTE ONE®

Cost to build? See page 374
to order complete cost estimate
to build this house in your area!

Design 3471
First Floor: 3,166 square feet
Second Floor: 950 square feet
Guest Living Area: 680 square feet
Total: 4,796 square feet

L

● Western farmhouse-style living is captured in this handsome design. The central entrance leads into a cozy parlor—half walls provide a view of the grand dining room. Entertaining's a cinch with the dining room's built-in china alcove, service counter and fireplace. The country kitchen, with a large island cooktop, overlooks the gathering room with its full wall of glass. The master bedroom will satisfy even the most discerning tastes. It boasts a raised hearth, porch access and a bath with a walk-in closet, separate vanities and a whirlpool. You may want to use one of the additional first floor bedrooms as a study, the other as a guest room. To round out the first floor, you'll also find a clutter room with a pantry, freezer space and access to storage space. Two family bedrooms and attic storage make up the second floor. Note, too, the separate garage and guest house which make this such a winning design.

Design 3425

First Floor: 1,776 square feet
Second Floor: 1,035 square feet
Total: 2,811 square feet

● Here's a two-story Spanish design with an appealing, angled exterior. Inside is an interesting floor plan containing rooms with a variety of shapes. Formal areas are to the right of the entry tower: a sunken living room with a fireplace and a large dining room with access to the rear porch. The kitchen has loads of counter space and is complemented by a bumped-out breakfast room. Note the second fireplace in the family room and the first-floor bedroom which could also be a guest suite. Three second-floor bedrooms radiate around the upper foyer, including the deluxe master suite. Among its many amenities; a private balcony, a walk in closet and a sumptuous bath.

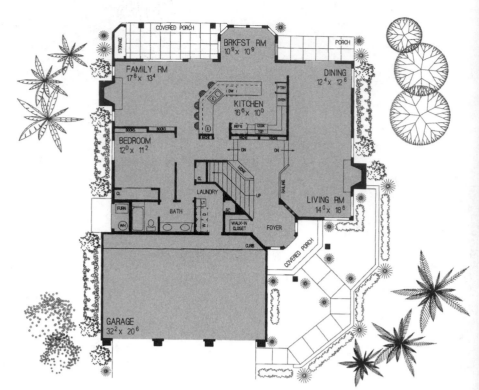

Width 52'
Depth 64'-4"

Design by
Home Planners

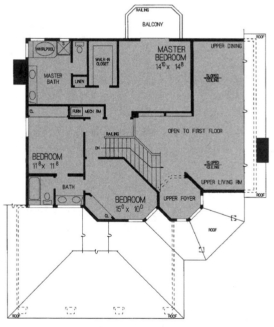

Cost to build? See page 374 to order complete cost estimate to build this house in your area!

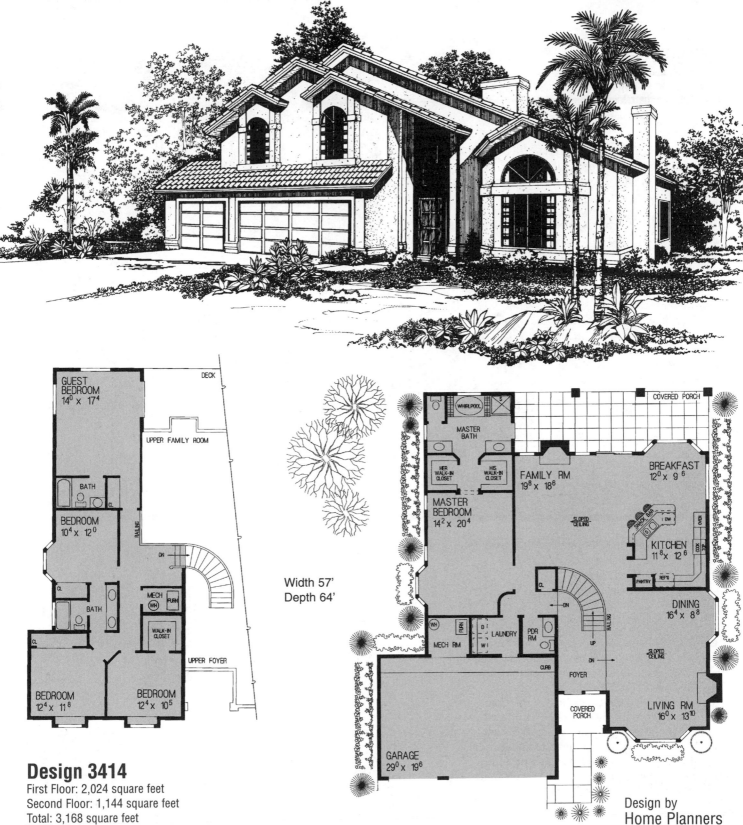

GUEST BEDROOM 14⁰ x 17⁴

DECK

UPPER FAMILY ROOM

BATH

BEDROOM 10⁴ x 12⁰

RAILING

DN

BATH

MECH FURN WH

WALK-IN CLOSET

UPPER FOYER

BEDROOM 12⁴ x 11⁸

BEDROOM 12⁴ x 10⁵

Width 57'
Depth 64'

WHIRLPOOL

MASTER BATH

HER WALK-IN CLOSET

HIS WALK-IN CLOSET

COVERED PORCH

FAMILY RM 19⁸ x 18⁶

BREAKFAST 12⁰ x 9⁶

SLOPED CEILING

SNACK BAR

DW

MASTER BEDROOM 14² x 20⁴

KITCHEN 11⁸ x 12⁶

COOK TOP OVEN

PANTRY

REF'G

CL

DN

RAILING

DINING 16⁴ x 8⁸

WH FURN

D W

LAUNDRY

PDR RM

UP

DN

SLOPED CEILING

MECH RM

CURB

FOYER

LIVING RM 16⁰ x 13¹⁰

COVERED PORCH

GARAGE 29⁰ x 19⁶

Design 3414

First Floor: 2,024 square feet
Second Floor: 1,144 square feet
Total: 3,168 square feet

Design by
Home Planners

● Though seemingly compact from the exterior, this home gives a definite feeling of spaciousness inside. The two-story entry connects directly to a formal living/dining area, a fitting complement to the more casual family room and cozy, bayed breakfast room. Located on the first floor for privacy, the master suite is luxury defined. A bayed sitting area, His and Hers walk-in closets, a whirlpool tub and twin vanities all combine to provide a lavish retreat. Upstairs, three family bedrooms share a full hall bath, while a large guest room waits to pamper with its private bath and access to its own deck. A three-car garage will protect both the family fleet and visitor's vehicles.

QUOTE ONE®

Cost to build? See page 374
to order complete cost estimate
to build this house in your area!

Design 3639

First Floor: 2,137 square feet
Second Floor: 671 square feet
Total: 2,808 square feet

L

● This stucco home provides a wealth of livability for the entire family. Inside, a formal living room and a formal dining room open to a covered entertainment area outside. The family room—with a fireplace—delights with open views to the kitchen and breakfast nook. On the left side of the plan, the master bedroom suite delights with a full, private bath and a lanai perfect for a spa. A large den could easily double as a study. Two bedrooms and a full bath are located upstairs.

Design by
Home Planners

Cost to build? See page 374 to order complete cost estimate to build this house in your area!

Width 75'-6"
Depth 62'-6"

Design 2801

First Floor: 1,172 square feet
Second Floor: 884 square feet
Total: 2,056 square feet

L **D**

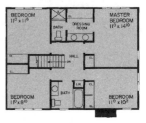

● An arched entry welcomes you to a sunny courtyard and leads you into a charming stucco home. Inside, to the left of the foyer, the sunken great room will be the place for wonderful gatherings with its beam ceiling, central fireplace and access to a rear terrace. Dining areas reign at the rear of the plan; a formal dining room, a U-shaped kitchen and a breakfast nook. Upstairs, three family bedrooms share a full hall bath while a master bedroom revels in its own private bath.

Design by
Home Planners

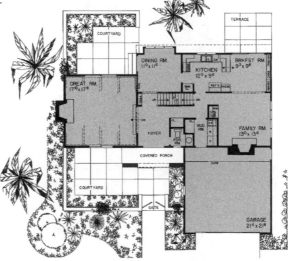

Width 54'-4"
Depth 47'-8"

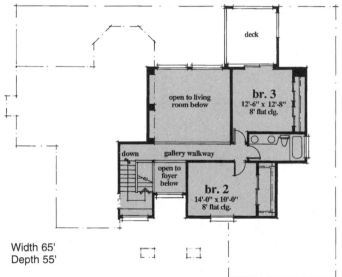

deck

open to living room below

br. 3
12'-6" x 12'-8"
8' flat clg.

down

gallery walkway

open to foyer below

br. 2
14'-0" x 10'-0"
8' flat clg.

Width 65'
Depth 55'

nook
11'-0" x 8'-4"
14' flat clg.

lanai
53'-0" x 12'-4" avg.

leisure
16'-0" x 14'-10" avg.
14' flat clg.
fireplace

kitchen

living
15'-6" x 14'-10"
17'-4" flat clg.

master suite
13'-0" x 18'-6"
8' flat clg.

desk

1/2 wall

up

dining
12'-0" x 12'-8"
14' flat clg.

foyer

entry

utility

workshop

garage
20'-8" x 22'-8"

©The Sater Group, Inc.

Design 6613

First Floor: 1,840 square feet
Second Floor: 608 square feet
Total: 2,448 square feet

● This stylish stucco home caters to even the most discriminating tastes. Inside, plant shelves lend a touch of comfort to both the formal and informal areas. Note the stair landing; arched glass and a window seat provide a quiet spot for reflective thoughts or a good book. The informal living area makes the most of the lanai. Other areas with access to the lanai include the spacious leisure room with its welcoming fireplace, the bay-windowed nook overlooking the rear grounds and the open kitchen complete with a walk-in pantry and a planning desk. The formal dining room is separated from the kitchen by a half-wall, thus making entertaining easy. The secluded master suite opens to the lanai also and features a huge walk-in closet and a master bath with a raised corner tub, a separate shower and dual vanities. The second floor contains two secondary bedrooms, a full bath and a rear deck.

Design by
The Sater
Design Collection

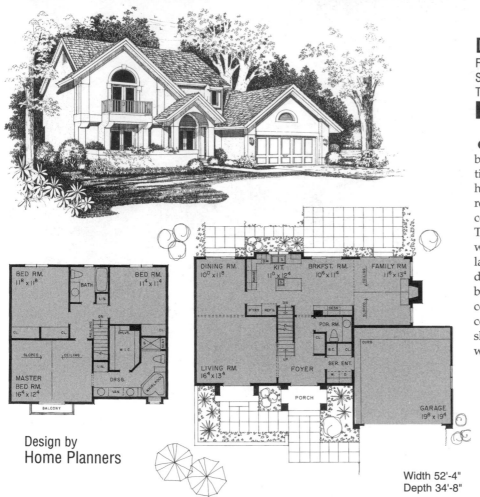

Design 3563

First Floor: 1,023 square feet
Second Floor: 866 square feet
Total: 1,889 square feet

L D

● This wonderful transitional plan combines the best of contemporary and traditional styling. Its stucco exterior is enhanced by arched windows and a recessed arched entry plus a lovely balcony off the second floor master bedroom. The double front doors open to a foyer with a hall closet and powder room. The large living room adjoins directly to the dining room. The family room is set off behind the garage and features a sloped ceiling and fireplace. Sleeping quarters consist of two secondary bedrooms with a shared bath and a generous master suite with well-appointed bath.

QUOTE ONE®
Cost to build? See page 374
to order complete cost estimate
to build this house in your area!

Design by
Home Planners

Width 52'-4"
Depth 34'-8"

Design 8640

First Floor: 1,485 square feet
Second Floor: 697 square feet
Total: 2,182 square feet

● Two facades, one floor plan! The double-door entry foyer of this stucco home has a seemingly unlimited view of the huge great room. This living area comes complete with fireplace and media center. The formal dining room is perfect for quiet candlelight dinners. The kitchen and nook areas overlook the outdoor living space and the great room. The master suite on the first floor features a lavish bath which includes a soaking tub, adjacent shower and private toilet. Bedrooms on the second floor are ample; Bedroom 4 can be used as a loft area or activity room for the kids.

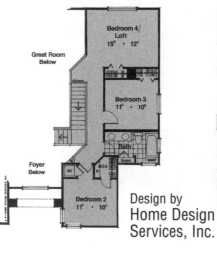

Design by
Home Design
Services, Inc.

Width 42'-4"
Depth 58'-4"

ALT. ELEVATION

354

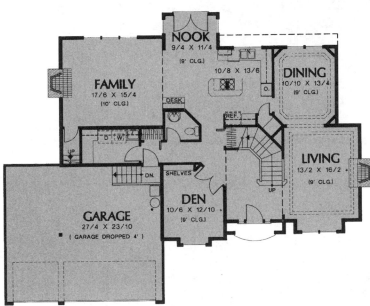

Design 9561

First Floor: 1,564 square feet
Second Floor: 1,422 square feet
Total: 2,986 square feet
Bonus Room: 430 square feet

● Designed for a slightly sloping lot, this dramatic stucco plan is the height of luxury. The main level contains a formal living room and dining room, both with special detailing. A family room allows a large space for everyday living. The central kitchen features a central cooktop, planning desk and large pantry. A cozy den with built-in bookshelves could serve as space for a home office. Upstairs, the master suite is raised a few steps above the main hallway. It has a lavish bath with a spa tub and also features a huge walk-in closet. Three family bedrooms share a full bath with twin vanities. A sizable bonus room above the garage can be developed into hobby or study space. A three-car garage further enhances the plan.

Width 63'
Depth 51'

Design by
Alan Mascord
Design Associates, Inc.

Design 6608

First Floor: 2,368 square feet
Second Floor: 428 square feet
Total: 2,796 square feet

● This grand two-story stucco home will be as delightful to live in as it is to look at. Practical planning combines the dining room and grand room to meet both formal and informal entertaining needs. The kitchen and bayed nook will become a favorite space for family conversations and informal dining. The master bedroom features space for a bayed sitting area and opens to the lanai. His and Hers walk-in closets lead the way to the master bath highlighted by a charming garden tub and a separate shower. Bedroom 2 completes the first floor. Bedroom 3, a loft and a full bath are contained on the second floor as well as an optional deck.

Design by
The Sater
Design Collection

QUOTE ONE®
Cost to build? See page 374
to order complete cost estimate
to build this house in your area!

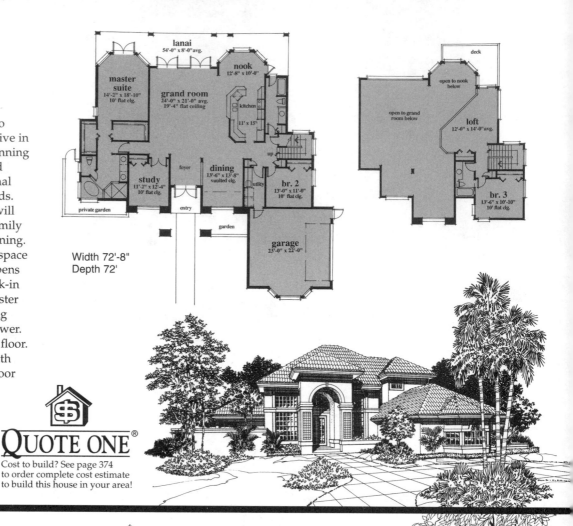

Width 72'-8"
Depth 72'

Width 52'
Depth 55'

Width 52'
Depth 55'

Design 8618

First Floor: 1,352 square feet
Second Floor: 1,000 square feet
Total: 2,352 square feet

Design by
Home Design
Services, Inc.

● A covered porch shades the entry to the foyer of this home—it is lit by an arched window. Double doors to the right open to a guest room with an arched picture window. The great room, open to the level above, has a wet bar; a large rear patio also offers a wet bar. The tiled kitchen provides a serving bar for the breakfast room. French doors in the master bedroom open onto a deck. The spacious bath here includes a walk-in closet, twin vanities and spa tub. Two additional bedrooms and a bath complete the second level. The front bedroom includes a study and opens onto a deck. The plan can be built with a flat-tiled or barrel roof.

This unique Floridian design brings all of the major living areas to the rear for extended outdoor livability. The separation of formal living areas adds excitement to dinner parties. A sunken living room leads to the covered patio. Unique detailing is shown by the coffered ceiling in the sunken dining room. The large, efficient kitchen has a planning desk and is convenient to the dining room and a sunny breakfast room. A bayed den invites relaxation. Luxury abounds in the master suite which includes a bath fit for a king: two walk-in closets, dual vanities, a whirlpool tub and a shower. The second floor houses three more bedrooms, one with a sitting room, and two full baths.

Design 8650

First Floor: 1,828 square feet
Second Floor: 906 square feet
Total: 2,734 square feet

Width 67'-4"
Depth 59'-8"

Design by
Home Design Services, Inc.

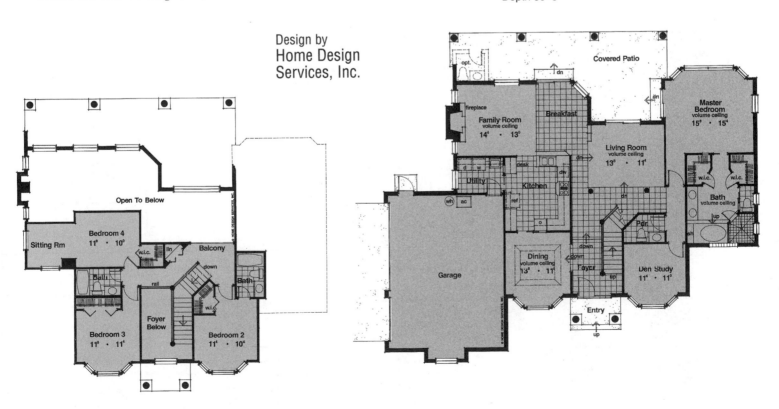

Design 8623

First Floor: 2,014 square feet
Second Floor: 975 square feet
Total: 2,989 square feet

● Arched, multi-pane windows inset in a stucco veneer give this home the ambience of a Mediterranean palazzo. The tiled, brightly illuminated foyer opens to the great room and the dining room, where columns heighten the sense of spaciousness. A high ceiling enhances the tiled kitchen and adjoining breakfast area with a bay window and a built-in desk. A full bath is located nearby and has access to the rear yard. Double doors open to the first-floor master suite with a lavish bath featuring a dual vanity, spa tub and a walk-in closet. Upstairs, a loft opens to the great room and foyer below. Clustered around it, two bedrooms and a study share a full bath.

Design by
Home Design
Services, Inc.

Patio

Breakfast
desk

Bath

volume ceiling
bar

Utility

Kitchen
pantry

Double Garage

fireplace

Great Room
volume ceiling
21⁰ · 16⁴

Master
Bedroom
16⁰ · 15⁰

Bath

w.i.c.

linen

Dining
13⁰ · 11⁰

Foyer

Living Room
12⁴ · 12⁰

Entry

Width 67'-4"
Depth 61'-4"

Deck

Great Room
Below

Bedroom 2
13⁴ · 11⁰
window seat

Loft
16⁸ · 11⁰

Study/Den
14⁴ · 13⁸

Foyer
Below

storage

Bath
window seat

Bedroom 3
12⁰ · 10⁰

© 91 HOME DESIGN SERVICES, INC.

J. V. HANSEN R.T.L.

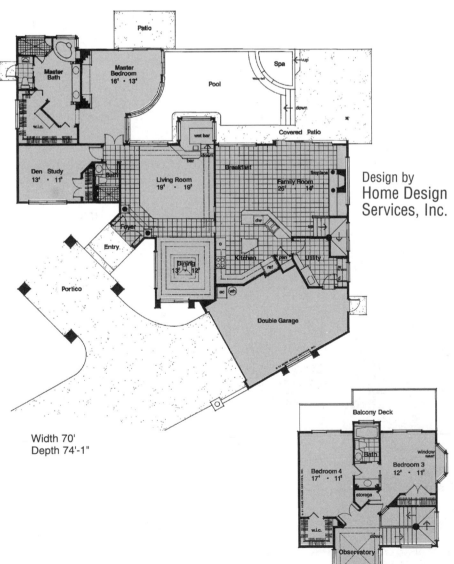

Design by
Home Design
Services, Inc.

Width 70'
Depth 74'-1"

Design 8652

First Floor: 2,212 square feet
Second Floor: 675 square feet
Total: 2,887 square feet

● As you drive up to the porte cochere entry of this home, the visual movement of the elevation is breathtaking. The multi-roofed spaces bring excitement the moment you walk through the double-doored entry. The foyer leads into the wide glass-walled living room. To the right, the formal dining room features a tiered pedestal ceiling. To the left is the guest and master suite wing of the home. The master suite with its sweeping curved glass wall has access to the patio area and overlooks the pool. The master bath, with its huge walk-in closet comes complete with a columned vanity area, a soaking tub and a shower for two. Two large bedrooms on the second floor—one with a bay window and one with a walk-in closet—share a sun deck, a full bath and an activity area.

359

Design 8658

First Floor: 2,219 square feet
Second Floor: 1,281 square feet
Total: 3,500 square feet

● This home demands a lifestyle that enjoys living spaces separated not by walls but by activities. The huge great room fills the bill nicely and includes a warming fireplace, plenty of windows and access to the wrap-around deck. A private library also complements this area. A step-saving kitchen works well with both the nearby formal dining room and the bayed breakfast nook.

The bedroom on this level, with its full bath, would be perfect for a guest suite. The master suite provides total luxury on the second floor. It has a private balcony, a corner fireplace, a lavish bath and a huge walk-in closet. Two family bedrooms are also found on the second floor and share a full bath. This home includes a basement and accommodates a sloping lot for rear-yard access.

Design by
Home Design
Services, Inc.

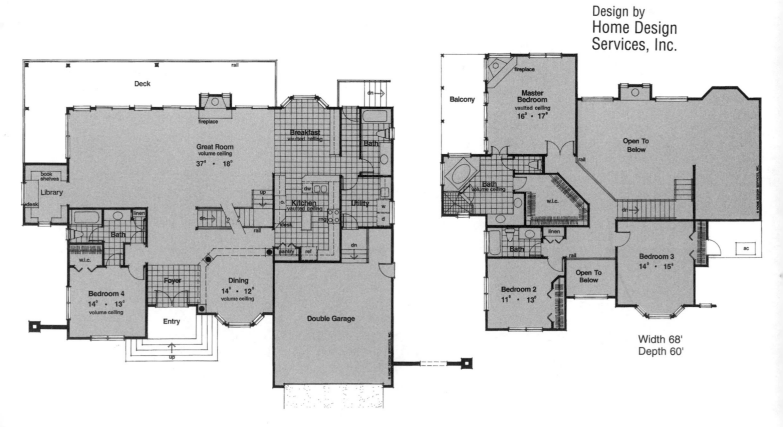

Width 68'
Depth 60'

Design 3628

First Floor: 1,731 square feet
Second Floor: 554 square feet
Total: 2,285 square feet

● Varying roof planes of colorful tile surfaces make a dramatic statement. Privacy fences add appeal and help form the front courtyard and side private patio. The kitchen has an island cooktop, built-in ovens, a nearby walk-in pantry and direct access to the outdoor covered patio. The living room is impressive with its centered fireplace with long, raised hearth. The high ceiling permits a fine view of the second-floor loft. This room, too, functions through French doors with the rear patio. At the opposite end of the plan is the master bedroom. It has a walk-in closet with shoe storage, twin lavatories in the bath, plus a whirlpool and stall shower. Not to be overlooked is the access to the private patio and the rear patio. The two secondary bedrooms upstairs each have direct access to a bath with twin lavatories and a loft for play times.

Width 90'-2"
Depth 69'-10"

Design by
Home Planners

Cost to build? See page 374
to order complete cost estimate
to build this house in your area!

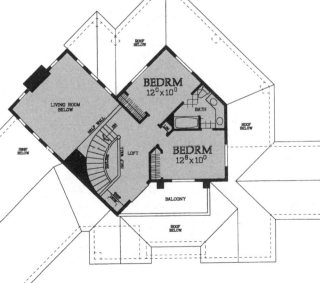

Design 3449

First Floor: 1,336 square feet
Second Floor: 1,186 square feet
Total: 2,522 square feet

L

● A covered porch leads inside this stucco two-story home to a wide, tiled foyer. A curving staircase makes an elegant statement in the open space between the formal living and dining rooms. A through-fireplace warms the nook and the family room which has access to the rear terrace. Also look for a wet bar and glass shelves here. Upstairs, the master bedroom suite includes a sitting area, two closets and its own deck. Two family bedrooms share a full bath with a double-bowl vanity.

QUOTE ONE®

Cost to build? See page 374 to order complete cost estimate to build this house in your area!

Design by
Home Planners

Width 58'-9"
Depth 54'-10"

Design 3437

First Floor: 1,522 square feet
Second Floor: 800 square feet
Total: 2,322 square feet

L

● This two-story Spanish Mission-style home has character inside and out. The first-floor master suite features a fireplace and gracious bath with a walk-in closet, a whirlpool, a shower, dual vanities and linen storage. A second fireplace serves both the gathering room and media/library room. The kitchen, with an island cook top, includes a snack bar and an adjoining breakfast nook. Three bedrooms—one a wonderful guest suite—and two full baths occupy the second floor.

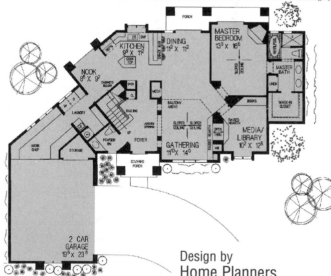

QUOTE ONE®

Cost to build? See page 374 to order complete cost estimate to build this house in your area!

Design by
Home Planners

Width 69'-6"
Depth 61'

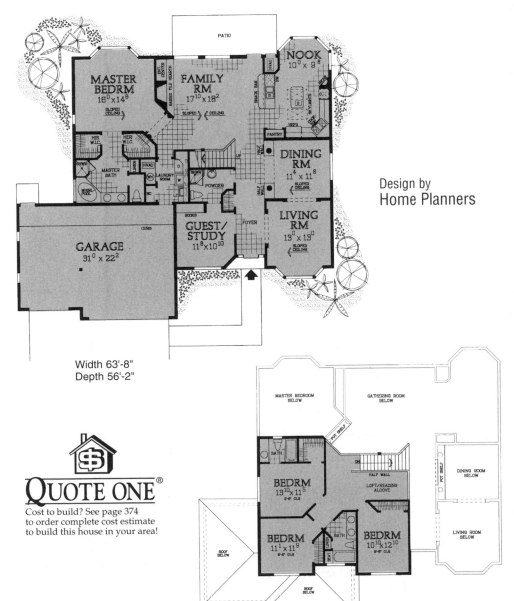

Width 63'-8"
Depth 56'-2"

Design by
Home Planners

Design 3441

First Floor: 2,022 square feet
Second Floor: 845 square feet
Total: 2,867 square feet

L

● Special details make the difference between a house and this two-story home. A two-story foyer ushers you into a comfortable layout. A snack bar, an audio-visual center, a fireplace and a high, sloped ceiling make the family room a favorite place for informal gatherings. A desk, an island cook top, a bay and skylights enhance the kitchen area. The dining room features two columns and a plant ledge. The formal living room is graced by a sunny bay window, while across the hall a cozy study encourages quiet times. The first-floor master suite includes His and Hers walk-in closets, a spacious bath and a bay window. On the second floor, one bedroom features a walk-in closet and private bath which makes it perfect for a guest suite, while two additional bedrooms share a full bath.

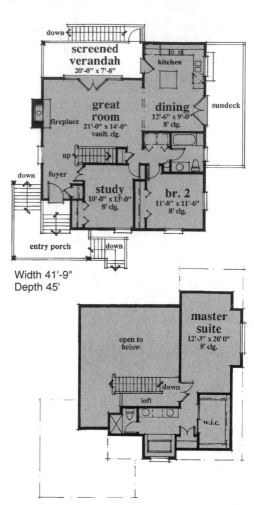

Width 41'-9"
Depth 45'

screened verandah 20'-0" x 7'-8"
kitchen
great room 21'-0" x 14'-0" vault. clg.
dining 12'-6" x 9'-0" 8' clg.
sundeck
fireplace
up
foyer
down
down
study 10'-0" x 13'-0" 8' clg.
br. 2 11'-8" x 11'-6" 8' clg.
entry porch
down

open to below
master suite 12'-3" x 20'-0" 8' clg.
down
loft
w.i.c.

Design 6616

First Floor: 1,136 square feet
Second Floor: 636 square feet
Total: 1,772 square feet

Design by
The Sater Design Collection

● The covered entry of this coastal design with its dramatic transom window leads to a spacious great room highlighted by a warming fireplace. To the left, the dining room and kitchen both provide access to a side deck through double doors. Two bedrooms and a full bath complete the first floor. The luxurious master suite is located on the second floor for privacy and features an oversized walk-in closet and a pampering master bath that enjoys a relaxing whirlpool tub, a double-bowl vanity and a compartmented toilet.

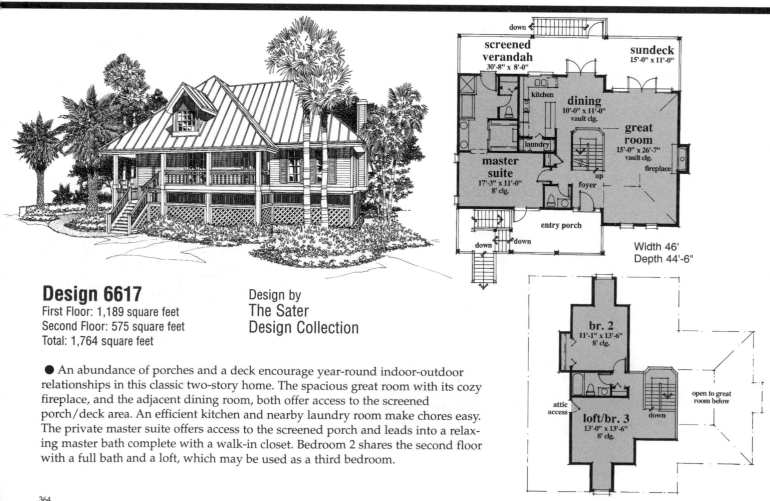

down
screened verandah 30'-8" x 8'-0"
sundeck 15'-0" x 11'-0"
kitchen
dining 10'-0" x 11'-0" vault clg.
great room 15'-0" x 26'-7" vault. clg.
laundry
fireplace
master suite 17'-3" x 11'-0" 8' clg.
up
foyer
entry porch
down down

Width 46'
Depth 44'-6"

br. 2 11'-1" x 13'-6" 8' clg.
attic access
loft/br. 3 13'-0" x 13'-6" 8' clg.
open to great room below
down

Design 6617

First Floor: 1,189 square feet
Second Floor: 575 square feet
Total: 1,764 square feet

Design by
The Sater Design Collection

● An abundance of porches and a deck encourage year-round indoor-outdoor relationships in this classic two-story home. The spacious great room with its cozy fireplace, and the adjacent dining room, both offer access to the screened porch/deck area. An efficient kitchen and nearby laundry room make chores easy. The private master suite offers access to the screened porch and leads into a relaxing master bath complete with a walk-in closet. Bedroom 2 shares the second floor with a full bath and a loft, which may be used as a third bedroom.

Design 6615

First Floor: 1,736 square feet
Second Floor: 640 square feet
Lower Level: 840 square feet
Total: 3,216 square feet

QUOTE ONE®

Cost to build? See page 374
to order complete cost estimate
to build this house in your area!

Design by
**The Sater
Design Collection**

● Lattice door panels, shutters, a balustrade and a metal roof add character to this delightful coastal home. Double doors flanking a fireplace open to the side sun deck from the spacious great room sporting a vaulted ceiling. Access to the rear veranda is provided from this room also. An adjacent dining room provides views of the rear grounds and space for formal and informal entertaining. The glassed-in nook shares space

with the L-shaped kitchen containing a center work island. Bedrooms 2 and 3, a full bath and a utility room complete this floor. Upstairs, a sumptuous master suite awaits. Double doors extend to a private deck from the master bedroom. His and Hers walk-in closets lead the way to a grand master bath featuring an arched whirlpool tub, a double-bowl vanity and a separate shower. This home is designed with an island basement.

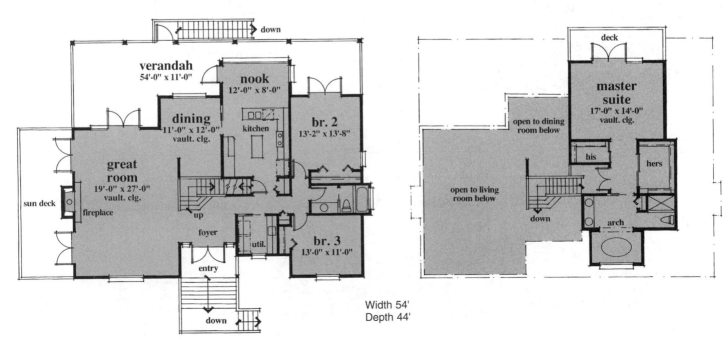

Width 54'
Depth 44'

Design 6621

First Floor: 1,642 square feet
Second Floor: 927 square feet
Total: 2,569 square feet

● Luxury abounds in this
Floridian home. A recreation
room greets you on the first
floor. Up the stairs, an open
grand room, a bayed nook and a
deck stretch across the back of
the plan. Two bedrooms occupy
the right side of this level and
share a full hall bath. The master
retreat on the upper level pleases
with its own reading room and
a morning kitchen.

Design by
**The Sater
Design Collection**

QUOTE ONE®

Cost to build? See page 374
to order complete cost estimate
to build this house in your area!

Width 60'
Depth 44'-6"

Design 6654

First Floor: 1,342 square feet
Second Floor: 511 square feet
Total: 1,853 square feet

● Amenities abound in this delightful
two-story Floridian. The foyer opens
directly onto the fantastic grand room,
which offers a warming fireplace and
two sets of double doors to the rear
deck. The dining room also has access to
this deck, and to a second deck shared
with Bedroom 2. A convenient kitchen
and another bedroom also reside on this
level. Upstairs the master bedroom
reigns supreme. Entered through double
doors, it pampers with a luxurious bath,
a walk-in closet, a morning kitchen and
a private balcony.

Design by
**The Sater
Design Collection**

Width 44'
Depth 40'

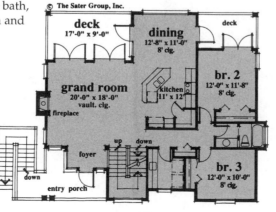

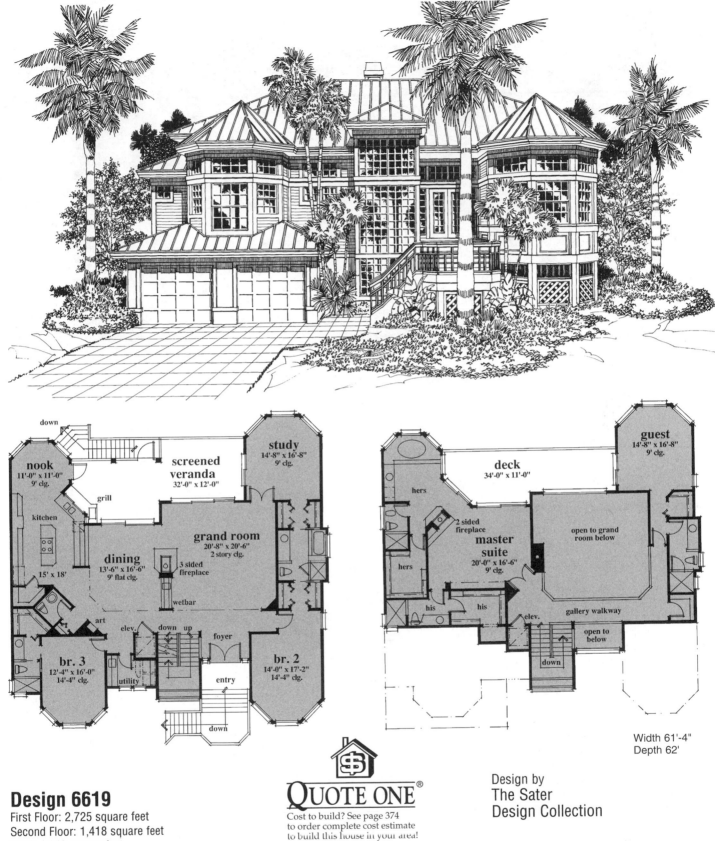

nook
11'-0" x 11'-0"
9' clg.

down

kitchen

15' x 18'

grill

screened veranda
32'-0" x 12'-0"

study
14'-8" x 16'-8"
9' clg.

dining
13'-6" x 16'-6"
9' flat clg.

grand room
20'-8" x 20'-6"
2 story clg.

3 sided fireplace

wetbar

art

elev.

down up

foyer

br. 3
12'-4" x 16'-0"
14'-4" clg.

utility

entry

br. 2
14'-0" x 17'-2"
14'-4" clg.

down

---

guest
14'-8" x 16'-8"
9' clg.

deck
34'-0" x 11'-0"

hers

hers

2 sided fireplace

master suite
20'-0" x 16'-6"
9' clg.

open to grand room below

his

his

elev.

gallery walkway

open to below

down

Width 61'-4"
Depth 62'

Design 6619

First Floor: 2,725 square feet
Second Floor: 1,418 square feet
Total: 4,143 square feet

Quote One®
Cost to build? See page 374
to order complete cost estimate
to build this house in your area!

Design by
**The Sater
Design Collection**

● Florida living takes off in this grand design. A grand room gains attention as a superb entertaining area. A through-fireplace here connects this room to the dining room. Sets of sliding glass doors offer passage to an expansive rear deck. In the bayed study, quiet time is assured—or slip out onto the deck for a breather. A full bath connects the study and Bedroom 2. Bedroom 3 sits on the opposite side of the house and enjoys its own bath. The kitchen is fully functional with a large work island and a sunny connecting breakfast nook. Upstairs, the master bedroom suite is something to behold. His and Hers baths, a through-fireplace and access to an upper deck all characterize this room. A guest bedroom suite with a bay window is located on the other side of the upper floor and will make visits a real pleasure.

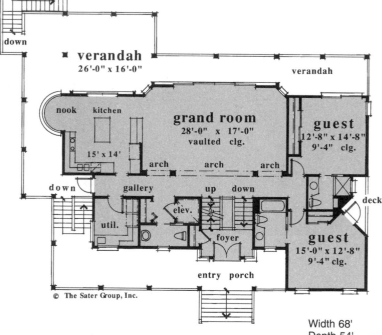

verandah
26'-0" x 16'-0"

verandah

nook   kitchen

grand room
28'-0" x 17'-0"
vaulted clg.

15' x 14'

guest
12'-8" x 14'-8"
9'-4" clg.

down

arch   arch   arch

gallery

up   down

down

util.

elev.

foyer

deck

guest
15'-0" x 12'-8"
9'-4" clg.

entry porch

© The Sater Group, Inc.

Width 68'
Depth 54'

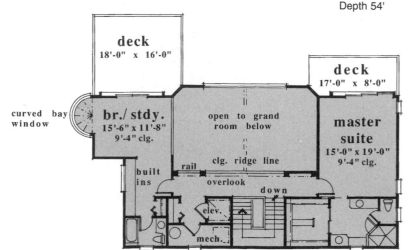

deck
18'-0" x 16'-0"

deck
17'-0" x 8'-0"

curved bay
window

br./stdy.
15'-6" x 11'-8"
9'-4" clg.

open to grand
room below

master
suite
15'-0" x 19'-0"
9'-4" clg.

built
ins

rail

clg. ridge line

overlook

down

elev.

mech.

© The Sater Group, Inc.

Design 6618

First Floor: 1,944 square feet
Second Floor: 1,196 square feet
Total: 3,140 square feet

● In the deluxe grand room of this Floridian home, family and friends will enjoy the ambience created by arches and access to a veranda. Two guest rooms flank a full bath—one of the guest rooms also sports a private deck. The kitchen serves a circular breakfast nook. Upstairs, a balcony overlook furthers the drama of the grand room. The master suite, with a deck and a private bath opening through a pocket door, will be a pleasure to occupy. Another bedroom—or use this room for a study—sits at the other side of this floor. It extends a curved bay window, an expansive deck, built-ins and a full bath. The lower level contains enough room for two cars in its carport and offers plenty of storage and bonus room. This home is designed with an island basement.

Design by
The Sater
Design Collection

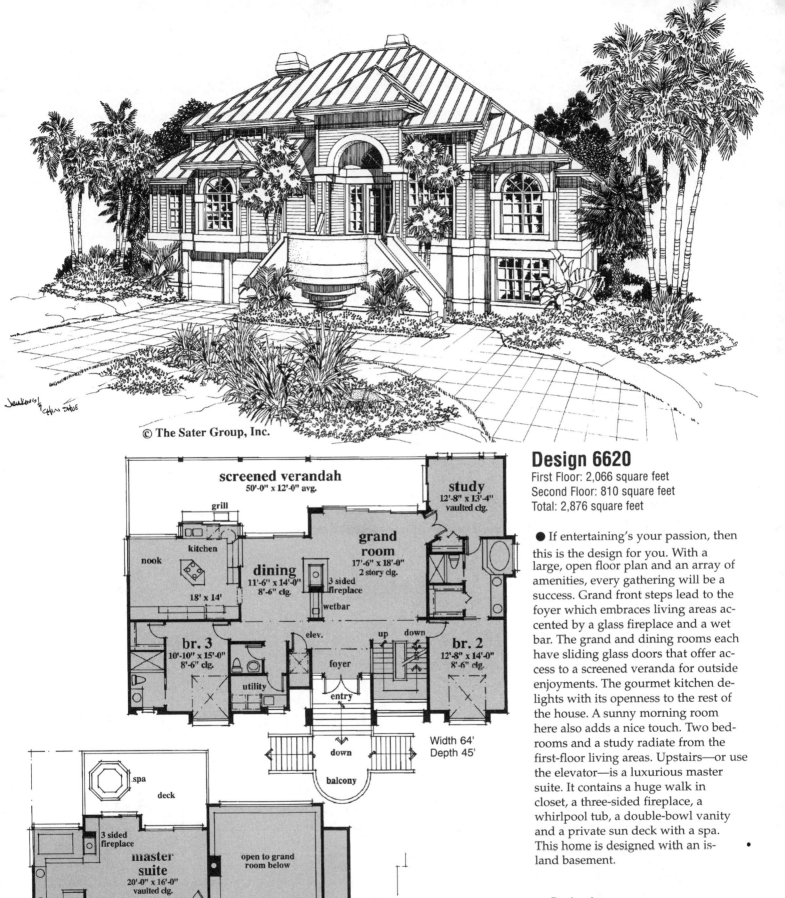

© The Sater Group, Inc.

screened verandah
50'-0" x 12'-0" avg.

grill

kitchen

nook

grand room
17'-6" x 18'-0"
2 story clg.

study
12'-8" x 13'-4"
vaulted clg.

dining
11'-6" x 14'-0"
8'-6" clg.

18' x 14'

3 sided fireplace

wetbar

br. 3
10'-10" x 15'-0"
8'-6" clg.

elev.

up   down

br. 2
12'-8" x 14'-0"
8'-6" clg.

utility

foyer

entry

down

balcony

Width 64'
Depth 45'

spa

deck

3 sided fireplace

master suite
20'-0" x 16'-0"
vaulted clg.

open to grand room below

elev.   gallery walkway   storage

w.i.c.

open to below

down

Design 6620
First Floor: 2,066 square feet
Second Floor: 810 square feet
Total: 2,876 square feet

● If entertaining's your passion, then this is the design for you. With a large, open floor plan and an array of amenities, every gathering will be a success. Grand front steps lead to the foyer which embraces living areas accented by a glass fireplace and a wet bar. The grand and dining rooms each have sliding glass doors that offer access to a screened veranda for outside enjoyments. The gourmet kitchen delights with its openness to the rest of the house. A sunny morning room here also adds a nice touch. Two bedrooms and a study radiate from the first-floor living areas. Upstairs—or use the elevator—is a luxurious master suite. It contains a huge walk in closet, a three-sided fireplace, a whirlpool tub, a double-bowl vanity and a private sun deck with a spa. This home is designed with an island basement.

Design by
**The Sater
Design Collection**

Design 3645

First Floor: 2,024 square feet
Second Floor: 800 square feet
Total: 2,824 square feet

L

● Tame the wild west with this handsome adobe-style home. Suitable for side-sloping lots, it contains a wealth of livability. A bee-hive fireplace graces the living room to enhance formal entertaining. Enjoy the family room, which opens to outdoor spaces. Four bedrooms include a guest room. Split styling puts the master bedroom suite on the right side of the plan. Here, a walk-in closet, curved shower and dual vanities bring a touch of luxury.

Design by
Home Planners

Width 80'-10"
Depth 54'

QUOTE ONE®

Cost to build? See page 374
to order complete cost estimate
to build this house in your area!

Design by
Home Planners

Width 77'-8"
Depth 62'

Design 3403

First Floor: 2,240 square feet
Second Floor: 660 square feet
Total: 2,900 square feet

L

QUOTE ONE®

Cost to build? See page 374
to order complete cost estimate
to build this house in your area!

● There is no end to the distinctive features in this Southwestern contemporary. Formal living areas are concentrated in the center of the plan; the kitchen and family room function well together as a working and living area. Also note the separate laundry room. The optional guest bedroom or den and the master bedroom are located to the left of the plan. Upstairs, the remaining two bedrooms are reached by a balcony overlooking the living room and share a bath with twin vanities.

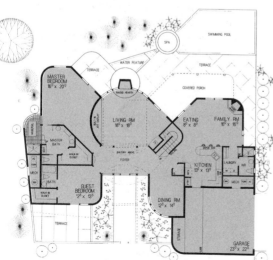

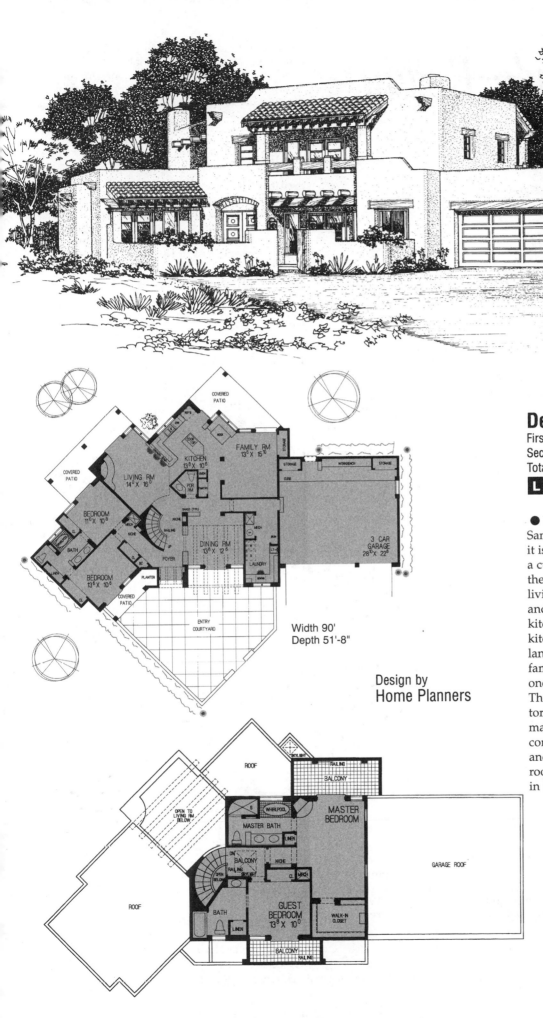

Design 3432

First Floor: 1,966 square feet
Second Floor: 831 square feet
Total: 2,797 square feet

L

● Unique in nature, this two-story Santa Fe-style home is as practical as it is lovely. The entry foyer leads past a curving staircase to living areas at the back of the plan. These include a living room with a corner fireplace and a family room connected to the kitchen via a built-in eating nook. The kitchen furthers its appeal with an island cooktop and a snack bar. Two family bedrooms on this level include one with a private covered patio. They share a full bath with dual lavatories and a whirlpool. Upstairs, the master suite features a grand bath, a corner fireplace, a large walk-in closet and a private balcony. A guest bedroom accesses a full bath. Every room in this home has its own outdoor area.

Width 90'
Depth 51'-8"

Design by
Home Planners

QUOTE ONE®

Cost to build? See page 374 to order complete cost estimate to build this house in your area!

371

When You're Ready To Order . . .

Let Us Show You Our Home Blueprint Package.

Building a home? Planning a home? Our Blueprint Package has nearly everything you need to get the job done right, whether you're working on your own or with help from an architect, designer, builder or subcontractors. Each Blueprint Package is the result of many hours of work by licensed architects or professional designers.

QUALITY

Hundreds of hours of painstaking effort have gone into the development of your blueprint set. Each home has been quality-checked by professionals to insure accuracy and buildability.

VALUE

Because we sell in volume, you can buy professional-quality blueprints at a fraction of their development cost. With our plans, your dream home design costs only a few hundred dollars, not the thousands of dollars that custom architects charge.

SERVICE

Once you've chosen your favorite home plan, you'll receive fast, efficient service whether you choose to mail or fax your order to us or call us toll free at 1-800-521-6797. For customer service, call toll free 1-888-690-1116.

SATISFACTION

Over 50 years of service to satisfied home plan buyers provide us unparalleled experience and knowledge in producing quality blueprints. What this means to you is satisfaction with our product and performance.

ORDER TOLL FREE 1-800-521-6797

After you've looked over our Blueprint Package and Important Extras on the following pages, simply mail the order form on page 381 or call toll free on our Blueprint Hotline: 1-800-521-6797. We're ready and eager to serve you. For customer service, call toll free 1-888-690-1116.

. . . .

Each set of blueprints is an interrelated collection of detail sheets which includes components such as floor plans, interior and exterior elevations, dimensions, cross-sections, diagrams and notations. These sheets show exactly how your house is to be built.

Among the sheets included may be:

Frontal Sheet
This artist's sketch of the exterior of the house gives you an idea of how the house will look when built and landscaped. Large ink-line floor plans show all levels of the house and provide an overview of your new home's livability, as well as a handy reference for deciding on furniture placement.

Foundation Plan
This sheet shows the foundation layout includ-

SAMPLE PACKAGE

ing support walls, excavated and unexcavated areas, if any, and foundation notes. If slab construction rather than basement, the plan shows footings and details for a monolithic slab. This page, or another in the set, may include a sample plot plan for locating your house on a building site.

Detailed Floor Plans
These plans show the layout of each floor of the house. Rooms and interior spaces are carefully dimensioned and keys are given for cross-section details provided later in the plans. The positions of electrical outlets and switches are shown.

House Cross-Sections
Large-scale views show sections or cut-aways of the foundation, interior walls, exterior walls, floors, stairways and roof details. Additional cross-sections may show important changes in

floor, ceiling or roof heights or the relationship of one level to another. Extremely valuable for construction, these sections show exactly how the various parts of the house fit together.

Interior Elevations
Many of our drawings show the design and placement of kitchen and bathroom cabinets, laundry areas, fireplaces, bookcases and other built-ins. Little "extras," such as mantelpiece and wainscoting drawings, plus moulding sections, provide details that give your home that custom touch.

Exterior Elevations
These drawings show the front, rear and sides of your house and give necessary notes on exterior materials and finishes. Particular attention is given to cornice detail, brick and stone accents or other finish items that make your home unique.

Frontal Sheet

Foundation Plans

Detailed Floor Plans

Exterior Elevations

Interior Elevations

House Cross-Sections

Important Extras To Do The Job Right!

Introducing eight important planning and construction aids developed by our professionals to help you succeed in your home-building project.

MATERIALS LIST

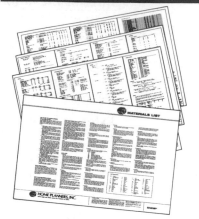

(Note: Because of the diversity of local building codes, our Materials List does not include mechanical materials.)

For many of the designs in our portfolio, we offer a customized materials take-off that is invaluable in planning and estimating the cost of your new home. This Materials List outlines the quantity, type and size of materials needed to build your house (with the exception of mechanical system items). Included are framing lumber, windows and doors, kitchen and bath cabinetry, rough and finish hardware, and much more. This handy list helps you or your builder cost out materials and serves as a reference sheet when you're compiling bids.

SPECIFICATION OUTLINE

This valuable 16-page document is critical to building your house correctly. Designed to be filled in by you or your builder, this book lists 166 stages or items crucial to the building process. It provides a comprehensive review of the construction process and helps in making choices of materials. When combined with the blueprints, a signed contract, and a schedule, it becomes a legal document and record for the building of your home.

QUOTE ONE®

Summary Cost Report / Materials Cost Report

A new service for estimating the cost of building select designs, the Quote One® system is available in two separate stages: The Summary Cost Report and the Materials Cost Report.

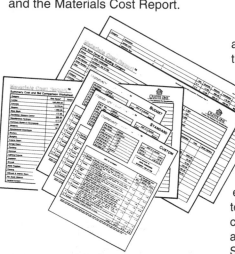

The Summary Cost Report is the first stage in the package and shows the total cost per square foot for your chosen home in your zip-code area and then breaks that cost down into ten categories showing the costs for building materials, labor and installation. The total cost for the report (which includes three grades: Budget, Standard and Custom) is just $19.95 for one home, and additionals are only $14.95. These reports allow you to evaluate your building budget and compare the costs of building a variety of homes in your area.

Make even more informed decisions about your home-building project with the second phase of our package, our Materials Cost Report. This tool is invaluable in planning and estimating the cost of your new home. The material and installation (labor and equipment) cost is shown for each of over 1,000 line items provided in the Materials List (Standard grade) which is included when you purchase this estimating tool. It allows you to determine building costs for your specific zip-code area and for your chosen home design. Space is allowed for additional estimates from contractors and subcontractors, such as for mechanical materials, which are not included in our packages. This invaluable tool is available for a price of $110 ($120 for a Schedule E plan) which includes a Materials List.

The Quote One® program is continually updated with new plans. If you are interested in a plan that is not indicated as Quote One®, please call and ask our sales reps, they will be happy to verify the status for you. To order these invaluable reports, use the order form on page 381 or call 1-800-521-6797.

CONSTRUCTION INFORMATION

If you want to know more about techniques—and deal more confidently with subcontractors we offer these useful sheets. Each set is an excellent tool that will add to your understanding of these technical subjects.

Plan-A-Home®

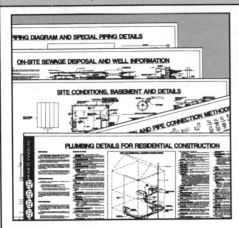

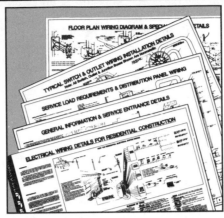

PLUMBING

The Blueprint Package includes locations for all the plumbing fixtures in your new house, including sinks, lavatories, tubs, showers, toilets, laundry trays and water heaters. However, if you want to know more about the complete plumbing system, these 24x36-inch detail sheets will prove very useful. Prepared to meet requirements of the National Plumbing Code, these six fact-filled sheets give general information on pipe schedules, fittings, sump-pump details, water-softener hookups, septic system details and much more. Color-coded sheets include a glossary of terms.

ELECTRICAL

The locations for every electrical switch, plug and outlet are shown in your Blueprint Package. However, these Electrical Details go further to take the mystery out of household electrical systems. Prepared to meet requirements of the National Electrical Code, these comprehensive 24x36-inch drawings come packed with helpful information, including wire sizing, switch-installation schematics, cable-routing details, appliance wattage, door-bell hookups, typical service panel circuitry and much more. Six sheets are bound together and color-coded for easy reference. A glossary of terms is also included.

Plan-A-Home® is an easy-to-use tool that helps you design a new home, arrange furniture in a new or existing home, or plan a remodeling project. Each package contains:

- **More than 700 reusable peel-off planning symbols** on a self-stick vinyl sheet, including walls, windows, doors, all types of furniture, kitchen components, bath fixtures and many more.

- **A reusable, transparent, 1/4-inch scale planning grid** that matches the scale of actual working drawings (1/4-inch equals 1 foot). This grid provides the basis for house layouts of up to 140x92 feet.

- **Tracing paper** and a protective sheet for copying or transferring your completed plan.

- **A felt-tip pen,** with water-soluble ink that wipes away quickly.

Plan-A-Home® lets you lay out areas as large as a 7,500 square foot, six-bedroom, seven-bath house.

CONSTRUCTION

The Blueprint Package contains everything an experienced builder needs to construct a particular house. However, it doesn't show all the ways that houses can be built, nor does it explain alternate construction methods. To help you understand how your house will be built—and offer additional techniques—this set of drawings depicts the materials and methods used to build foundations, fireplaces, walls, floors and roofs. Where appropriate, the drawings show acceptable alternatives. These six sheets will answer questions for the advanced do-it-yourselfer or home planner.

MECHANICAL

This package contains fundamental principles and useful data that will help you make informed decisions and communicate with subcontractors about heating and cooling systems. The 24x36-inch drawings contain instructions and samples that allow you to make simple load calculations and preliminary sizing and costing analysis. Covered are today's most commonly used systems from heat pumps to solar fuel systems. The package is packed full of illustrations and diagrams to help you visualize components and how they relate to one another.

To Order,
Call Toll Free
1-800-521-6797

To add these important extras to your Blueprint Package, simply indicate your choices on the order form on page 381 or call us Toll Free 1-800-521-6797 and we'll tell you more about these exciting products. For customer service, call toll free 1-888-690-1116.

L The Landscape Blueprint Package

For the homes marked with an **L** in this book, Home Planners has created a front-yard landscape plan that matches or is complementary in design to the house plan. These comprehensive blueprint packages include a Frontal Sheet, Plan View, Regionalized Plant & Materials List, a sheet on Planting and Maintaining Your Landscape, Zone Maps and Plant Size and Description Guide. These plans will help you achieve professional results, adding value and enjoyment to your property for years to come. Each set of blueprints is a full 18" x 24" in size with clear, complete instructions and easy-to-read type. To view the designs, call us to order your copy of *The Home Landscaper* which shows all 40 front-yard designs in full color.

Regional Order Map

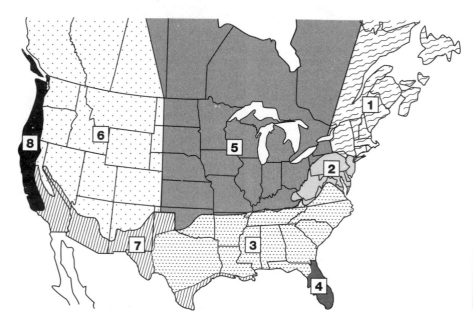

Most of the Landscape Plans are available with a Plant & Materials List adapted by horticultural experts to 8 different regions of the country. Please specify Geographic Region when ordering your plan.

Region	1	Northeast
Region	2	Mid-Atlantic
Region	3	Deep South
Region	4	Florida & Gulf Coast
Region	5	Midwest
Region	6	Rocky Mountains
Region	7	Southern California & Desert Southwest
Region	8	Northern California & Pacific Northwest

D The Deck Blueprint Package

Many of the homes in this book can be enhanced with a professionally designed Home Planners' Deck Plan. Those home plans highlighted with a **D** have a matching or corresponding deck plan available which includes a Deck Plan Frontal Sheet, Deck Framing and Floor Plans, Deck Elevations and a Deck Materials List. A Standard Deck Details Package, also available, provides all the how-to information necessary for building *any* deck. Our Complete Deck Building Package contains 1 set of Custom Deck Plans of your choice, plus 1 set of Standard Deck Building Details all for one low price. Our plans and details are carefully prepared in an easy-to-understand format that will guide you through every stage of your deck-building project. To view all 25 designs in our portfolio, call us to order your copy of our *Deck Planner* book.

Deck Plans Price Schedule

CUSTOM DECK PLANS

Price Group	Q	R	S
1 Set Custom Plans	$25	$30	$35
Additional identical sets	$10 each		
Reverse sets (mirror image)	$10 each		

STANDARD DECK DETAILS

1 Set Generic Construction Details ....$14.95 each

COMPLETE DECK BUILDING PACKAGE

Price Group	Q	R	S
1 Set Custom Plans, plus 1 Set Standard Deck Details	$35	$40	$45

Landscape Plans Price Schedule

Price Group	X	Y	Z
1 set	$35	$45	$55
3 sets	$50	$60	$70
6 sets	$65	$75	$85

Additional Identical Sets.....................................$10 each
Reverse Sets (mirror image)...........................$10 each

Price Schedule & Plans Index

House Blueprint Price Schedule
(Prices guaranteed through December 31, 1998)

Tier	1-set Study Package	4-set Building Package	8-set Building Package	1-set Reproducible Sepias	Home Customizer® Package
A	$350	$395	$455	$555	$605
B	$390	$435	$495	$615	$665
C	$430	$475	$535	$675	$725
D	$470	$515	$575	$735	$785
E	$590	$635	$695	$795	$845

Prices for 4- or 8-set Building Packages honored only at time of original order.
Additional Identical Blueprints in same order ....$50 per set
Reverse Blueprints (mirror image) ....$50 per set
Specification Outlines...$10 each

Materials Lists (available only from those designers listed below):
- ▲ Home Planners Designs...$50
- ● The Sater Design Collection $50
- ✳ Larry Garnett Designs $50
- ≠ Larry E. Belk Designs $50
- † Design Basics Designs $75
- ✴ Alan Mascord Designs $50
- ◆ Donald Gardner Designs $50
- ■ Design Traditions Designs $50

Exchanges...........$50 exchange fee for the first set; $10 for each additional set
$70 total exchange fee for 4 sets
$100 total exchange fee for 8 sets

Materials Lists for "E" price plans are an additional $10.
To Order: Fill in and send the order form on page 381–or call us Toll Free 1-800-521-6797.

Index

To use the Index below, refer to the design number listed in numerical order (a helpful page reference is also given). Note the price index letter and refer to the House Blueprint Price Schedule above for the cost of one, four or eight sets of blueprints or the cost of a reproducible sepia. Additional prices are shown for identical and reverse blueprint sets, as well as a very useful Materials List for some of the plans. Also note in the Index below those plans that have matching or complementary Deck Plans or Landscape Plans. Refer to the schedules above for prices of these plans. All Home Planners' plans can be customized with Home Planners' Home Customizer® Package. These plans are indicated below with this symbol: 🏠. See page 381 for information. Some plans are also part of our Quote One® estimating service and are indicated by this symbol: 🏠 . See page 374 for more information.

To Order: Fill in and send the order form on page 381—or call toll free 1-800-521-6797 or 520-297-8200.

DESIGN	PRICE	PAGE	CUSTOMIZABLE	QUOTE ONE®	DECK	DECK PRICE	LANDSCAPE	LANDSCAPE PRICE	REGIONS
▲1318	A	114	🏠						
▲1361	A	13	🏠		D117	S	L225	X	1-3,5,6,8
▲1482	A	176	🏠						
▲1715	B	113	🏠		D100	Q	L204	Y	1-3,5,6,8
▲1728	C	111	🏠						
▲1791	B	159	🏠	🏠	D114	R	L205	Y	1-3,5,6,8
▲1868	B	112	🏠						
▲1956	A	113	🏠	🏠	D117	R			
▲2145	A	157	🏠	🏠			L209	Y	1-6,8
▲2162	A	161	🏠		D103		L202	X	1-3,5,6,8
▲2188	C	155	🏠						
▲2250	C	141	🏠						
▲2356	D	211	🏠		D119	S	L219	Z	1-3,5,6,8
▲2427	A	177	🏠						
▲2488	A	340	🏠	🏠	D102	Q			
▲2490	A	343	🏠	🏠					
▲2520	B	160	🏠		D105	R	L201	Y	1-3,5,6,8
▲2540	B	115	🏠		D113	R	L205	Y	1-3,5,6,8
▲2543	D	266	🏠		D107	S	L218	Z	1-6,8
▲2563	B	163	🏠	🏠	D114	R	L201	Y	1-3,5,6,8
▲2571	A	168	🏠		D114	R	L202	X	1-3,5,6,8
▲2585	B	110	🏠		D113	R	L205	Y	1-3,5,6,8
▲2610	C	155	🏠		D114	R	L204	Y	1-3,5,6,8
▲2622	A	109	🏠	🏠	D103	R	L200	X	1-3,5,6,8
▲2639	C	142	🏠		D114	R	L215	Z	1-6,8
▲2650	B	53	🏠		D117	S	L201	Y	1-3,5,6,8
▲2659	B	107	🏠	🏠	D112	R	L205	Y	1-3,5,6,8
▲2661	A	164	🏠		D112	R	L202	X	1-3,5,6,8
▲2662	C	153	🏠				L216	Y	1-3,5,6,8
▲2665	D	305	🏠	🏠					
▲2667	B	135	🏠				L216	Y	1-3,5,6,8
▲2668	B	125	🏠				L214	Z	1-3,5,6,8
▲2682	A	166	🏠	🏠	D115	Q	L200	X	1-3,5,6,8
▲2683	D	138	🏠	🏠	D101	R	L214	Z	1-3,5,6,8
▲2686	C	132	🏠		D112	R	L209	Y	1-6,8
▲2687	C	156	🏠		D117	S	L204	Y	1-3,5,6,8
▲2690	C	143	🏠						
▲2694	C	128	🏠	🏠			L209	Y	1-6,8
▲2699	C	162	🏠	🏠			L211	Y	1-8
▲2711	B	340	🏠	🏠	D105	R	L229	Y	1-8
▲2733	B	114	🏠	🏠	D100	Q	L205	Y	1-3,5,6,8
▲2774	B	47	🏠	🏠	D100	Q	L207	Z	1-6,8
▲2776	B	87	🏠	🏠	D113	R	L207	Z	1-6,8
▲2781	C	338	🏠		D121	S	L230	Z	1-8
▲2801	B	352	🏠		D105	R	L232	Y	4,7
▲2826	B	317	🏠		D116	R			
▲2854	B	217	🏠	🏠	D112	R	L220	Z	1-3,5,6,8
▲2855	B	209	🏠	🏠	D103	R	L219	Z	1-3,5,6,8
▲2870	A	150	🏠						
▲2889	D	134	🏠	🏠	D107	S	L215	Z	1-6,8
▲2898	C	131	🏠		D118	R			
▲2905	B	23	🏠	🏠	D121	S	L229	Y	1-8
▲2907	B	52	🏠				L224	Y	1-3,5,6,8
▲2908	B	57	🏠		D117	S	L205	Y	1-3,5,6,8
▲2920	D	339	🏠	🏠	D104	S	L212	Z	1-8
▲2921	D	46	🏠	🏠	D104	S	L212	Z	1-8
▲2926	D	309	🏠						
▲2927	B	219	🏠	🏠	D100	Q			
▲2939	B	210	🏠		D108	R			
▲2940	E	288	🏠		D114	R	L230	Z	1-8
▲2945	B	56	🏠						
▲2946	C	49	🏠	🏠	D114	R	L207	Z	1-6,8
▲2952	E	276	🏠				L235	Z	1-3,5,6,8
▲2953	E	301	🏠	🏠	D111	S	L223	Z	1-3,5,6,8
▲2954	E	300	🏠				L223	Z	1-3,5,6,8
▲2955	E	298	🏠						
▲2957	D	299	🏠		D107	S	L218	Z	1-6,8
▲2959	B	208	🏠	🏠					
▲2964	B	208	🏠	🏠					
▲2967	B	216	🏠				L217	Y	1-8
▲2968	B	289	🏠				L227	Z	1-8
▲2969	C	206	🏠		D100	R	L223	Z	1-3,5,6,8
▲2970	D	195	🏠	🏠			L223	Z	1-3,5,6,8
▲2973	B	183	🏠				L223	Z	1-3,5,6,8
▲2981	D	129	🏠				L224	Y	1-3,5,6,8
▲2984	E	281	🏠				L214	Z	1-3,5,6,8
▲3307	C	65	🏠	🏠	D111	S	L207	Z	1-6,8
▲3309	B	205	🏠	🏠			L209	Y	1-6,8
▲3311	C	336	🏠	🏠	D109	S	L220	Y	1-3,5,6,8
▲3313	B	171	🏠	🏠			L200	X	1-3,5,6,8
▲3316	A	170	🏠	🏠			L202	X	1-3,5,6,8
▲3318	B	169	🏠	🏠	D111	S	L202	X	1-3,5,6,8

Before filling out the coupon at right or calling us on our Toll-Free Blueprint Hotline, you may want to learn more about our services and products. Here's some information you will find helpful.

Quick Turnaround
We process and ship every blueprint order from our office within 48 hours. Because of this quick turnaround, we won't send a formal notice acknowledging receipt of your order.

Our Exchange Policy
Since blueprints are printed in response to your order, we cannot honor requests for refunds. However, we will exchange your entire first order for an equal number of blueprints at a price of $50 for the first set and $10 for each additional set; $70 total exchange fee for 4 sets; $100 total exchange fee for 8 sets . . . *plus* the difference in cost if exchanging for a design in a higher price bracket or *less* the difference in cost if exchanging for a design in lower price bracket. One exchange is allowed within a year of purchase date. **(Sepias are not exchangeable.)** All sets from the first order must be returned before the exchange can take place. Please add $18 for postage and handling via ground service; $30 via Second Day Air; $40 via Next Day Air.

About Reverse Blueprints
If you want to build in reverse of the plan as shown, we will include an extra set of reverse blueprints (mirror image) for an additional fee of $50. Although lettering and dimensions will appear backward, reverses will be a useful aid if you decide to flop the plan.

Revising, Modifying and Customizing Plans
The wide variety of designs available in this publication allows you to select ideas and concepts for a home to fit your building site and match your family's needs, wants and budget. Like many homeowners who buy these plans, you and your builder, architect or engineer may want to make changes to them. Some minor changes may be made by your builder, but we recommend that most changes be made by a licensed architect or engineer. If you need to make alterations to a design that is customizable, you need only order our Home Customizer® Package to get you started. As set forth below, we cannot assume any responsibility for blueprints which have been changed, whether by you, your builder or by professionals selected by you or referred to you by us, because such individuals are outside our supervision and control.

Architectural and Engineering Seals
Some cities and states are now requiring that a licensed architect or engineer review and "seal" a blueprint, or officially approve it, prior to construction due to concerns over energy costs, safety and other factors. Prior to application for a building permit or the start of actual construction, we strongly advise that you consult your local building official who can tell you if such a review is required.

About the Designers
The architects and designers whose work appears in this publication are among America's leading residential designers. Each plan was designed to meet the requirements of a nationally recognized model building code in effect at the time and place the plan was drawn. Because national building codes change from time to time, plans may not comply with any such code at the time they are sold to a customer. In addition, building officials may not accept these plans as final construction documents of record as the plans may need to be modified and additional drawings and details added to suit local conditions and requirements. We strongly advise that purchasers consult a licensed architect or engineer, and their local building official, before starting any construction related to these plans.

Local Building Codes and Zoning Requirements
At the time of creation, our plans are drawn to specifications published by the Building Officials and Code Administrators (BOCA) International, Inc.; the Southern Building Code Congress (SBCCI) International, Inc.; the International Conference of Building Officials; or the Council of American Building Officials (CABO). Our plans are designed to meet or exceed national building standards. Because of the great differences in geography and climate throughout the United States and Canada, each state, county and municipality has its own building codes, zone requirements, ordinances and building regulations. Your plan may need to be modified to comply with local requirements regarding snow loads, energy codes, soil and seismic conditions and a wide range of other matters. In addition, you may need to obtain permits or inspections from local governments before and in the course of construction. Prior to using blueprints ordered from us, we strongly advise that you consult a licensed architect or engineer—and speak with your local building official—before applying for any permit or beginning construction. We authorize the use of our blueprints on the express condition that you strictly comply with all local building codes, zoning requirements and other applicable laws, regulations, ordinances and requirements. **Notice:** Plans for homes to be built in Nevada must be re-drawn by a Nevada-registered professional. Consult your building official for more information on this subject.

Foundation and Exterior Wall Changes
Most of our plans are drawn with either a full or partial basement foundation. Depending on your specific climate or regional building practices, you may wish to change this basement to a slab or crawlspace. Most professional contractors and builders can easily adapt your plans to alternate foundation types. Likewise, most can easily change 2x4 wall construction to 2x6, or vice versa.

Disclaimer
We and the designers we work with have put substantial care and effort into the creation of our blueprints. However, because we cannot provide on-site consultation, supervision and control over actual construction, and because of the great variance in local building requirements, building practices and soil, seismic, weather and other conditions, WE CANNOT MAKE ANY WARRANTY, EXPRESS OR IMPLIED, WITH RESPECT TO THE CONTENT OR USE OF OUR BLUEPRINTS, INCLUDING BUT NOT LIMITED TO ANY WARRANTY OF MERCHANTABILITY OR OF FITNESS FOR A PARTICULAR PURPOSE.

Terms and Conditions
These designs are protected under the terms of United States Copyright Law and may not be copied or reproduced in any way, by any means, unless you have purchased Sepias or Reproducibles which clearly indicate your right to copy or reproduce. We authorize the use of your chosen design as an aid in the construction of one single-family home only. You may not use this design to build a second or multiple dwellings without purchasing another blueprint or blueprints or paying additional design fees.

How Many Blueprints Do You Need?
A single set of blueprints is sufficient to study a home in greater detail. However, if you are planning to obtain cost estimates from a contractor or subcontractors—or if you are planning to build immediately—you will need more sets. Because additional sets are cheaper when ordered in quantity with the original order, make sure you order enough blueprints to satisfy all requirements. The following checklist will help you determine how many you need:

____ Owner

____ Builder (generally requires at least three sets; one as a legal document, one to use during inspections, and at least one to give to subcontractors)

____ Local Building Department (often requires two sets)

____ Mortgage Lender (usually one set for a conventional loan; three sets for FHA or VA loans)

____ TOTAL NUMBER OF SETS

Have You Seen Our Newest Designs?

Home Planners is one of the country's most active home design firms, creating nearly 100 new plans each year. At least 50 of our latest creations are featured in each edition of our New Design Portfolio. You may have received a copy with your latest purchase by mail. If not, or if you purchased this book from a local retailer, just return the coupon below for your FREE copy. Make sure you consider the very latest of what Home Planners has to offer.

Yes! Please send my FREE copy of your latest New Design Portfolio.

Offer good to U.S. shipping address only.

Name _____

Address _____

City_____State_____Zip _____

HOME PLANNERS, LLC
Wholly owned by Hanley-Wood, Inc.
3275 WEST INA ROAD, SUITE 110
TUCSON, ARIZONA 85741

Order Form Key

| VT |

Toll Free 1-800-521-6797
Regular Office Hours:
8:00 a.m. to 8:00 p.m. Eastern Time, Monday through Friday
Our staff will gladly answer any questions during regular office hours. Our answering service can place orders after hours or on weekends.

If we receive your order by 4:00 p.m. Eastern Time, Monday through Friday, we'll process it and ship within 48 hours. When ordering by phone, please have your charge card ready. We'll also ask you for the Order Form Key Number at the bottom of the coupon.

By FAX: Copy the Order Form on the next page and send it on our FAX line: 1-800-224-6699 or 1-520-544-3086.

Canadian Customers
Order Toll-Free 1-800-561-4169

For faster service and plans that are modified for building in Canada, customers may now call in orders directly to our Canadian supplier of plans and charge the purchase to a charge card. Or, you may complete the order form at right, adding 40% to all prices and mail in Canadian funds to:

The Plan Centre 60 Baffin Place
Unit 5
Waterloo, Ontario N2V 1Z7

OR: Copy the Order Form and send it via our Canadian FAX line: 1-800-719-3291.

The Home Customizer®

"This house is perfect...if only the family room were two feet wider." Sound familiar? In response to the numerous requests for this type of modification, Home Planners has developed **The Home Customizer® Package**. This exclusive package offers our top-of-the-line materials to make it easy for anyone, anywhere to customize any Home Planners design to fit their needs. Check the index on pages 377-380 for those plans which are customizable.

Some of the changes you can make to any of our plans include:

- exterior elevation changes
- kitchen and bath modifications
- roof, wall and foundation changes
- room additions and more!

The Home Customizer® Package includes everything you'll need to make the necessary changes to your favorite Home Planners design. The package includes:

- instruction book with examples
- architectural scale and clear work film
- erasable red marker and removable correction tape
- ¼"-scale furniture cutouts
- 1 set reproducible, erasable Sepias
- 1 set study blueprints for communicating changes to your design professional
- a copyright release letter so you can make copies as you need them
- referral letter with the name, address and telephone number of the professional in your region who is trained in modifying Home Planners designs efficiently and inexpensively.

The price of the **Home Customizer® Package** ranges from $605 to $845, depending on the price schedule of the design you have chosen. **The Home Customizer® Package** will not only save you 25% to 75% of the cost of drawing the plans from scratch with a custom architect or engineer, it will also give you the flexibility to have your changes and modifications made by our referral network or by the professional of your choice. Now it's even easier and more affordable to have the custom home you've always wanted.

For customer service, call toll free 1-888-690-1116.

 For information about any of our services or to order call 1-800-521-6797. Plus, browse our website: www.homeplanners.com

---
BLUEPRINTS ARE NOT RETURNABLE

Helpful Books & Software

Home Planners wants your building experience to be as pleasant and trouble-free as possible. That's why we've expanded our library of Do-It-Yourself titles to help you along. In addition to our beautiful plans books, we've added books to guide you through specific projects as well as the construction process. In fact, these are titles that will be as useful after your dream home is built as they are right now.

COUNTRY

1 200 country designs from classic to contemporary by 7 winning designers. 224 pages $8.95

BUDGET-SMART

2 200 efficient plans from 7 top designers, that you can really afford to build! 224 pages $8.95

MOVE-UP

3 200 stylish designs for today's growing families from 9 hot designers. 224 pages $8.95 NEW!

NARROW-LOT

4 200 unique homes less than 60' wide from 7 designers. Up to 3,000 square feet. 224 pages $8.95

REGIONAL BEST

5 200 beautiful homes from across America by 7 regional designers. 224 pages $8.95 NEW!

EXPANDABLES
6 200 flexible plans that expand with your needs from 7 top designers. 240 pages $8.95 NEW!

BEST SELLERS

7 NEW! Our 50th Anniversary book with 200 of our very best designs in full color! 224 page $12.95

NEW ENGLAND

8 260 of the best in Colonial home design. Special interior design sections, too. 384 pages $14.95

AFFORDABLE

9 430 cost-saving plans specially selected for modest to medium building budgets. 320 pages $9.95

LUXURY
10 154 fine luxury plans-loaded with luscious amenities! 192 pages $14.95

ONE-STORY

11 448 designs for all lifestyles. 860 to 5,400 square feet. 384 pages $9.95 NEW!

TWO-STORY

12 460 designs for one-and-a-half and two stories. 1,245 to 7,275 square feet. 348 pages $9.95

VACATION

13 345 designs for recreation, retirement and leisure. 312 pages $8.95 NEW!

MULTI-LEVEL
14 312 designs for split-levels, bi-levels, multi-levels and walkouts. 224 pages $8.95 NEW!

OUTDOOR

15 42 unique outdoor projects. Gazebos, strombellas, bridges, sheds, playsets and more! 96 pages $7.95 NEW!

DECKS
16 25 outstanding single-, double- and multi-level decks you can build. 112 pages $7.95

ENCYCLOPEDIA
17 500 exceptional plans for all styles and budgets—the best book of its kind! 352 pages $9.95

MODERN & CLASSIC
18 341 impressive homes featuring the latest in contemporary design. 304 pages $9.95

TRADITIONAL

19 403 designs of classic beauty and elegance. 304 pages $9.95

VICTORIAN
20 160 striking Victorian and Farmhouse designs from three leading designers. 192 pages $12.95

SOUTHERN
21 207 homes rich in Southern styling and comfort. 240 pages $8.95 NEW!

WESTERN
22 215 designs that capture the spirit and diversity of the Western lifestyle. 208 pages $9.95

EMPTY-NESTER

23 200 exciting plans for empty-nesters, retirees and childless couples. 224 pages $8.95

STARTER
24 200 easy-to-build plans for starter and low-budget houses. 224 pages $8.95

Landscape Designs

FRONT & BACK

25 The first book of do-it-yourself landscapes. 40 front, 15 backyards. 208 pages $12.95

BACKYARDS

26 40 designs focused solely on creating your own specially themed backyard oasis. 160 pages $12.95

EASY CARE

27 NEW! 41 special landscapes designed for beauty and low maintenance. 160 pages $12.95

Design Software

BOOK & CD ROM

28 NEW! Both the Home Planners Gold book and matching Windows™ CD ROM with 3D floor-plans. $24.95

HOME ARCHITECT

29 The only complete home design kit for Windows™. Draw floor plans and landscape designs easily. Includes CD of 500 floor plans. $42.95

Interior Design

HOME DECORATING
30 Special effects and creative ideas for all surfaces. Includes simple step-by-step diagrams. 96 pages $8.95

BATHROOMS

31 An innovative guide to organizing, remodeling and decorating your bathroom. 96 pages $8.95

KITCHENS
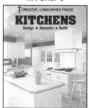
32 An imaginative guide to designing the perfect kitchen. Chock full of bright ideas to make your job easier. 176 pages $12.95

Design Software

BOOK & CD ROM	3D DESIGN SUITE	ENERGY GUIDE	BATHROOMS	KITCHENS	HOUSE CONTRACTING	WINDOWS & DOORS	CONTRACTING GUIDE

   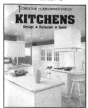  

33 Both the Home Planners Gold book and matching Windows™ CD ROM with 3D floorplans. $24.95

34 Home design made easy! View designs in 3D, take a virtual reality tour, add decorating details and more. $59.95

35 The most comprehensive energy efficiency and conservation guide available. 280 pages $35.00

36 An innovative guide to organizing, remodeling and decorating your bathroom. 96 pages $8.95

37 An imaginative guide to designing the perfect kitchen. Chock full of bright ideas to make your job easier. 176 pages $14.95

38 Everything you need to know to act as your own general contractor...and save up to 25% off building costs. 134 pages $12.95

39 Installation techniques and tips that make your project easier and more professional looking. 80 pages $7.95

40 Loaded with information to make you more confident in dealing with contractors and subcontractors. 287 pages $18.95

ROOFING	FRAMING	VISUAL HANDBOOK	BASIC WIRING	PATIOS & WALKS	TILE	PLUMBING	TRIM & MOLDING

41 Information on the latest tools, materials and techniques for roof installation or repair. 80 pages $7.95

42 For those who want to take a more-hands on approach to their dream. 319 pages $19.95

43 A plain-talk guide to the construction process; financing to final walk-through, this book covers it all. 498 pages $19.95

44 A straight forward guide to one of the most misunderstood systems in the home. 160 pages $12.95

45 Clear step-by-step instructions take you from the basic design stages to the finished project. 80 pages $7.95

46 Every kind of tile for every kind of application. Includes tips on use installation and repair. 176 pages $12.95

47 Tackle any plumbing installation or repair as quickly and efficiently as a professional. 160 pages $12.95

48 Step-by-step instructions for installing baseboards, window and door casings and more. 80 pages $7.95

Additional Books Order Form

To order your books, just check the box of the book numbered below and complete the coupon. We will process your order and ship it from our office within 48 hours. Send coupon and check (in U.S. funds).

YES! Please send me the books I've indicated:

☐ 1:VO $9.95	☐ 25:SW $10.95
☐ 2:VT $9.95	☐ 26:WH $9.95
☐ 3:VH $8.95	☐ 27:ECL $14.95
☐ 4:VS $8.95	☐ 28:HL $14.95
☐ 5:FH $8.95	☐ 29:BYL $14.95
☐ 6:MU $8.95	☐ 30:YG $7.95
☐ 7:NL $8.95	☐ 31:GG $7.95
☐ 8:SM $8.95	☐ 32:DP $7.95
☐ 9:BS $8.95	☐ 33:HPGC $24.95
☐ 10:EX $8.95	☐ 34:PLANSUITE . . $59.95
☐ 11:EN $9.95	☐ 35:RES $35.00
☐ 12:AF $9.95	☐ 36:CDB $8.95
☐ 13:E2 . . . . $9.95	☐ 37:CKI $14.95
☐ 14:VDH $12.95	☐ 38:SBC $12.95
☐ 15:EL $8.95	☐ 39:CGD $7.95
☐ 16:LD2 . . . . $14.95	☐ 40:RCC $18.95
☐ 17:NA $8.95	☐ 41:CGR $7.95
☐ 18:HPG $12.95	☐ 42:SRF $19.95
☐ 19:WEP $17.95	☐ 43:RVH $19.95
☐ 20:CN $9.95	☐ 44:CBW $12.95
☐ 21:ET $9.95	☐ 45:CGW $7.95
☐ 22:EC $9.95	☐ 46:CWT $12.95
☐ 23:NES $14.95	☐ 47:CMP $12.95
☐ 24:SH $8.95	☐ 48:CGT $7.95

Canadian Customers
Order Toll-Free 1-800-561-4169

Additional Books Sub-Total $_____
ADD Postage and Handling $____3.00____
Sales Tax: (AZ, CA, DC, IL, MI, MN, NY & WA residents, please add appropriate state and local sales tax.) $_____
YOUR TOTAL (Sub-Total, Postage/Handling, Tax) $_____

YOUR ADDRESS (Please print)

Name _____

Street _____

City _____ State _____ Zip _____

Phone (_____) _____—_____

YOUR PAYMENT
Check one: ☐ Check ☐ Visa ☐ MasterCard ☐ Discover Card
Required credit card information:
Credit Card Number_____

Expiration Date (Month/Year) _____/_____

Signature Required _____

 Home Planners, LLC
Wholly owned by Hanley-Wood, Inc.
3275 W Ina Road, Suite 110, Dept. BK, Tucson, AZ 85741

VT

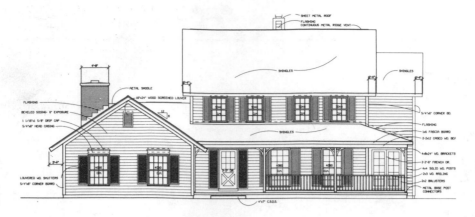

OVER 3 MILLION BLUEPRINTS SOLD

"We instructed our builder to follow the plans including all of the many details which make this house so elegant... Our home is a fine example of the results one can achieve by purchasing and following the plans which you offer... Everyone who has seen it has assured us that it belongs in 'a picture book.' I truly mean it when I say that my home 'is a DREAM HOUSE.'"

S.P.
Anderson, SC

"We have had a steady stream of visitors, many of whom tell us this is the most beautiful home they've seen. Everyone is amazed at the layout and remark on how unique it is. Our real estate attorney, who is a Chicago dweller and who deals with highly valued properties, told me this is the only suburban home he has seen that he would want to live in."

W. & P.S.
Flossmoor, IL

"Home Planners' blueprints saved us a great deal of money. I acted as the general contractor and we did a lot of the work ourselves. We probably built it for half the cost! We are thinking about more plans for another home. I purchased a competitor's book but my husband only wants your plans!"

K.M.
Grovetown, GA

*"We are **very** happy with the product of our efforts. The neighbors and passersby appreciate what we have created. We have had many people stop by to discuss our house and kindly praise it as being the nicest house in our area of new construction. We have even had one person stop and make us an unsolicited offer to buy the house for much more than we have invested in it."*

K. & L.S.
Bolingbrook, IL

"The traffic going past our house is unbelievable. On several occasions, we have heard that it is the 'prettiest house in Batavia.' Also, when meeting someone new and mentioning what street we live on, quite often we're told, 'Oh, you're the one in the yellow house with the wrap-around porch! I love it!'"

A.W.
Batavia, NY

"I have been involved in the building trades my entire life... Since building our home we have built two other homes for other families. Their plans from local professional architects were not nearly as good as yours. For that reason we are ordering additional plan books from you."

T.F.
Kingston, WA

"The blueprints we received from Home Planners were of excellent quality and provided us with exactly what we needed to get our successful home-building project underway. We appreciate Home Planners invaluable role in our home-building effort."

T.A.
Concord, TN